Wisconsin

Picture Research by Tom Capp
"Partners in Progress" by Jocelyn Riley

Produced in cooperation with the Wisconsin Manufacturers
and Commerce Service Corporation

Windsor Publications, Inc.
Northridge, California

Wisconsin

PATHWAYS TO PROSPERITY

SHIELA REAVES

Windsor Publications, Inc.—History Books Division
Editorial Director: Teri Davis Greenberg
Director, Corporate Biographies: Karen Story
Design Director: Alexander E. D'Anca

Staff for *Wisconsin: Pathways to Prosperity*
Editor: Jerry Mosher
Photo Editor: Susan L. Wells
Assistant Editor: Jeffrey Reeves
Assistant Director, Corporate Biographies: Phyllis Gray
Editor, Corporate Biographies: Brenda Berryhill
Production Editor, Corporate Biographies: Una FitzSimons
Editorial Assistants: Didier Beauvoir, Thelma Fleischer, Michael
    Nugwynne, Kathy M.B. Peyser, Pat Pittman, Theresa Solis
Sales Representatives, Corporate Biographies: Rita Baril, Tim Burke,
    Sandee Franks, Rubin Turner
Layout Artist, Corporate Biographies: Mari Catherine Preimesberger

Designer: Christina Rosepapa

Library of Congress Cataloging in Publication Data
Reaves, Shiela, 1954-
Pathways to prosperity
Includes chapter: Partners in progress / by
Jocelyn Riley.
Bibliography: p. 328
Includes index.
1. Wisconsin—History. 2. Wisconsin—Description
and travel—Views. 3. Wisconsin—Industries.
I. Riley, Joselyn. II. Title.
F581.R38 1988 977.5 87-3391
ISBN: 0-89781-236-0

Windsor Publications, Inc.
Elliot Martin, Chairman of the Board
James L. Fish, Chief Operating Officer
Hal Silverman, Vice-President/Publisher

*Previous page: Clouds billow in
a bright blue sky above this alfalfa field and farm. Photo by
R. Hamilton Smith*

*Page six: Frost glistens in the sun-
light above pure snow in this
winter scene. Photo by R. Hamilton Smith*

CONTENTS

For two businessmen with a
passion for history—
my grandfather, Jordan B. Reaves and
my father, J. Ben Reaves

*The first permanent streetcar
lines in the United States were installed in Appleton, Wisconsin,
in 1886 and also in Mobile, Alabama. Courtesy, State Historical
Society of Wisconsin*

ACKNOWLEDGMENTS

If the reader finds this history to have the ring of authority to it, then it is because I am standing on the shoulders of Wisconsin's scholars. I am indebted to the detail-loving historians that Wisconsin has produced since Frederick Jackson Turner's seminars in the early 1900s at the State Historical Society of Wisconsin. My hope is to draw these voices together into one voice that reflects the richness of Wisconsin.

I am also indebted to Pat Blankenburg, as well as my editors at Windsor, for giving me the opportunity to write this book; it has been a labor of love. I also wish to thank the following people for their help: Bill Redmond of the Wisconsin Association of Manufacturers and Commerce who, together with Pat Blankenburg, helped me at a critical stage for getting corporate information about large and small businesses; Jean Lang of the University of Wisconsin's University-Industry Research Program (UIR); Peg Geisler and her staff of the University of Wisconsin—Madison's Wisconsin Idea Seminar (which should be a prerequisite for all faculty); Bill Kraus, who is still missed in Wisconsin; Bill Durkin of the Wisconsin Insurance Alliance; Roger Nacker and Pat McMahan of the Department of Development; Peter Canon of the Legislative Reference Bureau; Joe Warnemuende of the UW-Madison's College of Engineering; John Halverson of the Janesville Gazette.

Wisconsin is blessed with dedicated local historians and I wish to thank the following who offered their help: Robert Billings of Clintonville; Timothy Siebert and William Paul of Stevens Point and Portage County; Charles Wallman of Watertown; Oliver Reese, Jr. of Wisconsin Dells; Peter Laun of Elkhart Lake.

And finally I'd like to acknowledge the professionalism of the library and iconography staffs of the State Historical Society of Wisconsin and the Milwaukee Public Library.

INDIAN LAND, EUROPEAN BOUNTY

In the seventeenth century Indians throughout the fur-trading region of the western Great Lakes supplied beaver pelts to the French fur traders. As the beaver was hunted to extinction in the East, the fur trade moved west into Wisconsin. By 1616 Ottawa and Huron Indians had established fur-trading centers in Chequamegon Bay in northern Wisconsin. Courtesy, State Historical Society of Wisconsin

The ancestors of Wisconsin's
Indians gathered wild rice in
the Fox and Wisconsin river valleys. These wild rice beds still
exist today. Courtesy, Milwaukee County Historical Society

The river banks were obscured by stalks of wild rice, and the river itself was broken by many swamps and small lakes. It was easy to get lost, but the two Indian guides led the seven French explorers safely to the portage. From there supplies and two birch canoes were carried 2,700 paces to a new river. And then the Indians turned back, "leaving us alone," wrote Father Jacques Marquette in 1673, "in this unknown country, in the hands of Providence."

During the portage of less than two miles, Father Marquette may have reflected on the advice the Menominee Indians gave before he and Louis Joliet began their journey. The river was dangerous, the Indians said. It was full of horrible monsters and even a demon. The river was watched by warrior Indians, the Menominees warned, and the heat was

Marquette and Joliet to the Mississippi, there had been only rumors of a great river in the western wilderness. Other explorers had surely crossed the Mississippi, but no one had recorded it. Marquette, a Jesuit priest, and Joliet, a fur trader, traveled down the river until they reached an Arkansas village and discerned that the Indians were trading with Europeans. The Mississippi, they decided, emptied into the Gulf of Mexico. Rather than risk being captured by the Spaniards, who claimed the Gulf of Mexico, they returned by way of the Illinois River.

The charting of the Wisconsin River opened a trade route to the Mississippi and helped map the unknown wilderness. Wisconsin took its name after the river Marquette first described, but the origin of the word may never be known. Instead of

By 1697 Jesuit priest-explorers such as Louis Hennepin had helped map the Upper Great Lakes. In 1673 Father Jacques Marquette and fur trader Louis Joliet had journeyed down the Fox and Wisconsin rivers and discovered the Mississippi River. Courtesy, State Historical Society of Wisconsin

so excessive that it could cause their deaths. In his journal Marquette wrote he had scoffed about the demon and the marine monsters. And then he had said a prayer.

Marquette called this unknown river the Meskousing, later known as the Wisconsin River. He and Joliet did not meet hostile Indians on their journey. Instead they saw deer and buffalo on banks that changed from woods to prairies and hills. And then on June 17, 1673, Joliet and Marquette floated in their canoes into the fabled Mississippi River, "with a joy that I cannot express," wrote Marquette.

Until the uncharted Wisconsin River led

referring to Joliet and Marquette's river as the Meskousing, French and English explorers later called Marquette's river "Ouisconsing" or "Ouisconsin." In 1822 the name "Wisconsin" was applied to the entire land, but scholars cannot explain the origin or meaning of the Indian word. Apparently the original ending, "ing," signified "place." However, that is where agreement ends. Speculation has offered "wild, rushing channel" or "gathering of the waters," but students of Indian languages have not been able to confirm these explanations.

Rivers had shaped European discovery of the

Above
The first house was built by Europeans in the Wisconsin area sometime between 1650 and 1660. Pierre-Esprit Radisson explored Wisconsin and settled for a brief period on Chequamegon Bay, which was Chippewa territory. Courtesy, State Historical Society of Wisconsin

Above right
This map of North America from 1635 shows the land known to Europeans at the time of Jean Nicolet's voyage to Wisconsin. The Great Lakes were unknown, as was the Mississippi River. However, in 1635 Jean Nicolet returned from Green Bay to Montreal with news that the Great Lakes were not a pathway to the Orient. Courtesy, State Historical Society of Wisconsin

Indian lands in the Northwest. Finding a trade route to China had been the first impetus for French exploration of the New World. In 1534 Jacques Cartier explored the St. Lawrence River looking for the Northwest Passage to the Far East but found only Woodland Indians. Envious of the Spanish bounty in Mexico, the French monarch Francis I originally was interested only in Indians who possessed gold, but fur proved to be an equally valuable source of riches. Trading developed between Indians, who wanted metal knives and hatchets, and Europeans, who prized beaver skins for making felt for fashionable hats.

As the trade in furs grew, the governor of New France, Samuel de Champlain, continued to dream of finding the Orient. The founder of Quebec, explorer-geographer Champlain wrote in 1618 that New France was the route to "the Kingdom of China and the East Indies, whence great riches could be drawn." In 1634 Champlain sent Jean Nicolet to find the route to the South Seas and to arrange peace among western tribes for future trading. In particular he wanted to make contact with the nation called the "People of the Sea," whom Champlain hoped could lead Nicolet to the Orient.

In the service of a French trading company, Nicolet had lived among Huron and Algonkian Indian tribes for eleven years along the Ottawa River. Nicolet spoke their language and knew their customs. Accompanied by seven Huron, Nicolet traveled along the northern shore of Lake Michigan, becoming the first European to explore the great lake.

The People of the Sea, most likely the Winnebago, beheld a sight when Jean Nicolet stepped ashore in Green Bay in 1634. From a narrative written during Nicolet's lifetime, we have a vivid description. Brandishing two pistols, Nicolet "wore a grand robe of China damask, all strewn with flowers and birds of many colors." The Indians were impressed with the guns, the women and children fleeing "at the sight of a man who carried thunder in both hands." The Indians held feasts for Nicolet, but the only seas they could point to were the Great Lakes. Satisfied with his mission, Nicolet returned to Quebec in 1635, a few months before Champlain died.

The People of the Sea did not encounter another European for 20 years. When explorer Pierre-Esprit Radisson visited the land around Lake Michigan in about 1659 he wrote of its natural beauty. "The country was so pleasant, so beautifull & fruitfull," Radisson said, "that it grieved me to see that the world could not discover such inticing countrys to live in. This I say because the Europeans' fight for a rock in sea against one another."

GLACIERS AND THE ICE AGE

The land Radisson found so beautiful was carved by glaciers, whose melting wake left the extensive waterways and wetlands through which he canoed. Wisconsin is world renowned for its well-preserved glacial features, which cover approximately three-fourths of the state. The Ice Age formed the Great

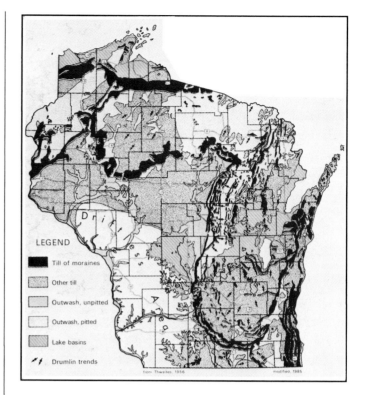

The accumulation of glacial drift formed hills and ridges called moraines, which show the advance of the glaciers into Wisconsin. The Ice Age began approximately one million years ago and ended about 10,000 years ago. Wisconsin's Ice Age formations are world renowned. Courtesy, Wisconsin Geological and Natural History Survey

The glacier's last visit to Wisconsin ended approximately 10,000 years ago, and as the environment warmed, animals such as woolly mammoths followed the blossoming vegetation. Painter George Peter portrayed the Paleo-Indians hunting these massive animals in this 1930s painting. Courtesy, Milwaukee Public Museum

Lakes and bequeathed to Wisconsin more than 14,000 lakes—9,000 of which are larger than 20 acres. Glaciers flattened hills and filled valleys, changed the course of rivers, and created gently rolling land.

But the glacial ice sheets missed southwestern Wisconsin, creating a dramatic contrast in landscape. Called the Driftless Area, the land is naturally lakeless and steeper with mounds, valleys, bluffs, and cliffs. The Driftless Area offers a glimpse back through time, and perhaps shows what Wisconsin looked like before the Ice Age.

The Ice Age began approximately one million years ago in eastern Canada around Hudson Bay. Snow accumulated faster than it melted. The snow turned to ice and, by the pressure of its own weight, could move. Great ice sheets formed—in some places as deep as two miles—and slowly the ice advanced. Glaciers also retreated. This glacial waxing and waning falls into four major stages; the last stage is called the Wisconsin Age, which began 70,000 years ago.

The glacier's last visit to Wisconsin, which ended 10,000 years ago, is still etched on the land. Although glaciers evoke an image of crystalline whiteness, underneath they are dirty, vacuuming up the topsoil and carrying this debris along. At the edges of the crushing sheets of ice, this unsorted pile of rock, sand, and gravel bulges outward into what geologists call moraines. During the last advance of the ice, these moraines formed a string of hills, which since have eroded to mounds and ridges. Moraines clearly outline the farthest advances of the ice sheet into northern and central Wisconsin.

The fertility and variability of Wisconsin soils is due to the glaciers that chewed and spread the earth. The glacier, which could grind rock into dust, spread top soil called glacial drift. Ranging from boulders to powder, glacial drift enriched Wisconsin's soil with a variety of rocks, which continuously broke down and released fresh nutrients into the soil.

As the glacier began its retreat, tundra-like plants began to grow on the exposed, damp land. According to geography professor Gwen Schultz, the first trees to appear in Wisconsin were spruces, willows, and tamarack, which were tolerant of moisture. Animals followed the vegetation, and soon caribou and musk-ox appeared along with the woolly mammoth—that shaggy, elephant-like behemoth who probably used its long curved tusks to find hardy plants in the snow.

The mastodons lived in the slowly returning forests. The giant beaver, seven-feet high and weighing up to 500 pounds, lived in the wetlands.

The first people appeared in Wisconsin during the late Ice Age. Their ancestors had been part of the migration of people who trekked across the thin strip of land that would later submerge into the Bering Strait. From Asia and Siberia people migrated to Alaska, becoming the first explorers of North America as far back as 11,000 years ago.

The Paleo-Indians (paleo comes from Greek for "ancient") who lived in Wisconsin from about 8500 B.C. were nomadic. They hunted deer, moose, caribou, beaver, and hare, supplementing their diet with vegetation as the environment began to blossom.

As historian Louise Kellogg declared, the first miners in Wisconsin were the Indians. From 3000 to 1000 B.C. people living in the northern part of the state began to mine copper from the Lake Superior area. They hammered raw copper into ornaments and jewelry, fish hooks, spear points, and knives. These copper artifacts were an important part of burials and the attending ceremonialism of what archeologists call the "Old Copper" culture. Archeologists have suggested that these graves may have been forerunners of the elaborate mound building of the later Woodland Indians.

The first gardeners in Wisconsin may have lived as early as 300 B.C. While there is no evidence of large-scale farming, early Indian cultures did store seeds and plant food. The Woodland Indians, who lived from about 1000 B.C. to 1100 A.D., distinguished themselves from the earlier forest-dwellers by making pottery, which provides archeologists with a glimpse of their daily routine. In northern Wisconsin people settled next to lakes and used nets for spring and summer fishing. As winter approached the villages dispersed to follow the winter game of moose, bear, and caribou.

From 300 B.C. to 400 A.D. Wisconsin was part of a commercial and artistic phenomenon known as Hopewell. A commercial trade network developed among Indians from New York to Florida to the Midwest. Commerce thrived on exotic tastes in mica, freshwater pearls, Gulf conch shells, obsidian from Yellowstone, sharks teeth and alligator from Florida, and copper from Lake Superior. Artists took these raw materials and made ornaments, headdresses, and superb carvings. The Hopewell florescence, which created one of the earliest trade networks, was centered in Ohio and the Illinois River Valley, producing some of the finest prehistoric art in North America. The Indians living along the Mississippi in Wisconsin, who were part of Hopewell, were the only prehistoric people to use silver in their jewelry.

The Hopewell traditions provide the first evidence of wealth and power among different ranks of people. In Hopewell an elite arose who wore finely crafted jewelry, furs, robes, and woven cloth. This wealth, ostentatious and reserved only for the few, was buried alongside the elite in mounds that were often built into geometric earthworks.

Southern Wisconsin was the primary setting for effigy mound builders who designed birds and animals in the earth. These three-foot high mounds were shaped into panthers, turtles, birds, and bears. Buried treasure was not a part of mound-building among the Indians who came after Hopewell. Some archeologists believe these mounds may have served as territorial boundary markers. The effigy mound builders, who began building the unique mounds as early as 300 A.D. and as late as 1642, usually chose lakes, rivers, and wetlands as their setting. In the

Madison area, which has the highest concentration of effigy mounds, one scholar counted more than 1,000 mounds near and around the four lakes in 1937.

Using the river for trading, a group of Mississippian Indians migrated from Southern Illinois to present-day Jefferson County in southern Wisconsin, where they built a fortified village. The people were vigilant and defensive. Their village was rectangular and surrounded on three sides by a high fence of stakes, with watchtowers every 80 feet. The fourth side was protected by the Crawfish River. Inside the people built three pyramid-shaped, flat-topped mounds for religious ceremonies. They grew corn and made pottery that included bottles,

Painter George Peter depicted the 1673 French discovery of the Mississippi River by Jesuit Priest Jacques Marquette and fur trader Louis Joliet, an event that opened the Upper Great Lakes region to the fur trading industry. Courtesy, Milwaukee Public Museum

beakers, bowls, and jars. The Wisconsin pioneer who first described the site, Nathaniel Hyer, called it Aztalan which evoked images of an Aztec legend about a northern colony. However the only southern connection to Aztalan is Cahokia, Illinois. The people of Aztalan lived within their barricaded walls from about 1100 to 1300, and like so many Indian cultures, vanished without a clue for archeologists.

Until contact with the Europeans created the fur trade, the Woodland Indians of Wisconsin—including the Winnebago and the Menominee—continued their rhythmic responses to the seasons. In the spring and summer they formed semi-permanent villages by lakes and rivers where they fished and hunted. They tapped the maple trees for maple sugar, gathered wild berries and nuts, and grew small gardens of corn, squash, and beans. In the late summer they harvested wild rice in the wetlands. By winter they had broken into smaller groups, following the deer and moose. Bear were hunted and killed with great ceremony, for the bear was revered. One tribe, the Chippewa, did not cultivate food. Found in the Lake Superior region in northern Wisconsin, this nomadic hunting people refined the canoe for travel.

TRADE AND COLONIZATION

The fur trade began to irrevocably change Indian life as it built an empire for France. Farming became less important to the Indian economy compared to hunting lucrative furs. "In truth," said one Indian chief, "my brother the beaver does everything to perfection. He makes for us kettles, axes, swords, knives and gives us drink and food without the trouble of cultivating the ground." The Indians traded for items that improved their own customs. Metal tools replaced stone tools, and metal cooking utensils were preferred to pottery. The Indians acquired guns and rifles and gradually abandoned the bow and arrow.

As the beaver was hunted to extinction in the eastern Great Lakes, the fur trade moved west into Wisconsin. By 1660 the Ottawa and Huron Indians, the middlemen for the French, had established permanent trading centers at Chequamegon Bay in northern Wisconsin that served the upper Mississippi Valley and western Great Lakes.

Competition for furs erupted into warfare among the tribes of the region. The Winnebagos of Wisconsin were nearly decimated in the 1630s in a trade dispute with the eastern Ottawa and Huron. From 1640 to 1660 the French and their Ottawa and Huron allies were thwarted by the powerful Iroquois from upper New York. Armed by Dutch traders, the Iroquois fought for possession of trading routes throughout the St. Lawrence River. The Iroquois wars drove the Algonkian-speaking Fox, Sauk, and Potawatomi into Wisconsin. Other refugees from the eastern Great Lakes region were the Miami, Kickapoo, and Mascouten.

The French built forts at strategic sites to control vital waterways and subdue hostile tribes. The central fort of the Northwest wilderness was at Mackinac, which housed a missionary and a royal notary. For French traders, a trip to Mackinac was a visit to one of the farthest outreaches of the French regime.

The French were not interested in forming colonies but in hunting and trading for furs to take back to New France. The largest French settlement in Wisconsin was around Fort La Baye, which was built in 1717 in present-day Green Bay. There may have been a few permanent French dwellers in Prairie du Chien along the Mississippi River, but not many before 1761.

In order to survive in the Wisconsin wilderness the French fur traders adopted Indian ways. They traveled by canoe, snowshoe and toboggan; they learned Indian languages and ate native food. Their knowledge of Indian ways ensured their survival and also improved business. Some married into tribes. The official traders were licensed by the crown and called voyageurs. They gathered furs or arranged for the Indians to bring the furs to the annual fairs at Montreal and Quebec. The interlopers were unlicensed and called coureurs de bois, or "wood rangers." Because wood rangers were unlicensed they sold furs to either licensed traders who did not want to travel deep into the woods, or else to the English.

One of the most influential traders in New France and Wisconsin was Nicolas Perrot, who visited Chequamegon Bay and Green Bay around 1667 to form alliances between the French crown and the Indians. Perrot established posts along the Mississippi and served as interpreter at peace negotiations with the Wisconsin Indians, building a reputation for diplomacy. "The savages could not understand why these men came so far to search for their worn-out beaver robes," he wrote. "Meanwhile they admired all the wares brought to them by the French, which they regarded as extremely precious." The French traders preferred worn beaver robes, which were supple and brought better prices at the market than the stiff new robes.

French traders mingled easily with the Indians, but the black-robed Jesuit missionaries mystified the Indians. Father Rene Menard, the first Jesuit sent to Wisconsin, died in the dense forests of northern Wisconsin in 1661 while searching for a Huron village near Lac Court Orielles. Father Claude Allouez opened a mission on Chequamegon Bay in 1665, which would later be run by Father Jacques Marquette, and another at Green Bay. Despite the missionaries' zeal, the Indians remained content with their indigenous religion. "I spoke their language," Father Claude Allouez said about his parish at Green Bay. "But alas, what difficulty they have in apprehending a law that is so opposed to all their customs!" Except for a token crucifix, it was often difficult to distinguish between a Christian Indian and a pagan.

While at Chequamegon, Father Allouez reported the vast copper mines around Lake Superior, prompting a search by, among others, Louis Joliet. The Indians were unwilling to reveal the exact locations of mines, and tribal warfare prevented exploration of mines and transportation routes.

Whether the Indians became Christian or not, their lands became France's on June 14, 1671, at Sault Ste. Marie, the post between lakes Superior and Huron. The French proclaimed Louis XIV king of the Great Lakes region and ruler of the lands "to be discovered." With Nicolas Perrot as translator, 14 Indian tribes witnessed the ceremony, acknowledging to Father Claude Allouez and others that they were subjects of the French Sun King. Eighteen years later Nicolas Perrot proclaimed Louis XIV king of the Wisconsin area at Lake Pepin. The English would contest the Sun King's claims.

Competition in the fur trade intensified. The English had allied themselves with New France's old enemies, the Iroquois, and this alliance interrupted New France's near monopoly in furs. The English consistently undercut French prices and exchanged guns and supplies for fewer pelts. In Montreal one gun cost five pelts, but in Albany a gun cost only two pelts. With prices so good, even French wood rangers traded with the English.

This rivalry was not limited to the New World. In Europe, France and England began the first of four wars they would fight between 1689 and 1763. After King William's War ended in 1697, the French realized the need to protect their trade in the western Great Lakes. The sites they chose to build forts grew to become Chicago and Detroit. In 1701 they built Fort Detroit to serve as a primary trade center and also to guard against British incursions. But peace was not in sight.

The Fox Indians, who dominated the lower Fox River in Wisconsin, resented the French for trading directly with the Sioux on the Mississippi. The Fox, who wanted to serve as middlemen, exacted tolls along the Fox and Wisconsin rivers and jealously controlled access to the Mississippi. About 1,000 reluctant Fox were persuaded to settle in Detroit, built by the French as a trade center and fort to guard against British incursions.

During the winter of 1711-1712, however, a fight erupted between the Fox and Ottawa that escalated into a 19-day siege. The French supported the Ottawa and eventually slaughtered almost all of the Fox. The few survivors fled to Wisconsin, their vengeance igniting the Fox wars against the French that lasted intermittently for 25 years. Travel was hazardous along the Wisconsin waterway to the Mississippi. After peace was negotiated in 1716, the French built Fort La Baye in Green Bay to maintain the Fox-Wisconsin route. But new Fox wars erupted again from 1727 to 1738. Wisconsin trade remained in turmoil and the French looked to other trade routes.

The Fox never drove the French from Wisconsin, but they did slow their advance westward across the country. The French turned their attention to Illinois and the Ohio Valley for trading. In the Ohio Valley the French met the English colonists for their final conflict in the New World. The French and Indian War, also called the Seven Years War, was fought from 1756 to 1763 and decided who would control North America.

THE FRENCH AND INDIAN WAR
The Fox having closed expansion in the West, the

French built forts in the Ohio Valley, a region already being colonized by the English. In 1755 the English, who had aligned themselves with the Iroquois, struck back, attacking Fort Duquesne near present-day Pittsburgh. However, the French and their western Indian allies prevailed at Fort Duquesne, killing the English general Edward Braddock and 1,400 British soldiers. The following May and June of 1756, France and Britain formally declared war on each other. The western Indians, led by Charles de Langlade (who was half French and half Ottawa), fought with the French in several key battles. Langlade, a French officer from Mackinac, became one of the first permanent settlers in Green Bay.

New France was hard pressed for supplies and soldiers. Corruption within New France's government had taken its toll. British sailors waged war on Quebec and it fell in 1759. When Montreal fell the next year, Canada succumbed to the British. British sea power cut France from her claims in America, Africa, India, and the Far East. When Spain decided to ally itself with France late in the war, the British wrested Cuba and the Philippines.

Following their victory in 1763, the British claimed all the land east of the Mississippi, except for New Orleans. In the fur-rich land that had been New France, the French retained only two fishing islands off New Foundland. The Mississippi River, which the French had explored and mapped, now became the dividing line between Spanish Louisiana and England's American colonies. The French fur traders and Canadian-born settlers who wanted to trade with the Indians and develop the wilderness, chose to remain in British North America rather than migrate to French territory.

In Wisconsin there were no white residents to make a decision of remaining or leaving. The land west of Lake Michigan was untouched by settlers seeking to make homes. Wisconsin had been valuable only for its water routes to the Mississippi and also in its forts that protected the trade routes. But even though the French had proclaimed Louis XIV ruler of these lands ninety years before, the land remained Indian.

With the French government vanquished, the Indians became alarmed for several reasons. The French had been interested in trade, not land. The English, on the other hand, were colonists lured to the New World by farming. In seeking to control the fur trade, on which they were economically dependent, the Indians could no longer play the French against the English as they had for more than a century.

The Indians revolted against the English in 1763, the year the British signed the peace treaty with France. The sudden uprising, which spread from Mackinac to Niagara, was begun by Chief Pontiac of the Ottawa, who planned a coup against the British in Detroit. Pontiac was rebuffed, but five other forts fell, including Mackinac. In Wisconsin, the English Lieutenant James Gorrell at Green Bay placated the Indians with food, gun powder, and diplomatic speeches. Elsewhere, in the bordering settlements, the uprising was unnerving to the whites who feared Indian torture.

To quell Indian fears, a line was drawn that stopped white settlement from the summit of the Alleghenies to the Mississippi River. Called the Proclamation Line of 1763, it reserved western lands for Indians that would be guarded by the military. The Stamp Act of 1765 required the colonies to help pay for the garrisons along the west. But as tensions between the Crown and the colonists grew, the British paid less attention to the western territories.

Although the British owned the Wisconsin wilderness, they were absentee landlords. The British had abandoned Green Bay to aid besieged Mackinac during Pontiac's uprising in 1763 and never formally returned. The fur trade continued in Green Bay, with Charles de Langlade and his family building a French community. Trade along the upper Mississippi thrived. One fur trader, Peter Pond, reported that 1,500 pounds of fur were sent from the Fox village of Prairie du Chien to Mackinac during the summer of 1774.

The fur trade was relatively unhampered by the Revolutionary War. Britain's yield remained higher during the Revolution than during the seven years preceding the war. There were some difficulties in transporting pelts from Mackinac to Montreal, but both the British and the traders were resourceful. The British continued to trade with the Indians not only to obtain revenue but also to secure their support during the war.

THE REVOLUTIONARY WAR

Wisconsin Indians and British fur traders were dispatched to fight in the Revolutionary War. Charles de Langlade, who had become a captain in the British Indian service, led contingents into the St. Lawrence Valley. While the Indians of southern Wisconsin were considered to be sympathetic to the Americans, the British continued their fur trade along the Fox-Wisconsin route. The bulk of trade to Montreal came from Prairie du Chien and Green Bay during the American Revolution.

The Revolution was a distant sound in Wisconsin. When the British relinquished control over the colonies in 1783, they set the Mississippi River as the western boundary of the new nation. But it took Jay's Treaty, ratified in 1795, for the British to leave their border posts and abandon their lucrative fur trade. Canadian trade was undisturbed because all fur traders—Canadian, Indian, and American—were free to travel on either side of the borders to do business.

Wisconsin's fur trade had always been tied to Montreal, whether controlled by the French or the British. The North West Company, a Canadian company headquartered in Montreal, dominated the field that included Madeline Island in northern Wisconsin and Fond du Lac on Lake Winnebago. Traders who formed small partnerships in the

Above
Rachel Grignon, of the early
Green Bay fur-trading family,
was the daughter of a
Chippewa woman and John
Law, a prominent fur trader.
Courtesy, State Historical
Society of Wisconsin

Left
Fur trader Augustin Grignon
was a member of Green Bay's
founding family. Grignon was
the grandson of Charles de
Langlade, who became
Wisconsin's first permanent
settler in 1764. Courtesy, State
Historical Society of Wisconsin

Charles de Langlade, whose house is pictured in 1890, became the first permanent settler in Wisconsin, and his son-in-law, Pierre Grignon, continued Wisconsin's fur-trading heritage with his family of five sons, who also became fur traders. Courtesy, State Historical Society of Wisconsin

Minnesota-Wisconsin area also prospered. The Langlade family of Green Bay were prominent fur traders in the 1790s, due to Charles Langlade's son-in-law, Pierre Grignon, and his sons. Prairie du Chien was dominated by Canadian fur traders.

Business continued to boom in furs. However, in 1809 the Non-Intercourse Act closed American ports to British and French ships. Montreal's Michilimackinac Company was banned from trade with Green Bay and Prairie du Chien. To circumvent this ban, the Canadians merged their company with John Jacob Astor's American Fur Company. The new firm, the South West Company, Americanized the fur trade in Wisconsin. Following the War of 1812, Astor created an American monopoly in the Upper Great Lakes that would last for 20 years.

THE WAR OF 1812

Relations between the American and British governments were deteriorating, and a chief dispute was trade relations. Competition for furs was keen. Along the frontier, American traders resented the freedom with which the British crossed the border and traded directly with the Indians. In Wisconsin, traders who refused to deal with Astor had to smuggle Canadian goods into the land. Many traders in Wisconsin were bitter.

Tempers among American frontiersmen were also aroused when they saw the British encourage the Shawnee chief Tecumseh. Tecumseh was gathering Indian support from Wisconsin to Alabama with the goal of ousting Americans from Indian land. Indian revolt was a dangerous threat according to Nicholas Boilvin, Prairie du Chien's Indian agent appointed by the U.S. War Department to monitor the Indian fur trade. Boilvin complained of the Canadians' large gifts of supplies to the Indians, which he saw as a sign of war. Indians continued to make pilgrimages to Mackinac, where they received gifts from the British.

Tecumseh had support in Wisconsin. The Winnebago, Sauk, and Potawatomi Indians were hostile to American claims. The governor of the Indiana Territory and future U.S. president, William Henry Harrison, became Tecumseh's archrival. In 1811, Harrison fought Tecumseh on Indiana's Tippecanoe River. Though the battle was a draw, it resulted in Tecumseh losing face among his Indian supporters and never regaining the support he needed. And although Harrison did not win the battle, he and his running mate John Tyler had a winning slogan for the 1840 presidential election: "Tippecanoe and Tyler, too!"

The Americans declared war against the British in June 1812. In Wisconsin the largely Canadian fur traders supported the British. One Prairie du Chien trader, Robert Dickson, recruited Indians for the British. Much of his time was spent finding food and keeping Indian loyalties. Indian support wavered after 1813 when the tide turned in favor of the Americans. Commodore Perry and the Americans beat the British navy in the strategic battle at Lake Erie in September 1813. A month later, at Canada's Thames River, the Americans beat the British in the battle where Chief Tecumseh was killed.

In 1814 American troops arrived in Prairie du Chien to build Fort Shelby and challenge the British along the Fox and Wisconsin rivers. On June 19, 1814, the first American flag to grace a Wisconsin building was raised. The flag's tenure was brief. A three-day skirmish that wounded eight changed the flag to British the following month. The only battle of the War of 1812 to be fought on Wisconsin soil yielded Fort Shelby to the British, who renamed it Fort Mckay after their victorious British colonel. Major Zachary Taylor later tried to reclaim Fort Shelby but was turned back by Sauk Indians at Rock Island.

No boundary changes occurred when the War of 1812 ended in a draw in December 1814. However, President James Madison did close access to the Mississippi River from Canada into American territory. British and Canadian traders were no longer welcome in America's fur trade. The dominance of Great Britain in the Great Lakes region had ended, and the British traders departed, leaving Wisconsin virtually untouched by settlement. For Europeans, Wisconsin had been valuable because of its fur, not its land. Wisconsin's water routes had connected the wilderness to Montreal in a great commercial empire. But the Europeans had always considered the wilderness Indian land. Neither the French or British had left much of an imprint, except that the Indian pathways were more worn and the fur-bearing animals less abundant.

SETTLEMENT AND STATEHOOD

Fort Howard, built in 1816, firmly established American interests in Green Bay, a settlement that had been dominated by French Canadians and Indians. Courtesy, State Historical Society of Wisconsin

Land that Solomon Juneau bought on the east bank of the Milwaukee River in 1833 for $1.25 an acre was being sold for up to $4,000 an acre by 1836. Courtesy, Milwaukee County Historical Society

The next pathfinders into the Wisconsin wilderness would come not by canoe, but by steamboat. In successive waves, new explorers would build upon the Indian trails and eventually force the Indians out. The new pathfinders would not blend into the wilderness, as the fur traders did, but instead would try to put a Yankee stamp on it. Land, not furs, was the new bounty.

Land speculation would become a frontier fever and have devastating effects on the national economy. A crisis in banking, based on easy credit for land sales, would plunge the entire country into depression. One of the most hotly debated issues of territorial Wisconsin would be banking, an issue that would dominate political debate even through the attainment of statehood.

The storms of change were gathering, but the Wisconsin frontier of 1815 was still Indian land. Wisconsin's great frontier historian, Frederick Jackson Turner, described the course of Wisconsin's development. "The Indian village became the trading post, the trading post became the city. The trails became our early roads," he wrote in 1891. "In a word, the fur trade closed its mission by becoming the pathfinder for agriculture and manufacturing civilization." As railroads connected the coasts of the United States, a U.S. senator remarked on the evolution of the buffalo trail: "Science now makes her improved roads exactly where the buffalo's foot first marked the way and the hunter's foot afterwards followed him."

Few frontier historians have matched the eloquence of Frederick Jackson Turner. When the U.S. Census in 1890 proclaimed there was no longer a frontier line, Turner was the first to recognize this as "the closing of a great historic movement." The American frontier, he argued, helped shape the American character: "This perennial rebirth, this fluidity of American life, this expansion westward with its new opportunities, its continuous touch with the simplicity of primitive society, furnish the forces dominating American character."

In 1815 the American frontier consisted of the Illinois Territory, which encompassed Wisconsin. The Indians who lived there were hostile to American claims. The few whites who lived in Wisconsin had allegiance to French and British Canada. One family from New York who settled in Prairie du Chien in 1816 considered themselves the only American residents in the village as late as 1827.

The upper Mississippi, which had been an enclave for the British, was a strategic waterway for the new nation. The American military built three forts along the river in 1816: Fort Crawford in Prairie du Chien, Fort Edwards at the Des Moines River, and Fort Armstrong at the Rock River. Two more forts were built in Wisconsin after a Winnebago uprising

Left
Fort Winnebago was built in 1827 on the portage between the Fox and Wisconsin rivers after an Indian uprising known as the Winnebago War of 1827. Courtesy, State Historical Society of Wisconsin

Below
John Jacob Astor was the founder of the American Fur Company. After the War of 1812 his company established a national monopoly in the fur trade. Astor died in 1834, about the same time that the fur trade in Wisconsin was declining. Courtesy, State Historical Society of Wisconsin

in 1827. Fort Howard was built in Green Bay, and Fort Winnebago was built at the portage between the Fox and Wisconsin rivers.

The U.S. government, protective of its control in the fur trade, passed a law in 1816 that prohibited foreigners from trading with the Indians on U.S. land. At Green Bay and Prairie du Chien the United States government installed two trading posts, called government factories, that sold goods to Indians at prices that substantially undercut those of private traders. Since 1795 factories had aimed at currying loyalty with the Indians and forming ties against the British. In 1822, several years after the British left, the factory system that outraged private traders was abolished.

John Jacob Astor, the eastern fur magnate who had urged both congressional laws, was jubilant. He had revived the American Fur Company and bought out his Canadian partners in the American-based South West Company. The industry once controlled by the French and British would now be American. Astor forged a monopoly in furs that blanketed the Great Lakes frontier. The fur traders in Wisconsin had no choice; if they wanted to work they either had to declare allegiance to the United States, or work for Astor under a licensed clerk. Many traders did both, and they became part of the monopoly that was known as the "Fist in the Wilderness." Bad wages and job insecurity were part of Astor's grip, which lasted until his retirement in 1834.

This trading post of John Jacob
Astor's American Fur Company
was depicted in about 1820.
The company Americanized an
industry that had been controlled by the French and the British. Courtesy, State Historical
Society of Wisconsin

INDIAN LAND CESSION

By the 1830s the fur trade, a wilderness industry, was in decline. White settlement was encroaching and clamors for Indian land cessions were sounding. "The Indian must go," was the vociferous cry of many settlers moving westward. The U.S. government began its removal policy in Wisconsin in 1825 when it arranged an intertribal council at Prairie du Chien. No land changed hands, but Indian tribes were asked to identify the boundaries of their lands as the first step in negotiations.

Tensions were building between Indians and whites. The Winnebago resented whites digging in their lead mines of southeastern Wisconsin, which they had been working years before Nicholas Perrot arrived in 1695. Miners drifting north from the Missouri mines gathered around Galena on the Fever River, an area the U.S. government had bought in 1804 from the Sauk and Fox. From there they continued to move north illegally into Winnebago territory.

Above
The 1825 Treaty of Prairie du Chien, between the U.S. government and several Wisconsin Indian tribes, marked the start of land negotiations between the government and individual tribes. This treaty began the process of removing the Indians from land that could then be settled by whites. Courtesy, State Historical Society of Wisconsin

Left
Winnebago Chief Yellow Thunder (seated) told the pioneer photographer H.H. Bennett in 1867 that his age was 110. Courtesy, the H.H. Bennett Studio

*This Winnebago Indian camped
with his wigwam and canoe in
about 1880. Because Indian practices changed very slowly, this
photo probably reflects how
Winnebago Indians traveled
and camped in earlier times. Courtesy, the H.H. Bennett Studio*

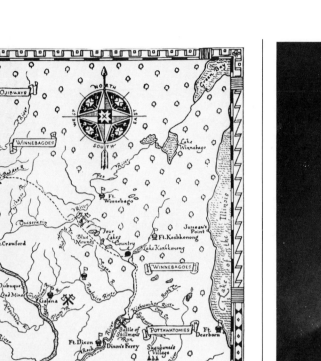

Tensions burst in Prairie du Chien when a Winnebago named Red Bird murdered two white men and scalped a child, who miraculously survived. The military moved to quell the uprising, known as the Winnebago War of 1827, and built a fort on Winnebago land. Red Bird surrendered and a full-scale war was averted. Red Bird later died in prison, and in 1829 the lead-mining region south of the Wisconsin River was ceded to the U.S. government.

Land cessions began in southern Wisconsin in 1829, opening the way for miners, farmers, and lumberjacks to claim land. By 1848 all Indian lands had been ceded by treaty, except for negotiated Indian reservations. During the 1830s two eastern tribes, the Stockbridge-Munsee and the Oneida, were removed to Wisconsin. These new tribes completed the present-day roster of Indians living in Wisconsin: the Chippewa, Potawatomi, Menominee, Stockbridge-Munsee, Oneida, and Winnebago. The Menominee of

Above
Chief Black Hawk was leader of the final Indian insurrection in the Wisconsin region. His defeat at Bad Axe River near the Mississippi River in 1832 ended the Black Hawk War and led to white settlement of Wisconsin. Courtesy, State Historical Society of Wisconsin

Above left
This early map of Indian tribes in the Illinois and Wisconsin region also shows the path of Chief Black Hawk in 1832. Courtesy, State Historical Society of Wisconsin

This sketch of the lead-mining region of southwestern Wisconsin appeared in Harper's Monthly *in 1853. By 1836 lead mining had brought a rush of 10,000 people to southwestern Wisconsin. Courtesy, State Historical Society of Wisconsin*

Wisconsin were able to negotiate a reservation on a portion of their original homeland, making them the oldest known continuous residents of Wisconsin.

The Indians anguished over leaving the homelands they revered. In Wisconsin the Black Hawk War of 1832 was a final convulsion for more than 1,000 Sauk and Fox who despaired at leaving their Illinois home. Serving in the military units that pursued the aging warrior Black Hawk were Abraham Lincoln, Jefferson Davis, and Zachary Taylor. Yet no heroes emerged. Historians have viewed the Black Hawk War as a combination of bungling mistakes and ruthlessness in which almost 850 Indians were killed. Black Hawk, who escaped the army's massacre of the Indians at Bad Axe River, explained his dilemma over land treaties in an autobiography that he later dictated:

My reason teaches me that land cannot be sold. The Great Spirit gave it to his children to live upon, and cultivate, as far as is necessary for their subsistence; and so long as they occupy and cultivate it, they have the right to the soil —but if they voluntarily leave it then any other people have a right to settle upon it. Nothing can be sold, but such things can be carried away.

Initially lead in southwestern Wisconsin was mined close to the surface of the land. But after 1840 the surface lead was depleted and the mineral needed to be brought up from deeper below the ground, as shown in this lithograph of a cross section of a lead mine in 1844. Many Cornish immigrants came to southwestern Wisconsin bringing with them the hard-rock mining techniques from England necessary to mine the remaining lead deposits. These lead miners work below the surface using hard-rock mining techniques in about 1850. Courtesy, State Historical Society of Wisconsin

Since 1787 Wisconsin had been a part of the shifting sands of the Northwest Territory. While part of the Indiana Territory created in 1800, in effect it was controlled by the British until after the War of 1812. In 1809 Wisconsin became part of the Illinois Territory, and in 1818 was annexed to the Michigan Territory after Illinois became a state. The Northwest Ordinance of 1787 detailed the procedure by which settlers could turn the frontier into states. The government would appoint a territorial governor plus three judges, each of whom had to own from 500 to 1,000 acres in the territory. Once there were 5,000 voters in the territory, the government granted a territorial legislature. The government deemed settlers to be voters if they were male, free, 21 years old, owned 50 acres of land, and were residents of the territory for two years. Once the territory reached 60,000 voters it could petition for statehood.

In 1830 the U.S. census counted 31,600 whites in the Michigan Territory, only about 3,000 of whom lived in the land that became Wisconsin. Wisconsin had only two small villages, Green Bay on Lake Michigan and Prairie du Chien on the Mississippi River. The residents were primarily descendents of the original fur traders, a mix of French-Canadian and Indian blood.

THE LEAD INDUSTRY

The opening of the Erie Canal in 1825 connected the Great Lakes to eastern markets. Once more Wisconsin was part of an important water route. Lead ore was the magnet for much of American settlement in Wisconsin. Lead was the basic ingredient for paint and bullets, perhaps two of the frontier civilization's primary tools. The region's lead, or "galena," lay close to the surface, often exposed on hill sides and ravines. These loose pieces, called "floats," alerted miners to hidden lodes. One resident from Galena in northern Illinois noted that "mining is as simple a process as the common method of digging wells."

Lead fever sparked a rush of 10,000 people by 1836. In 1829 more than 13 million pounds of refined lead were produced by the tri-state region of present-day Wisconsin, Iowa, and northern Illinois. The government did not sell the land but instead leased permits to miners, and only licensed smelters could

Above
Cornish lead miners settled in and around Mineral Point during the lead rush of the 1820s and 1830s. A Cornish miner's home is restored on Mineral Point's Shakerag Street. Courtesy, State Historical Society of Wisconsin

Right
Land sales swept Wisconsin during the 1830s and 1840s, and Cyrus Woodman and Cadwallader C. Washburn of Mineral Point were prominent promoters. Courtesy, State Historical Society of Wisconsin

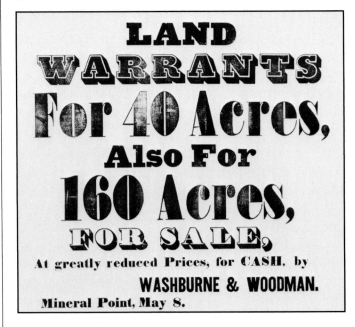

refine the lead ore. The government then collected 10 percent of the lead from the smelter as a royalty.

In the lead region, farming was permitted only where it did not interfere with mining. The government leasing system forbade miners to buy land; only land barren of minerals could be sold. But the lead region was also prime agricultural land. Many miners, farmers and investors wanted to buy land; there are reports that land was declared mineral-free after being examined blindfolded.

A depression in lead prices from 1829 to 1831 forced a revision in the government's land policy. With sinking lead prices and soaring food prices, many people turned to farming to make a living. In 1829 flour cost $15 a barrel, the price of 5,000 pounds of lead. The land offices that opened in 1834 in Mineral Point and Green Bay encouraged more farming. By 1847 the leasing system was dead and all land was for sale, including mineral reserves.

Lead production peaked in 1845 with 24,300 tons. However, this yield plummeted by 50 percent within five years. The accessible veins of ore had been exhausted and the deeper ore needed elaborate equipment to mine. The lead from the deep mining was mixed with what miners considered worthless zinc, which would not have a profitable market until 1900.

Though some miners were lured away by the California Gold Rush, the Cornish kept the lead industry productive after 1840, when most of the surface lead was gone. The tin mines in Cornwall, England had trained generations of miners who were used to hardrock mining and problems with water drainage. As Cornwall's tin industry declined, about 7,000 miners were attracted to the Mineral Point region of Wisconsin by the prospect of working for themselves. Among the innovations they introduced was the safety fuse for blasting.

The lead miners are credited with giving Wisconsin its nickname of the Badger State. Before Wisconsin reached statehood a 35-page history of Wisconsin was published in 1845 called *The Home of the Badgers*. According to tradition, many miners dug holes into hillsides during the cold and, like the badger, set up housekeeping. One pioneer, Daniel Parkinson, described the hillside homes of New Diggings, a village in southwestern Wisconsin. "They usually lived in dens or caves; a large hole or excavation covered with poles, grass, and sods," wrote Parkinson in 1827. "In

Solomon Juneau, a French-Canadian fur trader, built his first trading post on what would become Wisconsin's most valuable real estate, downtown Milwaukee. In 1833 Juneau became Milwaukee's first resident. Courtesy, State Historical Society of Wisconsin

Right
Land speculator James Doty was Wisconsin's second territorial governor. In 1836 Doty maneuvered the first territorial convention into selecting Madison as the capital of Wisconsin. Courtesy, State Historical Society of Wisconsin

Below
This map of Milwaukee in 1836 shows that the majority of platted land surrounded the Milwaukee River. Solomon Juneau's trading post of 1833 had swelled dramatically under the spell of land speculation. Courtesy, State Historical Society of Wisconsin

MAP OF
MILWAUKEE
SHOWING LOCATION OF ITS PRINCIPAL
BUILDINGS IN THE SPRING OF 1836
AS RECOLLECTED BY
Dr ENOCH CHASE, U B SMITH & OTHERS
Indicates Law Lands

these holes or dug-outs, families lived in apparent comfort and the most perfect satisfaction for years, buoyed by the constant expectation of soon striking a big lead."

Just as the fur industry gave rise to Green Bay and Prairie du Chien, the lead industry gave rise to towns such as Mineral Point, Platteville, and Dodgeville. Mineral Point, well-placed between the lead metropolis of Galena and ports on the Wisconsin River, was named the county seat in 1830, and in 1834 it became the site for one of the territory's two land offices. The frontier was home to the itinerant miners who named their temporary villages Red Dog, Burlesqueburgh, Nip-and-Tuck, Hoof Noggle, Hard Scrabble, Grab, and Trespass. As the area became farmlands, many communities were renamed.

THE LAND RUSH AND THE PANIC OF 1837

After lead, the land rush was the biggest business in Wisconsin. The sparsely populated interior of Wisconsin was first surveyed around Green Bay and Mineral

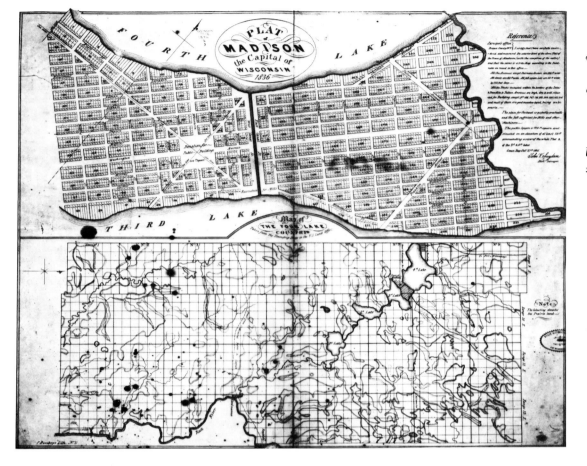

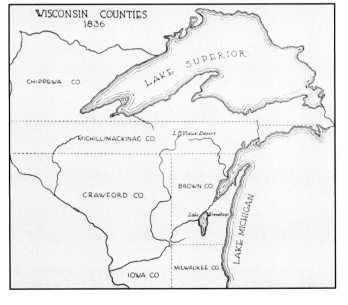

Left:
Many people were shocked when the legislators voted for Madison in 1836 as the permanent capital, because it was uninhabited wilderness. This map shows an optimistic view of the platted land, which quickly became a reality under the leadership of James Doty, land speculator and former judge. Doty would become Wisconsin's second territorial governor. Courtesy, State Historical Society of Wisconsin

Below:
When Wisconsin was declared a territory in 1836, it comprised parts of what are now Iowa and Minnesota. Courtesy, State Historical Society of Wisconsin

Henry Dodge, who became Wisconsin's first territorial governor in 1836, prided himself on being an Indian fighter in the Black Hawk War. Courtesy, State Historical Society of Wisconsin

Point. All land had to be surveyed before it could be sold for $1.25 an acre. Land speculators were the biggest buyers, but squatters also made claims to land. Many homesteaders cleared land before it was ready for public sale. Speculators with sales receipts inevitably clashed with homesteaders who were already living on the land. The Jackson administration passed four laws between 1830 and 1838 that gave some homesteaders protection. Finally, prompted by frontier agitation for a comprehensive law, the Pre-emption Act of 1841 gave all western homesteaders rights to the land they had claimed before the land was surveyed for public sale.

From 1835 to 1837 much of the country became a crazy quilt of squatters, resident landowners, and outside land speculators. The favorite targets for land speculation were the prospective towns that studded the Mississippi Valley. "Speculator," a pejorative term generally reserved for absentee owners, usually was not applied to residents buying large tracts of land. Of the 38 million acres of public land sold in the country from 1835 to 1837, 29 million acres probably belonged to speculators. In Wisconsin one active land agent, Moses Strong of Mineral Point, estimated that of the 878,014 acres sold through 1836, three-fourths went to speculators.

As land speculators tried to divine where the best land was, most promoters agreed the prime sites in Wisconsin were on waterways. Much of Wisconsin was a dense wilderness, with uncharted forests and streams separating Prairie du Chien on the Mississippi from Green Bay on lake Michigan. The Wisconsin River was the only highway between the two in 1832, during the Black Hawk War. Congress then appropriated $5,000 for a road to connect Fort Howard in Green Bay to Fort Crawford in Prairie du Chien, including Fort Winnebago in the portage between the Fox and Wisconsin rivers. Built by the soldiers of the three posts, the Military Road bridged streams and filled in swamps for 234 miles. The route it followed was south of the Fox and Wisconsin rivers, which had been heavily trafficked by the fur trade. In many places the road was no more than a lane through forests, but it attracted settlers who helped to maintain the road and keep it passable. Most settlers in Wisconsin, however, would still be attracted to the port cities.

Solomon Juneau, a French-Canadian fur trader, was astonished to discover that his fur trading post

In 1842 New Yorker Jerome I.
Case followed the wheat frontier to Racine. He brought with
him six wheat threshers, the
start of spectacular growth in
wheat threshers and harvesting machines. Case built his empire in
part by traveling through roadless Wisconsin and selling
threshers to farmers. Courtesy,
State Historical Society of
Wisconsin

was sitting on valuable land. His solitary building, surrounded by Indian wigwams, was located next to the Milwaukee River, which flowed into Lake Michigan. "His first hint of the prospective value of his location at Milwaukee came from me," recalled Morgan L. Martin, a Green Bay land speculator originally from New York. "He was so incredulous that it was sometimes difficult to prevent his sacrificing his interest to the sharks who soon gathered around him." In a verbal agreement, Martin formed a partnership with Juneau and claimed squatter's rights to 289 acres under President Jackson's 1834 pre-emption law that protected homesteaders.

The land that became downtown Milwaukee was first developed as Juneautown on the east bank of the Milwaukee River. A land surveyor from Ohio, Byron Kilbourn, built Kilbourntown on the west bank. Within three years of talking to Martin in 1833, Juneau's Indian village had increased to 50 houses and 1,208 villagers. Wisconsin writer Increase Lapham, who mapped the village in 1836, exclaimed, "Eighteen months ago there were but two families!" The land Juneau had bought for $1.25 an acre was selling for up to $4,000 an acre in 1836.

Wisconsin was declared a territory in 1836, during one of the biggest land sales in the history of the United States. Banks flooded the country with bank notes borrowed by speculators to buy public land, which they would then use as collateral to borrow more money for more land. Speculators could not afford to use hard currency for payment, but paper money was abundant. The bubble of land speculation broke in 1837.

The nationwide land speculation fever suffered a panic, following a New York City bank crash in May 1837 that spread to banks throughout the country. Banks lost confidence in bank notes and refused to accept them as payment. In July 1837 the U.S. Secretary of the Treasury issued the Specie Circular, a proclamation that required all lands sales to be paid in gold and silver only. The days of buying land on credit and with inflated bank notes were over. The Panic of 1837 destroyed almost all the banks in the Middle West, including Wisconsin. The country plunged into a severe depression that would last until about 1843.

Wisconsin became a territory in 1836 with all the optimism of boom times in land sales and prosperity of the lead rush. The next year Wisconsin felt the panic of the depression. In 1837 Wisconsin's first territorial governor, Henry Dodge, urged a one-year stay on court judgments that involved debtors. A stay of execution "would prevent the ruin of many whose property will be liable to sale at great loss," said Dodge, a flamboyant Indian fighter and faithful Jacksonian Democrat. The reason for Wisconsin's predicament was what Dodge called "the present embarrassed state of the currency in this Territory." There simply wasn't enough money around. Wisconsin's prosperity was further diminished in 1838 when the land incorporating Iowa and much of Minnesota became the Iowa Territory, removing nearly one-half of the Wisconsin Territory's industrious mining population.

The decision of where to locate the Wisconsin Territory's new capital was the first dispute between Dodge and James Doty, a Yankee land speculator who became Wisconsin's second territorial governor in 1840. In July 13 1836, Dodge chose Belmont as the temporary capital on the advice of a hopeful promoter. Belmont, off the beaten path in the southwest mining region, invoked so many complaints that Dodge promised to automatically approve the Legislature's decision on the permanent capital.

Doty had real estate interests in the area known as the City of the Four Lakes, soon to be named Madison. On July 1, 1836, on the way to Belmont's only legislative convention, he and a surveyor drew a plat of the "Town of Madison." Doty proved himself a master lobbyist, giving choice parcels of land in Madison to each legislator who promised to vote for Madison. An isolated wilderness town sitting on four lakes, Madison was virtually uninhabited, yet thanks to Doty's diligent campaigning, it was chosen as the new capital. To ensure that Madison would remain the capital, Doty quickly sold lots to prominent dignitaries, including the chief justice of the Wisconsin Supreme Court and Governor Dodge's son.

The most pressing problem in settling Wisconsin was transportation. Traveling on a stagecoach between Madison and Milwaukee, Swedish author Frederika Bremer described the well-used road in 1849: "I was shaken, or rather hurled, unmercifully hither and thither upon the newborn roads of Wisconsin, which are no roads at all, but a succession of hills, holes, and waterpools." Businessman Jerome I. Case, selling his wheat threshers throughout the region, found the roads in 1851 "soft with no bottoms in places."

The first building of the Wisconsin Marine and Fire Insurance Company, in Milwaukee, was not officially a bank. Because of the political backlash against wildcat banking, Wisconsin was bankless from 1841 to 1853. But certificates from George Smith's Wisconsin Marine and Fire Insurance Company were treated as paper money and were popularly called "George Smith's money." Courtesy, State Historical Society of Wisconsin

Another traveler described the bridges: "They get two huge trees 50 to 60 feet long, and lay across from bank to bank of creeks or small rivers. Then they lay small poles across, just to stop a horse's foot from going through, and that's all."

To stimulate financial capital for development of roads into the wilderness, the Legislature granted corporate charters for both banks and transportation companies. According to business historian George Kuehnl, of the 35 charters granted from 1836 to 1840, 7 were for banks and 11 were for canals and railroads. From 1841 to 1848, 29 of the 38 charters were related to transportation: piers, bridges, canals, steamboats, railroads, plankroads, and turnpikes. These large projects required more money than could be collected by a few investors during the depression, and canals and railroads required government land grants. By the time Wisconsin reached statehood in 1848, no canals had been dug and no railroads had been built.

After the tremendous success of the Erie Canal, which brought Yankee settlers into the Great Lakes region, many developers dreamed of connecting Wisconsin's rivers by canals. Promoters had plans to connect the Fox River with the Wisconsin River at the portage, but the Wisconsin River proved to be too shallow. Byron Kilbourn worked to connect the Milwaukee River to the Rock River and then across land into the lead region. James Doty wanted to connect Lake Winnebago to the Rock River and then on to the four lakes of Madison, where he held substantial real estate. Competing for scarce capital, Governor Doty was able to block Kilbourn's canal route, though the dam Kilbourn constructed became a source of power for Milwaukee's pioneer flour-milling industry.

BANKING

Banking would become a highly contested issue as Wisconsin entered statehood in 1848. Much of the animosity derived from Green Bay's Bank of Wisconsin, chartered in 1835, and the Bank of Mineral Point, chartered in 1836. These frontier banks engaged in wildcat banking, the cavalier policy of issuing bank notes in high quantities regardless of actual deposits held. The trick was to keep from having the bank notes redeemed. Many of the stockholders looked upon these banks as easy ways to capitalize their land speculations. When the Wisconsin attorney general seized the assets from the Bank of Wisconsin in 1839, the hard currency in the bank's vault amounted to $86.20 compared to liabilities of $100,000. Following this episode the public remained suspicious of banks, viewing them as inventors of worthless bank notes.

Reflecting public opinion, the Wisconsin Legislature refused to charter banks, from 1841 to 1853. In 1852 Wisconsin was one of seven states that did not have any incorporated banks. Yet hard currency was scarce, and the territory's struggling economy needed basic banking services such as loans and credit.

George Smith, a Scottish real estate speculator in Chicago and Milwaukee, devised a way to bring banking services to Milwaukee. He proposed to the Legislature the formation of the Wisconsin Marine and Fire Insurance Company. This famous shadow bank was granted a charter by the Legislature in 1839 as an insurance company. The charter provided the right to accept deposits and make loans, though banking services were prohibited. Smith, ignoring this contradiction, built a million-dollar business issuing certificates that the company was always prepared to redeem in gold. As Smith's reputation grew, his certificates of deposit were redeemable in gold in Chicago, Detroit, St. Louis, and as far away as Buffalo and New York City.

Smith and his partner, Alexander Mitchell, also helped Wisconsin settlers to buy land and farmers to sell their crops. The company would buy the land in gold from the government and sell it to the settlers on a contract basis. George Smith's certificates of deposit became the pioneer's paper money. Farmers could sell wheat to New York and accept certificates of deposit, instead of waiting for the buyer to send gold after re-selling the wheat to the eastern markets. In Wisconsin and the Middle West, the business community was grateful for "George Smith's money," as it was popularly known. However, the Legislature investigated the insurance company and in 1846 pressed for repeal of the company's charter. Alexander Mitchell defended the company by pointing out that investors received moderate returns and that the company did not engage in speculation. In addition, the company argued that the Legislature had no basis to repeal a charter unless its power to repeal was stipulated in the original charter. While this argument was supported by the Legislature's Judiciary Committee Council, the charter was repealed.

George Smith ignored the repeal of his company's charter and continued business. Four years later the attorney general ruled the repeal was unconstitutional. By 1852 the public sentiment against banking had changed among the voters, in large part due to the reputation of George Smith. The Legislature voted to allow banking again, and the Wisconsin Marine and Fire Insurance Company reorganized under the new law. George Smith sold his holdings to his partner, Alexander Mitchell, and returned to Scotland with a fortune estimated at $10 million.

IMMIGRATION

As the country recovered from the depression in 1843, New England Yankees packed their bags and moved West in search of land and new opportunities. Together with pioneers from the Middle Atlantic states, 103,000 Yankees settled in Wisconsin between 1840 and 1850; by 1850 one-fourth of Wisconsin's population was New Yorkers. While some migrants were drawn to Wisconsin by its rich, abundant farmland, many easterners had economic and political connections that helped them become entrepreneurs and politicians in the West. For example, of the largest names in land speculation, C.C. Washburn and Cyrus Woodman were from Maine, and Moses Strong was from Vermont. James Doty, Wisconsin's second territorial governor, was from New York. Wisconsin's first elected governor, Nelson Dewey, was a lawyer from Connecticut. As the 1846 state convention clamored for statehood, 46 of the 124 delegates were native New Yorkers, and 72 had some New York connection through education, residence, or business experience.

Between 1840 and 1850, Wisconsin's population increased ten-fold to 305,000. During this period sail and steam boats through the Erie Canal brought 106,000 Europeans to Wisconsin. Social reformer Margaret Fuller observed their arrival in Milwaukee in 1843: "During the fine weather the poor refugees arrive daily, in their national dresses all travel-soiled and worn. The night they pass in rude shantees, in a particular quarter of the town, then walk off into the country—the mothers carrying their infants, the fathers leading the little children by the hand, seeking a home where their hands may maintain them." Immigrants during this decade included 38,000 Germans, 9,000 Scandinavians, 21,000 Irish, and 28,000 English, Scots, and Welsh. Many of the Germans stayed in Milwaukee, and by 1850 the German-born accounted for 40 percent of Milwaukee's population.

STATEHOOD

With these sharp increases in population Wisconsin moved closer to statehood. By 1845 Wisconsin had more than the 60,000 voters required for statehood as suggested by the Ordinance of 1787. The framers of the state constitution met in 1846 to decide on government structure and conclude debates concerning boundaries between Illinois, Michigan, and Minnesota as drawn by President Polk's administration.

The most bitterly debated issue at the three-month constitutional convention was banking. While no one was in favor of wildcat banking, Whigs generally supported the concept of banks and Democrats rejected all banking. The article set before the convention banned all banks and paper money. Opponents of the article tended to agree that Wisconsin, while it did not need banks at the time, might need them in the future. Politicians ignored the business community's assertion that by forbidding paper money or banks, the article was preventing future prosperity.

Rufus King, editor of the *Milwaukee Sentinel and Gazette*, strongly denounced the proposed ban on banking, arguing in an editorial campaign that the banking article "will add immediately to the glittering heaps of those who have already amassed stores of coin. It will assuredly make the rich richer; but it will, as assuredly, keep the poor, still poor; if it does not make them poorer." King was one of many opponents who saw the need for credit and loans in a growing economy.

Persuaded by the arguments of King and others,

the voters rejected the proposed constitution. Its nemesis was the article banning banks, according to historian Robert Nesbit. In 1847 the delegates met again, anxious for Wisconsin to become a state in time for the 1848 presidential election. The new compromise gave the voters the right to accept or reject any legislation on banks by special referendum. The constitution was accepted, and on May 29, 1848, Wisconsin became the thirtieth state.

Wisconsin had become a state amid tumultuous economic times. The boom period of land speculation had crashed in the Panic of 1837, and countless businesses were ruined in the nationwide depression that followed. Upon statehood Wisconsin was bankless and virtually roadless, but European and Yankee settlers had dreams of prosperity in a wilderness of rivers, forests and rich farmland.

Cassville became a home of Nelson Dewey, Wisconsin's first elected governor. This lithograph is from a drawing by the German artist Henry Lewis, who in 1854 published an illustrated book Das Illustrirte Mississpithal. *Courtesy, State Historical Society of Wisconsin*

THE PIONEER ECONOMY

*A Norwegian family near Madison uses a
reaper to harvest wheat fields in about 1873.
Courtesy, State Historical Society
of Wisconsin*

An early photo of a log jam in Chippewa Falls in 1869 shows the dilemma loggers had when it came to unraveling the wooden gridlock. Courtesy, State Historical Society of Wisconsin.

During the years of frontier settlement, the Wisconsin economy took root in the growing wheat fields. "King Wheat," according to the *Prairie Farmer* in 1850, "pays debts, buys groceries, clothing, lands, and answers more emphatically the purposes of trade than any other crop." Even in the lead region of southwestern Wisconsin, farming gradually replaced mining.

Until the wheat belt moved westward in the late 1860s, Wisconsin was one of the nation's leading wheat producers. In 1860 farmers produced 29 million bushels of wheat, about one-sixth of the nation's total. Wheat, Wisconsin's great cash crop, commanded good prices at the Great Lakes ports. Wheat was also the ideal crop for pioneer farmers, who needed time to clear and break the land. It was easily sown and could be ignored until harvest. While the fields turned from tender green to burnished gold, the settlers could fence and build.

The problem for wheat farmers was in harvesting the crop. The basic tool, the scythe, was essentially unchanged since biblical times. The scythe was woe-fully inadequate for large fields of wheat, which needed to be harvested within days, and gathered by hand into sheaves for storage before threshing. The farmer needed either a large workforce, which meant wages, or better tools for harvesting. During the 1840s Wisconsin inventors improved threshers and harvesters, laying the groundwork for Wisconsin's farm machine industry.

As lead mining began to decline around 1845, farming became the main occupation in Wisconsin. In 1850 the state had more than 40,000 farmers, the largest occupational group in a population of 305,000. Wheat was grown in all Wisconsin counties, with the southeastern and south-central counties being the largest producers. Oats and corn were grown for livestock and became major crops, particularly in the southwestern region. By 1840 potatos became a crop for domestic use, and by 1850 the potato yield would exceed 1.4 million bushels. Settlers continued the Indian tradition of producing maple syrup, and in 1839 more than 135,000 pounds were produced. By 1850 more than 600,000 pounds of maple syrup reached the market, coming from all but eight counties.

Location was one of the pioneer farmer's primary concerns in roadless Wisconsin. "Strangers looking for a home ought to look more to location and proximity to market than to the price," advised guidebook writer John Gregory in 1855. The best lands had a combination of forest and prairie. The woods supplied lumber for barns and fences, while the prairie was broken for crops. Forested lands were usually less expensive because the land had to first be cleared of trees and stumps. By 1850 prices for land ranged from $3 to $30 per acre based on proximity to markets and the amount of settlement on the land.

GROWTH OF EARLY INDUSTRIES
In frontier Wisconsin, business and industry were spurred by a growing population and an abundance of natural resources that didn't require large capital to exploit. Wisconsin's population more than doubled from 305,000 in 1850 to 776,000 in 1860. Settlers clustered largely in the southern counties, the sites of early manufacturing. In 1860 the counties lying south and east of Green Bay contained more than 82 percent of the state's 776,000 population and produced more than 83 percent of the $11 million in goods.

Processing raw materials, specifically wheat and lumber, dominated Wisconsin's early manufacturing. In 1850 flour and lumber mills contributed about 40 percent of manufacturing, with flour surpassing lumber. A decade later, lumber and flour would continue to dominate with 42 percent, with lumber exceeding flour milling. The average firm employed fewer than five men.

As a major industry, flour and grist mills were a natural extension of Wisconsin's bounty in wheat and water power. Every village located on a stream with enough power to turn a water wheel boasted a flour mill. Milwaukee and Racine, which emerged early as flour milling centers, drew on three advantages: water power, access to the wheat crops, and harbors that served as ports to the larger markets. Inland counties could also build markets from the local wheat fields. Jefferson County in south-central Wisconsin was in the wheat belt, and towns such as Watertown and Jefferson had thriving flour mills.

During the 1850s flour milling would gradually centralize in Milwaukee and the lower Fox River Valley, as wheat farming moved north and railroads connected Milwaukee across the state. By 1860 the villages of Neenah and Menasha would produce 50,000 barrels of flour, ranking second to Milwaukee. Wheat flour in 1860 accounted for almost 19 percent of Wisconsin's manufacturing.

The thick forests of northern Wisconsin, ribboned with rivers and streams, were a haven for Wisconsin's early lumberjacks. This was the land carved by the Ice Age. The glaciers which had formed Wisconsin's lakes and streams also pulverized rocks into sand, the soil on which white pine thrives. Most of the forests belonged to the Indians, and during the 1830s, when fur trading and lead mining dominated, there was a scarcity of building materials in the settled regions of southern Wisconsin, as logging was done only on a small scale. When the first territorial capitol was built in 1836, the lumber was imported from Pennsylvania. Land treaties with the Indians in 1836 and 1837 opened the thick pine forests of northern Wisconsin, which became the domain of the loggers. The lumber industry, which soon superseded the fur trade and lead mining, was concentrated north of Manitowoc to Portage and upward to the St. Croix River. Before the arrival of the railroads the rivers of Wisconsin divided the state into six lumbering districts: Green Bay and Wolf River districts in the northeast, and Wisconsin, Black, Chippewa, and St. Croix districts in the northwest.

The prized wood was pine, and the forest that blanketed the northern three-fifths of Wisconsin was called the pinery even though there were mixed conifers and hardwood. White pine is a softwood that cuts easily and smoothly. It is strong for its weight, and resists rot because it's resinous. Pine was the carpenter's first choice in building houses. The treeless states of Illinois, Iowa, and the Great Plains were markets for Wisconsin pine sent down the Mississippi River. The annual production of Wisconsin lumber in 1853 was an estimated 200 million board feet.

In 1831 a Green Bay entrepreneur built a sawmill on the Wisconsin River, and by 1847 there were 24 sawmills on the Wisconsin River, plus 5 on the Chippewa River and 5 on the St. Croix River. The lumber industry was moving westward, and lumberjacks from Maine and other eastern states were following. A Maine congressman complained of "the stalwart sons

of Maine marching away by scores and hundreds to the piny woods of the Northwest." Wisconsin pioneer lumber barons—Philetus Sawyer of Vermont, Isaac Stephenson of New Brunswick and Orrin H. Ingram of New York—learned the business in the East.

Lumber towns now flourished in the region once prized by Indians and trappers for beaver. Chippewa County in northwestern Wisconsin, which had only 615 residents in 1850, had more than 10,000 settlers in 1860. In 1840 the Chippewa River Valley contained an estimated one-sixth of all white pine west of the Appalachians, which translated into a potential 20 billion board feet. Eau Claire County became one of the major lumber-processing regions, and the towns of Oshkosh, La Crosse, Eau Claire, Chippewa Falls, and Stillwater developed into important sawmilling centers.

URBAN GROWTH

By the time of statehood in 1848, Wisconsin had a constellation of five urban centers: Platteville, Janesville, Kenosha, Racine and Milwaukee. The growth of these towns, each of which boasted more than 2,500

Above
Flour mills were one of Wisconsin's pioneer industries, as Wisconsin was a leading wheat producer before the 1870s. Built in Green Lake Prairie, this flour- and gristmill was moved to Alto around 1896. Courtesy, State Historical Society of Wisconsin

Right
Between the Fox and Wisconsin rivers, Portage was historically a crossroads for travelers sojourning in Wisconsin. In 1829 Army Lieutenant Jefferson Davis wrote, "I and the file of soldiers who accompanied me were the first white men who ever passed over the country between the Portage of the Wisconsin and Fox rivers and the then village of Chicago." Courtesy, State Historical Society of Wisconsin

residents, reflected the growth of the state economy. Platteville, like its rival Mineral Point, was built near a rich lead lode close to the Mississippi River. Surrounded by timber and growing farm lands, Platteville became a center for Grant County's manufacturing of flour and sawmilling in addition to lead mining. Janesville, located on the Rock River in the heart of the wheat belt, used its water power for mills, its roads placing it between the bustling commercial center at Racine and the southwestern lead mining region. Kenosha, originally named Southport by the New Yorkers who settled it, competed to become a port city in the 1840s for exporting wheat, lead, and lumber. Nearby Racine, whose roads into the interior connected it to the wheat belt, became the second largest manufacturing center after Milwaukee.

By 1850 Milwaukee had been transformed into Wisconsin's urban center. Solomon Juneau's fur post had grown from an Indian village to a metropolis of

Artist L.E. Blair conveyed the feeling of a frontier town in this sketch of Dodgville in 1859, which he drew for the State Highway Commission. Wisconsin's first territorial governor, Henry Dodge, settled on Indian territory south of what became the village of Dodgville in the late 1820s. Courtesy, State Historical Society of Wisconsin

20,000. Commerce was the key to Milwaukee's initial growth, just as manufacturing was the key to its future. Its largely "wheat and hog" economy used rails and lake transport to ship wheat to the East and Canada's eastern market. With the trafficking in wheat, 14 flour mills sprang up in Milwaukee by 1860. During the Civil War, Milwaukee would become the largest flour-milling city in the West.

While primarily a commercial port city, Milwaukee was setting down roots of industry. By 1860 Milwaukee County contributed more than 27 percent of the state's nearly $30 million dollars in manufactured goods. As historian Margaret Walsh noted, diversification distinguished Milwaukee industries from those of other Wisconsin towns. While other sites depended on one industry, such as lumber in northern Wisconsin, Milwaukee had a broader base. In 1850 six industries contributed to half of Milwaukee's manufactured goods: flour milling, clothing, construction material, iron, furniture, and shoes. In 1860 five in-

Above
A county fair may have been the occasion for Janesville's crowded Court and Main streets in the late 1860s. Janesville was in Wisconsin's wheat belt and by 1870 had a population of 8,789. Courtesy, State Historical Society of Wisconsin

Right
By 1860 Oshkosh had a population of 6,100 and its economy was rapidly growing, thanks to its location on Lake Winnebago and the Wolf River basin. Lumbering and sawmilling were important industries. Courtesy, State Historical Society of Wisconsin

industries provided half the output in manufactured products: flour milling, iron products, clothing, liquors, and shoes. Yet despite Milwaukee's promise of large industry, in 1860 only 7.5 percent of Milwaukee's population engaged in manufacturing.

Building materials were a substantial part of Milwaukee's early growth during the 1840s. Brickmaking became an early specialty, and the famous yellow bricks from the city's clay beds gave Milwaukee the title of "the Cream City." By 1850 there were 11 brick yards employing 95 workers who produced more than 11 million bricks. Wood manufacturing was important to the city's economy, and planed pine lumber imported from northern Wisconsin was used throughout the city.

Milwaukee dominated Wisconsin's developing meat packing industry. Wisconsin farmers were raising about 160,000 hogs and 185,000 cattle in 1850, creating a foundation for meat packing. While problems with refrigeration kept meat packing small-scale and local, by 1860 Milwaukee was responsible for three-quarters of Wisconsin's meat packing. Milwau-

The New Yorkers who founded Kenosha originally named the port city "Southport" in 1841 because it was the southernmost natural harbor in Wisconsin. By 1860 Kenosha would boast a population of 4,000. Courtesy, State Historical Society of Wisconsin

"To Sell is the Watchword, and Never to be undersold their Motto."

BONESTEEL'S

Take your time, and you shall all be served in your turn.

CHEAP CASH STORE

CALL AND TRY.

GREAT RUSH AGAIN AT BONESTEEL'S

CHEAP CASH STORE,

Since they received their

NEW GOODS

At No. 187 East Water Street,

Where they are opening a large and choice selection of DRY GOODS AND GROCERIES, adapted expressly for the Western Trade, and solicit the attention of purchasers to the examination of their stock, as they would find it very much to their advantage in making their selection, both in regard to quality and price. Their stock is new, and selected with the greatest care, and bought at a time when there were many failures in the eastern cities, and while the prices of Goods of all descriptions were continually falling, therefore they can offer greater facilities in making selections, and be enabled to sell at less prices than those who keep a small stock and sell less goods.

Above
An ad in the first Directory of the City of Milwaukee, in 1847, featured an advertisement for a grocery store, Bonesteel's Cheap Cash Store. Courtesy, Milwaukee County Historical Society

Right
This 1856 bird's-eye view of Milwaukee emphasizes its port, one of the major reasons for its growth. Milwaukee's economy was based on commerce from its port to Eastern markets. Industries such as brewing, tanning, meat-packing, and manufacturing represented only 7.5 percent of Milwaukee's economy by 1860. Courtesy, State Historical Society of Wisconsin

kee exported meat northward to lumber camps and also to eastern markets, and as railroads connected the city to Wisconsin's hinterland, cattle and hogs could be shipped to Milwaukee alive for slaughtering. The tanning of leather goods, such as saddles and harnesses, was also an important processing industry, and Milwaukee had 13 tanneries by 1860.

The German art of brewing beer expanded rapidly in the 1850s, becoming Wisconsin's fourth leading industry in 1860. By 1855 more than 50,000 barrels were produced by 20 breweries. Two years later there were six more breweries, and the total output of beer jumped to 75,000 barrels. Much of the beer was consumed locally, but Milwaukee's brewers exported as many as 35,000 barrels to Chicago in 1857.

Capital, the fuel for manufacturing, was scarce in the frontier, forcing Milwaukee to export most of its raw materials instead of manufacturing products within the city. Milwaukee and towns throughout Wisconsin created their own markets for locally produced clothing, shoes, and furniture. These businesses

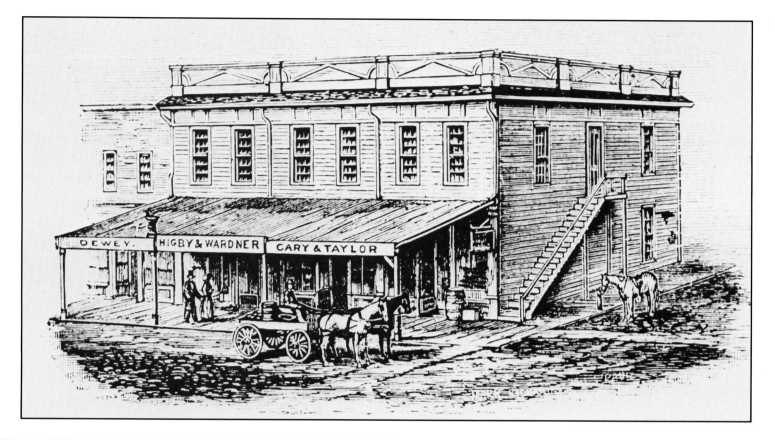

Above
The Milwaukee Sentinel *reported on pioneer life, and in 1848 it was the main customer for Wisconsin's first paper mill. The Milwaukee mill recycled old rags for printing the news. Courtesy, State Historical Society of Wisconsin*

Right
Milwaukee's largest early German beer garden, the Milwaukee Garden, opened in 1855. Beer gardens were social centers for the German community where customs were preserved. Courtesy, Milwaukee County Historical Society

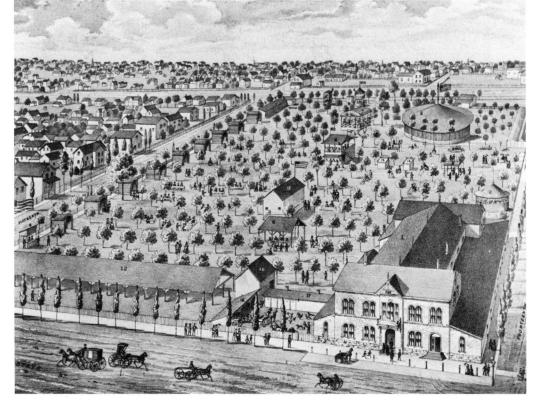

Below
A Jerome I. Case horse-powered threshing machine, produced in about 1850, enabled farmers to harvest their wheat fields quickly. Since wheat ripens all at once, harvesting became a critical time for pioneer farmers. Courtesy, State Historical Society of Wisconsin

developed on a small scale as family establishments. Despite a large population and promise of manufacturing, Milwaukee continued to import furniture, farm machines, wool, boots, harnesses, and stoves.

Wisconsin inventors revolutionized wheat harvesting. Jerome I. Case of Racine, who added a fan to help threshers separate grain from the outer chaff, built his own factory in 1847, producing a thresher with a two-horse tread power. Case's ten-horse sweep power threshers became the standard throughout the wheat-growing regions in the 1850s. The *Wisconsin Farmer* reported in 1850 that Case was building 100 threshing machines a year. By 1853 his market reached westward beyond the Mississippi. Case's company produced 300 threshing machines in 1860, 500 in 1865, and 1,300 in 1870.

Another Wisconsin inventor, George Esterly, produced what may have been the first successful American harvester in 1844. His Whitewater factory, built in 1857, produced reapers in Wisconsin until 1893, when Esterly decided Minneapolis was more centrally located to the railroads that served the wheat fields. Esterly is also credited with the invention of mowing machines and self-rake reapers, plus improved plows and seeders. In 1878, after years of tinkering, John Appleby of Walworth County devised the twine binder, which was adapted to harvesters to safely bind sheaves of wheat without hazardous wire. Other Wisconsin manufacturers, the Van Brunt Company

Above
Byron Kilbourn's first endeavor in Wisconsin was to develop Kilbourn Town on the west bank of the Milwaukee River in the 1830s. In 1851 Kilbourn built Milwaukee's first railroad, which ran between Milwaukee and Waukesha. Courtesy, State Historical Society of Wisconsin

of Horicon and the Rowell Company of Beaver Dam, each produced approximately 1,300 seeders by 1866.

Wisconsin's farm machinery and iron castings industries were already part of a westward regional market in 1860. These heavy-goods industries, accounting for almost 8 percent of the state's manufacturing in 1860, were the progenitors of the factory system in Wisconsin. However, growth in the Milwaukee-based iron industry, which produced castings and machinery, was slow because foundries required capital for machinery and labor.

RAILROADS COME TO WISCONSIN

Settlers, businessmen, and farmers all agreed that railroads were crucial to prosperity. In virtually roadless Wisconsin, a railroad could guarantee growth and commerce for any community. Citizens voted for revenue-raising bands in hopes of putting their town on the map. Farmers had the largest stake in rail transportation, for railroads could get their harvests to market. One historian estimated that an average harvest of 500 bushels of wheat for a Rock County farmer could require up to 20 round trips by wagon to Racine.

Milwaukee out-distanced its Wisconsin competitors in attracting railroads. Milwaukee rails stretched south to Chicago in 1855 and west to the Mississippi River. By 1860 the Milwaukee and Mississippi Company reached to Prairie du Chien and the La Crosse and Milwaukee Company reached to La Crosse. The Legislature granted charter to more than 100 railroad companies during the 1850s. A report from the Milwaukee Board of Trade observed that the proposed rails, "when laid upon the map make Wisconsin look like a spider's web." By 1860, as the Civil War broke, Wisconsin had 891 miles of railway.

Wisconsin's first rails were built in 1851 by Byron Kilbourn's company, optimistically named the Milwaukee and Mississippi. The cost was $550,000 and the tracks ran for only ten miles between Milwaukee and Waukesha when the project ran out of money. To continue Kilbourn's railroad, a Milton farmer proposed that farmers mortgage their farms in exchange for stock in the railroads. The company would sell the farmer's mortgages as collateral for its railroad bonds from eastern money markets. From 1850 to 1857 approximately 6,000 farmers mortgaged their farms, raising almost $5 million. The farmers, however, did not know that their mortgages were sold in the East for 50 to 75 percent of their face value. The railroad promoters were not honest in their dealings with farmers, and this would have a serious impact after 1857.

Fraud riddled railway promotion. "In the history of the financial speculations of this country," said Wisconsin Governor Alexander Randall in 1861, "so bold, open, unblushing frauds, taking in a large body of men, were never perpetrated. There was, and is, no law to punish them; because such rascality could not have been anticipated." This statement was not political hyperbole. The previous governor, Coles Bashford, left for Arizona after receiving $50,000 worth of railroad bonds that Byron Kilbourn had given him. To win a charter for the La Crosse and Milwaukee Railroad, Kilbourn and Moses Strong had also bought 59 assemblymen, 13 senators, and a supreme court judge. There was a legislative investigation, but no one was punished. Kilbourn explained that competition with Chicago railroads necessitated the bribes. Kilbourn was perhaps the most flamboyant of the railroad promoters, but corruption and gross mismanagement plagued the building of all of Wisconsin's early railroads.

The railroads were riding on a gossamer of financial stability. In 1857 a nationwide panic was touched off by the failure of an eastern bank, the Ohio Life Insurance and Trust Company, causing a string of bank failures throughout the country. The Panic of 1857, which was followed by a depression, bankrupted every railroad in Wisconsin. The Milwaukee and Mississippi Railroad, for instance, carried a mortgage debt of $6 million in bonds and $3.5 million in capital stock. Revenue did not come close to what was needed to survive in a depression. In the reorganization that followed, railroad lines were consolidated despite cries of monopoly. One of the two future railroad giants, the Chicago and Northwestern, was organized in 1859. The other giant, the Milwaukee and St. Paul, was organized by Milwaukee's financier, Alexander Mitchell, in 1863.

By 1867 Alexander Mitchell had secured control of all the railroad lines running east and west from Wisconsin's lake ports to the Mississippi River, including the La Crosse and Milwaukee, the Milwaukee and Mississippi, and smaller lines such as the Milwaukee and Watertown and the Racine and Mississippi. The antimonopoly sentiment incited several incidents of vandalism to tracks and bridges in 1865, prompting the Milwaukee and St. Paul to temporarily abandon running trains at night. To offset charges of monopoly, Mitchell pointed to his Chicago-based competitor, the Chicago and Northwestern, which ran north in Wisconsin. Mitchell's supporters preferred a monopoly based in Milwaukee rather than an outsider's financial control of rails in Wisconsin.

The railroads' bankruptcy was a calamity for Wisconsin's farmers. The farmers who had sold their mortgages to finance the railroads were left holding worthless stock, and they began receiving foreclosure notices from strangers out East. The farmers felt swindled. Governor Randall voiced their sentiment when he declared in 1861, "The railroad mortgages were conceived in fraud, executed in fraud, and sold or transferred in fraud."

A political solution to the farmers' dilemma was sought. Legislators abandoned the idea of the state assuming the farmers' debt because it would have required a state constitutional amendment. Instead the Legislature enacted stay-of-execution laws that released the farmer from debt if he could prove fraud in the contract. However, as one economic historian has pointed out, in most cases the eastern investors were innocent third parties who were unaware of the fraudulent representations of the railroad agent. Nevertheless, from 1858 to 1863 the Legislature passed 14 separate measures that released farmers, outraging the eastern investors. The state Supreme Court ruled these laws unconstitutional in 1860 and again in 1862. Many perplexed mortgageholders compromised with the farmers, but investors became less willing to support ventures in Wisconsin and capital grew even more scarce.

BANK REFORM

Wildcat banks that issued worthless paper money also discouraged capital. After banking became legal again in 1853, Wisconsin once more had problems with wildcat banking, the practice of issuing bank notes unsupported by assets. A feature of wildcat banking was having redemption centers in remote places. In less populated northern Wisconsin, there were up to 20 times more bank notes issued than around the populated areas of Milwaukee and Madison.

In 1858 45 state banks formed the Association of Banks of Wisconsin to encourage bank reform. With Alexander Mitchell as president, the association agreed that a central redemption center for bank notes was crucial. While nothing came of this resolution, a state law was ratified by voters in 1858 that required the state comptroller to issue bank notes only to banks doing business in towns of at least 200 voters. However, the state comptroller noted the existence of wildcat banks with no regular place of business as late as 1861. One bank, called the Bank of Green Bay, its name proudly bannered on its bank notes, was actually in La Crosse.

In April 1861 the Bankers' Association decided to weed out the wildcat banks, devising a blacklist of 37 banks whose discredited bank notes it refused to honor. With an eye to self-interest, the banks affiliated with the Bankers' Association immediately floated the unlucky bank notes from the blacklisted banks into their communities. Before the bank blacklist was published, however, an unusually high number of repudiated bank notes were placed in the pay envelopes of Milwaukee's labor force. Believing that their employees had been privy to inside information, angry German laborers marched to Alexander Mitchell's bank. Neither Mitchell nor the mayor of Milwaukee could appease the crowd and the two men exited, leaving four Civil War troops in training to control the crowd. A small bonfire was set to another bank's furniture, but the worthless bank notes might just as well have been tossed into the flames. Citizens were left holding worthless paper.

The ability to form a united front enabled the Bankers Association to police wildcat banking. In the fall of 1862, as business began to recover from the Panic of 1857, the Bankers Association watched for sound currency practices among new banks. Members of the association collected the bank notes of offending banks and sent the notes to Milwaukee. When a large number were collected, the notes were presented to the wildcat bank for redemption. Once the bank's assets were drained of hard currency, the remaining bank notes forced the bank to liquidate.

Despite these efforts at bank reform, the frontier economy was still considered a risk by big investors. Wisconsin's major manufacturing concentrated on the boom industries of processing lumber and wheat. The household industries such as furniture making

This sketch by Milwaukee Socialist Frederic Heath in 1897 depicts Milwaukee's bank riot of 1861. The riot was caused by "wildcat" bank notes given to workers in their pay envelopes and found to be worthless. Courtesy, State Historical Society of Wisconsin

and clothing were supported only by local markets. The promising industries of meat packing, farm machines, iron products, and brewing were constricted by elusive capital and credit. The railroads had failed to provide the panacea of easy transportation to reach new markets.

CIVIL WAR

As the Civil War broke, the frontier economy was still depressed from the Panic of 1857. Although recovery was rapid in the industrial East, growth in Wisconsin's economy was interrupted by the war, which stopped trade and commerce in the Mississippi River Valley. Immigration dropped, fewer than 100 corporations were chartered during the war, and only 130 miles of railroad tracks were built.

During the Civil War agriculture continued to dominate Wisconsin's economy. Half of Wisconsin's labor force were farmers or farm laborers, accounting for 125,000 of the 233,000 tabulated occupations. In wheat production Wisconsin ranked second only to Illinois throughout the Civil War decade. From 1860 to 1865, Wisconsin's farmers grew 100 million bushels of wheat and exported about two-thirds of that yield.

Growth in the dominant industries of lumber and flour milling was at a standstill during the Civil War. Flour milling in Milwaukee produced more than 200,000 barrels in 1860 but output did not increase through 1865. Deprived of markets in the lower Mississippi River Valley, Wisconsin lumber was not in demand until about 1863, and prices continued to fluctuate throughout the decade.

Wood products, however, were boosted during the Civil War in the production of machine-made wooden shingles. Before 1860, German and Belgian shingle weavers in the northeastern counties fashioned shingles by hand from pine logs considered too remote in the forest to haul out. During the Civil War machine-sawed shingles became popular in Chicago, creating a market for the shingle-makers of Manitowoc and Green Bay who were close to the pineries and ports. Wisconsin became the largest shingle maker in the country by the end of the decade, producing more than 801 million shingles.

The trauma of sending young Wisconsin men to war was expressed by English novelist Anthony Trollope, who visited Camp Scott in Milwaukee during the summer of 1861: "Ten thousand men fit to bear arms carried away from such a land to the horrors of civil war is a sight as full of sadness as any on which the eye can rest." Wisconsin sent 96,000 soldiers to the Civil War; 12,216 did not return.

During the war women helped in traditional areas by making bandages and working in hospital care. However, women also entered into industry. The 1860 census records only 773 women employed in industry, but by 1870 the number had risen to 3,967. Over 360 women worked in sawmills, while others worked in light manufacturing.

The Civil War dramatically forced the spread of labor-saving farm equipment, even among those farmers who were suspicious of new fangled machines. The *Wisconsin State Journal* urged farmers to buy reapers since farm laborers, "the very bone and sinew of the harvest fields, will be called away to other fields of toil and danger." Every good reaper, the newspaper said, equaled five to ten men in the field. The Wisconsin State Agricultural Society reported that about 3,000 reapers were sold in 1860. At the beginning of the Civil War the J.I. Case company was one of the largest producers of threshers in the Northwest, selling 1,500 ten-horse threshers annually. By the end of the decade Case was one of the largest companies in the country.

Farmers responded to war-induced demands for particular crops. They grew African sorghum and Chinese imphee as substitutes for sugar cane from the South. In 1866 the *Wisconsin Farmer* reported that nearly one million gallons of sorghum were produced. However, the Wisconsin summer was simply too short for ripening the cane, and when the war ended Wisconsin could not compete with Ohio, Indiana, and Missouri in sorghum production. Beer became popular during the war and farmers responded by growing hops until the hop louse migrated from New York, plaguing Wisconsin farmers. With cotton shut out from the South, farmers experimented with flax until cotton came back after the war's end.

Clothing and feeding the Union soldier's helped to stimulate Wisconsin's economy. Wisconsin wool, with its coarse fleeces, was in special demand for the production of soldier's uniforms. Wool also replaced the North's need for cotton, and the prices continued to climb throughout the war, from 25 cents a pound in 1860 to more than one dollar a pound in 1864. By 1865 Wisconsin farmers produced more than four million pounds of wool from more than one million sheep. Wisconsin farmers looked eagerly to rivaling Ohio in the wool industry. However, peace brought back cotton, and prices for coarse wool plummeted to 29 cents a pound within two years.

The Union Army ate a diet of salted pork and beef, and this boded well for the meat packers of Milwaukee. As part of the wheat and hog economy of Milwaukee, meat packers processed 60,000 hogs in 1860 and more than 133,000 hogs in 1866. By the end of the decade Milwaukee was the fourth largest pork packing center in the country, with more than 313,000 hogs dressed for salting. Barreled pork, hams, and lard were sent to the East as well as to England. The tanneries, an extension of the meat packing industry, processed shoe leather for army boots and harnesses. In 1860 Milwaukee had 13 tanneries; by 1872 it was the largest tanning center in the West, with 30 tanneries producing more than $2.5 million in leather.

Beer became more popular during the Civil War, in part because Congress imposed a severe excise tax on whisky in an effort to raise revenue. As the tax on beer and ale was milder, Yankees discovered these beverages for the first time. The *Wisconsin Farmer* observed in 1868, "The taste for beer and ale, and the custom and fashion making it 'respectable' to drink it, is largely growing." By 1872 Milwaukee had become the largest beer-exporting center in the West, especially since Chicago's fire of 1871 had destroyed competitive breweries.

The Civil War did not industrialize Wisconsin, but it did encourage a few important industries that helped to diversify the state's economic base. From the days of settlement in the 1830s through the Civil War, Wisconsin's economy depended on extracting and processing natural resources. Lumbering would remain in Wisconsin, but the golden wheat fields were moving westward as Wisconsin soil became exhausted. Farmers eventually would rebound, but it would be a slow process.

NEW LIVES, NEW INDUSTRIES

The Joseph Schlitz brewery in Milwaukee was the third largest in the country in 1895, behind Pabst and Anheuser-Busch. Courtesy, the H.H. Bennett Studio

These brewery wagons lined up in the Pabst Brewery shipping yards around the turn of the century. Beer wagons were used to deliver barrels of beer to local taverns. Courtesy, Milwaukee Public Library

The younger son had returned to Germany to persuade the entire family to emigrate to America. He and his older brother were succeeding in Milwaukee, he told them. Their vinegar factory was prosperous. The younger son urged his father to move the family business to America. Times were bad in the Rhineland, but in Milwaukee 1843 had been a good year. Jacob Best, Sr., believed his sons were right, and in 1844 the family bought a factory in Milwaukee. However, the Jacob Best family business wasn't vinegar. It was beer. By 1892 their brewery would sell more than one million barrels of Pabst Blue Ribbon beer.

GERMAN BREWERIES DOMINATE WISCONSIN ECONOMY

No other ethnic culture had such a direct impact on Wisconsin's economy as did the Germans with their mastery of lager beer. Milwaukee's brewers, the first to export beer to a regional market, reigned nationally after German beer became one of the country's favorite beverages. The most spectacular growth of any Milwaukee business after the Civil War was in brewing lager beer, which by 1890 was the city's leading industry in both sales and money invested. In Wisconsin, German breweries remained family enterprises. As historian Thomas Cochran observed of the Jacob Best brewery, management was strictly a family affair, and disputes could be resolved at the family dinner table.

Jacob Best, one of the 38,000 German-born immigrants in Wisconsin in 1850, moved his family to Milwaukee primarily for financial reasons. But in a letter home to Germany in 1847, his son Philip described the political and religious freedoms found in the new land: "One beholds here how the farmer lives without worries, one seldom finds a farmer who doesn't have a newspaper in his house every week. In Germany no one knows how to appreciate the liberty to which every human being is entitled. Here officials and priests are dependent upon the people, and in Germany the people are dependent upon the officials and priests. The preacher's business is a poor trade here."

Until the mid-nineteenth century when Best and other Germans began immigrating to the United States, most American brewers were non-German. The predominant American beers, called common beer, were similar to the heavier British ales and porters. In the 1850s German brewmasters, who used a longer fermentation process, introduced a sparkling beer that was lighter than the quick-fermenting British ale. The Germans called their beer "lager" derived from the German verb lagern, meaning "to store." This light lager of German brewmasters grew in popularity after the Civil War, and by 1866 there were 216 breweries in Wisconsin.

Left
Wilhelm Strothman, Milwaukee's first German immigrant, arrived in 1835. By 1870 Milwaukee had the largest German population in the United States. Courtesy, Milwaukee Public Library

Below left
The old Plank Road Brewery in Milwaukee was purchased by Frederic Miller in 1855. He managed the brewery until his death in 1888. Courtesy, Milwaukee Public Library

Below
Frederic Miller bought the Plank Road Brewery in 1855 from Jacob Best's sons, Charles and Lorenz. Courtesy, Milwaukee County Historical Society

Milwaukee, the city made famous by its beer and advertising, listed 12 breweries in 1850. Jacob Best's brewery was the fourth largest, producing 2,500 barrels by its four employees. That same year Jacob's sons, Charles and Lorenz Best, had formed a partnership to establish the Plank Road Brewery, which produced 1,200 barrels in 1850.

In 1855 the Plank Road Brewery was sold to Frederic Miller, a German immigrant fresh from working in the Royal Brewery at Sigmaringen, Hohenzollern. On Miller's death in 1888, the Frederic Miller Brewing Company, managed by Miller's three sons and one son-in-law, was producing 80,000 barrels per year.

Milwaukee's beer production increased from 20,000 barrels to more than 100,000 barrels during the nationwide boom of the 1850s. Beer was a social product, and in German communities beer gardens flourished in breweries. Beer gardens were places where families could gather and enjoy free music, singing, and even theater. Besides providing social life, beer gardens introduced the immigrant to New World outlooks and customs.

By 1860 the four largest brewers in Milwaukee would be Charles Melms, Valentin Blatz, Phillip Best, and Joseph Schlitz. During the 1850s both Valentin Blatz and Joseph Schlitz had acquired an established

Above
The Blatz Brewing Company, a nineteenth-century pioneer in distributing beer nationally, marked its 50th anniversary in 1895. Courtesy, Milwaukee Public Library

Top
Milwaukee's Blatz Brewing Company sold beer in the 1870s to markets in New York, Boston, and Chicago. Courtesy, Milwaukee County Historical Society

brewery through marriage. Blatz married John Braun's widow in 1851 and merged with Milwaukee's second-largest brewery, becoming a leading pioneer in exporting bottled beer nationally. Milwaukee brewer August Krug had employed Schlitz for his brewery's bookkeeping. Upon Krug's death in 1856, Schlitz took over the brewery and two years later married Krug's widow, Anna. Krug's brewery was changed to the Joseph Schlitz Brewing Company in 1874, and the next year Joseph and Anna Schlitz drowned in a shipwreck during a voyage to Germany. The Schlitz Brewing Company was inherited by August Krug's nephews, August, Henry, Edward, and Alfred Uihlein.

Jacob Best, Sr., died in 1860, but like many Wisconsin breweries, his remained a family business. Jacob's son, Phillip Best, retired in 1866 and left the Best Brewing Company to the management of his son-in-law, steamer ship captain Fred Pabst, who had married Jacob Best's granddaughter Maria in 1862. Until his death in 1904, Fred Pabst steered Jacob Best's brewery to become a national producer of beer.

In 1869 Pabst bought the Charles Melms' brewery for $100,000 after Melms died. Pabst later acquired another competitor, the Falk, Jung and Borchert Brewing Company, whose business operations were disrupted by fires. Historian Thomas Cochran observed that these bold decisions by Fred Pabst may have accounted for the continuing national leadership of the Best brewery, which by 1872 had become the second-largest national beer producer. In 1889 the Phillip Best Brewing Company's name was changed to the Pabst Brewing Company, by then the largest beer producer in the United States. With the name change came a new advertising slogan: "He drinks BEST who drinks PABST."

Other pioneer Milwaukee breweries included the Adam Gettelman Brewing Company and the Cream City Brewing Company. Begun in the 1850s, the Adam Gettelman Brewing Company was known for its "$1,000 Natural Process" beer and the $1,000 reward if anyone could disprove that the beer was made with pure malt and hops. The Miller Brewing Company would later buy the Gettelman family's brewery in 1961. The Cream City Brewing Company, founded in 1879, took its name from Milwaukee's acclaim as "the Cream City" built from pale yellow bricks. The

Above
Joseph Schlitz took over the management of a Milwaukee brewery owned by August Krug upon Krug's death in 1856. In 1858 Schlitz married Krug's widow, Anna. In 1874 the brewery was named the Joseph Schlitz Brewing Company. Courtesy, Milwaukee County Historical Society

Right
An advertisement for Schlitz beer in 1908 tried to extol the medicinal qualities of beer. Courtesy, Milwaukee Public Library

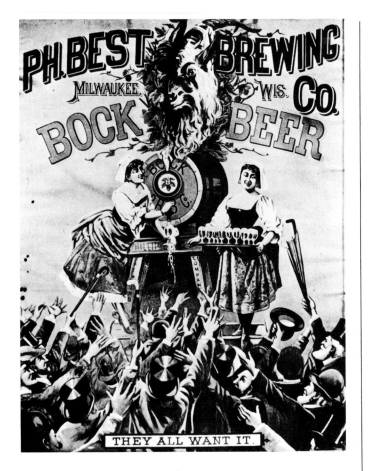

Above
An 1880s advertisement for the
Phillip Best Brewing Company
of Milwaukee, the forerunner of
the Pabst Brewing Company,
was for the brewery's bock beer,
a heavier and darker beer
traditionally made in the spring.
Bock is the German word for
goat, so the goat was used as a symbol on many bock beer labels.
Although the origin of the word
bock is disputed, one explana-
tion says that the beer came
from Einbeck, Germany, in
about 1250. Courtesy, Milwaukee Public Library

Above right
An early ad for the Joseph
Schlitz Brewing Company
played on a slogan the company
used since the 1870s: "The beer
that made Milwaukee famous."
Courtesy, State Historical Society of Wisconsin

Cream City Brewing Company was operated by different groups until it closed in 1937.

Thomas Cochran suggests that Milwaukee's limited market spurred its brewers to export Milwaukee beer earlier and with more aggressiveness than other competitors. In 1870 Milwaukee had a population of only 70,000. In contrast, brewers in New York had a market of 1.4 million; in Philadelphia, 674,000; in St. Louis, 311,000; in Chicago, 299,000; and in Cincinnati, 216,000. The lack of a large local market may have pushed Milwaukee brewers into marketing their product in these more populous cities. By 1891 Milwaukee brewers were shipping 100 carloads of beer by rail daily.

Chicago was a prime market for Milwaukee beer. The Chicago Fire of 1871 destroyed many Chicago breweries, and Milwaukee brewers eagerly supplied Chicago with beer. Sales for Milwaukee brewers increased 44 percent in 1872, and production was up to nearly 192,000 barrels. After Chicago's fire Schlitz adopted its slogan, "Schlitz, the Beer That Made Milwaukee Famous." During the 1880s, the Anheuser-

Right
The ice business grew from the beer industry and also from Chicago and Milwaukee meat packing, which required several million tons of ice each year. Most ice harvesting was done on lakes closest to railroad lines. Courtesy Milwaukee Public Museum

Below right
Workers the bottling house in Milwaukee's Phillip Best Brewing Company cleaned, filled, and capped bottles. Demand for bottled beer increased during the 1880s as Milwaukee's brewers found ways to keep bottled beer from spoiling. Courtesy, Milwaukee Public Library

Busch Brewery of St. Louis would provide fierce competition in Chicago.

Competition among national brewers encouraged the development of labels, trademarks, and promotion. Pabst's "Blue Ribbon" label was promoted as early as 1892, when the company hand-tied more than 300,000 yards of blue silk ribbon around white bottles. A woman perched on a crescent moon became the symbol for the Miller Brewing Company in 1903. Brewers competed in fairs and world expositions. At the Paris World Exposition in 1878 the Phillip Best Brewing Company was awarded a gold medal along with Anheuser-Busch of St. Louis.

In 1895 Pabst, Schlitz, and Blatz ranked first, third, and seventh, respectively, in U.S. beer production, turning out a total of about 2.1 million barrels of beer. In 1900 the three brewers obtained court injunctions to stop New York brewers from advertising their eastern product as "Milwaukee beer," which enjoyed a national reputation for quality.

Milwaukee brewers were able to sustain a national market by solving the problems of transporting beer. Steaming tanks were used for heating the beer and pasteurizing it for better stability in shipping long distances by rail. They also developed techniques for large-scale bottling, which could guarantee larger markets in New York, Philadelphia, Kansas City, and New Orleans. German lager that remained sparkling in bottles was difficult to achieve. As the demand for bottled beer increased during the 1880s, the process became more mechanized to prevent bacteria contamination.

The first significant breakthrough in preventing early spoilage was the introduction of Goulding bottle-washing machines in 1884. Improvements on bottle-washing machines included the Birkholz-Theurer soak tanks, in which bottles were immersed overnight in a hot soda solution. Over 1,500 kinds of bottle stoppers competed in the bottling business, but the metal bottle cap was introduced in 1892 and later perfected.

As beer became big business, German businessmen won the respect of Milwaukee's Yankee business community. In 1865 Fred Pabst and Valentin Blatz were made members of the Milwaukee Chamber of Commerce. Charles Melms, the third-largest brewer in Milwaukee in 1865, had been the first German to be elected to the Chamber of Commerce in 1861.

The Pabst Brewing Company became one of the earliest American companies to develop a worldwide reputation for its beer. As early as 1888 Pabst was exporting several thousand quarts and pints of beer to Mexico, Australia, China, and South America. In 1893 Pabst shipped more than 600 barrels to Cuba. Until Prohibition in 1919, Pabst continued to emphasize its international market.

Successful German brewmasters outside of Milwaukee also founded breweries that have survived into the present time. Gottlieb Heileman had brewed beer in Wurttemberg, Germany before emigrating to Milwaukee. Although he was not hired as a brewmaster for the Pabst Brewing Company as he had hoped, he met his future wife Johanna Bantle, who was a domestic servant in the Pabst household. In 1858 Gottlieb Heileman became a partner with John Gund and began the City Brewery in La Crosse on the Mississippi River. The City Brewery was renamed the G. Heileman Brewing Company after John Gund left to form another brewery in 1872. Gottlieb Heileman died in 1878, and his wife Johanna headed the business until her death in 1917. When the G. Heileman Brewing Company was incorporated in 1890, Johanna Heileman became one of the first women presidents of a corporation in Wisconsin. In 1902 Johanna Heileman copyrighted Old Style Lager.

In 1867 Jacob Leinenkugel established the Spring Brewery in Chippewa Falls in northwestern Wisconsin. Leinenkugel's father, Matthias, had originally opened a brewery in Sauk City, after emigrating with his family from the Rhineland in Germany. Matthias Leinenkugel's five sons operated other Leinenkugel breweries in Wisconsin, including one in Baraboo and two in Eau Claire. In 1899 Jacob Leinenkugel's son and sons-in-law incorporated the Jacob Leinenkugel Brewing Company in Chippewa Falls. The brewery, which still promotes the fact that its water is from Big Eddy Springs, is headed by grandchildren and great-grandchildren of Jacob Leinenkugel.

The Joseph Huber Brewing Company of Monroe, in southern Wisconsin, traces its origins back to 1848. The brewery was run by different owners until Adam Blumer took over in 1891 and renamed it the Blumer Brewing Company. In 1927 the brewery hired Joseph Huber as its new brewmaster. Huber had moved from Bavaria in 1923 and worked for the Blatz Brewery. The brewery remained in the Blumer family

*In the early 1900s German cooper-
age tradesmen made beer barrels
for Milwaukee's Pabst Brewery.
This turn-of-the century photo
shows all stages of barrel making. Courtesy, Milwaukee
Public Library*

until 1947, when Joseph Huber acquired the stock of the business and renamed the brewery. The brewery remained in the Huber family until it was sold in 1985 to two former Pabst executives.

John Walter founded his brewery in Eau Claire in 1889. His brothers and their sons founded other plants throughout the state: the Geo. Walter Brewing Company of Appleton (1880-1972); the Walter Bros. Brewing Company of Menasha (1889-1956); and the West Bend Lithia Company of West Bend (1911-1972). There was also a Walter Brewing Company established in Pueblo, Colorado (1898-1975). John Walter's brewery of Eau Claire became Hibernia Brewing. Since its founding in the 1850s, the Stevens Point Beverage Company has had several German brewmasters among its many owners.

Beer was Wisconsin's third-largest industry in 1890, after lumber and flour milling. Beer production directly affected the industries of barrel making or cooperage, ice harvesting, brewery equipment, bottling, saloon furnishings, and shipping.

ICE HARVESTING

Wisconsin's brewers were the primary cause for the rise of Wisconsin's ice harvesting industry. A large natural resource in ice gave Wisconsin brewers year-round production and an advantage over other national brewers. However, Wisconsin brewers were not interested in harvesting ice; they preferred to contract separately for ice, which was used for beer production and shipping. Blocks of ice were cut and stored in large ice houses in breweries and near railroad depots. Along with Chicago and Milwaukee meat packers, Milwaukee brewers demanded several million tons of ice each year.

Ice harvesting thrived on lakes near railroads, which were the primary carriers of ice. Pewaukee Lake, because of its location just west of Milwaukee, became a prime center for ice harvesting. The primary ice carrier was the Chicago, Milwaukee and St. Paul Railroad, whose main line was 500 feet from Pewaukee Lake. In northeastern Wisconsin, on Lake Winnebago, ice was cut for railroad lines in Fond du Lac and Oshkosh. In south-central Wisconsin, Madison, built on four lakes and served by three major railroad lines, also attracted ice harvesters. Lakes Monona, Wingra, and Waubesa exported ice, while Lake Mendota was harvested primarily by local ice companies since it was farther away from the railroad lines.

Ice harvesting began to decline after 1900, when artificially made ice, using compressed liquid ammonia and local water, came into vogue. Refrigeration machinery businesses, such as Weisel and Vilter of Milwaukee, began selling machines to breweries, meat packing houses, and ice plants. Mechanical improvements eventually made artificially produced ice cheaper and safer than natural ice, which was dependent on winter's erratic chill.

Because of a tradition of apprenticeships in their homeland, Germans contributed more than beer to Wisconsin's economy. One specialty proved to be cigar making. The Herman Segnitz Cigar Manufacturing Company alone employed 700 men and women during the 1880s. By 1912 Milwaukee's city directory listed 217 cigar manufacturers, ranging from producers nestled in home attics to large halls.

One of the the many immigrants who fled Germany's turbulent politics after the revolution of 1848, Daniel Kusel, Sr., brought substantial gold with his family plus a solid background in tin and brass goods.

Kusel re-established himself in the tinware business in Watertown, according to historian Charles Wallman, and as a sideline began a hardware store. Kusel later helped to establish a Lutheran church and in 1864 a Lutheran seminary, now Northwestern College. Kusel's descendents continued the family business, which changed to sheet metal and later to the manufacturing of dairy supplies as the Kusel Equipment Company of Watertown.

"English Spoken Here," a common sign in German shops, was important in assimilating German businesses into the marketplace. German employees were also expected to be bilingual. This combination of trade skills and language assimilation helped German business owners reach a wider market than their German neighborhood. By 1900 Milwaukee businessman John Pritzlaff had built his hardware wholesale company into the third largest in the nation. Originally from Pomerania, Pritzlaff preferred German employees but assumed they spoke English, a normal expectation in Milwaukee.

Germans did business with each other, a built-in advantage when competing against Yankee businessmen. Ethnic loyalty could help a new business because the German market was so large in Milwaukee. By 1870 native Germans made up one-third of Milwaukee's 71,440 population. Although only 17 percent of Milwaukee's population was German-born by 1910, more than 50 percent of the city's 373,857 population identified with a German heritage.

TANNING

By 1872 Milwaukee had become the largest tanning center in the West with 30 tanneries, of which 70 percent were German-owned. Tanners exploited Wisconsin's abundance of hemlock bark, oak, and sumac, which were used as chief tanning agents. Leather tanneries, like breweries, tended to be family-run businesses, and nearly all the successful ones were owned and managed by German immigrants. Albert Trostel emigrated from Wurttemberg, Germany, and began his Milwaukee tannery in 1852. His two sons, Albert and Gustav, carried on the family business, which continues to the present time. August F. Gallun emigrated from Germany in 1854, and his family business continues to produce calfskin leather in Milwaukee. Similarly, Fred Vogel, Jr., and his family carried on the

Milwaukee business begun by his father, Fred Vogel, Sr.

In 1880 there were 73 tanneries throughout the state, employing 815 workers. A decade later there were only 38 tanneries, but the number of workers rose to 2,570. Milwaukee had 15 tanneries in 1890, but Kenosha, Fond du Lac, and Sheboygan were also centers for tanning. The Wisconsin Leather Company in Two Rivers built a national reputation for harness leather and shoe leather. Edward P. Allis, Milwaukee's biggest industrialist in the 1880s, was one of the early investors in George and William Allen's tannery, which claimed to be the largest tannery in the world in the 1870s.

Milwaukee tanners took advantage of their access to Chicago's meat packing industry. Chicago was the nation's hide market, and Milwaukee tanners could buy hides and process leather while still making a profit. By 1890 Milwaukee would be the world's largest producer of plain leather. In overall leather goods Milwaukee ranked fourth in the country, processing 622,456 hides.

The Pfister and Vogel Tannery of Milwaukee emerged as the giant in the field, employing more than 600 tanners in 1890. Guido Pfister and Fred Vogel emigrated from Wurttemberg, Germany, to Milwaukee in the 1840s. By 1857 they had merged their tanneries and combined their business strengths in producing and marketing leather. The reputation of Pfister and Vogel opened markets in New York and Pennsylvania, and by 1906 Pfister and Vogel had branches in Boston, New York, London, Paris, and Milan. Many other tanneries were later begun by former employees of Pfister and Vogel.

MEN'S CLOTHING

Men's clothing manufacturing was another industry in which German entrepreneurs in Milwaukee excelled; 70 percent of Milwaukee's manufacturers of men's garments were German in 1870. By 1890 clothing manufacturers employed the largest labor force in the city, including those who worked at home or in tailor shops. Milwaukee was fourth in the production of hosiery and knitted garments, the latter necessitated by the cold climate and outdoor occupations such as the lumber industry.

Many Jewish Germans who settled in Milwaukee

Right
An employee at Milwaukee's Pfister & Vogel tannery worked with calf skins. The leather-tanning industry was dominated by German immigrants, who had made Milwaukee the largest tanning center in the West by 1872. Courtesy, State Historical Society of Wisconsin

Left
In 1888 tanneries lined the Milwaukee River in Milwaukee. Courtesy, State Historical Society of Wisconsin

Below
This 1892 advertisement displayed Pfister & Vogel Tanneries in Milwaukee. Pfister & Vogel was a giant in Milwaukee's prosperous tanning industry and employed more than 600 tanners in 1890. Courtesy, Milwaukee Public Library

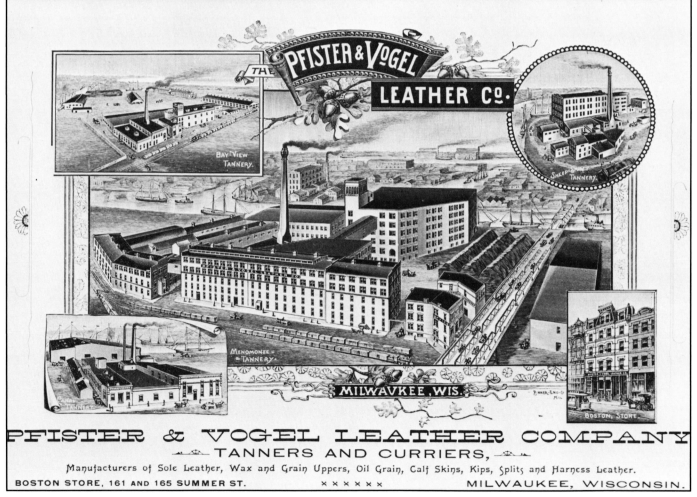

The German culture in Wisconsin was a ready market for the beer Wisconsin brewers produced. The Liederkranz singing society in Wausau in 1913 preserved the tradition of the German biergarten. Courtesy, State Historical Society of Wisconsin

became manufacturers of men's clothing. By 1880 the top three men's clothing manufacturers were owned by German and Austrian Jews, employing more than 1,400 employees. In 1847 Henry and Elias Friend, Jewish immigrants from Bavaria, began Friend Brothers, which by 1880 had become the largest Milwaukee manufacturer of men's clothing. The second-largest manufacturer, David Adler and Sons, was begun in Milwaukee during the 1850s by the Adler family, who were Jewish Austrians. Emanuel Silverman, the third-largest manufacturer in 1880, was a German Jew who had emigrated during the 1850s.

Milwaukee did not have the corner on successful clothing manufacturing. In Oshkosh, overalls would became a national symbol under the marketing of a company begun in 1895 as the Grove Manufacturing Company, and later changed to Oshkosh B' Gosh. In Sheboygan, H.J. Holman, a Russian tailor who had immigrated in 1890 made overalls in his house and delivered them to customers by horse and wagon. His 13-year-old son, George, was called "the knee pants salesman" because he also sold clothing in the family business, which later changed its name to Lakeland.

IMMIGRATION CONTINUES

Wisconsin's government actively welcomed immigrants. A commissioner was sent to New York City in 1852 to open an office that advertised the benefits of settling in the wilderness state, where there were ample opportunities fo people willing to clear the land and build towns. Wisconsin's office was maintained from 1867 to 1900, and its efforts to attract immigrants were successful. By 1870 two-thirds of Wisconsin's 1,054,670 population were immigrants and their children, half of them Germans.

Germans were keenly interested in all aspects of life in America, particularly Wisconsin and the Midwest. One book by Christian Ficker, published in 1853, was titled *Friendly Adviser for All Who Would Emigrate to America and Particularly Wisconsin*. Another book, *Hints for the Immigrant*, persuaded a German immigrant, William Rueping, to settle his leather tannery in Fond du Lac because it was "The Land of Paradise."

The influx of immigrants into Wisconsin continued, and by 1890 the foreign-born made up more than 30 percent of the state's 1,686,880 population, with Germans continuing to dominate. By 1895 there were 268,469 German-born, and 106,900 Scandinavian born. The Poles, who emigrated in large numbers during the 1890s, were more difficult to count since the country was divided among Germany, Russia, and Austria-Hungary. The census in 1900 counted 27,644 Polish or Slavic immigrants in Milwaukee County and 2,750 in Portage County in the center of the state.

The Norwegians were the earliest and largest group of Scandinavians to settle in Wisconsin. Indeed, by 1850, 70 percent of the Norwegians in the United States lived in Wisconsin. Norwegian immigrants tended to cluster into tight communities. By 1910 13,694 Norwegians in Dane County had settled in south-central Wisconsin; in western Wisconsin 7,795 Norwegians were living in Trempealeau County and almost 6,000 Norwegians in Vernon and La Crosse counties.

Over 68 percent of the Scandinavians arriving in the United States migrated to the Midwest. By 1910 there were 128,000 Norwegians, 48,000 Swedes, and 32,000 Danes in Wisconsin who were either foreign-

The Norwegians, and later the Swedes, were primarily farmers. Norwegians, who tended to be poorer than German immigrants, often were left with less favorable farmland. Nevertheless, historian Joseph Schafer credits the industrious Norwegians with building up Wisconsin agriculture. Norwegian farmers would become part of Wisconsin's dairy industry and also grew tobacco.

The British and Irish, who were also early immigrants, easily assimilated into Wisconsin's predominantly Yankee environment. The British, in particular the English and the Scottish, usually settled among the Yankees. While the Irish were the larger group with 50,000 in 1860, their numbers significantly declined

The Carl de Haas house in 1847, on Calumet Harbor in Lake Winnebago, became a familiar site to German immigrants. In 1848 De Haas wrote a two-volume book that was popular among German immigrants. It was called Nordamerica, Wisconsin Calumet, Winke fuer Auswanderer. *Courtesy, State Historical Society of Wisconsin*

born or children of foreign-born parents. Swedes settled primarily in northwestern Wisconsin from the Chippewa River basin north to Bayfield County. In 1910 the largest Danish settlement was in Racine County with 7,000. Danes also settled around Lake Winnebago in Oshkosh and Neenah.

Scandinavians tended to be parochial, preferring to isolate themselves into separate communities. English remained a foreign language to many Scandinavian immigrants. One Norwegian guide book warned that this could be a distinct disadvantage: "Before having learned the language fairly well, one must not expect to receive so large a daily or yearly wage as the nativeborn American."

thereafter. In 1850 Milwaukee's population was 14 percent Irish, but a decade later it was 7 percent and by 1890 it was down to 1.7 percent. The Irish were mobile and tended to be either small-town farmers, loggers, or urban laborers. Irish influence was felt in local and state politics, where they were devoted and savvy Democrats.

The Cornish settled primarily in the lead region in southwestern Wisconsin. In 1850 approximately 7,000 of the 27,000 British in Wisconsin were Cornish, most of whom came to mine lead. By 1850 4,319 Welsh had settled in Wisconsin, first settling in Racine and Waukesha counties and later moving northwest in search of cheaper farmland.

Above and top
At Stevens Point's Market Square, Polish immigrants buy food from farmers. Polish immigrants, who were the third-largest group to settle in Wisconsin, arrived in large numbers during the 1890s. They settled largely in the Stevens Point area and Milwaukee County. Courtesy, State Historical Society of Wisconsin

Right
Norwegians were the largest ethnic group in Stoughton. The Isham & Hale store suggests that business owners were still of German and Yankee heritages in 1890. Courtesy, State Historical Society of Wisconsin

In Wisconsin, particularly in Milwaukee, business leaders were most often Yankee, British, or German. These groups had considerable influence over jobs, since they owned or controlled key industries—metal, tanning, brewing, and meat packing. According to historian Gerd Korman, the Yankees, British, and Germans were the factory masters and foremen, and they hired and trained labor according to their ethnic preferences.

Polish immigrants, who began arriving in large numbers after 1880, were at the bottom of the job hierarchy. In Milwaukee they joined the ranks of the unskilled and semi-skilled laborers. Supervisory positions above the rank of assistant foreman were seldom accessible to Poles and other southern Europeans. The Pabst Brewing Company, for example, staffed most of its departments with Germans and reserved the most unskilled tasks in the bottling department to non-Germans, usually Polish women.

Polish workers were courted by other employers, however. In 1893 Irishman Patrick Cudahy, of the Cudahy meat-packing company, recruited 1,000 Polish workers to live and work in Cudahy's new industrial

suburb on Milwaukee's south side. He promised employment to Poles who bought land from him, and he gave land to the Catholic church's local Polish parish.

Although the largest settlements of Polish immigrants were in Stevens Point and on Milwaukee's south side, Poles also settled throughout Wisconsin, including the towns of Berlin, Menasha, Manitowoc, Beaver Dam, and La Crosse. Nearly one-third of Wisconsin's Poles were farmers.

Another central European group, the Bohemians from the Czech portion of Czechoslovakia, also settled in large numbers in Wisconsin. As with the Poles, the number of Bohemians is difficult to trace because they lacked national sovereignty at the time. Bohemians were usually counted as Austrians. By 1870 Bohemians had settled next to Milwaukee in Racine County and also in southwestern Wisconsin in Grant, Crawford, and Richland counties. In 1890 the census takers counted 11,999 Bohemians in Wisconsin, though these official figures are most likely short of the actual number.

Smaller groups of Swiss, Belgians, and Dutch formed farming communities in Wisconsin. By 1890 there were 7,000 Swiss-born in Wisconsin, concentrating primarily in southern Wisconsin in Green County's New Glarus. The Belgians clustered in northeastern Wisconsin around the Green Bay counties of Brown, Kewaunee, and Door. In 1860 there were 4,600 Belgian-born immigrants, and by 1910 there were 14,000 Wisconsin residents of Belgian parentage. The Dutch also settled in the Green Bay area and in nearby Sheboygan and Fond du Lac counties, where many grew barley. By 1910 there were 7,379 Dutchborn Wisconsin residents and 16,554 of Dutch parentage.

Wisconsin's population was on the move in the 1890s. The 1895 census revealed that one out of four Wisconsin-born residents moved outside the state, usually West. According to historian Joseph Schafer, Americans and Irish tended to leave Wisconsin more readily, taking profits in real estate ventures and land improvements. Business owners apparently were as mobile as the immigrants who searched for better farmland. In a study of Trempealeau County in western Wisconsin, historian Merle Curti concluded that 75 percent of business owners and professionals who were present in the 1870 census were missing from the 1880 census.

Immigrants who wanted to farm had fewer choices, as good land was only available further north. But the beauty of the land in central Wisconsin impressed one Scottish immigrant. Conservationist John Muir, whose family moved to Marquette County in 1849 when he was eleven, remembered "the sunny woods overlooking a flowery glacier meadow and a lake rimmed with white water-lillies . . . Oh, that glorious Wisconsin Wilderness!

IMMIGRANTS AND WISCONSIN POLITICS

As immigrants helped build industries and settle the wilderness, they also affected Wisconsin's politics. The political parties and Protestant Yankees had to contend with an emerging Catholic population. Close to half the Germans were Catholic, in addition to Catholic Irish, Poles, Bohemians, Swiss, and Belgians.

Anti-Catholic and anti-immigrant sentiment had found political expression in the nineteenth century, even in the more tolerant frontier states. During the 1850s, the nativist American Party, popularly called the Know-Nothings, advocated the exclusion of foreigners and Catholics from political office. During the height of nativism, a sermon delivered at Milwaukee's Plymouth Church in 1856 warned parishioners of great suffering if "we visit their dance-house on the Sabbath, saturate ourselves with their lager beer, and place ourselves . . . under the control of the Romanish Church."

Wisconsin had few collisions between nativists and immigrants, owing largely to the fact that the nativist was out-numbered in Wisconsin by nearly three to one in 1890. Wisconsin's ethnic community, however, did join together to fight the Bennett Law of 1889, a compulsory school law that decreed that reading, writing, arithmetic, and American history had to be taught in English. Germans saw the Bennett Law as a move to extinguish the German language; Catholics and Lutherans saw it as a threat to parochial education. Scandinavians, who usually voted Republican, allied with German Catholics and Lutherans to vote the Republicans out of office in 1890. The Republicans lost the governor's chair, the Legislature and all but one of the congressional districts. If anything else, the reaction to the Bennett Law notified party bosses about the swift fury of democracy.

THE AGE OF LUMBER AND METAL

East Water Street in Milwaukee circa 1890.
Courtesy, the H.H. Bennett Studio

The roar of log drives along Wisconsin rivers and the roar of blast furnaces in Wisconsin's cities were the sounds of prosperity in the nineteenth century. The state's industrial base was built on lumber and metal. In northern Wisconsin pines fell at a ferocious rate, and paper mills began to replace flour mills on the Fox River. In the southeast, Wisconsin's foundry workers forged iron and steel castings for an expanding market. No longer would Wisconsin be dependent primarily on wheat and flour. Lumbering, factories, and the dairy industry would establish an economic base that would carry Wisconsin into the modern economy of the twentieth century.

Lumber and flour milling, Wisconsin's pioneering industries since statehood, continued as Wisconsin's top two industries from 1870 to 1900. However, while the primary producers of lumber and wheat

The Reliance Iron Works was world renowned in the late nineteenth century for its production of heavy steam engines. Courtesy, the H.H. Bennett Studio

were moving further west, the state's producers of cheese and metal found markets that continued to expand. By 1910 metal castings and dairy products were, respectively, the second- and third-ranked industries in Wisconsin. In contrast, flour fell from second to sixth place among Wisconsin's industries and by 1920 lumber plummeted from first to seventh place.

Two business recessions slowed Wisconsin's industrialization. The Panic of 1873 was in part due to overextension of bank credit after the Civil War plus excessive speculation in stock market securities. In Wisconsin the panic touched off a depression that kept prices down for about six years. The Panic of 1893 was more severe, causing a worldwide depression. In Wisconsin 27 banks closed permanently, and many more banks closed temporarily. In Milwaukee George Smith and Alexander Mitchell's famous pioneer bank, the Wisconsin Marine and Fire Insurance Company, temporarily failed. The closing of Wisconsin's largest bank shocked residents and business leaders. Alexander Mitchell's son John and bank president John Johnston pledged their personal fortunes to reopen the bank six months later. Their bank survived to become the statewide Marine Banks of the Marine Corporation.

THE AGE OF INVENTION

The mid-nineteenth century was an age of invention. The U.S. Patent Office issued four times as many patents in the 1860s as it had since its inception in 1790. During the next two decades the number of patents doubled again. Many Wisconsin inventions were innovations of industrial machines such as Bruno Nordberg's poppet valve in the 1890s, which enabled heavy steam machines to attain constant speeds. Attracting many financial backers in Milwaukee, Nordberg ventured forth from E.P. Allis to rent space above another struggling foundry shop, Pawling and Harnischfeger. Both fledgling shops would grow into worldwide manufacturers of heavy machinery. In contrast, one

Above
Christopher Latham Sholes invented the typewriter in Milwaukee during the period from 1868 to 1872. The Panic of 1873 stymied sales, and Sholes sold his interest in his invention to former Oshkosh newspaper editor James Densmore. During the 1880s the typewriter became an office fixture. Courtesy, State Historical Society of Wisconsin

Right
The first typewriter was built in the Kleinsteuber machine shop by Christopher Sholes in Milwaukee. Courtesy, Milwaukee County Historical Society

unpatented invention important to the dairy industry was first eaten in 1881 in Two Rivers. Edward Berner put chocolate syrup on ice cream for a low-priced dessert he reserved only for Sundays, later known as the sundae.

Another Wisconsin invention was inspired perhaps by Wisconsin's winters. Warren Johnson, a professor of natural science at Whitewater State College, grew tired of his classrooms that fluctuated from hot to cold. In 1883 he invented the all-electric thermostat, and in 1885 he founded Johnson Electric Service to market his invention. Johnson's curiosity led him to tinker with clock towers, invent puncture-proof tires, and build steam and electric trucks. By 1890, however, his thermostat had won renown from Germany to Spain and Moscow, and his company would become Johnson Controls, a worldwide marketer of temperature controls.

The typewriter was invented in Milwaukee by a former Kenosha newspaper editor, Christopher Latham Sholes. James Densmore, a friend and former Oshkosh newspaper editor, helped finance Sholes' invention, which went through several designs from 1868 to 1872. Densmore arranged for the gun factory of E. Remington & Sons of New York to produce typewriters, one of which was purchased by Mark Twain. The Panic of 1873 stymied sales, and Sholes, lacking confidence in the profitability of his invention, eventually sold his interest to Densmore. During the

1880s the typewriter became an office fixture. "Whatever I may have thought in the early days, of the value of the typewriter," said Sholes in 1888, "it is very obviously a blessing to mankind, and especially to womankind. I am very glad I had something to do with it."

Perhaps the most dramatic invention was electricity, evolving from Ben Franklin's rain-swept kite to Thomas Edison's incandescent lamp in 1879. In New York City on September 4, 1882, Edison switched on the first electrical power station. On September 30, Appleton businessmen, headed by paper manufacturer H.J. Rogers, turned on the second Edison power station. Driven by water, the Appleton station was the first hydroelectric plant in the country.

The electric light was a popular novelty in Wisconsin even before Edison had completed his power station. Civic leaders in downtown Oshkosh had lit the streets with electricity, and town boosters were proud of their new night life as residents strolled the streets beneath strings of lights. The *Appleton Post* reported that "the electric light is perfectly safe and convenient, and is destined to be the great illuminating agent of the near future." Daytime use was the key to profit for electricity companies. Electric streetcars would become one of the first daytime users. The first

Electric-powered streetcars, such as this 1890s Eau Claire streetcar, were one of the first daytime users of electricity. The first permanent electric-streetcar line in the nation was installed in Appleton in 1886. Courtesy, State Historical Society of Wisconsin

permanent streetcar lines in the nation were installed in Appleton and in Mobile, Alabama, in 1886.

In the mid-1880s more Wisconsin communities were exchanging gas light for incandescent lights. New utility companies entered the field, and local businesses brought electricity to their own towns. From 1887 to 1901 the Baker Manufacturing Company, a water pump and windmill manufacturer in south-central Wisconsin, supplied steam-generated electricity for the village of Evansville from dusk until 11 p.m. Throughout the state a number of electrical plants began as outgrowths of water-powered lumber mills and flour mills.

RAILROADS

Wisconsin's industrialization was fueled by heavy railroad construction. From 1872 to 1893 Wisconsin's railroads increased to nearly 6,000 miles of tracks. Wisconsin's initial 2,000 miles of tracks ran largely westward, connecting Milwaukee to Prairie du Chien and to La Crosse. After the Panic of 1857 bankrupted every railroad in the state, Milwaukee financier Alexander Mitchell stepped in to consolidate two major Wisconsin lines, the Chicago, Milwaukee and St. Paul Railroad, which ran primarily westward, and the Chicago and Northwestern Railroad, which ran primarily northward, connecting Janesville to Fond du Lac.

The flurry of construction after 1873 stretched Wisconsin's rails northward into the lumber towns. Many lumbermen and pine owners bought railroad stocks and bonds and encouraged local governments to vote financial aid. The West Wisconsin Railroad, popularly known as the Wisconsin Lumber Line, connected many of the pineries in the north with markets in Omaha. Although the Chicago and Northwestern bought a majority of its stock in 1882, the Wisconsin Lumber Line continued its separate existence.

Above right
The Chicago, Milwaukee &
St. Paul Railroad depot was pho-
tographed in Kilbourn City
(later named Wisconsin Dells).
In the 1880s tourists flocked to
this popular vacation region. Cour-
tesy, the H.H. Bennett Studio

Right
A sign near a railroad crossing
at Middleton, Wisconsin,
warned horse-drawn vehicles to
watch for railroad cars in 1883.
During the latter part of the nine-
teenth century, Wisconsin's
roads often were a combination
of mud and holes, incapable of con-
necting Wisconsin towns to the
outside business world. But be-
tween 1872 and 1893 Wiscon-
sin's railroads increased to
nearly 6,000 miles of track. Cour-
tesy, State Historical Society of
Wisconsin

The Wisconsin Central Line became another important railroad in 1877 when it completed a line from Milwaukee to Ashland, with branches to Green Bay and Portage. "Hurray for the cars of progress," was the sentiment expressed from Stevens Point as the Wisconsin Central Line first pulled into town. In 1875 Wisconsin Central built repair shops in Stevens Point, which for the next 25 years was a central stop for the line.

Railroads brought the rural populations such big-city advantages as commerce and industry, political campaigns in whistle-stop tours, and traveling theater troupes. Farm properties increased in value once the farm became accessible to an urban center. By 1890 Janesville was served by 30 trains daily, which was not unusual for cities in southern Wisconsin, according to historian Robert Nesbit. The placement of railroads was crucial to towns and businesses. When the Indiana railroads bypassed the town of Vincennes, one local department store owner and five of his brothers relocated to the boom town of Milwaukee. The family business they brought was Gimbel Brothers department store.

Left
In 1887 the Milwaukee office of the Chicago, Milwaukee & St. Paul Railway Company was in the Alexander Mitchell building. Alexander Mitchell created the railroad company by combining a number of railroads that had become bankrupt in 1857. Courtesy, State Historical Society of Wisconsin

*The business district in Mer-
rimac, Wisconsin, in Sauk
County was little more than a
few storefronts in 1890. Courtesy, State Historical Society of
Wisconsin*

WISCONSIN'S LUMBER BOOM

The railroads revolutionized Wisconsin's lumber industry. As historian Robert Fries observed, streams and rivers limited both the speed and quality of log transportation. Log jams were not a part of railroad transportation. But more strategically, railroads opened new markets for lumber. By 1870 much of the desirable timber had been stripped along Wisconsin's rivers. As railroads wound into Wisconsin's northern woods, trees far from rivers were no longer spared the ax. Rough logging railroads were built from remote timberlands to the main rail lines. By 1881 nearly two-thirds of the lumbermen along the pine-rich Chippewa River were shipping lumber by rail. By 1892 the railroads were carrying more lumber than the 3 million logs floated down the Chippewa River.

Chicago was Wisconsin's biggest customer for wholesale lumber during the 1870s and 1880s, receiving 85 percent of its lumber from Wisconsin and Michigan by way of Lake Michigan. As most of Wisconsin's eastern forests were exhausted by the 1890s, Chicago merchants looked to western Wisconsin for lumber, railroads overcoming the land barrier between Chicago and the Mississippi River.

Six lumber districts emerged from forests surrounding Wisconsin's main rivers. The two pineries of northeastern Wisconsin, Green Bay and the Wolf River, were Wisconsin's earliest sources of lumber be-cause of the older settlements. By the 1870s Oshkosh, "the Sawdust City," and Fond du Lac were considered old, established lumber towns. Railroads and closer markets spurred these towns to diversify in producing furniture, wagons, and doors. By 1890, however, the forests around the Wolf River were exhausted.

Four Wisconsin rivers became logging streams feeding into the Mississippi: the Wisconsin, winding down the center of the state; the Black, which joins the Mississippi just north of La Crosse; the Chippewa, which gave rise to Eau Claire and Chippewa Falls; and the St. Croix, which borders Minnesota. Enormous rafts of lumber the size of ten city blocks were not uncommon sights along the Mississippi River.

Along the Wisconsin River there were more than 100 sawmills by 1857, and the towns of Wisconsin Rapids, Stevens Point, and Wausau became early sawmill centers. The Wisconsin River district had an advantage because it had access to older settlements. As the Wisconsin River's many bends and rapids limited large-scale rafting, railroads became the main transportation in the district.

The Black River attracted lumberman Nathan Myrick, who founded La Crosse in 1841. By 1860 La Crosse had a population of 3,800, which doubled to 7,785 a decade later. The years between 1870 and 1890 were boom times for La Crosse as the lumber town grew to 25,000. In 1885 La Crosse, the state's

The Fox River had caused Green Bay to become the gateway to the Mississippi in the seventeenth century. In the nineteenth century the Fox River remained a prime waterway for Green Bay's pinery and diverse industries in paper, meat-packing, and agriculture. Courtesy, State Historical Society of Wisconsin

Above
The Wisconsin River had many dangerous passages, including the dam at Kilbourn, through which pilot Archie Young is shown maneuvering. Courtesy, the H.H. Bennett Studio

Right
Rafting pilots like Archie Smith, steered rafts that were divided into sections called "cribs" and measured 16 feet long. Cribs were then attached together to form strings or "rapids pieces" that were seven cribs long. Several of these rapids pieces could be connected to form a complete raft. Rafting pilots had to know every inch of the river, and their expertise was rewarded with wages of four dollars to $15 a day. Courtesy, the H.H. Bennett Studio

Above and left
Each raftsman built simple
wooden bunks for housing.
Blankets provided a little
warmth on cold mornings.
Courtesy, the H.H. Bennett
Studio

Above left
Another hazardous spot along
the Wisconsin River was The Nar-
rows at the Wisconsin Dells,
where turbulent water could
force rafts against the rocky
banks. Courtesy, the H.H.
Bennett Studio

Right
The Wisconsin River was famous for its shallow depths and shifting sandbars. When a raft would get lodged on a sandbar, the entire crew's effort would be required to extricate it. Courtesy, the H.H. Bennett Studio

Below right
H.H. Bennett titled this final rafting picture "Trip Finished." Early sawmills produced only rough lumber for river rafting, since water transportation damaged finished lumber. However, each sawmill had to weigh the risks of water damage against the extra profit gained from finished lumber. Water transportation, for all its dangers, was the cheapest transportation. Courtesy, the H.H. Bennett Studio

Below
These raftsmen take a drink after steering the raft oar, which required experience and strength. Courtesy, the H.H. Bennett Studio

*The cook for H.H. Bennett's raft-
ing photo story had an assistant, Bennett's son Ashley, who
is the young man holding the
ax. Courtesy, the H.H. Bennett
Studio*

largest producer of wooden shingles, and nearby Onalaska were sending out by rail an average of two million board feet of lumber weekly.

The Chippewa River, with its many tributaries, drains an area of about one-sixth the state. It extends north to within 25 miles of Lake Superior in Ashland County and reaches south to the Mississippi River above Lake Pepin where the French monarch, Louis XIV, was proclaimed king of the area in 1689. Of the lumber towns, Chippewa Falls was the chief sawmill town since 1836 when the first mill was built. By 1890 5 lumber companies in Eau Claire were producing about 20 to 40 million feet of lumber each year. The Chippewa valley timberlands contributed more than 500 million feet of lumber in 1885.

Loggers at Alma, Wisconsin, along the Mississippi River in 1890 needed to retrieve logs that had been stranded on a sandbar. The Mississippi River was a major highway for transporting Wisconsin logs to the treeless states of the Great Plains. Courtesy, State Historical Society of Wisconsin

Further north, the St. Croix River lumber district was largely held by Minnesota lumbermen, who had controlled access to the area's water power as early as 1837. On the Wisconsin side of the river the chief mill towns were St. Croix Falls, Hudson, and Prescott.

The lumber boom populated northern Wisconsin's towns and turned several lumbermen into tycoons. Orrin Ingram of Eau Claire made his fortune in the Chippewa Valley district. Philetus Sawyer of Oshkosh, who later became a U.S. senator, had also speculated in the Chippewa valley and was worth $4 to $5 million by the time he died in 1900. Isaac Stephenson of Marinette made millions in the Menominee River district.

Frederick Weyerhaeuser began his lumber empire in the Midwest, though he later became a far bigger giant in the Pacific Northwest. While in Wisconsin, he helped to settle the Beef Slough skirmishes during the 1870s. An inlet at the mouth of the pine-rich Chippewa River, the Beef Slough was used for storing and sorting logs for transport down the Mississippi River. Local lumbermen fought "outsiders" from the Mississippi River valley who attempted to control logging at the slough. Both groups tried to monopolize the slough through legislative charters. Arriving from Illinois in 1870, Weyerhaeuser sided with the Mississippi River lumbermen, overwhelming all

Above
Isaac Stephenson of Marinette became a multi-millionaire from lumber in the Menominee River district. He was later a financial supporter of Robert La Follette—in part because he wanted to become a U.S. senator, a goal he finally achieved in 1908. Courtesy, State Historical Society of Wisconsin

Above left
The Oshkosh lumber baron, Philetus Sawyer, was also a Republican party boss who became U.S. senator in 1881. Courtesy, State Historical Society of Wisconsin

Left
The United States' demand for lumber caused towns like Eau Claire to boom. Rafts of lumber lie in front of two mills that merged to become the Empire Lumber Co. Courtesy, State Historical Society of Wisconsin

competitors by the amount of capital he could pour into the lumber district. Weyerhaeuser later devised a log-sharing plan that regulated log cutting and transportation among his disgruntled Chippewa River valley competitors.

Wisconsin may have lost as many trees to fires as it did to lumberjacks. Loggers took only the choicest parts of trees while the remainder dried into kindling. Forest fires burned unchecked as people stood helpless to fight them. So great was the devastation from fires that historian Robert Fries suggested Wisconsin might have kept a thriving lumber industry if the forests' slash had been piled and carefully burned.

Between 1885 and 1891 fires destroyed more than $2 million worth of sawmills. In 1905 alone there were 1,435 fires in the northern counties of Wisconsin, creating a pall of smoke that impeded travel on Lake Michigan. On the same October night in 1871 that Chicago burned to the ground, Wisconsin had its deadliest fire. It swept through the drought-ravaged Peshtigo area, killing more than 1,000 people in a

Wisconsin Land & Lumber Company employees pose atop a pile of logs that scaled 13,562 board feet. Courtesy, State Historical Society of Wisconsin

These loggers in Barron County in northern Wisconsin used oxen to haul a load of white pine. Around 1900 it was more common for loggers to use horses for such hauling. The lumberjacks on top of the logs are shown with the canterhooks used to pull logs onto the piles. By 1900 the lumber industry, which had been Wisconsin's leading industry since territory days, was in decline. Courtesy, Milwaukee Public Library

swath 10 miles wide and 40 miles long. Over a half dozen counties were burned in the fire, and Peshtigo was razed.

Wisconsin's forests were a one-time resource. By the mid-1880s the lumber industry was moving westward to find untouched forests. Wisconsin's peak harvest was in 1892—more than four billion feet—but as the forests began to disappear, population growth in northern counties slowed dramatically. Ashland County had increased 1200 percent during the 1880s, but grew at only 9 percent during the 1890s. Eau Claire County, whose population had repeatedly doubled during the 1860s and 1870s, increased only 3 percent in the 1890s. The last log roll down the Chippewa River was in 1910. Weyerhaeuser's sawmill at Chippewa Falls, hailed as the "largest mill in the world," closed in 1911.

The lumber industry obliterated Wisconsin's pine forests, but not against the public's will. Wisconsin lumber built prairie homes throughout the treeless Great Plains. Wisconsin's northern counties were populated, railroads were finally built, and thousands of immigrants found ready jobs. At its peak from 1888 to 1893, the lumber industry paid one-fourth of all wages in Wisconsin.

The legendary Paul Bunyan had moved west. He was born in Maine, reached maturity in the Old Northwest that included Wisconsin, and he died on the Pacific Coast. But historian Richard Current points to the argument that Paul Bunyan is buried in a grave near Wausau, Wisconsin. Paul Bunyan had a reputation for being a very large man, and the dirt on the grave piled pretty high. It formed Rib Mountain.

WOODWORKING AND PAPER MILLS

Even before the pineries disappeared, towns looked for industries to replace and augment the lumber trade. Woodworkers used Wisconsin's hardwood trees—maple, birch, oak—for a variety of new businesses. By the 1880s Oshkosh was already the country's biggest manufacturer of wooden doors, window sashes, blinds, matches, wagons, and carriages. Fond du Lac was known for iceboxes made from the hardwoods. Along Lake Michigan's ports rose the furniture-producing centers. During the 1890s Kenosha produced wooden beds, and Port Washington built swing rockers. Sheboygan manufactured so many wooden chairs that it became popularly known as Chair City.

Many present-day woodworking businesses began during the lumber era and show the diversity of the industry. The Richardson Brothers of Sheboygan Falls, which began as a sawmill business in 1848, expanded to include furniture making and remained a family-owned business. The Eggers Plywood Co. of Two Rivers was begun in 1848 by Fred Eggers, who emigrated from Germany and whose grist mill grew into a veneer and plywood manufacturing business. In 1883 Porter B. Yates began producing woodworking

The Cereal Mills Company and other mills called Wausau home by the turn of the century. Courtesy, State Historical Society of Wisconsin

machines such as the first successful drum sander. The Yates-American of Beloit continues to manufacture heavy woodworking machinery. In 1892 more than 30 residents of the agricultural community of Kiel formed a woodworking company to produce jobs. The Kiel Furniture Company was reorganized as the A.A. Laun Furniture Company in 1935. Begun as a community venture, A.A. Laun remains a family business. In Chippewa County in 1897, August Lotz of Boyd raised honey bees as a hobby, and he decided to use the abundant supply of basswood to manufacture wooden honey frames. Furniture parts are now the principal product of the August Lotz Company.

Wisconsin's paper industry did not emerge from the lumber trade. Wood was not a primary ingredient in papermaking until the 1890s, and by then the Fox River Valley had more than 25 paper mills alone. According to historian Maurice Branch, water power was the major factor for developing the paper industry among Great Lakes paper manufacturers during the pioneer days of papermaking, from 1834 to 1890.

Water provides the solution in which cellulose fibers form a mat which becomes paper once the water is removed.

Rags and straw were the primary ingredients for paper before 1890. These raw materials were usually in short supply for the demand, and even corn husks were considered a possible source. Clean cotton rags worked best because the yield was 91 percent cellulose, the stuff of paper.

Wisconsin's first paper mill, begun in Milwaukee in 1848, recycled old cotton rags for printing the *Milwaukee Sentinel and Gazette.* However, the paper industry quickly centered in the Fox River valley in central Wisconsin because of access to water power supplied by the Lake Winnebago reservoirs. Most of these mills developed from converted flour mills. Decreasing wheat yields in Outagamie and Brown counties, combined with the competition from Minneapolis mills, made papermaking attractive to mill owners of the Fox River valley.

In 1871 a German innovation reached Wisconsin that would eventually change the course of papermaking. Discovered in 1840, the groundwood process enabled papermakers to extract wood pulp for paper. Two Appleton businessmen began a groundwood pulp mill in 1871, using hemlock wood discarded by nearby lumber mills. Because wood such as hemlock, balsam, and spruce had to be ground first, it was not a popular choice over rags and straw until the 1890s. The sulphite process, which chemically converted wood into pulp, was introduced from Europe in 1884, but the import taxes for European sulphite discouraged growth until the 1900s.

As wood became an option for making paper, mills sprang up along the forested Wisconsin River valley and throughout northern Wisconsin. Wisconsin Rapids, Rhinelander, Tomahawk, Mosinee, and Merrill became paper mill towns. By 1910 Wisconsin would be ranked third as a national producer of paper, with 57 paper mills that employed 6,000.

FOUNDRY PRODUCTS AND HEAVY INDUSTRY

The success of one industry often spawned the demand and growth of later industries. Wisconsin foundry masters responded first to the needs of the flour and lumber industries, reflecting changing demands as Wisconsin's economy changed. During the 1850s one Beloit papermaker, Sereno Merrill, had trouble getting parts for his English-made machinery. In 1858 his brother Orson started a machine shop that specialized in repairing and making parts for his brother's papermaking machinery. As paper became an important industry, the company grew into the Beloit Corporation, which today is one of the largest manufacturers of custom-designed papermaking machines.

Agricultural machinery was one of the earliest products of Wisconsin foundries and metal workers. Entrepreneurs such as Jerome I. Case of Racine produced quality threshers for wheat farmers and later turned out steam-powered agricultural machines. By the 1900s the J.I. Case Company could proclaim, "There is not a spot in the civilized world where grain is grown that is not touched or cannot be quickly reached by the departments of our organization."

Lumber and saw milling required specialized machinery, and local foundry shops eagerly supplied the demands. Local newspapers and business leaders urged the public and business community to support new foundries. And as steam power transformed lumber and flour milling, steam engines became a Milwaukee specialty. Railroad construction also spurred new demands for iron products. Essential equipment such as rails, wheelbarrows, picks, and shovels could not be shipped economically from the East. Local manufacturers filled the orders.

From 1880 to 1910 the foundry and machine industries were Wisconsin's fastest-growing industries, outstripping brewing and even dairying. In 1880 foundry and machine shops ranked ninth among Wisconsin's industries; by 1890 they ranked fifth and at the turn of the century they had become the third-largest industry in Wisconsin. In 1910 foundry and machine shops ranked second in the state after the lumber industry, which would plummet to seventh place in the following decade. Clearly, Wisconsin's strength as a manufacturing state rested in the custom-designed engines and farm implements whose roots were present even during the early days of statehood.

Despite this industrial growth, Wisconsin was not blessed with conditions to become an industrial state. Wisconsin had no coal and would prove to have no petroleum or natural gas. The village of Oil City in southwestern Monroe County is a testimony to Wisconsinites' optimism that oil could eventually be

Above
The casting-room floor at Fairbanks, Morse and Company, a
prominent Beloit manufacturing
firm in 1890, was originally
part of a facility producing wind-
mills that was launched by a Con-
gregational missionary in 1867.
Courtesy, State Historical Society of Wisconsin

Right
A Beloit minister invented a windmill in 1867 that he began manufacturing as the Eclipse Wind Engine Company of Beloit. A
Vermont firm that made scales
bought the windmill factory,
and Beloit's Fairbanks, Morse
and Company was launched as
a large manufacturer. Courtesy,
State Historical Society of
Wisconsin

*The North Chicago Rolling
Mills in the Bayview area of Milwaukee is pictured here in
1890. Courtesy, the H.H. Bennett Studio*

This cartoon promotes the potentials of Superior in 1885. Its booster-ism was backed by the brief boom in Wisconsin's iron mines and the boom in shipbuilding. Courtesy, State Historical Society of Wisconsin

found. But like the speculator's hoax that founded the city in 1866, hope soon evaporated, prompting the sentiment that "if God had designed Wisconsin to be chiefly a manufacturing state, instead of agricultural, he could have endowed her more richly for that purpose."

Wisconsin's iron mines in northern Ashland County enjoyed a brief boom in the 1880s, attracting John D. Rockefeller, who was in competition against steel masters Henry Frick and Andrew Carnegie. The village of Superior would swell from 2,700 to 44,000 people as the iron boom also gave rise to iron works and ship building. Rockefeller had acquired control of the American Steel Barge Company and an interest in Alexander McDougall's steel steamer ships, known as the whalebacks. This smooth-sailing ship also had the capacity to be used as a tanker for oil. Superior's 2,700 shipyard workers launched 27 whalebacks during the 1890s. Unfortunately, McDougall's whaleback became known as McDougall's folly after new technology made the whaleback's design obsolete for loading grain and cargoes.

Above
These steamers navigate the Milwaukee River in 1890. Courtesy, the H.H. Bennett Studio

Left
In the 1880s and 1890s the McDougall Whaleback steamers were built in this shipyard of the American Steel Barge Company at Superior. John D. Rockefeller owned the controlling interest in the company. Courtesy, State Historical Society of Wisconsin

Facing page
Milwaukee's rise as a manufacturing center depended on its easy access to Eastern coal. In the 1890s men unloaded coal from ships one wheelbarrow at a time. Courtesy, the H.H. Bennett Studio

Below
The launching of well-made ships like the City of Racine in 1889 helped prepare Manitowoc's expert shipyards for the boom in shipbuilding during World War I. Courtesy, State Historical Society of Wisconsin

Rockefeller returned to oil after losing in his bid to corner steel. Wisconsin's iron ores ran too deep and required more expensive mining methods. Superior's booming iron works disappeared although individual businesses such as the Lidgerwood Manufacturing Company, which has produced industrial hoists since 1873, managed to survive.

Wisconsin's shipwrights throughout the state returned to building wooden tugs, fishing boats, packets, and launches. For the most part Superior, Manitowoc, Sturgeon Bay, and Milwaukee shipyards would remain quiet until the twentieth century's two world wars stimulated new demand.

Milwaukee, and later southeastern Wisconsin, emerged as the state's center for foundry and heavy industry. While Milwaukee had no early advantages in power sources, it had access to iron, the essential raw material that was obtained first from Dodge County's Iron Ridge in the 1850s and later from eastern imports. With the advent of steam engines during the

E.P. Allis, the most successful foundry owner in Wisconsin during the 1880s, established the E.P. Allis Company, which made sawmill equipment and became world famous for producing heavy engines. In 1901 the company became Allis-Chalmers. Courtesy, State Historical Society of Wisconsin

1840s, coal became the main source of power for engines. Milwaukee was the chief benefactor of eastern coal because transporting the coal further west made the fuel very expensive for western Wisconsin foundries. Despite the expense of shipping, there were more than 30 foundries scattered throughout the state by 1880. Most towns seldom had more than one foundry; La Crosse and West Bend each had three. In contrast, Milwaukee had 17 foundries in 1880.

By 1880 Milwaukee had grown from a commercial port city into the country's fourteenth-largest manufacturing center, with a population of 115,587. By 1903 there were 53 foundries in Milwaukee, which had an industry-wide reputation for modern foundry equipment and progressive methods. Milwaukee founders produced some of the heaviest castings in foundry history. In 1907 Milwaukee boasted the two largest steel foundries in the country, the Falk Company and the George H. Smith Steel Casting Company.

Capital and entrepreneurial talent were the terms for survival in the foundry business, and inventiveness became the hallmark of Wisconsin's foundry masters. Adapting to the changing business climates was essential to makers of specialty machinery. John Bonnel's machine shop in Fond du Lac began as a small repair shop for local sawmills, but it continued to adapt its products to heavy-industry machine tools. Bonnel's shop grew into Giddings & Lewis, which would become one of the largest machine tool builders in the United States.

Milwaukee's most successful foundry owner, Edward P. Allis, had both imagination and access to capital, and his company would achieve national acclaim for the quality of its manufacturing in flour mills, lumber mills, and power engines. Yet when Allis entered the foundry business he knew nothing about it; his background had been in leather tanning and real estate. As historians have noted, his success was based upon a simple formula: find the men who could envision the highest state of the art and then provide them with the most modern equipment, enough money, and a free hand. Allis' factory buildings may have been flimsy, but inside no expense was spared on modern equipment and skilled personnel.

Allis escaped the Panic of 1857 unscathed—he had just sold his interest in his leather tannery. In 1861 he bought the Reliance Works and later one of his

*In the 1880s produce vendors
sold their goods wholesale in Milwaukee's North Broadway
market. Courtesy, Milwaukee
County Historical Society*

This advertisement attracted customers to John Plankinton's and Patrick Cudahy's large Milwaukee meat-packing company, the Plankinton Packing Company. In 1888, upon Plankinton's retirement, the company was taken over by brothers Patrick and John Cudahy. Courtesy, Milwaukee County Historical Society

leading competitors, the Bay State Iron Manufacturing Company of Milwaukee, which was twice the size of Allis' company. In the following decade consolidation and expansion forced Allis to overextend himself, and he would not escape the Panic of 1873. In 1876 Allis declared bankruptcy. His reputation as a community leader helped him through bankruptcy. His creditors, aware that he had one of Milwaukee's largest payrolls, settled his debts at a considerable discount and ensured that he would retain control of his company.

By the 1880s the Allis Company was the acknowledged giant in the field of sawmill equipment. Allis machinery had become the standard in the lumber industry. The steam engines produced by chief engineer and manager Edwin Reynolds were consistently innovative and reliable. The Reynolds-Corliss low-speed heavy engine would make the Allis Company world famous. By 1882 steam engines and pumping equipment accounted for about two-thirds of the company's sales.

As Milwaukee's largest industrialist, Allis was a risk taker who constantly expanded his company on borrowed money. When Allis died in 1889, his wisely invested life insurance policies helped absolve his debts in a company that employed nearly 1,500 workers. In 1901, the Edward P. Allis Company merged with Fraser & Chalmers Company of Chicago in order to expand production of more sophisticated engines with the advent of electricity.

As Wisconsin's only metropolitan city, Milwaukee was the leader of Wisconsin's industrial growth, contributing nearly one-half of the value of the state's manufacturing from 1870 to 1900. In contrast lumber, which contributed the majority of manufacturing, was widely dispersed throughout the state. Although most of Wisconsin's cities tended to be identified with only one or two industries, Milwaukee's industries had tremendous variety in their national markets, ranging from heavy machinery to frothy beer.

MEAT PACKING

Milwaukee's largest industry in 1880 was meat packing, adding $6 million worth of goods from seven companies. Meat packing had surged ahead of many industries during the Civil War. Salted pork and beef were shipped in barrels to Union troops by Milwaukee firms such as Plankinton and Armour, Layton and Company, and Van Kirk, McGeoch & Company.

Wisconsin's meat packers processed the hogs raised by Wisconsin farmers, who found that hogs were a perfect complement to the dairy business. The byproducts of cheese and butter—whey and buttermilk—provided a feast for portly pork bellies. Combined with dairy calves that were sold for veal, hogs helped Milwaukee to hold its own in the competition between regional meat packers.

One of Milwaukee's most flamboyant meat packers, Philip Armour, initiated a dramatic episode of speculation in pork bellies, according to historian Francis Bowman. Realizing the Civil War was drawing to a close in March of 1865, Armour convinced his partner, John Plankinton, that they should liquidate their entire stock of pork while the war prices were still high. Armour sold their pork barrels to eastern speculators for approximately $40 a barrel before the price plunged to $18 a barrel after peace was declared. Plankinton and Armour are reputed to have cleared $1.8 million from the wartime deal. Armour left Milwaukee eight years later to join Swift, Hammond and Morris in Chicago, which was growing into the meat packing center of the country.

Irishman Patrick Cudahy took Armour's place in the partnership of John Plankinton and Company. When Plankinton retired in 1888, the Cudahy brothers eventually gained control. In 1893 Patrick and John Cudahy moved their plant to their new suburban development south of Milwaukee called Cudahy. Meat packing continued to be among the top four industries in Milwaukee from 1880 to 1910, along with the Layton Company, the Peter McGeoch Company, and the Bodden Packing Company.

Although John Armour moved south to Chicago to continue his meat packing empire, one Chicago meat packer relocated north to make Madison the center of its operations. Oscar Mayer began making Bavarian-style sausages and Westphalian-style hams in Chicago in 1883. By 1900 the business had grown to 43 employees processing and selling meats throughout Chicago. His son, Oscar F. Mayer, expanded the family business in 1919 when he purchased a meat packing plant in Madison, which would grow into one of the largest and most efficient in the country. The company's headquarters were moved to Madison in 1957.

FAMILY BUSINESSES, HOUSEHOLD NAMES

Many family businesses begun in Wisconsin during the nineteenth century have survived into the twentieth century. In Janesville a teacher of telegraphy repaired his student's pens as a hobby. He felt he could make a better pen, and in 1892 George S. Parker's "Lucky Curve" debuted. In 1903 the company began its first overseas distributorship in Scandinavia; manufacturing plants later were started in European and South American countries. Parker Pen built an international reputation designing dependable and luxury-line pens before moving its headquarters to England in 1985.

Floor wax was the principal product of another family-owned business that became a household word. Johnson Wax began in 1886 when Samuel C. Johnson bought a parquet flooring company from his employer, the Racine Hardware Company. Two years later he was advertising paste wax for wooden floors in the major magazines of the day. The founder's son, Herbert Fisk Johnson, continued to emphasize advertising. "Our goal is to have the housewife so conscious of the superiority of our products," declared a Johnson Wax vice president, "that dealers need only give them a good display to have a profitable year-round business with them." During the 1920s Johnson's advertising budget reached $1 million.

John M. Kohler's foundry business in Sheboygan began producing J.I. Case's farm machines in 1880, but then branched off to produce kitchen sinks. In the following decades Kohler specialized in bathroom and kitchen designs. The Kohler family is distinctive for having produced two governors of the state, Walter J. Kohler, Sr., (1929-1931) and Walter J. Kohler, Jr., (1951-1957).

The Kohler Company is also well-known for its planned community, begun in 1900 when the company moved its factory four miles away from Sheboygan. The founder's son, Walter J. Kohler, Sr., had dreams of a garden-industrial community. In 1913 he and Milwaukee architect Richard Philipp traveled to Europe to study European cities. In England they met Sir Ebenezer Howard, a major promulgator of the theory that planned communities could avoid the congestion and slums of industrialized cities. When Kohler returned to Wisconsin he hired the Olmsted Brothers of Boston, who helped plan New York City's Central Park, and the first foundations were laid in 1917. The village differed from its European counterparts in that the Kohler employees owned their homes. The vision of Walter J. Kohler, Sr., turned a large manufacturing plant into a gardened community. Perhaps English writer John Ruskin's observation, which hung in Kohler's office for 25 years, sums up the industrialists philosophy: "Life without labor is guilt, but labor without art is brutality."

Manufacturing had taken firm root in Wisconsin by the turn of the century. In 1900 there were approximately 16,000 manufacturing establishments in the state. Many of these manufacturers were isolated sawmills, but the number of companies with 100 or more employees had increased substantially during the 1880s and 1890s. In 1894 Wisconsin had 227 companies that employed more than 100 workers. The lure of success offered by business and industry inspired the growth of business schools. There were only two business schools listed in 1873; however, by the 1890s there were 20 business schools located in 14 communities. Milwaukee had six business schools, while Eau Claire had three and Janesville had two.

WISCONSIN'S BIG TOPS

For circus lovers, the world of private enterprise probably pales next to the dazzle of Wisconsin's early entertainment business. Baraboo and Delavan were both homes of the "Greatest Show on Earth." From Delavan, the earliest circus center, came the originators of the P.T. Barnum Circus, and from Baraboo rose the Ringling Brothers Circus.

In the late 1840s Ed and Jerry Mabie of New York brought their circus to their Delavan farm each winter. As the Mabies' circus grew, several employees, among them a bareback rider and an animal trainer, began their own circuses. Over the years 26 circuses were organized in Delavan and additional ones in other towns, including Portage, Beaver Dam, Watertown, Janesville, Burlington, Evansville, Whitewater, and Wonewoc.

Two Delavan circus owners, manager William Cameron Coup and clown Dan Castello, convinced Phineas T. Barnum, the world's greatest showman, to go into the circus business. P.T. Barnum, the discoverer of Tom Thumb, had never sponsored a traveling tent show. In 1871 Coup and Castello took Barnum's tent show on the road. It was Coup's idea to add a second

and third circus ring, and he set another precedent by having the circus travel by train in special railroad cars. In 1875 Barnum's decision to divide his circus into two traveling shows prompted Coup and Castello to leave. P.T. Barnum's circus was later managed by James A. Bailey, becoming Barnum & Bailey's "Greatest Show on Earth." W.C. Coup, the originator of Barnum's circus, died penniless in Florida, the owner of a dog and pony show. He is buried in Delavan.

The "World's Greatest Show" was born in Baraboo. Albrecht Ringling was the son of a harness maker from Germany, and he grew up watching traveling circuses as his family moved from Baraboo to Iowa, Prairie du Chien, and later back to Baraboo. During the 1870s Al Ringling learned to juggle and walk tightropes in a professional troupe. But his dream was to start a circus, and on May 19, 1884, Al Ringling's circus premiered in front of the Sauk County Jail in Baraboo.

Four of Al Ringling's seven brothers doubled as performers and Al's wife, Louise, was the snake charmer. Their first tour by wagon caravan took them to Black Earth, Mt. Horeb, Mt. Vernon, and New Glarus. "The boys are on the road to fortune," predicted the *Baraboo Republic* after the brothers' third year. The newspaper was right. In 1890 the Ringling Brothers Circus pulled out of Baraboo in 18 railroad cars. Five years later the three-ring circus opened in Chicago before touring major cities across North America. In 1907 the Ringling Brothers bought the Barnum & Bailey Circus from Bailey's widow for $410,000—a price earned back the following season.

The Ringling Brothers Circus continued to spend winters in Baraboo, the town Al Ringling loved, while the Barnum & Bailey circus headquartered in Bridgeport, Connecticut. Al Ringling died in 1916, and three years later the Ringling Brothers Circus train pulled out of Baraboo for the last time. The "Greatest Show on Earth" became the Ringling Brothers and Barnum & Bailey Combined Shows. In 1959 the State Historical Society of Wisconsin opened a museum to Baraboo's most glamorous business. The Circus World Museum is located on the same grounds that once housed the Ringling Brothers' winter quarters. The sound of noisy calliopes has not vanished.

This clever 1890s advertisement
for a tailor in Milwaukee employed a well-dressed boy, two
goats, and a wagon. Courtesy,
the H.H. Bennett Studio

AGRICULTURE IN AMERICA'S DAIRYLAND

Around 1890 a Milwaukee a farmers'
market provided city residents access to fresh
farm products. Courtesy, the H.H. Bennett
Studio

Cows, a cow governor, and a cow college brought Wisconsin's economy into the twentieth century. Wisconsin's dairy revolution built a modern industry based on science, marketing, and specialization. Dairying began fitfully in the 1870s, but by 1909 Wisconsin would produce almost half of the country's cheese and by 1919 almost two-thirds. The dairy farm would produce a pastoral industry that by the 1920s was Wisconsin's strongest manufacturer and the nation's largest producer of dairy products.

Wisconsin became America's Dairyland because farmers could find no other solution to the vanishing wheat fields. They had tried wool. They had tried flax and sugar. But these demands had been spurred by the Civil War. Once the South returned to the Union, these products were produced more cheaply elsewhere. Farmers had also planted hop fields, but they later watched helplessly as their crops were destroyed by the eastern hop louse.

In the 1870s, a vocal group of Yankees preached the advantages of dairying in stimulating Wisconsin's sagging agricultural economy. Wheat farmers were skeptical—cows could be as profitable as wheat? The acceptance of dairying by Wisconsin's farmers was a process of education and persuasion. "Speak to a cow as you would to a lady," advised Kenosha cheese maker W.C. White. This whimsical advice hid the difficulties facing the men and women who, within twenty years, would make dairying a Wisconsin specialty.

A loyal wheat farmer could easily object to becoming "tied to a cow." The pioneer's cow had been valued chiefly because she could produce oxen for breaking sod. If she provided milk beyond the needs of her calf, that was a happy coincidence. The job of a farmer was to grow crops; milking and butter making was considered "women's work."

Wheat had been the farmer's boom crop. Indian corn was usually the first crop the pioneer planted on his wilderness land. After breaking a few acres of sod the farmer would make ax-cuts at regular intervals, deposit a seed and step on it. "Sod corn," sometimes planted between stumps of freshly cut trees, gave the family ears of roasting corn and winter feed for oxen.

For years wheat had been the state's cash crop. "Wheat is king and Wisconsin is the center of the Empire," proclaimed the *Milwaukee Sentinel* in 1861. Yet poor soil management eventually robbed the soil of

In 1895 a promotional photo
showed a family who decided to
farm in northern Wisconsin.
The photo was included in a pamphlet, Northern Wisconsin: a
Handbook for the Home-
seeker, that promoted northern
Wisconsin's cutover region as
potentially good farmland. Courtesy, State Historical Society of
Wisconsin

nitrogen, and by the 1870s Wisconsin's wheat fields were moving westward. Alert farmers knew they had to diversify, but they resisted dairying, which required them to go into debt to buy cows and equipment. Moreover, dairy farming demanded a rigorous routine seven days a week, including holidays. Cows required milking twice a day, every day, in addition to feeding and attending them. In contrast, wheat farmers had the luxury of free time between planting and harvesting.

PIONEERS OF DAIRYING

The early leaders of dairying in Wisconsin were originally from New York. By 1850 New York produced 25 percent of the nation's butter and more than half of its cheese. Many New Yorkers who settled in Wisconsin brought with them the know-how for produc-

Above
In 1878 a rural cheese factory in the Village of Pipe on Lake Winnebago in Fond Du Lac County was an early member of an industry that would transform Wisconsin from a wheat-growing state to "America's Dairyland." Courtesy, State Historical Society of Wisconsin

Right
As the Seymour Brooks farm of 1873 in East Troy shows, not everything profitable in Wisconsin agriculture mooed. Brooks settled in East Troy in 1843 and became a breeder of cattle, sheep, and pigs. Courtesy, State Historical Society of Wisconsin

ing quality butter and cheese, skills that would help to solve the problem of marketing dairy products. The problems of pioneer dairy farmers were immense: the product was perishable, the work was seasonal, and the market was difficult to reach.

The first hurdle for Wisconsin's dairy industry was building a reputation for quality. Casual dairying was common, and the popular name for pioneer butter was "western grease," literally used as axle grease for wagons. In 1885 the publication *Prairie Farmer* illuminated the conditions of many butter-makers. Bad butter began with cows that slept in beds of manure and never knew the comforts of a brush and wash. Unclean hands would wet the teats with milk for milking, adding filth to the milk pail. Inside the house, pans of milk set out for the cream to rise shared the same space as muddy boots, family pets, wet laundry, and cooking smells. These odors became part of the butter that farm wives sold to grocers. Wholesome butter was also made, but the grocer didn't make distinctions and would combine the good butter with the inferior butter. Butter often turned rancid at the grocery store due to unclean containers and lack of refrigeration.

Butter was the most common way for farmers to market milk. Butter was easier to handle than fluid milk, and it was easy to make. Grocers traditionally accepted butter in exchange for groceries. Even with the rise of commercial creameries that offered fresh wholesome butter at higher prices, individual farms were the most common butter producers. By 1899 there would be more than 8,000 creameries in the United States, yet farms continued to produce more than two-thirds of the country's butter.

Cheese making, which required a steady supply of milk, equipment, storage space, and skill, separated the casual milk producer from the serious dairy farmer. The chemical processes involved in cheese making were still not understood. However if properly made, cheese lasted longer than butter and traveled farther in shipping. The cheese factory, pioneered in New York in 1851, improved the consistency and quality of cheese. As the milk producer concentrated on high-quality milk, the competent cheese maker divined the process of making consistent cheese. Due to bad roads and bumpy horse-drawn transportation, the cheese factory had to be close to the milk producer—a radius of not more than three miles. And in order to be economical the cheese factory needed at least 200 cows.

In 1872, recognizing the importance of dairying, seven industry pioneers met in Watertown in Jefferson County to form the Wisconsin Dairymen's Association. Their prospectus was ambitious: to improve dairy products and dairy herds; to develop markets and ways to reach those markets; and to build dairying into a permanent industry. The chief organizer, William Dempster Hoard, later became a governor of Wisconsin from 1889 to 1891. A fiery orator as well as a tireless campaigner for dairying, he is perhaps most

William Dempster Hoard was Wisconsin's governor from 1889 to 1891; however, he made his largest contribution to Wisconsin with his trailblazing leadership as a builder of Wisconsin's dairy industry. He was not a farmer but rather the editor of Hoard's Dairyman, *which campaigned for the scientific manufacturing of milk, cheese, and butter. Courtesy, State Historical Society of Wisconsin*

famous for his outstanding publication, *Hoard's Dairy-man*, which he started in 1885 and which reached a circulation of 70,000 by World War I.

Though not a farmer, W.D. Hoard understood the problems besetting dairying's latent industry. Hoard never tired of promoting scientific, businesslike dairying, advising farmers to specialize in milk products, not to diversify with other agriculture. Hoard, "the cow candidate" who became governor in 1889, was defeated for re-election in 1891 largely due to the anger caused by the Bennett Law, which required that school children be taught only in English. Hoard misjudged the political climate, but he was a visionary in helping to transform Wisconsin's agriculture.

Wisconsin's white gold came from cows throughout the state. In Appleton on the Black Creek Road in 1915 a line of milk producers also marks the transition from horses to horseless carriages. Courtesy, State Historical Society of Wisconsin

One of Hoard's early campaigns was against the milk-and-beef cow. All a dual-purpose cow gave, he said, was "a little beef, a little milk and a little butter. The result is a cow whose main product is littleness all around." Gradually the beef cow disappeared from Wisconsin's dairy herds. At first the Jersey was the favorite milking breed; by 1900 the Holstein dominated, followed by the Guernsey.

Hoard experimented with alfalfa crops, a choice feed for cows, on his vacant lots in his hometown of Fort Atkinson. "Another of Hoard's notions," scoffed an agricultural expert, "alfalfa won't grow here." But Hoard was experimenting with a new yellow-flowered variety brought by Wendelin Grimm, a German immigrant, to Minnesota. Grimm's alfalfa, which thrived in Wisconsin's cold climate, not only fed the cows but also put nitrogen back into the soil that wheat had stolen.

In the 1870s dairying was still seasonal work because farmers had no way to feed milking cows during the winter. In 1879 French research on silage, the nutritious green winter feed that keeps cows milking year round, was translated into English and available to American farmers. One of the first Wisconsin silos, used for storing silage, was built by Fort Atkinson farmer Levi P. Gilbert. He built a pit six feet square

In 1929 this Plymouth, Wisconsin, cheese worker stirred Swiss cheese in copper kettles. Courtesy, State Historical Society of Wisconsin

and filled it with alternate layers of green cornstalks and rye straw. He reported that by using silage, three cows could be fed for what it had previously cost to feed one cow.

Despite well-publicized research by a few farmers and the state university, most farmers were very slow to accept silage. Farmers argued that silage would cause cattle to lose teeth, complicate calving, and eat away at the cow's stomach. As late as 1904, when Wisconsin was a leading dairy state, there were still only 716 silos. However, farmers eventually saw the advantages of silage, and by 1924 there were more than 100,000 silos, accounting for two-thirds of Wisconsin's farms. The silo had gradually taken flight from the ground to become the familiar tower.

CHEESE MAKING

While Wisconsin's farmers may have balked at silage, they were innovative when making cheese. Wisconsin's immigrants quickly introduced cheeses from the Old Country. Swiss and Limburger mingled on the market with the popular English cheddar. Two Wisconsin cheesemakers invented varieties from cheddar and Limburger. In Dodge County during the mid-1870s, Swiss immigrant John Jossi created Brick cheese, a milder version of Limburger. In 1885 Joseph Steinwald experimented with cheddar in the Black

River lumber district of Clark County. His new cheese, which was milder and moister, found an immediate market. He named this popular new cheese after his township, Colby, which had taken its name from the construction president who had built the Wisconsin Central railroad through the village. Gardner Colby's business was railroads, but his name graces one of Wisconsin's best-known cheeses.

Although the majority of Wisconsin's dairy farmers made butter in 1880, the state's industrialized dairies made cheese. By 1888 cheese manufacturing was largely concentrated in three counties: Sheboygan, Jefferson, and Green. Sheboygan County had 87 factories, Green County, 47; and Jefferson County, 36. The next three ranking counties were Walworth, Manitowoc, and Dodge. Sheboygan County built an early reputation for fine cheese, producing twice as much as its nearest rival.

Sheboygan County's newspaper reflected the importance of cheese making in that area. In 1882 the *Sheboygan County News* began a front-page column called "Dairy Notes." Beginning in 1886 the weekly printed on its masthead that it was "The Official Paper for the Dairy Interests." In 1901 the newspaper reflected the scope of its dairy coverage by changing its name to the *Sheboygan County News and Dairy Market Reporter*. The next year it dropped the first part of its name. By 1929 the *Dairy Market Reporter* alerted its audience of its final specialization by changing its name to *The Cheese Reporter*, which now publishes for the dairy industry from Madison.

A worthy rival to Sheboygan County was Jefferson County, which had developed commercial dairying before the Civil War. According to historian Eric Lampard, Jefferson County may have produced the first cooperative cheese factory. As early as 1870 a dozen farmers built a cheese factory two miles north of Lake Mills. One farmer was elected to manage the cheese maker, supplies, and accounting. Dividends were divided among the owners at the end of each year.

Green County, an enclave of Swiss immigrants, actually made very little Swiss cheese. Limburger, popular among German and Swiss, comprised half the county's total production, while Swiss cheese made up less than 10 percent. Since Green County never formed a board of trade, cheese did not become the export business that it was for Sheboygan and Jefferson counties.

To reach eastern buyers directly, the Wisconsin Dairymen's Association formed a dairy board of trade in 1872 in Watertown. They wanted to prevent middlemen from buying Wisconsin cheese and selling it as New York cheese, which kept Wisconsin from claiming its rightful reputation. In 1873 Sheboygan County, through its board of trade, began to develop a direct trade with the British and helped standardize methods of marketing.

MARKETING

Marketing was critical to pioneer cheese makers. Although Wisconsin cheese was cheaper than New York's, freight rates kept Wisconsin from being competitive. In 1874 the Wisconsin Dairymen's Association sent W.D. Hoard to Chicago to persuade the railroads to lower their rates. Hoard was successful in having the fees reduced by more than 50 percent, which allowed cheese to be shipped east on express cars in only one week. By 1880 more than 3,000 refrigerated freight cars carrying Wisconsin cheese shuttled between Chicago and the Eastern Seaboard.

England was Wisconsin's first large market, sparking the dairy revolution in Wisconsin. Cheese was regarded more as a relish in the United States, where meat was abundant. In contrast, the British considered cheese a substitute for meat. British tastes were

a salvation for American cheese makers, who during the 1870s exported nearly half their cheese to England. By 1881 national exports peaked at 148 million pounds of cheese.

The Wisconsin Dairymen's Association had achieved its goals in less than two decades. By 1890 the wheat fields had almost disappeared from Wisconsin and farmers had learned to specialize. Dairying was dominant in southern and eastern Wisconsin, and it was starting to penetrate the northern and western parts of Wisconsin. Dairy cows were replacing wheat fields, sheep, and steers. In 1890 there were more than 1,000 cheese and butter factories throughout the state.

Ironically, one of the biggest threats to cheese makers came from themselves. Across the country farmers were making skim-milk cheese and passing it off as whole-milk cheese. Also called "filled cheese," this product contained lard or oleo, which was added to replace the missing butterfat content. When very fresh it was difficult to distinguish filled cheese from whole-milk cheese. But filled cheese deteriorated very quickly, a fact that became apparent in exports. As farmers' profits rose, reputations fell. British exports fell during the 1880s as fast as they had risen in the 1870s.

In 1881 the Wisconsin Dairymen's Association pressured the state Legislature to pass a law requiring that filled cheese be properly labeled. But without enforcement powers, the law was an empty gesture. And Wisconsin filled cheese could be sold out of state and repackaged as whole-milk cheese from Wisconsin. In 1895 the Legislature prohibited the manufacture of filled cheese. Although the foreign market never recovered, the domestic market had risen to more than offset the loss of overseas trade.

For butter makers the menace of oleomargarine could not be solved through legislation. Invented by a Parisian chemist in 1867, oleomargarine was first made from a cow's udder. It tasted remarkably like the butter of the times and was cheaper. By the time the first U.S. patent was obtained in 1873, the recipe for margarine had changed. Improved oleomargarine was made from fresh sheep's stomach, ground parts of beef, carbonate of potash, milk, and water. By 1880 there were 15 oleo factories in the United States. The Wisconsin dairy commissioner reported that by 1890 four to five million pounds of oleo were sold annually in Wisconsin.

The butter maker's agitation was nationwide. In 1902 Congress passed the Oleomargarine Act, which taxed yellow-colored oleo at ten cents a pound. Dealers who mixed oleo with butter were designated manufacturers and required a manufacturing license that cost $600.

Oleomargarine sales tripled between 1904 and 1914. The public simply preferred oleo, which was becoming a more wholesome product. About 3.5 million pounds of oleo were sold in Wisconsin during 1910. Wisconsin butter makers reacted by making higher-quality butter under cleaner conditions, and Wisconsin had become the largest producer of creamery butter by 1910. Despite Wisconsin's reputation, butter sales declined nationally after World War I. In 1950 Congress repealed the Oleomargarine Act of 1902. Oleo, once a product of the stockyards, was a preferred product over more expensive butter.

Wisconsin dairies spcecialized in other uses for whole milk such as dried, condensed, and pasteurized

During the 1880s it was the partnership between dairy leaders and the scientists at the University of Wisconsin that built the reputation of the university's College of Agriculture. This partnership also built Wisconsin's reputation for consistently excellent dairy products. In 1906 the dean of the College of Agriculture, William A. Henry, said, "The Wisconsin State Dairymen's Association is the true parent of the Wisconsin College of Agriculture of today." Courtesy, State Historical Society of Wisconsin

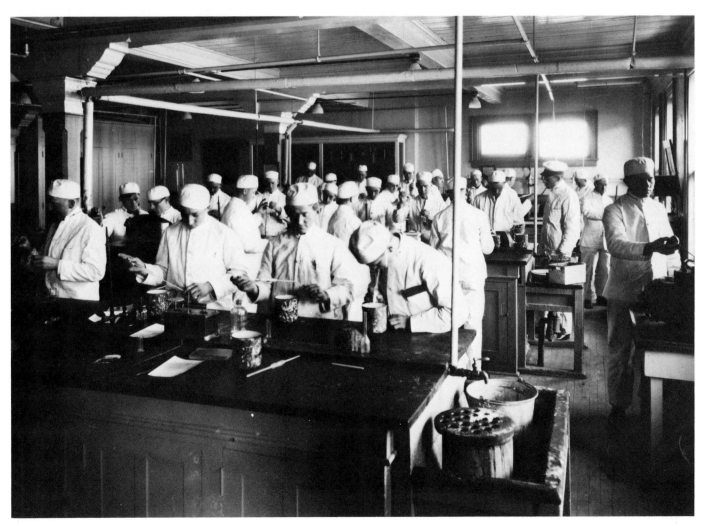

milk. In 1876 William Horlick of Racine combined dried milk with malted wheat in 1887, discovering a delicious beverage—malted milk. Horlick's Malted Milk Company later opened offices in New York City and his homeland, England. Wisconsin remained the principal home of Horlick's Malted Milk, but after World War II the English branch took control. Gail Borden opened Wisconsin's first condensery in Monroe in 1889. The New York company had 67 plants in the state by 1920, producing one-quarter of the country's condensed and evaporated milk.

AGRICULTURAL RESEARCH

During the growth of dairying Wisconsin had also become a world leader in agricultural science and nutrition. Like dairying, agricultural research had a fitful start. The College of Agriculture at the University of Wisconsin hired its first professor of agriculture in 1868; it graduated its first student 10 years later. The college had to wait another three years before its second student began school in 1881.

The dairy pioneers, who needed help in problem solving, rescued the university's program from a hostile Legislature, according to historian Robert Nesbit. In 1906, near the end of his career the dean of the College of Agriculture, William A. Henry called the Wisconsin State Dairymen's Association "the true parent of the Wisconsin College of Agriculture of today."

The detection of bovine tuberculosis was among the early scientific discoveries of the College of Agriculture and the Wisconsin Dairymen's Association. Unfortunately farmers were hostile to the tests for bovine tuberculosis because of the possibility of losing their prized herds if the tests proved positive. Pasteurization, introduced in the late 1890s, helped to prevent the spread of tuberculosis to humans, but it was not until after World War I that farmers were convinced the disease should be rooted out. U.S. pastures were not declared tuberculin-free until 1940.

The university's most famous contribution to dairying was the Babcock Test, which measures the quality of milk. Previous tests to determine the buttermilk content, which identifies high-quality milk from inferior milk, were laborious and required a chemist. The Babcock Test, which became world renowned, separated the butterfat without the aid of a

ESTABLISHED 1873

HORLICK'S FOO

DAIRIES,
LABORATORIES & FACTO
at Racine, Wis. U.S.A.

This 1890s letterhead represented Horlick's Food Company, maker of Horlick's malted milk. Malted milk was invented by William Horlick of Racine in 1887 when he combined dried milk with malted wheat. He eventually opened offices in New York City and in England, his homeland. Courtesy, State Historical Society of Wisconsin

University of Wisconsin Professor Stephen M. Babcock invented a device in 1890 that measured the butterfat content of milk. This test ensured high-quality dairy products, because milk could no longer be watered down before being sold. Babcock is shown here with his device, which he refused to patent. Courtesy, State Historical Society of Wisconsin

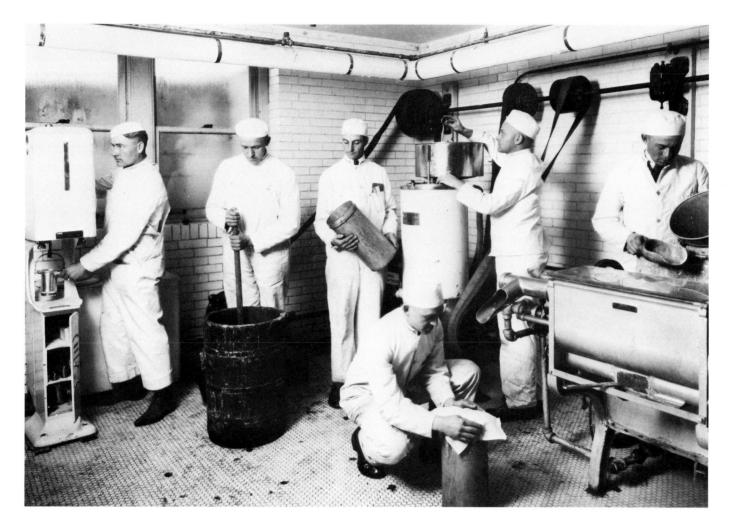

chemist.

In 1890 Professor Stephen M. Babcock discovered that sulphuric acid accurately separated butterfat from milk. When subjected to slight centrifugal
force, the butterfat would gather at the neck of the
gradient for easy measurement. The test, which Babcock refused to patent, was so simple and inexpensive
that anyone could measure milk quality on location
within five minutes. Farmers could no longer water
down their milk without detection. Indeed, as one
creamery owner stated, "the Babcock Test can beat the
Bible in making a man honest."

In 1895 Babcock and his associates devised the
"Wisconsin curd test," which measures the amount
of casein in milk for cheese making. Along with Harry
L. Russell, Babcock determined that this enzyme is responsible for the curing of cheese. Their experiments
with curing, salting, and packing had direct results in
raising the quality of Wisconsin cheese. From 1909
to 1911 Wisconsin cheese swept first, second, and
third place in almost every class in the international

*Students in dairying at the Univer-
sity of Wisconsin maintained Wisconsin's modern reputation for
clean, wholesome dairy products. Courtesy, State Historical
Society of Wisconsin*

competitions held at the state fairs at Chicago and Milwaukee.

In his experiments with cows, Babcock realized that corn-fed cows thrived while cows fed on nothing but wheat did poorly. Some mysterious factor X accounted for the difference, he concluded. One of his assistants, Dr. Elmer V. McCollum, discovered the factor in his research analyzing milk—vitamins. He isolated vitamins A and B and later discovered vitamin D, which proved capable of curing and preventing rickets.

But vitamin D—the sunshine vitamin—was available primarily through cod liver oil, which was both expensive and bad tasting. Another of Babcock's associates, Harry Steenbock, discovered how to infuse foods with vitamin D by the simple process of ultraviolet irradiation. Now milk, cereals, bread, and oleo could be a source for preventing rickets.

Steenbock's discovery, worth millions of dollars, assured profits to fund future university research. In 1927 Steenbock sold the patent for $10 to the Wisconsin Alumni Research Foundation. Steenbock's patent earned the university $8 million in royalties by the time it expired in 1945. Among the new developments funded through Steenbock's patent were the hybridization of sweet corn, the stabilization of iodine in table salt, and the nutritional treatment of anemia and pellagra.

The catalyst in making dairying one of Wisconsin's most brilliant industries was the partnership between the Wisconsin Dairymen's Association and the University of Wisconsin. W.D. Hoard tended the growth of both. In 1907 he was appointed to the university's Board of Regents and later served as president of the board.

NONDAIRY AGRICULTURE

Not everything profitable in Wisconsin farming mooed and chewed cud. Many farmers grew hogs for the meat packing industry, as hogs conveniently guzzled the whey left over from cheese making or the buttermilk from butter. Hogs complemented dairying and corn growing in the southern counties. At the turn of the century feed crops, especially hay, rye, barley, and oats, were grown throughout Wisconsin. The College of Agriculture was developing hybrids of sweet corn that could grow in Wisconsin's short growing season.

Many farmers, including dairymen, grew peas, a good cash crop because of canning. Vegetable canning had become possible in 1874 when the first pressure

In Dodge County a German farm family poses for a portrait during their sorghum harvest of 1901. Courtesy, State Historical Society of Wisconsin

cooker appeared on the market. In 1887 Albert Landreth, a pea-seed dealer from Pennsylvania, set up a small canning plant in Manitowoc, where Dutch and German immigrants had been growing peas for years. Landreth persuaded the area's farmers to grow more acres of peas, and three years later he built another plant in Sheboygan.

Canning was still often a mystery, but Wisconsin canners improved the primitive process. In 1894, when cans of peas exploded in Landreth's warehouse, the green spray and stench inspired Landreth to seek help from the College of Agriculture's Harry L. Russell, who devised a chart of temperature, pressure, and exposure times for safe canning and sterilization. By 1900 there were 20 small canneries in the state canning peas, sweet corn, and other vegetables. Wisconsin became the largest pea-canning state in 1913, and five years later the war economy spurred more production.

Potatoes, cranberries, and tobacco became unique specialties in parts of Wisconsin. Potatoes were first grown on large scale in the central counties of Portage, Waupaca, and Waushara. Central Wisconsin also had bogs where cranberries grew wild. Summer fires were a hazard for cranberry farmers due to the peat in bogs, and early frosts were a danger in the fall. But profits were good enough for growers to overcome the difficulties of building up bogs. As cranberry growing stretched north into the central sand counties, Indians were hired for the labor-intensive picking. Wisconsin Indians also continued their centuries-old tradition of harvesting wild rice from glacial lakes and wetlands. Wild rice has since become a local Wisconsin specialty.

Tobacco was introduced by Norwegian farmers in southern Wisconsin around Edgerton and Stoughton and later west into Vernon and Crawford counties. Norwegians were indifferent to the Yankee bias that tobacco was immoral. Norwegians' large farm families were well-suited to raising tobacco, which was temperamental and needed careful cultivation. But it was a good cash crop due to the German cigar-making factories, and in 1885 farmers grew 27,000 acres.

Many immigrants from northern Europe recognized the quality of Wisconsin's soil. The Ice Age's glaciers had caused the variability of soil in both northern Europe and Wisconsin. The Old Country also had boulders, rocks, and fine glacial drift; Wisconsin's lakes and marshes resembled European homelands. The sheets of ice had been "God's great plough," according to Swiss naturalist Louis Agassiz, who in his 1876 book *Geological Sketches* first asserted that the glaciers made the land fit for agriculture.

Norwegians and their large families became associated with tobacco growing in Wisconsin, although it was not a tradition in Norway. Tobacco was a good cash crop, and this 1905 photograph of Norwegian farmers in Jefferson County shows the harvest. Courtesy, State Historical Society of Wisconsin

Above
Farm communities like Black Earth were still horse-and-wagon economies in 1909. Courtesy, State Historical Society of Wisconsin

Right
A Norwegian farmer proudly displays his grain fields, farmhouse, and barn in this 1875 photo taken in Dane County. Courtesy, State Historical Society of Wisconsin

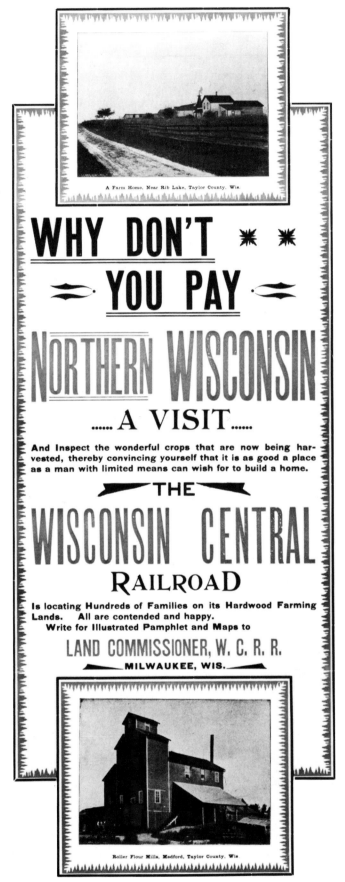

THE CUTOVER

Northern Wisconsin's pine forests had been reduced to stumps by the lumberjacks. And although hardwoods would eventually rot, pine stumps remained rooted as bleak scars on the land. This land of stumps, called "the cutover," was considered by some to be potential farmland. If people could be persuaded to move north, there was a chance of turning the grim landscape into farms.

"There is no royal road to farming in northern Wisconsin," wrote Dean Henry of the College of Agriculture in 1896. His pamphlet, *Northern Wisconsin: A Handbook for the Homeseeker*, encouraged hard-working, industrious farm families to try their luck. It was not for the faint of heart, he warned, and he was right. Some farmers had to haul 20 wagonloads of rocks before a field was ready, and removing the stumps was a back-breaking undertaking. Since many pine stumps were impervious to even horse pulling, the College of Agriculture introduced the use of dynamite in 1912.

Land companies had eagerly bought land from the railroads and lumber companies in anticipation of a land boom in 1900. In their letters to prospective clients, many promoters divided sections of the cutover into districts with optimistic names: The Great Cheese Section, The Great Hay and Potato Belt, Land of the Big Red Clover. Unfortunately for the boosters, settlers did not create a land boom. Many immigrants arrived, including Finns, Lithuanians, Bohemians, and Swedes, but many others quickly departed, and those who stayed often faced foreclosure. By 1920 there were 20,000 new farms, mostly in the southern tier of the cutover, but several million acres of land were still stumps and swamps.

Farm colonization had proved a failure. The pioneer's maxim that "farming follows forests" was not true for northern Wisconsin. Although some of the soil was rich, the growing season was too short and the markets were too distant. The great tragedy of the cutover land, according to historian Lucille Kane, is that no one figured out in advance which sections of land were good farm land. By then years had been wasted trying to farm stump land that wasn't meant for diversified crop farming.

In 1929 the Legislature authorized each county to study land use for farm, forests, and recreation. By 1941 more than half the counties had adopted zoning ordinances for controlling rural land. The Forest Crop Law, passed in 1927, taxed tree growers ten cents per acre. Once the trees were cut the tax was 10 percent of the crop's value. Much of this revenue went to the tax-starved counties. Reforestation began with the federal purchases of national forests and parks. In 1925 the state authorized the federal government to buy 100,000 acres for forests that might one day draw visitors to the north.

Isolation was one of northern Wisconsin's greatest problems, however it wasn't confined to just the north. Throughout rural Wisconsin there were secluded farms and villages. Until radio began to connect these hamlets with outside culture, the county fair was the main forum for reaching isolated farmers. County fairs alerted farmers to new farming techniques. The county fair widened the agricultural world for farmers who did not read farm journals or belong to agricultural societies.

Exhibits, machinery displays, and livestock judging were small seminars for exchanging information beyond a farmer's neighbor. Starting in 1886 the state fair settled in Milwaukee, but county fairs continued to reach a larger farm audience.

From county fairs to Hoard's Dairyman, education was the key to lifting Wisconsin agriculture from its pioneer roots in wheat. The cooperation between farmer, scientist, and visionary created the dairy industry that Wisconsin has dominated for 100 years.

A stump-pulling machine is used to remove stumps from the ground in the cutover lands of northern Wisconsin on the Medford farm of Chris Paustenbach. The 1895 photo was included in a pamphlet, Northern Wisconsin: a Handbook for the Homeseeker, *that promoted northern Wisconsin's cutover region as potentially good farmland. Courtesy, State Historical Society of Wisconsin*

PROSPERITY AND PROGRESSIVISM

The Northwestern Mutual Life Insurance
Company building in Milwaukee was photo-
graphed in about 1890. The business,
founded in 1857, was the first
insurance company in Wisconsin. Courtesy,
the H.H. Bennett Studio

In 1910 workers posed in front
of the Milwaukee Harvester
Works, which had become part
of International Harvester in
1904. Courtesy, State Historical
Society of Wisconsin

In 1900 it was still the Victorian Age in England and
the age of Robber Barons in the United States. The
fury of industrialization had brought an admixture of
unparalleled wealth and sweatshop toil to nineteenth-
century America. But this era was passing, and Wisconsin would play a role in shaping the new century.
In 1900 a giant of the Progressive movement, Robert
La Follette, was elected Wisconsin's governor. In the
social reform that followed, Wisconsin would remain
competitive in an industrial society as it helped to re-
shape how society treated its workers. The Wisconsin
Idea emerged as a vague concept attached to concrete
changes such as workers compensation and university
involvement in government and industry.

Wisconsin had become a prosperous and diversified state by 1910, ranking eighth nationally in industrial wealth. Its leading industries—lumber, foundry,
and dairy—were equal in production value. Southeastern Wisconsin was becoming part of an industrial
belt with vigorous political activity. In 1910,

Milwaukee—a blend of progressivism, labor activity, and German and American socialism—elected Victor Berger the first Socialist to the U.S. House of Representatives.

Wisconsin's heavy machine industries followed the national trend of industrial consolidation, according to Richard Nesbit. Milwaukee's pioneer industry, E.P. Allis, merged with four companies in 1901 to form Allis-Chalmers, an international combine. In 1904 Milwaukee Harvester became part of International Harvester. The Milwaukee Iron Company became a U.S. Steel subsidiary. The Bucyrus Company was a combine put together by the Morgan syndicate in 1911.

The age of steam was giving way to electricity and the internal combustion engine. During the transition from steam to gas engines, Wisconsin maintained its success in building large engines for heavy machinery. By 1914 Wisconsin ranked first in the country in producing large steam and gas engines.

The change from steam to gas caused a reshuffling of the hierarchy at Allis-Chalmers, Milwaukee's largest producer of engines. According to historian Walter Peterson, as early as 1902 the board of direc-

tors at Allis-Chalmers acknowledged the need for making gas engines, especially steam turbines that produced low-cost electricity. However, chief engineer Edwin Reynolds still believed in the Reynolds-Corliss engine that he had invented in 1877. In 1904 Reynolds and Allis-Chalmers' president Charles Allis—who also supported the steam engine—were removed from their original positions, and the board of directors elected Benjamin Warren, who had worked with steam turbines at Westinghouse, as president. A year later Allis-Chalmers installed its first steam turbine in a utilities plant, and by 1906 gas engines comprised more than one-fifth of Allis-Chalmers' unfilled orders.

The gas engine revolutionized agricultural machines. Gas engines, and the hulking tractors they moved, were quickly accepted by farmers who needed power in muddy fields. The harvesting combine, which cut and threshed grain without a troop of hungry workers, also became commonplace. Charles Hart and Charles Parr, two mechanical engineering students from the University of Wisconsin, moved to Iowa to produce the "gasoline traction engine," the tractor they had designed. The Wisconsin manufactur-

The first automobile in Antigo, Wisconsin, got stuck in the mud in 1905. Wisconsin's roads in the early part of the twentieth century were generally dirt trails. The good-roads movement, which would begin in 1911, was aimed primarily at helping farmers' horse-drawn wagons. Courtesy, State Historical Society of Wisconsin

Although cars were not familiar sights on Wisconsin roads in 1901, Racine workers pave North Main Street with bricks. The pioneers' wooden plank roads had proved useless because they were slippery and rotted easily. A town's prosperity could be measured in its brick roads. Courtesy, State Historical Society of Wisconsin

ers that competed with Iowa's Hart-Parr Company included Allis-Chalmers, Milwaukee Harvester, the Van Brunt Seeder Company, and J.I. Case. The age of steam evanesced from the farm fields.

The symbol of the modern age was noisy, unreliable, and it gave a bumpy Sunday ride. Among the terms describing the horseless carriage were motor fly, electrobat, and oleolocomotive. Early cars were made from borrowed parts of steam engines, carriages, and bicycles. At the turn of the century there were simply no manufacturers of automobile parts. According to historian Victor Clark, the wide-scale manufacturing of bicycles trained many mechanics for the problem-solving of early horseless carriages.

THE HORSELESS CARRIAGE

The horseless carriages of the nineteenth century were crude toys built in the workshop. In 1873 a Racine physician, Dr. Carhart, built a steam buggy he called "the Spark." Two years later the Wisconsin Legislature, in an effort to find a "cheap and practical substitute" for horses, offered a $10,000 award to the winner of a race using public roads between Green Bay and Madison. The 1878 race attracted two hulking entries, both powered by steam engines. The Oshkosh entry was able to finish the course, but the Legislature

was disappointed in the performance, and awarded the winners only $5,000.

Wisconsin became an early center of horseless carriages. There was certainly a demand for cars, as Wisconsin granted 1,492 auto licenses in 1905, with the number increasing to 5,600 within three years. Not all car producers survived the early years of the industry. The Kunz Auto and Motor Company of Milwaukee produced cars from about 1902 to 1905. The inventor of the all-electric thermostat, Warren Johnson, produced steam and electric cars and trucks from 1901 until 1911. After Johnson's death his company concentrated on temperature controls.

The J.I. Case company deviated for a time from its threshers and tractors to produce touring cars and sports cars. J.I. Case acquired the Pierce Auto Company of Racine after the small car producer defaulted on a loan from Case. Case continued to manufacture Pierce's expensive, custom-made autos. However, J.I. Case's main customers, farmers, could not always afford the cars, which cost three times more than Ford's Model T.

Many Wisconsin businesses adapted quickly to the coming revolution of the auto industry. In Milwaukee Arthur Oliver Smith, who manufactured bicycle frames, added automobile frames to his line in 1903. In 1916 his son Lloyd began to design the automatic

The Kunz car was built in
1902 by the Kunz Auto and
Motor Company of Milwaukee,
which closed in 1905. Courtesy,
Milwaukee Public Library

The luxurious Mitchell touring car was made by the Mitchell-Lewis Motor Car Company of Racine and sold for $1,500 in 1908. The company began as a wagon maker in the nineteenth century. Courtesy, Milwaukee Public Library

assembly line, which by 1920 substituted machines for men in producing car frames.

The popularity of cars forced some Wisconsin businesses to change their products, which catered to horse owners. In 1867 Justus Luther invented a machine that rolled horse whips in one-quarter the time it took to roll a whip by hand. A Berlin glove-making company invested in Luther's machine and in 1870 changed its name to the Berlin Whip Company. Horseless carriages dried up the demand for whips, and in 1900 the company reverted to hand-stitching gloves and mittens. In 1922 the Berlin Whip Company became the Berlin Glove Company. With the disappearance of hungry horses, another company was forced to adapt its product. Since 1882 Philip Orth's company in Sullivan had milled flour and horse feed. With the advent of autos, their sales in horse feed plummeted. Orth's son switched his emphasis from flour and feed to bakery supplies, eventually adding a complete line of machinery for bakers.

At the turn of the century a successful wagon

maker in Racine, Mitchell-Lewis, began building cars in addition to wagons. Henry Mitchell, an early settler of Racine, began his wagon business in 1854 and was joined by his son-in-law, W.T. Lewis, in 1864. Though it continued to build wagons as late as 1910, the Mitchell-Lewis Motor Company produced touring cars with fashionable gray bodies and red upholstery. By 1916 the Mitchell-Lewis Motor Company employed 2,000 workers in the Racine plant, which covered nearly 30 acres. The company was later bought by another Wisconsin-based auto producer, the Nash Motor Company, in 1925.

One of Wisconsin's prized custom-built cars—the Kissel Kar—was not available to Wisconsin buyers the year of its debut. Instead, brothers George and William Kissel of Hartford sold their entire production of 100 cars to a Chicago dealer. Each car cost $1,850, not including windshield, generator, gas lamps, or horn, which were extra. A detachable top, patented in 1922, would make the Kissel Kar an all-weather vehicle. The Kissel Kar, which won the 1910 Los Angeles-to-Phoenix race, maintained its reputation for durability and sportiness. A nostalgic article in *Road and Track* magazine called the Kissel Gold Bug

"the niftiest, raciest, and classiest American production car ever to hit the highways." Kissel Kars were made until 1931, when the family business could no longer compete against assembly-built cars and the Depression.

A bicycle manufacturer became the founder of Wisconsin's most successful auto company. Thomas L. Jeffery, who built bicycles he called Ramblers in Chicago, had been tinkering with cars since 1890. Jeffery sold his bicycle company in 1900 and moved to Kenosha, where he bought the Sterling bicycle factory. In 1902 Jeffery produced 1,500 new Ramblers—this time autos, not bikes. That year Oldsmobile in Detroit and Jeffery in Kenosha accounted for 4,000 of the 5,000 cars manufactured in the Midwest.

Thomas Jeffery died in 1910, and in 1916 his son decided to sell the company. The buyer, Charles W. Nash, had served as president of General Motors for four years, winning acclaim in Detroit by rescuing the Buick line from financial difficulties in 1910. After resigning from GM over policy differences, Nash acquired the Thomas B. Jeffery Company, making Kenosha the largest producer of motor cars outside of Detroit.

Hartford's Kissel Motor Car Company built four-wheel-drive trucks for the Army during World War I. Kissel had received a special contract to assemble the trucks, which usually were manufactured by the Four Wheel Drive Company in Clintonville. Courtesy, State Historical Society of Wisconsin

In World War I women took the place of men on the assembly lines at Nash Motors in Kenosha. During the war Nash was a large producer of trucks for the Army. Courtesy, State Historical Society of Wisconsin

Thomas Jeffery's converted bicycle factory was the genesis of Kenosha's modern auto industry. In 1917 Kenosha's Rambler plant began producing the Nash, which became a prized motor car. Plants were built in Racine, Milwaukee, and Pine Bluff, Arkansas. Nash negotiated a U.S. Army contract that made the Nash Motor Company one of the largest builders of trucks, producing 11,494 in 1918. The American Motors Corporation was created in 1954 when the Nash Motor Company merged with Hudson of Detroit. American Motors survived the post-World War II shake-out that eliminated other famous car makers such as Packard, Studebaker, and Kaiser.

But American Motors would not survive the modern marketplace. Kenosha's auto-assembly plant dated back to Thomas Jeffery's bicycle factory and an 1890s five-story mattress factory, making Kenosha the oldest operating auto plant in the country. Consumer

Above
This Nash sports car of 1922 was one of Charles Nash's many successful cars that would become Wisconsin classics. In 1954 the Nash Motor Company merged to become American Motors Corporation. Courtesy, State Historical Society of Wisconsin

Left
A common sight on Milwaukee streets in the 1920s was of trucks transporting automobile bodies for Nash Motors, the forerunner of American Motors Corporation. Auto bodies were transported from the Seaman Body Corporation to the Nash assembly plants in Milwaukee, Racine, and Kenosha. Courtesy, Milwaukee Public Library

RURAL HIGHWAYS

Poor roads put the family "in a rut" and keep it there.

Good roads mean opportunity for
1 Neighborhood social life
2 Consolidated schools
3 Prompt mail service
4 Church attendance
5 Prompt medical attendance
6 Cheaper hauling of produce

In 1909 less than 17 percent of Wisconsin's roads were paved; however, Wisconsin government realized that good roads would help the farmer. Cars were not the prime motive for improving roads under the 1911 State Aid Road Law. It would take another five years for officials to realize that autos were the next mode of transportation and that gravel roads were not adequate. Courtesy, State Historical Society of Wisconsin

tastes changed in the 1970s and 1980s. Foreign car makers offered efficient small cars from state-of-the-art tech nology, and American Motors could not compete. In 1987 Detroit's Chrysler Corporation ac quired AMC and its prosperous line of Kaiser-Jeeps. Despite Kenosha's exemplary work force, Chrysler unexpectedly cut 5,500 jobs in January 1988 and effectively shut down Kenosha as an auto producer.

General Motors had entered Wisconsin in 1918 when it bought the Janesville Machine Company, a tractor producer. Tractors continued to roll out of the plant, but inside engineers were developing the prototype of the Samson, a nine-passenger car with removable seats to make room for cargo. General Motors widely advertised the Samson but never approved it for production. Instead, the Janesville plant was converted for GM's Chevrolet company, and the first Chevrolet left the assembly line in 1923.

Four-wheel drive was invented in Clintonville, a small town in east-central Wisconsin. In 1906 William Besserdich and two friends became mired in sand on a trip to Embarrass, Wisconsin. Besserdich asked his friends to move the front wheels, and the car nimbly moved out of the sand pit. Impressed by the combination of force to all four wheels, Besserdich, a prosperous mechanic, suggested to his partner Otto Zachow that they invent a mechanism that empowered all four wheels of a vehicle. By 1908 they had a patent, and in 1909 they built "the Battleship," a 3,800 pound four-wheel drive behemoth.

Besserdich and Zachow's Four Wheel Drive Company launched Clintonville as a producer of heavy trucks. World War I provided the small town with an international market. In 1915 the British government bought 288 of the 3-ton trucks while the Russian government purchased 82. By the war's end, the British government had bought 3,000 heavy trucks. When the U.S. government entered the war the company produced 14,473 trucks. After World War I, Clintonville's Four Wheel Drive Company was manufacturing trucks ranging from 2 to 15 tons.

A bicycle with an engine was the beginning of Milwaukee's Harley-Davidson Motor Company. In 1903 William Harley and the Davidson brothers, William, Walter, and Arthur, designed their first motorized bicycle. By 1907 their company was producing about 150 bikes. Their two-cylinder engine, designed in 1909, became a company trademark. During World

Above
Wisconsin roads had impeded
transportation, and therefore economic growth, since pioneer
days. A spring rain could easily
turn a pathway into one muddy
ditch. Courtesy, State Historical
Society of Wisconsin

Left
When this accident happened in
1915 the rickety bridge was part
of what was considered a major
thoroughfare, Wisconsin's Highway 18. A truck from the Milwau-
kee-Waukesha Delivery Company broke through this wooden
bridge over the Wisconsin River
near Prairie du Chien and
blocked the road for two days.
Courtesy, Milwaukee Public
Library

War I production rose to 18,000 motorcycles, which the military used for dispatch work.

The iron horses of the nineteenth century—trains—did not see competition from the curious autos of the 1900s. Railroads serving Wisconsin offered to help improve the feeder roads to railway depots for farmers. In 1909 less than 17 percent of Wisconsin's roads were surfaced, and farmers had difficulty in maneuvering their wagons of grain, produce, or milk for export to markets. When the State Aid Road Law passed in 1911, railroads offered to haul highway construction materials at reduced rates.

Wisconsin's good roads movement of 1911 was aimed at helping farmers, not car owners. Automobiles were still a novel luxury in 1911, and the common improved road was made of gravel. By 1916, however, the state highway commission observed that "the automobile has introduced new problems into the business of road construction. Roads fit for old horse drawn vehicles are not at all fit for use with an automobile." The horseless carriage was no longer part-bicycle and part-wagon. Cement roads were a testament to the horse's modern replacement.

The first two decades of the twentieth century saw enormous change in Wisconsin's leading industries. The 1900 census ranked lumber and flour first and second among industries for the last time. Within the first two decades of the new century lumber and flour would steadily fall as dairies, foundries, and automobiles became the top industries.

THE PAPER INDUSTRY

Papermaking became an important industry in Wisconsin despite the depletion of Wisconsin's forests. By 1910 paper products, produced by the state's 57 mills, ranked eighth in Wisconsin, ahead of the tenth-ranked auto industry. In 1911, however, Wisconsin's thriving paper industry, which produced newsprint in abundance, faced a crisis that threatened its existence. Congress passed a reciprocal trade agreement with Canada that, among other things, allowed Canada's cheap newsprint into the country duty free. Canada later rejected the trade agreement, but in 1913 President Wilson allowed Canadian newsprint to enter the country on a duty-free list. American newspaper owners were elated, but Wisconsin papermakers were faced with a fight for survival.

Adapting to this market change, Wisconsin papermakers invented new varieties of paper, creating lightweight paper, toilet tissue, absorbent wadding, and insulating paper. Glazed, glassine, and serum-resisting paper joined high-quality magazine and book paper. Kimberly-Clark introduced Kleenex facial tissue in 1924, four years after it had introduced its Kotex feminine pads. According to historian James Clark, newsprint soon became a minor product as new demands forced Wisconsin to import wood from Canada, the western states, and even from Sweden and Finland. By 1930 Wisconsin was the second leading paper producer in the country after Maine.

Wisconsin's papermakers led the industry in its innovations of paper products. The chemical laboratory of Kimberly-Clark in 1922 was one of many research labs in the state for inventing products such as glazed, glassine, and serum-resisting paper. Courtesy, State Historical Society of Wisconsin

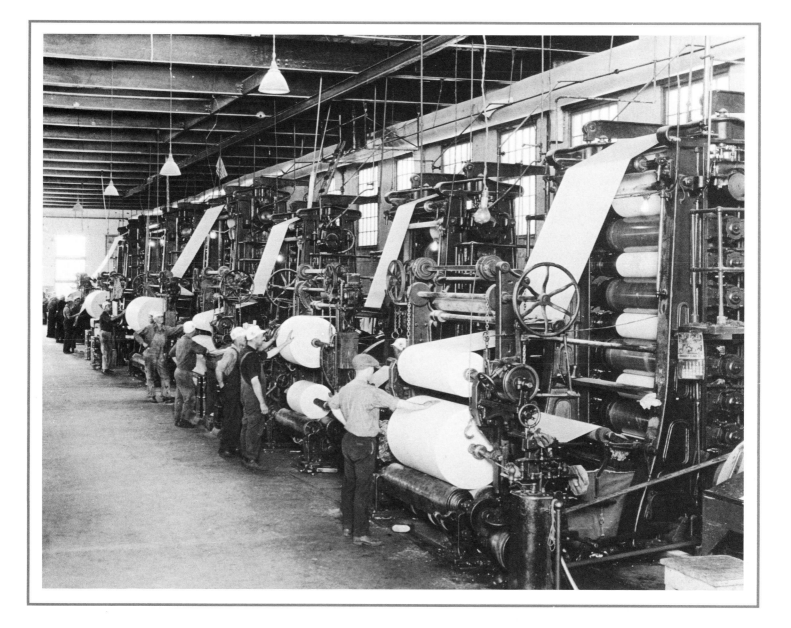

*Investment in calendaring
machines that smoothed paper,
such as Kimberly-Clark's in
1922, was one of the many financial commitments of Wisconsin
papermakers in maintaining
their leadership in the quality
and quantity of Wisconsin
paper products. Courtesy, State
Historical Society of Wisconsin*

Wisconsin National Guardsmen were positioned in the yards of Edward P. Allis' Reliance Works during the riots of May 1886. In the course of the riots in Milwaukee's industrial Bayview area nine workers died. The riots grew out of protests for an eight-hour workday. Courtesy, State Historical Society of Wisconsin

As the paper industry expanded, one small Wisconsin business had to adapt or shut down. Henschel, a maker of wooden cigar boxes in New Berlin since 1889, was threatened by the new demands for paper boxes and paper packages for cigarettes. As sales of wooden boxes dropped, the company began coating the bronze labels of its cigar boxes, later expanding to coat other printed papers.

WISCONSIN'S LABOR AND PROGRESSIVE MOVEMENTS

While business and industry adapted to changes in the marketplace, it also had to address the grievances of labor. Rapid industrialization had created deplorable working conditions, and worker demands included the eight-hour work day, safer work places, the abolition of child labor, and fair wages. In 1893-1894 alone, 44 workers died in Wisconsin from industrial accidents; "killed, wound up on shaft" were the words used to describe eight of these deaths.

Employers would not agree to the unions' demand that employees work for eight hours but be paid for ten hours. The general public found it hard to un-

Robert La Follette was a leader of the Progressive movement, which heralded reform in the early twentieth century. The era of Progressivism was also a time of economic prosperity for Wisconsin and the United States. By 1910 Wisconsin ranked eighth nationally in industrial wealth. Courtesy, State Historical Society of Wisconsin

derstand why urban workers should work fewer hours than farmers, who worked from dawn to dusk. Strikes supporting the eight-hour work day were often met with violence. The May 1886 agitation over the ten-hour work day resulted in violence at both Chicago's Haymarket Square and Milwaukee's Bay View. Nine people died in Milwaukee when the Wisconsin militia fired into the crowd of striking workers and supporters.

Wisconsin's reform movement was fragmented. In general, Robert La Follette's Progressive movement favored farmers and small businessmen. Wisconsin's labor groups united in the Wisconsin State Federation of Labor shortly after the formation of Samuel Gompers' American Federation of Labor. WSFL deviated, however, by orienting itself with Milwaukee's

Socialist party despite Gompers' hostility to socialism. In turn, Victor Berger and his Socialist party were suspicious and perhaps envious of La Follette's success in progressivism. Victor Berger, the principal reason for socialism's success among Milwaukee's German and labor communities, advocated democratic socialism in which the people gradually voted in Socialist platforms. A conservative among the country's Socialists, Berger is credited with Americanizing socialism. Milwaukee sent Berger to the U.S. Congress four times and elected two Socialist mayors, whose party became known primarily as the party of good municipal government. Socialist Daniel Hoan was mayor for 24 years, from 1916 to 1940.

The growth of socialism before World War I was a measure of the need for reform. The magazines of

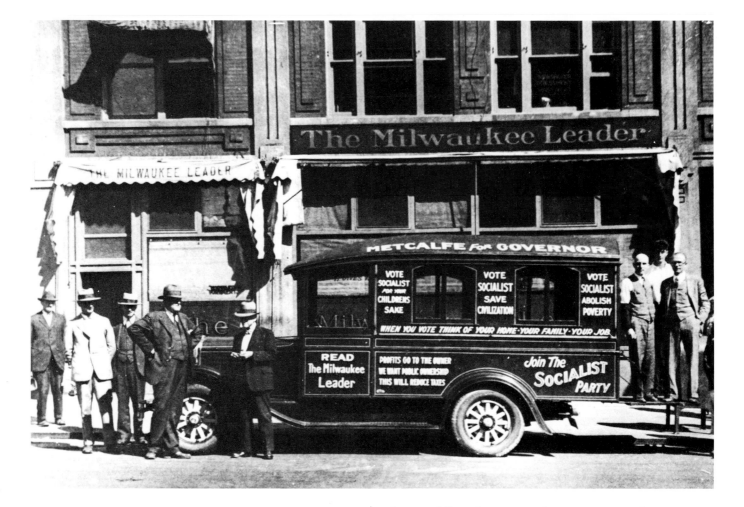

The delivery van for the Milwaukee Leader newspaper often served as a campaign billboard for Wisconsin Socialist candidates. The Leader was a Socialist daily newspaper begun by Victor Berger, the first Socialist elected to the U.S. Congress. Courtesy, Milwaukee County Historical Society

the middle class—*McClure's, Cosmopolitan, Everybody's, Collier's* and *American Magazine*—built national circulations by exposing corruption in government and big business. Insurance, the Standard Oil company, and meat packing were among the celebrated exposes. In 1906 President Theodore Roosevelt called this journalism "muckraking" and hinted that it aided socialism. The muckrakers were moralists, not radicals, but their command of facts proved that reform was needed in the industrialized nation. Progressivism was one response to the hue and cry for reform.

Robert M. La Follette, the catalyst for progressivism in Wisconsin, was governor of Wisconsin for three terms before he became a U.S. senator in 1906. Three issues dominated La Follette's gubernatorial administration: the direct primary, railroad taxation, and railroad regulation. Wisconsin's first governor to be born in the state, La Follette earned his nickname "Fighting Bob" during the battles to establish these changes. La Follette's pet issue, the direct primary, was a direct assault on the machine politics he hated. In battling the conservative Republicans who called themselves "the Stalwarts," La Follette campaigned for a slate of Progressive candidates in the 1902 election. During his last two years in office La Follette and his Progressives achieved passage of the direct primary and a railroad commission.

"The first pirates on land were the railroads," had been a common sentiment among the public. Railroads were a boon to small towns, but also a monopoly in transportation.

For all of La Follette's fire, he was pragmatic about railroad regulation. Wisconsin's first attempt at railroad regulation had been a fiasco. The 1874 Potter Law formed a commission that could only reduce rates, which proved useless when the railroad companies balked and was later repealed. In April of 1900 La Follette met with counsels of the railroads in Milwaukee, assuring them that Wisconsin's railroad commission, chaired by Professor Balthasar Meyer, would not reduce rates but only equalize them.

Lumber baron Isaac Stephenson was the Progressive party's financial angel. Stephenson, who became a millionaire in the Menominee River district, served three terms in the U.S. Congress. Angered with the Republican Stalwarts when they did not help him win the U.S. Senate seat in 1899, Stephenson became a Progressive. In 1901 he bought the *Milwaukee Free Press*, a daily newspaper that did battle with the *Milwaukee Sentinel*, owned by Stalwart leader Charles Pfister of the Pfister-Vogel tannery empire.

When Wisconsin's senate seat became open in 1905, La Follette rescinded his pledge to support Stephenson. Friends of La Follette undertook what Nesbit termed "the relatively easy task" of persuading the governor to keep the peace among Progressives by accepting the senate seat himself. Stephenson later won an expensive election to the U.S. Senate in 1908, admitting that he had spent $107,000.

La Follette and his successor, Francis McGovern, helped Wisconsin win national acclaim as a laboratory of reform. The direct primary, a successful income tax, worker's compensation, an industrial safety commission, and the legislative reference library were innovations issuing from the Wisconsin Legislature. Theodore Roosevelt wrote in *Outlook* magazine that Wisconsin was "a pioneer blazing the way along which we Americans must make our civic and industrial advance during the next few decades."

THE WISCONSIN IDEA

The spirit of reform in Wisconsin was called "The Wisconsin Idea," a vague term for trail-blazing changes. "The borders of the university are the borders of the state," perhaps best explains scholars and legislators working together for effective reform. Although the origin of the term is obscure, the geography of Wisconsin's capital might explain the Wisconsin Idea. Bascom Hill, the seat of the university, is about one mile away from the Capitol. State Street connects these centers of learning and legislation, and the walk between them—leading to an isthmus between two lakes—is exhilirating. The Wisconsin Idea sprang from university activism. John Bascom, president of the university from 1874-1887, was "forever telling us what the state was doing for us and urging our return obligation not . . . for our own selfish benefit, but to return some service to the state," wrote La Follette in his autobiography. During Bascom's tenure, the university began the Short Course, vocational seminars for farmers. The next university president, Thomas C. Chamberlain, declared, "Scholarship for the sake of the scholar is simply refined selfishness. Scholarship for the sake of the state and the people is refined patriotism."

The next generation of leaders acting on Bascom's and Chamberlain's philosophy gave birth to the Wisconsin Idea. In his 1903 inaugural address to the university, Charles Van Hise, a friend and former classmate of La Follette, proposed that professors be used as technical experts by the state government. His proposal took fire, and by 1912 46 professors served both the university and the state. Charles McCarthy, librarian of the Legislative Reference Bureau, wrote a book in 1912 titled *The Wisconsin Idea*, which included a forward by Theodore Roosevelt. McCarthy also helped legislators write bills, including the vocational education law that established vocational schools for adults in cities with populations of 5,000 or more. Reporter E.E. Slosson observed that "it is impossible to ascertain the size or location of the University of Wisconsin. The most that one can say is that the headquarters of the institution is at the city of Madison and that the campus has an area of about 56,000 square miles.

Wisconsin's progressivism was fueled by a new source of money—corporate income taxes. In 1911 Wisconsin became the first state to tax manufacturers. Connecticut followed Wisconsin's lead in 1915, and

Construction of Wisconsin's fourth state capitol began in 1907 after fire destroyed the third capitol in 1904. By 1911 the dome was not the only Wisconsin legacy under construction. The Wisconsin Idea, the partnership between university scholars and state legislators, turned Wisconsin into a laboratory of reform. Courtesy, State Historical Society of Wisconsin

Massachusetts and New York passed corporate income taxes in 1916 and 1917, respectively. It wasn't until the Great Depression that other industrial states followed suit.

There was little disagreement with the idea of taxing manufacturers. The tax burden fell mainly on large manufacturers, exempting the railroads, utilities, and insurance companies. Manufacturers such as Allis-Chalmers, Kimberly-Clark, and International Harvester opposed the tax, which also left them subject to local property taxes. Other non-manufacturing corporations, however, supported the measure, as they hoped to see their tax burden passed along. When the conservative businessman Emanuel L. Philipp became governor from 1915 to 1921 he left the corporate income tax intact, and his taxing of manufacturers differed little from the policies of the Progressive governor who followed him.

The business community was often allied with progressivism. Although railroad regulation had a radical ring, business leaders supported it in order to equalize competition. In 1904 La Follette's Progressives elected lumber baron William D. Connor, who had helped manage La Follette's campaigns in 1901 and 1903, as chairman of the Republican State Central Committee.

WORKERS COMPENSATION AND THE INSURANCE INDUSTRY

In 1911 businessmen and progressives worked together to form one of Wisconsin's most famous innovations, worker's compensation. Until Wisconsin's groundbreaking law, workers who were injured on the job had to sue their employers and prove extraordinary negligence in order to get any compensation. Common law said that employers were not liable for their dead or injured because workers undertook an implied risk when they accepted a job.

Worker's compensation was essentially conservative reform and was written by moderates who were sympathetic to both labor and business, according to historian Robert Asher. John R. Commons, University of Wisconsin professor of economics, was the architect of worker's compensation who won approval from both organized labor and the large employers. When a worker was injured or killed, the Industrial Commission investigated the cause of the accident and then awarded money according to a fixed scale. Though worker's compensation at first was voluntary, by 1931 it was mandatory for all employers.

John Commons helped design the Wisconsin Industrial Commission, which reviewed industrial safety and sanitation. Advisory committees of employers, labor, and outside experts devised safety codes for each industry. The commission grew in power when it became responsible for enforcing the worker's compensation law, which the courts ruled the law constitutional in 1911. Commons chose Charles W. Price of International Harvester to represent management's needs. Price, who had a national reputation for industrial safety and welfare, was among the growing list of industrialists who were beginning to realize the waste involved in workers' accidents and grievances. Although employers reluctantly gave up their common-law defenses for accidents, they realized that safety laws and accident prevention were efficient and in their self-interest.

A group of Wausau lumbermen, realizing the implications of worker's compensation, designed the first mutual insurance for Wisconsin employers. Mutuals are basically cooperatives in which a group of people pool their resources to share risks and, if successful, share in investment dividends.

On September 1, 1911, the day worker's compensation went into effect, Wausau's Employers Mutual Liability Insurance sold their first policy to the Wausau Sulphate and Fibre Company, later the Mosinee Paper Company. Employers Mutual opened its first branch office in Milwaukee in 1912, but Wausau remained its headquarters. Small, hometown America became Employers Mutual corporate identity, and in 1979 Wausau Insurance Companies became its trade name. Among the safety innovations of Wausau's Employers Mutual was the hiring of the first industrial nurse in 1928 to develop on-site medical care.

In 1906, as he was leaving for the U.S. Senate, Robert La Follette asked the Legislature to investigate Wisconsin's life insurance companies. In 1905 scandal had rocked New York's insurance giants. By 1907 more than 70 insurance bills were introduced in the Wisconsin Legislature. The bills that passed required more open elections of the companies' managers, stricter fiscal reporting, curbs on salaries, and more liberal policy provisions. In response 23 out-of-state insurance companies left Wisconsin, though many

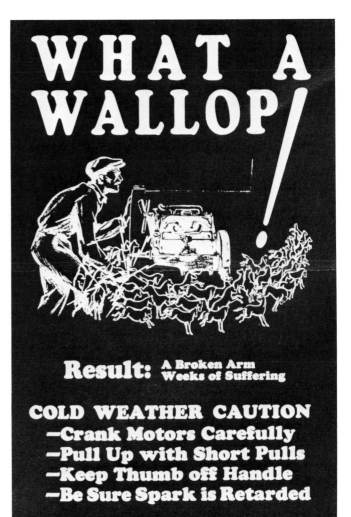

A poster from Employers Mutual Liability Insurance Company of Wisconsin was designed to help prevent accidents in the workplace. The insurance company, which began in 1911, the same year Wisconsin's Workmen's Compensation law went into effect, is now Wausau Insurance Companies. Courtesy, Milwaukee Public Library

returned in 1915.

Wisconsin's oldest and largest insurance company, Northwestern Mutual, emerged relatively unscathed from the legislative investigations. In 1907 Northwestern was the sixth largest insurance company in the country. Investigators found no corruption, and even praised Northwestern Mutual for its accounting procedures and cautious investments, though they did condemn unethical sales techniques that were common to the industry during that time.

Northwestern's name reflects Wisconsin's heritage as being the New World's original Northwest Territory. When New Yorker John C. Johnston founded the company in Janesville in 1857, Wisconsin was only six years old and still a frontier, hardly a likely birthplace for a major insurance company. However, Johnston was an eccentric with a small fortune he had earned in New York from selling insurance policies for Mutual Life of New York. At age 72 he came to Wisconsin and bought 3,000 acres of prime farm land in wheat-growing Rock County.

Johnston ignored conventional wisdom that insurance is a product of a mature economy. He was not concerned that frontier Wisconsinites had scant capital to make investments—or pay insurance premiums. In 1857, the year a financial panic bankrupted every railroad in Wisconsin, Johnston managed to gather the $200,000 worth of commitments needed to establish Mutual Life of Wisconsin, a virtual carbon copy of Mutual Life of New York.

Mutual Life of Wisconsin would grow to have more than 4,000 policy holders by the end of the Civil War, spurring its leaders to rename the company Northwestern Mutual in order to attract a regional market. The new name, "Northwestern," had the same familiar ring that the word midwestern has today.

The only snag for Johnston was the board of directors he chose. In 1859 the board of directors managed to engineer a vote that moved company headquarters from Janesville to Milwaukee. A small black trunk was enough to accomplish the move. In anger Johnston sold his interest and moved to Madison. He died in 1860 at 78, but his company, the first major insurance company born west of Philadelphia, was guided skillfully into the twentieth century by board member Henry L. Palmer.

Many of Wisconsin's oldest insurance companies were formed because of the high rates charged by eastern fire insurance companies. The widespread perception that eastern insurance companies were expensive and unfair encouraged the births of homegrown mutuals.

In 1897 two Lutheran pastors formed the Church Mutual Insurance Company in Merrill, Wisconsin. Churches were particularly vulnerable to fires because during the week they were often empty and unless a fire started on Sunday, few people would be around to notice a blaze beginning. First available only to Evangelical Lutherans or Norwegian Evangelical Lutherans, Church Mutual grew to become non-denominational and a nationwide specialist in church insurance.

Fire protection was expensive for hardware store owners because they stocked inflammable paint, linseed oil, and turpentine. But Wisconsin hardware dealers felt their premiums were too high in relation to the actual loss caused by fires. In 1904 the Wisconsin Retail Hardware Association formed a mutual insurance company in Berlin, Wisconsin. In 1912 the newly elected secretary-treasurer of the association, Peter J. Jacobs, decided to move the offices to his hometown of Stevens Point. In 1914 Hardware Mutuals joined the wave begun by worker's compensation and began to offer employers liability insurance. Later life insurance was added. In 1962 a new corporate symbol—a Revolutionary War minuteman—was introduced and in 1963 the trade name Hardware Mutuals was exchanged for Sentry Insurance.

Incensed by the high rates paid by jewelers for fire insurance, Andrew W. Anderson, secretary of Wisconsin Jewelers Association, helped found a mutual insurance group in 1913. Jewelers were grouped together with clothes-cleaning shops as bad risks because both used benzine for cleaning. However, jewelers used benzine for only cleaning watches. His Jewelers Mutual Insurance Company grew into the only insurance company devoted exclusively to protecting jewelers from fires to theft and personal jewelry coverage.

In 1927 the Farmer's Mutual Automobile Insurance Company was formed in Madison to meet the needs of farmers, who as a group didn't drive as much as urban dwellers during the winter. Their insurance premiums from Farmer's Mutual reflected this lower risk. Farmer's Mutual, like Sentry and Wausau, outgrew its initial prospect, and in 1958 was changed to

American Family Insurance.

Wisconsin's insurance industry enjoyed a unique, spectacular growth from small towns. The nature of insurance allows the industry to be located almost anywhere, which was proved by Northwestern's John Johnston in frontier Wisconsin in 1857. During the 1950s Wausau Insurance Companies began advertisements that alerted its national customers to its pride in its small-town origin and instructed them on how to spell Wausau. Carl N. Jacobs, who guided Hardware Mutuals as it swelled into Sentry, summed up why he decided to stay in Stevens Point, "I was a small-town boy, and decided to remain a small-town boy."

ALUMINUM

Wisconsin was equally an unlikely place for success in aluminum. Since 1888 aluminum had been the

Workers at the Vollrath Company of Sheboygan dipped enamel kitchenware, which was a familiar household product in Wisconsin. Courtesy, State Historical Society of Wisconsin

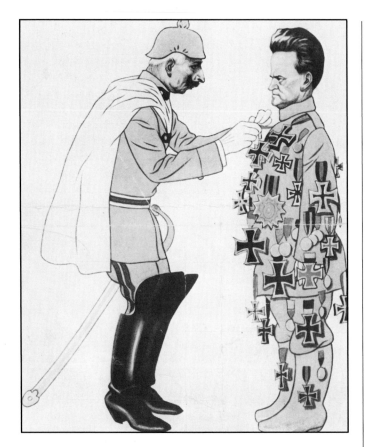

Because of the state's strong German heritage, World War I was a traumatic time for patriots in Wisconsin. Senator Robert La Follette was a vocal opponent of the United States' entry into World War I. Life's 1917 cover shows the Kaiser decorating Wisconsin's vocal senator. Resentment of German heritage even led one zealous patriot to call German beer "Kaiser brew." Courtesy, State Historical Society of Wisconsin

monopoly of the Aluminum Company of America (Alcoa) of Pittsburgh, which continued its grip on competition until World War II. Wisconsin entrepreneurs bought aluminum from Alcoa and made cookware, which by 1919 was close to becoming the most preferred cookware and utensilware. Wisconsin supplied more than 50 percent of the national market in aluminum cookware.

Aluminum was once the rare metal of kings. Denmark's King Christian X wore an aluminum crown and Napoleon III reserved an aluminum table service for special guests. Aluminum was treasured because it was extremely difficult and expensive to isolate from bauxite. Aluminum's lightness and pliability made it a luxury metal. In 1886 the electrochemical process was discovered that would eventually turn the dinner service of kings into the commonplace cookware.

Virtually unknown to the public at the turn of the century, aluminum was used for novelty items such as combs, mustache cups, cigar cases, salt and pepper shakers, and lucky pennnies ("Keep me and never go broke"). But Joseph Koenig, a German immigrant who settled in Two Rivers, was captivated by the German aluminum at the Chicago World's Columbian Exposition in 1893. Koenig spent the next two years designing machines, tools, and dies to produce aluminum novelties. He was helped by business leader J.E. Hamilton and later the city of Two Rivers, which wanted to keep the business in town. As Koenig's business flourished, several employees left to start their own aluminum enterprises. A rectangular strip from Two Rivers and Manitowoc to West Bend became the area known for Wisconsin's aluminum production.

Aluminum cookware helped to fill the vacuum created by the receding timber industries of eastern Wisconsin. Until the end of World War I only two Wisconsin manufacturers produced aluminum cookware—Koenig's company, which had merged with two of its competitors to form the the Mirro Aluminum Company, and the West Bend Aluminum Company, begun in 1911. West Bend marketed almost 50 percent of its production to Sears Roebuck and Company.

By 1920 the aluminum cookware industry was concentrated primarily in Ohio, Pennsylvania, and in eastern Wisconsin at Two Rivers and West Bend. The success of Wisconsin's aluminum industry reflected the general prosperity of the country. Although more

Chippewa Indians at Reserve, Wisconsin, celebrate the return of Indian soldiers from World War I. Although Indians were not eligible for the draft, many of them volunteered to fight; and the war heroes helped publicize the economic poverty of Indians. Courtesy, State Historical Society of Wisconsin

expensive than copper or enamelware, aluminum could be bought through catalogue companies and was in demand by the general public.

SHIPBUILDING

Wisconsin's quiet shipbuilding yards were boosted dramatically during World War I, becoming the twelfth leading industry in 1920. Wisconsin built wooden and steel rescue crafts, tugs, and harbor mine sweepers. Manitowoc and Sturgeon Bay were the primary shipyards, with 6,000 workers. The Manitowoc Shipbuilding company built 32 ocean freighters during the war. After the Armistice of 1919 smaller companies such as Burger Boats returned to making custom-built commercial boats and pleasure cruisers. Beginning in 1921 Norwegian-born Ole Evinrude revolutionized motorized boats with his twin outboard motor made in Milwaukee. By 1928 his four-cylinder outboard motors were used in racing boats.

WORLD WAR I

Wisconsin's large German community was torn apart in 1917 when the United States, breaking its policy of strict neutrality held since 1914, declared war on Germany. Nine of eleven congressmen from Wisconsin voted against declaring war, and Wisconsin's fighting senator, Robert La Follette, also voted against entering the war.

The German culture that had built Wisconsin was suddenly suspect during World War I, and freedom of discussion was severely curtailed. A Madison druggist paid a $2,000 fine for his overheard remark that the Kaiser was a better friend to his people than the U.S. government was to its people. The Espionage Act gave informants the opportunity to help return 92 indictments against Wisconsinites. These indictments included different and overlapping offenses: 35 for criticizing U.S. policy; 36 for praising Germany; 32 for saying it was "a rich man's war and the poor man's fight"; 19 for criticizing the sale of war bonds; and 9 for insults to the flag.

Ten million people died in World War I. The war virtually wiped out a generation of French men from 18 to 45 years old, and in the final 19 months of the war more than 100,000 Americans died, including 3,932 Wisconsinites. The emotional costs had been staggering, but peacemakers took comfort that the Great War had been "the war to end all wars."

PROHIBITION AND HARD TIMES

On April 6, 1933, thousands of Milwau-
keeans, including hundreds at this Schlitz Brewery open house, celebrated the legalization of
3.2 beer. The final end to Prohibition came
eight months later. Courtesy, Milwaukee
Public Library

On January 16, 1920, the proud brewmasters of Wisconsin found their profession outlawed. Brewing beer was Wisconsin's fifth largest industry in 1920, but for the next 13 years the Wisconsin breweries that survived Prohibition would publicly sell malt syrup, soda pop, tonic water, even cheese. The pride of Wisconsin was reduced to making non-alcoholic "near beer."

Home brewing grew. Eastern Wisconsin became notorious for selling wort, the malt liquid that required only yeast and time before it bubbled into beer. One of the treasured recipes for brewing five gallons of home beer was written by the braumeister of Cream City Brewing in Milwaukee. Written on company stationery for the brewery's scrub woman, Braumeister Gustav Hanke also advised the home brewer to "omit

waukee brewer Gustav Pabst wrote an article in *Cosmopolitan* magazine in 1908 asserting "temperance is civilization and intelligence, Prohibition is tyranny." By 1911 Pabst believed that the Prohibition movement was on the wane, but World War I and its anti-German rhetoric gave Prohibitionists a sudden advantage. America's German beer became "kaiser brew" for many dry patriots. A former lieutenant-governor of Wisconsin said in 1918, "We have German enemies in this country too. And the worst of all our German enemies, the most treacherous, the most menacing are Pabst, Schlitz, Blatz and Miller." As Paul Glad observed, World War I effectively neutralized German influence in American society.

Prohibition turned saloons into speakeasies and,

A sign outside a Milwaukee milling company from 1920 called for an end to Prohibition. The wish would not be granted until 1933. Courtesy, Milwaukee County Historical Society

fermentation in dry territory." Sixty days in a warm room was the difference between German lager and near beer.

Prohibition was a wet affair in Wisconsin, but the length of it strangled many small breweries. When Prohibition ended in 1933, Wisconsin had lost 40 percent of its breweries. The U.S. Census had counted 132 breweries in Wisconsin in 1914 but only 80 in 1933. The Great Depression toppled another seven breweries by 1939, including Milwaukee's venerable Cream City Brewery in 1937.

Many brewers believed that reforming bawdy saloons would diffuse the Prohibition movement. Mil-

officially, German lager into near beer. Milwaukee brewers marketed several brands of non-alcoholic near beer: Pablo by Pabst, Famo by Schlitz, and Vivo by Miller. Brewers were at first encouraged by near beer sales, which then dropped during the Roaring Twenties.

One Milwaukee gin distillery quickly adjusted to Prohibition. In 1919 the National Distilling Company —called the "Gin House of America"—became the Red Star Yeast and Products Company. National Distilling had marketed Red Star yeast since the 1890s, but yeast now took center stage. When Prohibition ended in 1933 Red Star Yeast returned to making

Members of Milwaukee's Brewery Workers' Union marched in the 1914 Milwaukee Labor Day parade protesting the growing Prohibition movement five years before Prohibition became law. Courtesy, Milwaukee County Historical Society

Above
In 1928 Milwaukee's Seven Master Lock Company shipped 147,000 padlocks to New York City for federal agents to use to lock up illegal taverns. Ironically, the locks were being produced in a building in Milwaukee owned by the Pabst Brewing Company, whose brewery was closed by Prohibition. *Courtesy, Milwaukee Public Library*

Right
In 1919 Milwaukee men mourned, in a mock funeral for John Barleycorn, the loss of alcohol to Prohibition. *Courtesy, Milwaukee County Historical Society*

small quantities of gin, though gin production was discontinued four years later. The company later became Universal Foods Corporation.

Violating the Eighteenth Amendment was as easy as making a toast. As one University of Wisconsin student observed of his hometown in 1930, "There has been, is, and always will be plenty of stimulating fluids in Viroqua. Wine is a mocker, strong drink is raging, and beer—beer is two bits a quart." The editor of the *Burlington Standard-Democrat* observed that "a beerless Milwaukee is like a beanless Boston—it can't be done."

Prohibition was in part a reaction to immigrants and their foreign ways. The Irish of the nineteenth century were often stereotyped as whiskey-loving drunks. Moreover, drinking openly on Sundays was a special sin to a great many Americans—and a cherished custom among Germans. Whether Lutheran or Catholic, German-Americans did not consider Sundays in the biergartens as sacrilegious.

During the Dry Decade Wisconsin had a resurgence of nativist activities—only this time members wore white sheets. The Ku Klux Klan attracted as many as 40,000 members in Wisconsin. The Klan

This Milwaukee freight-hauling truck had originally been used for bootlegging. It was confiscated by federal agents as it was delivering a shipment of beer to Manitowoc. Courtesy, Milwaukee Public Library

Zahringer's Malt Products Company's business went flat in 1919, because beer, which uses malt in the brewing process, could not be produced legally. Courtesy, Milwaukee Public Library

preached "100 percent Americanism," which appealed to nativists who objected to Wisconsin's large immigrant and Catholic population. The strongholds of the Ku Klux Klan were in Milwaukee, Kenosha, and Racine counties, which had received the twentieth-century influx of Polish, Italian, and Russian Jewish immigrants. Many German Socialists who opposed the Catholic clergy joined the Klan to the embarrassment of Socialist leader Victor Berger and Milwaukee's Socialist mayor, Daniel Hoan.

Madison was also an active Ku Klux Klan center in reaction to its Little Italy neighborhood, according to historian Robert Goldberg. Italian laborers had settled in Madison at the turn of the century during the construction of the State Historical Society and the Capitol. During Prohibition the Greenbush neighborhood, a community of about 500 Italians, was known for its bootlegging. In 1924 six men were killed

in the neighborhood during what local newspapers called a "rum war." The Ku Klux Klan promised to bring law and order to Madison and even burned two crosses along Lake Mendota in 1924. The anti-Catholic rhetoric failed to sustain passion, however, and by 1927 Wisconin's Ku Klux Klan had died out for lack of members.

THE GREEN BAY PACKERS

Even as Wisconsin's communities appeared splintered along ethnic lines, a new business was forming that united communities against a common foe. It inspired conversation among strangers and sparked enthusiasm that cut across ethnicity, class, and gender. In 1919 Curly Lambeau organized a football team.

Green Bay is known more for football than for being part of the historical waterway to the Mississippi River. Son of a Belgian-born building contractor, Earl Louis Lambeau spent most of his freshman year at Notre Dame playing football for Knute Rockne. When he returned home to Green Bay, Lambeau persuaded his employer, the Acme Meat Packing Company, to pay for the uniforms of a new football team. Lambeau was coach and star player. During their first season of 10-1, the players each earned $16.75 from the hat passed among the fans.

In 1921 the meat packing company paid the $50 needed to join the year-old National Football League, and Lambeau's team became the Green Bay Packers. They had winning seasons for the next eight years and won three league championships in 1929, 1930, and 1931. When their team was struggling financially in 1925, Green Bay residents bought 1,000 shares of stock at $5 a share, turning the football team into a community-owned enterprise.

Green Bay would continue to be the smallest city in the National Football League, and the fans were steadfast regardless of the Packers' record. In 1949 the city once again bought shares of stock and raised $100,000 to help its losing football team. The new community stockholders agreed not to receive stock dividends, preferring that profits be saved for bad times.

Curly Lambeau resigned in 1949 after a coaching career of 31 seasons, making way for a committee that steadily steered the team from one loss to the next. From 1948 to 1958 the Green Bay Packers were the goats of the league despite a multi-million dollar stadium subsidized by Green Bay in 1957.

In the 1960s, however, the Packers would bring honor to Green Bay. A Brooklyn meatcutter's son would make the Green Bay Packers the winningest team in football history. His approach to success would be simple—winning was not the main thing, it was the only thing. In 1959 Vince Lombardi would come to town.

URBAN GROWTH AND THE GENIUS OF FRANK LLOYD WRIGHT

The prosperity of the twentieth century belonged to the cities, and many rural Americans were leaving the country for urban life. In Wisconsin the urban population grew 163 percent from 1900 to 1955. In contrast the rural population grew only 26 percent during those years. The greatest population centers remained in the 13 counties of southeastern Wisconsin, the center of industry and jobs. In 1900 one-sixth of Wisconsin's two million population resided in Milwaukee County. However, by 1950 more than one-quarter of Wisconin's 3.4 million population lived in Milwaukee County alone.

One young man from rural Wisconsin went to Chicago although he would hate city life. However,

he earned a fortune in the city and it enabled him to return to the land he loved. In the process he made Wisconsin internationally famous.

The low, lean lines of Frank Lloyd Wright's architecture influenced design throughout the world. Together with Louis Sullivan, Frank Lloyd Wright was a fresh American voice from the prairie. Wright's Prairie Houses would reconstruct how Americans looked at homes.

Frank Lloyd Wright made his reputation in Chicago, but his nesting instincts drew him back to southern Wisconsin. Born in Richland Center in 1867, Frank Lloyd Wright spent his youth in Spring Green and Madison. It was in the Wyoming Valley near Spring Green that Frank Lloyd Wright worked on his first building, Unity Chapel, for his Unitarian minister uncle. When Wright was 20 he began working for Chicago's most innovative architect, Louis Sullivan, whom Wright referred to as "Dear Master." He learned from Sullivan that in design, form follows function, a philosophy evident in Wright's distinctive Prairie House, his signature in which a house grew organically from its environment. The elements of water, fire, and earth haunted Wright. At the center of many of his homes were cavernous fireplaces surrounded by interiors of bare brick and stone and unpainted wood. "Architecture . . . is no less a weaving and fabric than the trees," he wrote. Frank Lloyd Wright was always trying to escape the traditional rectangles of modern architecture, according to Peter Blake. The goal of Frank Lloyd Wright was breaking down "the insufferable limitations of the box."

In 1911 Frank Lloyd Wright returned to the Wyoming Valley and built a home he called Taliesin, the name of a Welsh poet that invoked Wright's Welsh ancestry. "I turned to this hill in the Valley as my grandfather before me had turned to America—as a hope and haven," said Wright in his autobiography. The Wyoming Valley is in Wisconsin's Driftless Area, the craggy, diverse region in southwestern Wisconsin that was not chewed and flattened by the Ice Age glaciers.

Taliesin was a haven for Wright, but in 1914 it became a nightmare. While Wright was in Chicago on business his Barbadian chef went beserk and burned Taliesin to the ground, killing seven people. Among the dead were Mamah Cheney, the woman for whom Wright had left his first wife, plus Cheney's two

Above
Although Frank Lloyd Wright became a famous international architect, he returned to his childhood home of Spring Green to found his school for architects, the Taliesin Fellowship. Courtesy, State Historical Society of Wisocnsin

Right
Frank Lloyd Wright's genius for using wood, stone, and light created his celebrated Prairie Houses. At Taliesin in Spring Green in 1957, Wright sits at his desk. Courtesy, State Historical Society of Wisconsin

Facing page
In Racine the Johnson Wax Company commissioned Frank Lloyd Wright to build a research tower in 1946, a decade after Wright designed Johnson Wax's administration building. Courtesy, State Historical Society of Wisconsin

children and four workers.

In 1923 Wright's genius was confirmed internationally when a devastating earthquake hit Japan. One hundred thousand people died and Tokyo was left in rubble—except for Wright's Imperial Hotel. A telegram from the hotel chairman informed Wright, "Hotel stands undamaged as monument of your genius—Hundreds of homeless provided for by perfectly maintained service—congratulations." In 1932 Taliesin, which Wright had rebuilt, became in part a school for architects called the Taliesin Fellowship.

Wisconsin's Johnson Wax Company commissioned Wright to design their Racine administration building in 1936 and a research tower in 1946. His last grand project was the Guggenheim Museum in New York City. Frank Lloyd Wright died in 1959, two months before his ninety-second birthday. He was buried near Unity Chapel, the first building on which he had worked. In 1985 his remains were transferred to Arizona to be interred next to his widow, Olgivanna, at their western home near Phoenix called Taliesin West.

Frank Lloyd Wright had retreated in comfort to the country after he had made his reputation in the city. It was a privileged choice born from his genius. However, few people had such unrestricted mobility.

WISCONSIN'S MINORITIES

Wisconsin had its share of inequalities. Wisconsin's Indians, isolated in reservations in central and northern Wisconsin, lived in rural poverty. Since 1890 Indians have consistently accounted for less than one percent of the state's population, their economic resources becoming increasingly scant. During the 1920s the Menominee tribe, living on an undivided reservation, owned a forest and lumber mill that could provide regular employment. The remainder of Wisconsin's tribes—the Chippewa, Winnebago, Oneida, Potawatomi, and Stockbridge-Munsee—did not fare as well, according to anthropologist Nancy Oestreich Lurie. For most tribes, work was seasonal and piecemeal.

During World War I many Indians, not eligible to be drafted, volunteered to fight. As some Indians became war heroes, the deplorable conditions of the reservations were publicized in the newspapers. In 1924 Congress granted Indians full citizenship and suffrage, although some traditional Indians were suspicious of this symbol of assimilation.

Just as Indians were overwhelmingly rural, Wisconsin's black population was primarily urban. Many of Wisconsin's first blacks had arrived as slaves of Southerners migrating to the lead region during Wisconsin's territorial days. By 1900 there were only 2,486 blacks in the state, but the 1920s saw a new influx of blacks from the South. Wisconsin's heavy industries in Milwaukee and Beloit encouraged migration during the 1930s despite the Depression, and there were nearly 9,000 blacks in Milwaukee just before World War II.

Like new immigrants before them, blacks got only the dirtiest jobs such as blast furnace work, according to labor historian Robert Ozanne. However, once white immigrants had learned English they were often promoted to foremen, whereas black Americans remained in the foundries. Labor unions were not agents of change for blacks until the 1930s. In fact during the nineteenth century blacks were often considered strikebreakers since few were allowed in unions, according to historian Robert Nesbit.

During the Great Depression blacks and other minorities would become first-class union members. In 1935 and 1937 both the federal government and Wisconsin passed labor relations acts that prevented employers from spying on workers and dismissing workers who led or organized labor unions. Collective bargaining was now sanctioned by law. In 1936 the Congress of Industrial Organization (CIO) and the American Federation of Labor (AFL) competed for votes in becoming a local union's representative. The competition for votes elevated blacks, women, and immigrants within the ranks of unions, according to Robert Ozanne.

The surge of unionism during the 1930s gave blacks better pay and benefits, but they were still given the least desirable jobs. However, blacks were often staunch supporters of unions. Although very few blacks were union officers, one black steelworker in Beloit did become a union officer in 1937.

Working women in Wisconsin had been traditionally employed either in domestic service or industries such as clothing manufacturing and cigar rolling. Their hours were just as long as men—60 hours a week—but their wages were usually half that of men's pay. It was presumed that women worked only until they could find a husband, and their employment was dismissed as transitory.

Because of their low wages women often were considered threats to unions. In 1898 the Oshkosh Woodworkers' Council asked the seven woodworking companies to stop hiring women. Refusing to acknowledge the fact that women and girls were replacing men at lower pay, the union wrote: "Believing that a woodworking factory is no place for the employment of either women or girls we respectfully ask that female labor be abolished." Women joined unions in large numbers during the 1930s, but wage and job discrimination against women continued in both blue-collar and white-collar jobs according to Ozanne.

When jobs became scarce married women were often fired. During the Depression women teachers who were married had a difficult time hanging onto their jobs. While the leadership of the Wisconsin State Federation of Labor opposed firing married women, local trade unions such as the Green Bay Federated Trades Council often were active in barring married women from teaching during the late 1920s and 1930s.

Discrimination also came in separate pay scales. During the 1920s and 1930s Wisconsin school boards often had three separate salary scales: one for women, a higher one for men, and the highest pay for married men. However, because women dominated the teaching profession, unionization eventually destroyed discriminatory pay scales. Women who worked in factories were not helped until the 1964 Civil Rights Act, which prohibited race, age, and sex discrimination in the workplace. After 1964 both unions and employers quickly adopted single pay scales.

Ironically Wisconsin's most famous strike occurred, not in the radical 1930s, but in the 1950s. The gardened company town of Kohler, Wisconsin's first planned community, was the site of worker unrest. In 1954 contract talks broke down at the Kohler Company, and approximately 1,400 workers went on a strike that lasted for six bitter years. Kohler's plumbing supplies were nationally recognized, and the conflict on the streets of Sheboygan and the village of Kohler attracted national attention. In 1958 a U.S. Senate committee, the McClellan Committee, held hearings in Washington, D.C. that lasted five weeks. In 1960 the National Labor Relations Board ruled that the Kohler Company had refused to bargain, and the

company paid $4.5 million in back pay and pension credits.

THE GREAT DEPRESSION

The 1920s had been a time of laissez-faire. During the Roaring Twenties, tax rates were low and the national debt was decreasing at a satisfactory rate. Many believed that the management of the Federal Reserve System had made depressions a thing of the past. When the stock market crashed on Black Thursday, October 24, 1929, many business leaders thought the business slump was only temporary. They were gravely mistaken.

Banks failed. In 1930 Wisconsin had 933 banks; by 1933 it had only 445. More than 500 banks were suspended, while 90 banks consolidated. Recovery was slow. From 1934 to 1936 there were 10 more suspensions and 43 more consolidations. Eventually nearly 200 suspended banks reopened their doors, but banking in Wisconsin would not exceed its pre-1929 strength until 1942.

Manufacturing plummeted. About 1,500 Wisconsin businesses shut down between 1930 and 1932. In 1929 the value of manufacturing in Wisconsin was $960 million, but in 1933 it fell to $375 million.

Unemployment skyrocketed. Within a dizzying three years, from 1929 to 1932, Wisconsin factories lost nearly 56 percent of their workers—from 264,745 workers to 116,525. Milwaukee alone lost about 44 percent of its wage earners. There were 117,658 employed in Milwaukee in 1929, but by 1933 there were only 66,010 with jobs.

Farmers struggled. Wisconsin farm income fell from $350 million in 1930 to $199 million in 1932. Using 1929 as the base index for farm commodities, prices dropped from 100 to 43 by 1932. Drought hit the Midwest in the early 1930s, and the 1934 drought became the most severe ever recorded in Wisconsin.

Dreams evaporated. The bottom fell out of the 1920s with such ferociousness that it scarred an entire generation of Americans. People who lived through the Great Depression tell stories of fear and insecurity that never quite healed. Some blocked the memories entirely. "We weren't affected," said a woman vaguely who failed to mention she took in boarders. The children of the 1930s grew up with such movie classics as the Wizard of Oz and Gone With the Wind—but

The bustling appearance of Appleton's Fox River belies the realities of the period when this air view was taken, the decade of the Great Depression. In 1929 the value of manufacturing in Wisconsin was $960 million, but in 1933 it fell to $375 million. Wisconsin factories lost more than 50 percent of their workers —from 264,745 workers in 1929 to 116,525 workers in 1932. Courtesy, State Historical Society of Wisconsin

Wisconsin farmers dumped an estimated $10-million worth of milk during their 1933 "milk strikes," which protested falling milk prices. Courtesy, Milwaukee Public Library

these children could also see breadlines and soup kitchens and the shantytowns of the homeless once called "Hoovervilles."

Apple vendors became a symbol of the depression in the summer of 1930 as a bumper crop of Oregon and Washington apples reached the country. Across the nation the unemployed sold apples for a nickel a piece. The vendor's profit for the day amounted to less than a dollar—if the vendor sold all the apples. Shoe shiners and street vendors became legion, selling everything from rubber balls to cheap neckties.

Drought and a decade of falling prices made Wisconsin's farmers desperate. Milk strikes in 1933 and 1934 showed the turmoil of the dairy farmers, revealing an underlying hostility between dairy farmers and dairy manufacturers. Most of Wisconsin milk was manufactured into dairy products such as cheese, butter, and ice cream products. As prices dropped, the dairy farmers of the radical Wisconsin Milk Pool in the Fox valley called three milk strikes in 1933 that tried to prevent milk from reaching the manufacturing plants. Two larger groups, the Farm Holiday Association and the Wisconsin Council of Agriculture, refused to join the strikes.

Milk was Wisconsin's white gold. As striking farmers poured their milk onto the ground they made a powerful statement. Two men died in the May strike of 1933, and Governor Schmedeman called in the state troops. One striker remembered, "Scenes of violence were being enacted elsewhere in the State, notably around Shawano and Appleton, and blood from noses was flowing almost as freely as milk." Although violent, the strikes were largely ineffective, as farmers could not agree on a unified strategy. The milk strikes were an angry release against an enemy no one could point to.

Beginning in 1933 Congress passed two bills designed by Franklin D. Roosevelt to help industry and agriculture. The National Industrial Recovery Act was largely a failure, falling victim to inside quarreling and outside criticism from both business and labor. The Supreme Court later invalidated the controversial act.

The Agricultural Adjustment Act (AAA) tried to curtail the abundance that caused falling prices. It identified nine basic crops and paid farmers to decrease acreage. This program helped some farmers, but small farmers or those who grew crops outside the chosen nine found themselves just as badly off, according to historian Paul Glad. In Wisconsin four AAA programs reached farmers—tobacco growers were paid to reduce their acreage by half, wheat growers were asked to reduce their yields about 15 percent, and corn and hog farmers reduced their yield approximately 30 percent.

Hunger and want in America's land of plenty was the Great Depression's greatest paradox. Critics of the New Deal could not forget the image of the the government buying six million pigs and having the meat butchered—much going to relief agencies—but much being dumped.

The Depression also emphasized the large disparity between urban and rural life. In 1930 only one in six Wisconsin farm homes had access to electrical power lines. Although 84 percent of Wisconsin farm families had automobiles, only 16 percent had indoor plumbing. The New Deal's Rural Electrification Administration began to provide electricity to rural areas, thus partially closing the gap between urban and rural dwellers.

Radio became America's new entertainment. The families that gathered around the large wooden radio were listening to the sounds of the modern era. Financial stability and better programming had made radio a mass advertising medium by 1929, and radio drew large audiences during the Depression years as people sought relief from their troubles. One of the longest-running shows sponsored by one advertiser was Johnson Wax's Fibber McGee & Molly, a comedy show that ran from 1935 to 1950.

As advertising hit the airwaves, people became more aware of the power of promotion. In 1932 Wilbur Carlson, a Wisconsin promoter attending an agricultural conference in Washington D.C., heard a representative from Maine talk about how the Pine Tree State was promoting itself as the Potato State. As Carlson listened, it struck him: Wisconsin was America's Dairyland. Carlson returned home and began lobbying. By the early 1940s Wisconsin's famous slogan was on its license plates.

The Depression years were not favorable times to start a print shop, let alone one that used the little-known process of photography to make smooth printing plates. During the 1930s most print shops and newspapers still used virtually the same process that Gutenberg had used to print his bibles in the fifteenth century—letterpress—where cast lead directly pressed onto paper. But W.A. Krueger, who opened his Milwaukee print shop in 1934, bet on the new photographic offset method, which now dominates all printing.

Children became the market for two of Wisconsin's oldest printers during the 1930s. In Menasha, the George Banta Company was launched as a leading publisher of "skill and drill" workbooks for elementary school children. tIn Racine, the Western Publishing Company signed an innovative contract in 1933 with cartoonist Walt Disney to print storybooks, and Disneyland's first castles nestled in the imaginations of the readers of Big Little Books.

Fascinated with letterpress printing, a young George Banta collected unwanted metal type from his hometown newspaper in Franklin, Indiana. After marrying a Menasha woman in 1886, he hand-printed an 1888 book of family-written stories and poems called *Flying Leaves*. Begun in 1902, his small shop printed insurance forms and in 1908 began to print college fraternity and sorority magazines. Scholarly works, with their demands for precision and accuracy, formed the Collegiate Press during the 1920s, and in 1929 Banta began printing disposable workbooks for school children.

The Three Little Kittens and *The Little Red Hen* were two of the greatest hits of the Little Golden Books of Racine's Western Publishing Company. The print shop, begun in 1907, accidentally fell into book marketing when a Chicago publisher could not pay its printing bill. Western Publishing easily sold the unpaid inventory of children's books. First published in 1942, the 25-cent books with the gold foil spine became a familiar sight in household toy boxes. The one-billionth Little Golden Book was printed in 1986. The ubiquitous Betty Crocker's Cookbook had been published by Western since the early 1950s.

WORLD WAR II

During the hard times of the Depression, war clouds gathered in Europe. In March 1938 Hitler's armies marched into Austria to proclaim the union of the German Reich. By July 1940 Germany occupied most of Europe, including Poland, Czechoslovakia, Denmark, Norway, Belgium, the Netherlands, and more than half of France, including Paris. Japan signed a Tripartite Pact with Germany and Italy in September 1940 that pledged mutual support.

The United States remained cautiously neutral until the morning of December 7, 1941, when Japanese warplanes attacked Pearl Harbor, leaving 3,500 servicemen dead. America's entrance into the war galvanized the nation's economy. Mass production and the country's assembly lines were crucial to the country's war effort, and after more than a decade of unemployment the United States now had a labor shortage. Government contracts were awarded only to businesses that could guarantee the required labor needed to meet the contract deadlines.

Wisconsin's largest single wartime industry was shipbuilding. The shipyards of Superior, Sturgeon Bay, and Manitowoc produced primarily small naval vessels. The Manitowoc Shipbuilding Company employed 7,000 shipbuilders to produce 28 submarines. Since the subs were too large for the St. Lawrence River and Erie Canal, they sailed to Chicago and then were towed via the Illinois Drainage Canal to the Mississippi River. The subs were floated downriver on pontoon docks until reaching the Gulf. Of the 28 submarines produced, only three failed to return at the end of the war.

The automobile industry throughout the country halted production on new cars in 1942 and began making tanks, aircraft, engines, weapons, and ammunition. Chrysler became a major builder of Sherman tanks, while General Motors became the country's largest single producer of weapons. Nash Motors of Kenosha, which merged to become American Motors in 1954, built aircraft engines for Pratt & Whitney. The plant in Janesville built shells, and a popular slogan at the plant was "Keep 'Em Firing."

World War II brought women into the factory jobs once reserved only for men. Rosie the Riveter became the symbol of women working in the foundries and on the assembly lines. In Wisconsin small business owners such as Jefferson's Ben Schweiger were forced to hire women for the first time. Schweiger's furniture-making business would soon comprise 400 workers, half of whom were women. Discovering that attention to detail was a trait found not only in men, Schweiger continued to hire women after the war. In 1943 the Wisconsin Legislature abandoned its 40-year-old prohibition against hiring female clerks. By the war's end, 35 percent of the national workforce was female.

The farmers of Wisconsin helped feed the U.S. armed forces. Wisconsin's farmers were the major producers of the cheese, vegetables, and dried and evaporated milk that were sent overseas. The canning industry boomed. In 1941 alone the government bought one million cases of Wisconsin canned peas for the army and navy. In 1945 Wisconsin, the leading producer of vegetables for canning, produced 15 million cases of peas and nearly 12 million cases of sweet corn, beets, and beans. After the war about 150 canneries continued to operate.

Wisconsin's industries sent diverse goods overseas, from mess kits and raincoats to guns and trucks. Many of the military's combat boots were made of Milwaukee's Trostel leather. In 1938 Albert Trostel, Jr., had visited Europe and was convinced that war was imminent. On his return to Milwaukee Trostel immediately converted production from calf leather to the tougher side leather in anticipation of the need for combat boots.

One Wisconsin company changed products because of World War II. The Green Bay Soap Company had been making soap since 1881, but soap's major ingredient—glycerine—was needed for explosives. Edward Meyer and his family began processing other animal byproducts such as tallow and cured hides. By 1950 the Green Bay Soap Company would discontinue laundry soap, and in 1978 it changed its name to Anamax.

Wisconsin sent 375,000 citizens into service during World War II, and the number of Wisconsin casualties at the war's end was 7,980. With the returning GIs, Wisconsin would be part of the boom in education, buildings, and babies. An expanding middle class would shape the tastes and patterns of a new, prosperous economy.

The Wisconsin Products Exposition of 1922 in the Milwaukee Auditorium proudly displayed the auto, dairy, and manufacturing products that had helped bring the Wisconsin economy into the twentieth century. Courtesy, State Historical Society of Wisconsin

THE WISCONSIN IDEA CONTINUES

Fleets of rowboats carried tourists and guides on the Wisconsin River in the 1870s at the Wisconsin Dells. The main attractions of the area are the many bluffs and rock formations along the shores of the river. Courtesy, the H.H. Bennett Studio

The full moon rises above the Silos on this productive Wisconsin farm. Photo by R. Hamilton Smith

The pathways of the glaciers and ancient Indians, fur traders and settlers are still alive in Wisconsin's newest major industry, tourism. Modern highways have replaced the Wisconsin River for getting around, but forest trails and crystal lakes still allow travelers to explore the land described by Nicolet and mapped by Marquette and Joliet in the seventeenth century.

Wisconsin's natural resources have allowed tourism to become part of Wisconsin's economic Big Three: manufacturing, which by 1986 produced approximately $59 billion in annual sales; agriculture, with a total annual product of $20 billion; and tourism, which brought in about $4.1 billion in 1984.

By the mid-1980s tourism in Wisconsin was a big business built on small and medium-sized establishments. Southeastern counties contributed to half of the state's total tourism, but in the northern one-third of Wisconsin tourism was the leading industry. Statewide the nearly 15 million visits by travelers created approximately 130,000 jobs in 1985. By 1995 the tourist industry is expected to add another 11,000 jobs, according to the Wisconsin Strategic Development Commission that studied the health of Wiscon-

sin tourism in 1985.

Water, and its promise of renewal, was Wisconsin's first attraction for tourists. In the 1870s the springs in southern Wisconsin became buried treasure as entrepreneurs, doctors, and quacks promoted the miraculous powers of mineral water. "Taking of the waters" was the genteel remedy for ailments and frazzled nerves throughout the nineteenth century.

Waukesha, which became famous for its mineral spas, was trumpeted as "the Saratoga of the West," after New York's lavish Saratoga Springs where the wealthy and powerful came to sip. Waukesha's fame began in 1868 when one rich New Yorker, Colonel Richard Dunbar, drank from a spring and felt unusually refreshed. A diabetic, Dunbar felt so rejuvenated that he moved to Waukesha and bought 40 acres of land surrounding the spring he called "Bethesda," referring to the biblical house of mercy. In 1869 Dunbar pronounced himself cured of diabetes. Two Chicago promoters built a dazzling hotel, Fountain Spring House, launching Waukesha as a watery haven for affluent visitors throughout the country, especially the South. One newspaper editor in 1873

Above
In the 1880s the tourist steamer
Dell Queen docked on the Wisconsin River at the Wisconsin
Dells near Kilbourn City. The
well-known Wisconsin pioneer
photographer H.H. Bennett is pictured third from the left. Courtesy, the H.H. Bennett Studio

Left
The tourist steamboat Alexander Mitchell *sailed on the Wis-*
consin River near Kilbourn City
(later called the Wisconsin
Dells) in the 1880s. Courtesy,
the H.H. Bennett Studio

The Bethesda Spa in Waukesha
was known in the 1880s and
1890s as a fashionable resort
where people came to drink the
curative waters. In its heyday
Waukesha aspired to be the
"Saratoga of the West." Courtesy, the H.H. Bennett Studio

"The Pride of Waukesha!"

FOUNTAIN SPRING HOUSE

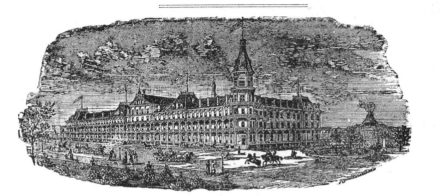

Finest Summer Hotel West of Saratoga Springs.

—o—

A New Hotel !   Elegantly Furnished !

—o—

Accommodations for 800 Guests

described a Sunday evening walk as a concentration of "at least $200,000 worth of jewelry, silks, satins, ribbons, laces, hair bustles, etc." Dunbar collected more than 1,000 orders for barrels of mineral water, providing area coopers with a beverage other than beer for filling their barrels.

Fashionable spas and bottles of Wisconsin water were not founded on a hoax. Wisconsin has some of the purest groundwater available because of its rock formation bequeathed by the glaciers. The Ice Age deposited vast amounts of sand and gravel mixed with snow. The porous sandstone rocks that formed were water bearers, or aquifers, which excell at transmitting clean groundwater. Sandstone covers most of Wisconsin, except for northern Wisconsin that has harder rock and the Driftless Area in southwestern Wisconsin where the glaciers did not form.

Wisconsin's clean, abundant groundwater gave competition to Dunbar's Bethesda Park. Healing springs were promoted in Sparta, Palmyra, Beloit, and Appleton. In Madison the Tonyawatha Springs Hotel on Lake Monona drew visitors. In Beaver Dam, the owner of the Vita Spring Pavilion, Dr. George Swan, declared, "I name this water Vita—or life—life to the whole urinary economy." Nine more springs discovered around Waukesha were given such fanciful names as Hygeia, Vesta, Lethean, Arcadian, Fountain, Clysmic, and Glenn. The well-known White Rock

continued to bottle Psyche mineral water after most resorts closed down at the turn of the century.

The railroads were the first to extensively promote vacations to Wisconsin. The Milwaukee Road claimed that its "palace cars" brought 8,000 to 10,000 passengers to Waukesha annually, and in the 1900s it advertised Lake Delavan as a vacation spot for Chicago tourists. In northern Wisconsin, the Wisconsin Central built the Chequamegon Hotel in Ashland and made a profit with its trainloads of vacationers and sportsmen. By 1915 the Milwaukee Road's "Guide to Summer Homes" featured 63 Wisconsin locations.

The crown jewel for vacationers to Wisconsin was Kilbourn City on the Wisconsin River, located amid eerie rock formations called the "Dalles" by the French fur traders. "Dalles," which means "a swift stream of water running between the high banks," was changed to "Dells" after the founding of Kilbourn City in 1856. Few settlers had seen these primeval vistas before the 1850s except for lumber raftsmen trying to survive the wild Wisconsin River. Parlour-room photography advertised the Wisconsin Dells and Devil's Lake long before Kilbourn City became a tourist spot. The Dells were captured in vivid three dimensions in double photographs called stereographs, which gave a startling sense of depth.

Kilbourn City's portrait photographer, Henry Hamilton Bennett, became one of the country's great

Right
The Lake Lawn Hotel was one of Delavan's retreats for Chicago tourists in 1900. Nearby Lake Geneva and Delavan have continued to attract Chicagoans eager to leave the city on a three-hour ride by train. Courtesy, State Historical Society of Wisconsin

Below right
The bluffs surrounding Devil's Lake were formed by the Ice Age and became a tourist attraction for vacationers also visiting Kilbourn City (later renamed Wisconsin Dells). Courtesy, State Historical Society of Wisconsin

A Pleasant Summer Resort.

RATES.
Per Day............ $ 2.00
Per Week............ 10.00

W. B. PEARL, PROPRIETOR.

CLIFF HOUSE, DEVIL'S LAKE, WISCONSIN.

Above
Madeline Island is the largest of the Apostle Islands of Chequamegon Bay, a popular spot for Ashland's tourists. Courtesy, State Historical Society of Wisconsin

Left
The Wisconsin Central Railroad advertised Ashland's Chequamegon Hotel in the 1880s. At the entrance to the Apostle Islands of Lake Superior, Ashland had a population of five in 1872. However, railroad surveyors and investors saw the tourist potential, and more than 200 buildings were constructed in the spring of 1872. Courtesy, State Historical Society of Wisconsin

A Wisconsin era ended with the last of the lumber rafts floating down the Mississippi River in 1915 at Prairie du Chien. Courtesy, State Historical Society of Wisconsin

landscape photographers. "You don't have to pose nature," said Bennett, "and it is less trouble to please." According to biographer Sara Rath, Bennett invented camera parts to simplify the bulky, complicated process of on-site photography. In 1886, using a shutter that could freeze action, he documented the active life of lumber raftsmen on the Wisconsin River, producing what is probably the first photographic essay.

By the 1870s Kilbourn City was a growing summer resort mainly because of Bennett's exciting stereographs. Bennett and Kilbourn City's tourism enjoyed a symbiotic relationship; the more tourists, the more portrait commissions for Bennett, who traveled with the sightseeing boats. In 1874 Bennett reported that he had sold more than 20,000 stereographs. Bennett was later hired by the Chicago, Milwaukee and St. Paul Railroad to photograph the scenery along the rail lines to attract railroad passengers. In 1931 Kilbourn City changed its name to Wisconsin Dells so that tourists could readily identify the town from railroad timetables and brochures.

Wisconsin's tourism evaporated each autumn, prompting resort owners to promote Wisconsin as a winter playground. In the 1920s Model-T Fords were converted into snowbuggies by exchanging wheels for skis. In 1927 Carl Eliason, of Lost Lake Resort in northern Vilas County patented a motorized toboggan that he called the "autoboggan." The modern snowmobile was designed in Canada in 1958, and Wisconsin became home to 6 of the 23 major producers. With its extensive trails and races, northern Wisconsin billed itself as the snowmobile capital of the world, and Wisconsin tourism became a year-round business.

After World War II Door County became one of the Midwest's most popular tourist destinations. Its 250-mile shoreline on Lake Michigan and its seacoast appeal also attracted artists, many of whom stayed to build art studios and galleries. Tourism gradually eclipsed commercial fishing and lumbering, which had sustained settlers and the large colonies of Belgians in the nineteenth century. The popular fish boils and active shipyards of Sturgeon Bay remind visitors of the peninsula's nautical past. Bountiful cherry trees and apple groves have also kept Door County a farming community.

The active State Historical Society of Wisconsin has helped protect Wisconsin's heritage, preserving the state's frontier architecture and Indian effigy mounds. In 1987 there were more than 1,000 Wisconsin listings on the National Register of Historic Places, including more than 80 historic districts.

Visitors can retreat to Wisconsin's pioneer past in historic sites preserved by the society. Madeline Island in northern Chequamegon Bay ventures back in time to the fur traders. In Baraboo the circus business is preserved in live performances at the Circus World Museum. Lead miners and the Cornish cut their presence at the Pendarvis and other Shake Rag Street sites in Mineral Point. The most elaborate site is Old World Wisconsin in Eagle, where nine farmsteads are traditionally farmed on 576 acres. Ethnic festivals during the summer add more color to Old World Wisconsin's celebration of the past.

The preservation of Wisconsin's unique Ice Age landscape was begun by citizens and private donations in the 1960s. In 1980 Congress declared it a National Scenic Trail, a designation given to famous pathways such as the Appalachian Trail. The 1,000-mile Ice Age Trail winds through bowl-shaped kettles, snake-like mounds called eskers, and elongated hills called drumlins. The trail follows the extensive mounds called end moraines that clearly outline the glaciers' last pathway into Wisconsin more than 70,000 years ago. Five of the nine units of the Ice Age National Reserve established in 1971 are open to the public: Horicon Marsh, Devil's Lake State Park, Interstate Park, Mill Bluff State Park, and the northern unit of Kettle Moraine State Forest.

Wisconsin was the first state to establish a park system, setting aside 50,000 acres in Lincoln County called "the State Park" in 1878. The land was later sold to lumber companies, but in 1900 Interstate Park was established along the St. Croix River, becoming Wisconsin's oldest park. During the 1930s the federal government purchased land that became the Nicolet and Chequamegon national forests, and by 1942 Wisconsin had eight additional state forests. By 1987 Wisconsin had 48 state parks, 9 state forests, 11 state trails, and 3 recreation areas.

In 1961 Wisconsin became a pioneer in conserving its natural resources, especially its single most important geological gift—water. The Outdoor Recreation Act Program (ORAP) pledged $50 million for cleaning the environment and buying land. Wisconsin's sand and gravel aquifer, which covers most of the state, is at the land's surface and therefore is particularly vulnerable to pollutants from industry, municipal waste, farm fertilizers, pesticides, landfills, and some types of mining. Water pollution became ORAP'S primary target, and by 1984 almost half of the total $332 million program had been spent on cleaning Wisconsin's water.

Two governors of the Great Lakes states have likened clean water of the Great Lakes to the oil boon.

When this picture of Fish Creek in Door County was taken in 1950, the 250-mile peninsula was quickly becoming one of the Midwest's most popular tourist spots. The lumber and fishing traditions of the nineteenth century were replaced by artists' studios and galleries and hotels. Courtesy, State Historical Society of Wisconsin

Logging had built Chippewa
Falls into a prosperous town by
1900, although the lumber industry was moving west. The challenge for logging towns was to
build a manufacturing base to replace the lumber trade. Courtesy, State Historical Society of
Wisconsin

"Water will be for the Midwest almost like oil is to the OPEC countries," said former Michigan Governor William G. Milliken. In 1987 Wisconsin's Governor Tommy Thompson described Wisconsin's strength in terms of water. "We have an abundance of natural resources, clean air and clean water," he said after bristling at the notion that Wisconsin is part of the "Rust Belt." Speaking to the Wisconsin Farm Equipment Association, Thompson said clean water is going to be "the new petroleum of the future."

Many of Wisconsin's industries, such as food processing, require abundant clean water. By 1983 Wisconsin industries were using 133 million gallons of groundwater each day. The six major industries that require clean water are pulp and paper, fruit and vegetable processing, cheesemaking, brewing, meat processing, and electroplating.

Wisconsin's paper industry, one of the chief polluters of water, has become a corporate leader in preventing the pollution that contaminates water and kills fish. Since the 1970s it has spent more than $450 million in environmental protection equipment, with operating costs for cutting pollution exceeding $115 million annually. Since the 1970s papermakers have cut 80 percent of BOD (biochemical oxygen demand) and 90 percent of TSS (total suspended solids) discharged—while increasing paper production more than 46 percent. By 1983 production of each ton of paper required 60 percent less water than the amount needed in 1960, and production of each ton of paper used 22 percent less energy than it required in 1972.

However, a new challenge for science and technology is unraveling the exact source of toxic waste pollution in water and providing dependable tests that measure toxic levels of pollutants such as PCBs and dioxin. Research and cooperation from municipalities and industry is crucial. In 1986 Neenah's Biodyne Chemicals and the University of Wisconsin-Madison were experimenting with a revolutionary sulfur-free paper process, which could help reduce acid rain and one source of water pollution.

Wisconsin's careful stewardship of its lakes, rivers and forests is essential for the growing tourist industry. Old World settlements in a glacial land of lakes make Wisconsin distinctive when competing for tourist dollars and business travelers. In 1986 business travel was beginning to eclipse pleasure trips in traditional resort towns such as Lake Geneva. Convention centers were built in cities such as Green Bay and Oshkosh with an eye to accommodating business travel.

The continued growth of Wisconsin tourism will rest on general prosperity plus the perception that Wisconsin is indeed a desirable place to trek. Wisconsin's unique landscape and ethnic history is one formula for positioning Wisconsin in the minds of vacationers and business travelers. The diversity of Americana is something Wisconsin has preserved in abundance—or often overlooked in many of its small cities and towns.

RECESSION AND RECOVERY

During the 1970s Wisconsin was such a prosperous state that in 1977 the *Wall Street Journal* called it the "Star of the Snow Belt." Wisconsin gained manufacturing jobs from 1970 to 1979 and matched the national growth in manufacturing jobs. The national newspaper asserted that Wisconsin could compete with the Sun Belt states because of its quality of life, low unemployment, and strategic business tax cuts.

And then the recession hit in 1979, and by the early 1980s Wisconsin's manufacturing economy was in a depression. Job layoffs in automobile and nonelectrical equipment boosted the state unemployment to 7.8 percent, causing Wisconsin to exceed the national level for the first time since 1958. Economists noted that Wisconsin's recovery began later and moved more slowly than the nation's during the recesssion years of 1980 to 1983. The continued downswing of manufacturers such as Allis-Chalmers indicated that Wisconsin's manufacturing was in a painful transition.

In 1984 Governor Anthony Earl formed the Wisconsin Strategic Development Commission, a group of corporate leaders and state officials, to evaluate Wisconsin's economic future. The 1985 final report, which concluded that manufacturing would continue to be the foundation of Wisconsin's economy, identified the strengths and weaknesses of Wisconsin's major existing industries. The commission believed that part of the key to preserving the existing job base lay in the Wisconsin Idea, the partnership between activist scholars and leaders in government and industry. In effect, argued the commission, the Wisconsin Idea could "improve the working relationship between faculty and private industry" through such programs as industrial-funded faculty chairs, expanded partnerships in the University-Industry Research Program

(UIR), and additional research for entrepreneurs and small business.

The markets that had fueled Wisconsin manufacturing—construction, farm, auto, mining, and oil machinery—remained in a stupor during the mid-1980s. Wisconsin's nonelectrical machinery industry, which produced farm and heavy machines for international markets, was Wisconsin's largest employer in 1983 with 92,000 workers, down from 1979's peak of 135,000 jobs. In other sectors, electrical machinery manufacturers employed about 49,000 people in 1984, a loss of about 10,000 jobs. The primary and fabricated metals sector, which employed about 65,000 people in foundries in 1983, lost nearly 25,000 jobs during the recession.

Recovery remained elusive. Modernizing industries was one costly avenue of recovery pursued by Wauwatosa's Briggs & Stratton, which invested $230 million in modernizing its production of small gasoline engines. The modernization by Briggs & Stratton, which reportedly had 60 percent of the U.S. market in small engines, helped to rejuvenate Wisconsin's strong tool and die makers. Tool and die makers are the ultimate machinists since they make the machines that make machines.

In competing for international customers, Wisconsin's Department of Development opened offices in Frankfurt, West Germany, and in Hong Kong. The department also began the Mentor-Mentee program which paired experienced Wisconsin exporters with new companies that needed advice on how to enter the exporting business.

The hard times of the 1980s brought one of Wisconsin's oldest manufacturers to its knees. In 1987 Wisconsin's pioneer mogul in heavy engines, the Allis-Chalmers Corporation, filed under Chapter 11 of the Bankruptcy Code for reorganization with a reported debt of $248.4 million.

PAPER AND PUBLISHING

During the devastating recession from 1979 to 1983, only the paper industry in Wisconsin achieved growth. Wisconsin's 46 mills produced 3.7 million tons of paper annually, or 11.6 percent of the nation's total, the highest of any state. The forest products industry—lumber, wood, and paper—was the second largest employer in the state in 1985, with 76,000 jobs, and the largest in 28 counties; in some northern towns a paper or pulp mill was the only employer.

Wisconsin also ranked first in the diversity of its paper products. Wisconsin's papermakers led the nation in the production of writing paper, laminated and coated process paper, and sanitary tissue products. Wisconsin's Consolidated Papers was the country's leading producer of high-quality coated paper used for magazines and commercial printing. Wisconsin's Fort Howard Paper Company invested $42 million in 1984 to operate the world's widest tissue-making machine.

Recycled paper, which has about 50 different grades, constituted about 25 percent of Wisconsin's papermaking. In 1985 Wisconsin became the national leader by producing 1.4 million tons of recycled paper, the majority of which was cardboard. As early as 1925 there were 13 recycling mills in Wisconsin—6 were rag mills and 7 used paper stock.

The dearth of valuable softwood trees for papermaking remained a concern of Wisconsin's forest industry. Wisconsin was blanketed with softwoods during the nineteenth century, but lumberjacks and forest fires eliminated most of the white pine, spruce, and fir. Modern forest management is by definition a patient industry, since it takes 30 to 40 years to grow trees for commercial use. By 1987 about 42 percent of Wisconsin's land, or 14.5 million acres, was commercial forest land, of which 82 percent was hardwood used for construction millwork and furniture. Only 22 percent of Wisconsin's softwood demands were supplied by Wisconsin's forests, forcing papermakers to import 155 million cubic feet of softwood from Canada or other states.

Wisconsin's leadership in paper was a perfect complement to one of the state's strongest emerging industries—printing and publishing. Wisconsin's industry grew 30 percent from 1969 to 1983, while nationally it grew 17 percent. The majority of Wisconsin's 1,200 companies, which provided 33,000 jobs in 1983, employed about 20 workers, reflecting the national trend. The largest sector was commercial printing, with 13,800 jobs in 1983, followed by newspapers, with 10,700 jobs, and book publishing, with 3,200 jobs. Weekly magazines such as *Time, Newsweek,* and *Sports Illustrated* filled the presses of one of Wisconsin's largest commercial printers, Quad/Graphics. Established in 1971 by Harry Quadracci of Pewaukee, Quad/Graphics demonstrated an ability to

Above
Established in 1867, the Leinen-kugel Brewery of Chippewa Falls had prospered with the lumber town. Times would change after World War I with Prohibition. Courtesy, State Historical Society of Wisconsin

Left
The Whiting paper mill in Mena-sha was part of the rapid growth of paper and pulp mills in Wisconsin during the late nine-teenth century. Courtesy, State Historical Society of Wisconsin

meet weekly deadlines, enabling it to quickly become a major printer of national magazines.

BEER, CHEESE, AND "BRATS"

Although Wisconsin's economic base remained in manufacturing, Wisconsin's national reputation rested on its beer, cheese, and brats. Wisconsin's pioneer reputation for beer and cheese survived into the twentieth century, although beer was no longer the family business it was in the nineteenth century. By 1983 dairy products led food production with more than 17,000 jobs, while meat packing provided 13,400. The beverage industry and the preserved fruits and vegetable sector each employed 9,800 people in 1983.

Modern consumer tastes had changed Wisconsin food production. By 1985 the poultry industry was expected to outpace meat shipments, although high-quality processed meats, such as the proud bratwursts of Sheboygan, still had markets. Madison's Oscar Mayer hotdog, promoted since 1963 by the famous "wiener jingle," continued as a national product. Wisconsin's canning industry was also changing. One of Wisconsin's oldest canning companies, the Larsen Company of Green Bay begun in 1890, began adapting to the consumer's growing preference for frozen vegetables. By the mid-1980s its nine Wisconsin plants were working to meet the goal of a 50-50 mix of frozen and canned vegetables.

Milwaukee's pioneer elixir—beer—had changed the most. National competition and fewer beer drinkers reshaped the beers that made Milwaukee famous. Consolidation turned many of Milwaukee's family breweries into historic anecdotes. Pabst was sold to a California millionaire in 1985; Schlitz's brewery was bought and closed by Stroh's of Detroit in 1982; the Miller brewery was bought by the Philip Morris Company in 1971; after closing in the late 1950s, Blatz was brought back by G. Heileman in 1969. In 1987 G. Heileman was bought by an Australian brewery.

Wisconsin remained a national beer producer in 1986 with Miller, Heileman, and Pabst breweries producing more than 15.6 million barrels. Miller, which ranked second in production after Anheuser-Busch, in 1987 planned to invest $12 million in a new hops plant in Watertown. However, the number of brewery jobs fell during the 1980s, largely due to the Schlitz closing and increased automation. By 1984 Wisconsin breweries employed 5,635 workers, down from 8,814 jobs in 1980.

The brewery begun in the hinterlands of Wisconsin in 1858, G. Heileman's of La Crosse, emerged as the fourth-largest brewer in the country by the mid-1980s. In 1960 the 39th-ranked brewery began acquiring more than one dozen small breweries across the country at favorable prices. By 1983 its breweries were producing about 26 million barrels of beer from Baltimore to San Antonio and Seattle. Combined with its bakery and snack food products, G. Heileman became one of Wisconsin's leading food and beverage producers.

The taste of Europe, which built Milwaukee into Beer City, began returning to some of Wisconsin's small breweries in the 1980s. These boutique beers were made in small batches and sold at import prices, tapping the Wisconsin tradition of pride in the hometown brew. G. Heileman decided to keep Blatz a small producer of custom-made beer, as was Sprecher Brewing of Milwaukee. Hibernia of Eau Claire and Capital Brewery of Middleton produced European-style beers, while Joseph Huber of Monroe became a regional producer of its Augsburger brand. Point Brewery of Stevens Point and Leinenkugel of Chippewa Falls had been well-established local breweries since the 1860s.

Cows remained big business in Wisconsin. In 1985 America's Dairyland produced 1.8 billion pounds of cheese, 35 percent of the nation's total. Wisconsin also led in butter production with 295.6 million pounds, and in condensed milk and whey products. Wisconsin's food processors in 1985 were a diverse group of nearly 1,100 companies, the majority of which employed less than 30 people.

Wisconsin's agricultural prosperity of the 1970s was not expected to return during the 1980s. Overproduction continued, food prices fell, and a strong dollar crippled farm exports. Dairy surpluses caused Congress to cut dairy supports, and farm income spiraled down. In 1983 Wisconsin ranked eighth nationally in farm receipts—small comfort for Wisconsin farmers, who earned an average of $12,756. In three harsh years Wisconsin lost 9,000 farms—in 1982 there were 92,000 farms and by 1985 there were 83,000. More and more farmers sought part-time jobs in the struggle

*Ginseng was a closely guarded
secret for Marathon County
farmers, who began exporting
the temperamental root to the Orient as early as the 1900s.
Growing ginseng is labor intensive and requires four years for
each harvest. Courtesy, State Historical Society of Wisconsin*

to keep their farms. Wisconsin's agriculture was based on medium-sized farms, the average being 213 acres compared to the 1985 national average of 433 acres.

The country's farm crisis also depressed makers of farm machinery, which stymied many Wisconsin manufacturers. Nearly one in four jobs in Wisconsin could be traced to the state's farms, since Wisconsin was also a leading producer of farm machinery and processed food.

In the 1980s Wisconsin farming entered the computer age, where skillful management and marketing was almost as crucial as rain. The traditional jargon of business—capital, cost reduction, demographics, new technology—would be part of the farms that survive, according to the task force that studied agriculture for the Wisconsin Economic Development Commission in 1985.

Some farmers had turned to specialty crops. While only 22 percent of farm revenues came from crops, Wisconsin was first in corn for silage and led the nation in green peas, beets, cabbage, and sweet corn for processing. Wisconsin ranked second in cranberries and third in maple syrup, with mint another specialty.

Some farmers turned to the Orient and invested in ginseng and shiitake mushrooms. Wisconsin's wild ginseng was domesticated by farmers in Marathon County during the early 1900s. Farmers guarded their secrets and exported the temperamental plant to New York and the Orient. By 1985 Marathon County had become the country's ginseng capital, producing more than 1.1 million pounds. Prized in the Orient for medicinal powers, ginseng sold for about $60 a pound in 1980, and farmers were willing to buy the expensive roots and invest the four years it took to produce the first crop. By 1986 overproduction had driven the price of ginseng down to approximately $30. Despite the drop in price, Marathon County exported 97 percent of the nation's ginseng to markets such as Hong Kong and Singapore.

Some agricultural officials were optimistic that shiitake mushrooms could grow into a billion-dollar industry nationally during the 1990s. Wisconsin had the oak suited for the exotic mushrooms, and in 1987 about 300 growers were investing in the spawns, which new techniques allowed to grow within six months. The success of shiitakes would ultimately depend on convincing the American consumer that they tasted better than familiar mushrooms—or that they cut cholesterol levels, as the Japanese believed.

Mink farms remained another Wisconsin specialty. In 1984 Wisconsin led Utah and Minnesota, two leading mink producers, with its 241 mink ranches, which produced 1.2 million of the 4.2 million pelts in the country. It required approximately 40 to 50 mink to produce one full-length mink coat.

BUSINESS GROWTH AND R&D

During the prosperity of the 1970s Wisconsin was considered by many business leaders to have a poor business climate, specifically because of its higher taxes. With the recession the criticsms grew sharper, and in 1983, after vocal criticism about Wisconsin's business climate, Darwin Smith of the venerable paper giant Kimberly-Clark moved his company's world headquarters from Neenah to Dallas, Texas.

Academia rallied to the defense of Wisconsin's business climate. According to William Strang, business professor at the University of Wisconsin-Madison, by objective standards Wisconsin's business climate in 1982 was average—"at worst." Peter Eisinger, professor of political science at the University of Wisconsin-Madison, found in a 1982 study of Fortune 500 companies that there was no clear relationship to tax rates and decisions to move—44 percent of the companies went to areas with lower tax rates, while 44 percent went to areas with higher rates.

Wisconsin was a top-ranking state for many new business opportunities, according to new criteria for measuring business climate devised by the Corporation for Enterprise Development that premiered in 1987. Wisconsin's high employment and income levels made it a good place to work. Although Wisconsin's financial resources such as venture capital were relatively scarce, its work force was high quality, making it more desirable for new and incoming businesses. The report concluded that Wisconsin needed a better partnership between business and state government, but the biggest need for improvement was entrepreneurial energy as measured by self-employment, new business growth, and women and minority business ownerships.

The newer criteria for business climate suggested that perhaps Wisconsin could recapture its "Star of the Snowbelt" stature. The Wisconsin Strategic

Development Commission, the partnership of business leaders and state analysts, concluded that Wisconsin should advertise its exemplary strengths in work force, education, natural resources, and quality of life. Wisconsin residents received a high standard of living in services, schools, and vocational education. The strong work ethic from the early immigrants survived in Wisconsin's reputation for productive workers and squeaky clean government.

Many Wisconsin analysts hoped that if the nation's service industries grew more prominent in the Midwest, Wisconsin could offer quality of life as its trump card. Wisconsin had preserved its natural beauty in parks, ranging from northern woods to city parks and historic preservations. Wisconsin's clean environment and pure groundwater could be found throughout the state, including the industrialized southeastern region. Its tradition of clean government had continued, following the earlier examples set by Robert La Follette's Progressives and Milwaukee's Socialist mayors.

Quality of life also meant that daily life was easier in Wisconsin, according to business professor Dowell Myers at the University of Wisconsin-Madison. Myers, who moved from Texas in 1986, observed that Wisconsin's quality of life made it easier for young families to pursue the American dream. Wisconsin's quality of life included diversity in leisure and recreation, low cost of living and housing, low crime rate, and even the low "hassle factor" of traffic.

The explosive growth of high-tech business was expected to continue in specific industries through 1995, according to analysts for the Wisconsin Strategic Development Commission. The commission pointed to the University of Wisconsin's international research reputation plus its dominance in attracting research funding as obvious advantages for high-tech firms.

In 1984 the National Science Foundation ranked the University of Wisconsin-Madison third nationally among universities in expenditures for R&D firms. Most firms were clustered in Dane County, where the University of Wisconsin-Madison is located. The campus had more than 5,000 research projects, and Wisconsin firms such as Agracetus, Agrigenetics, and Astronautics drew on university resources.

The university's Biotechnology Center, established in 1984, coordinated more than 150 faculty

In 1903 Charles Van Hise, the new president of the University of Wisconsin, proposed that scholars use their knowledge to help state government in problem solving. His proposal was not original; it echoed the advice of two earlier university presidents, John Bascom and Thomas Chamberlain. The Wisconson Idea was born during Van Hise's tenure. Courtesy, State Historical Society of Wisconsin

members in 15 different departments to explore new technology such as food processing and medical technology. Fitchburg's Nicolet Corporation, just south of Madison, worked with faculty in its advancements in hearing aids. In 1983 Fitchburg's Promega Corporation became the first biotechnology company to enter into a joint venture agreement with the People's Republic of China for establishing Chinese manufacture of enzymes.

The university's Wisconsin Center for Applied Microelectronics used faculty research for specific projects of several Wisconsin manufacturers. Dodgeville's Silicon Sensors received help in making devices that transform light into electrical energy. The center also designed new ways for monitoring flashlight batteries for Madison's Rayovac Corporation. Milwaukee's Rexnord Company received help in its pioneering process called X-ray lithography, while researchers were helping to modernize specific instruments of Milwaukee's Johnson Controls.

High-tech seeds also fell in northern Wisconsin. In 1984 two-thirds of the world's renowned supercomputers were designed and built in Chippewa County. Seymour Cray began Cray Research in his hometown of Chippewa Falls in the early 1970s. Although Cray moved his corporate headquarters to Minneapolis, supercomputer building in Chippewa County employed 1,700 people in 1987, rejuvenating the county's sagging economy. In Marinette, Cade Industries made aerospace component parts, and in 1987 Cade Industries was ranked by *Inc.* magazine as fourteenth of the 100 fastest-growing small public companies.

Not all businesses chose to locate in Wisconsin because of the university. Gary Comer of Dodgeville's Lands' End, a successful clothing and catalogue company, explained that he moved his firm from Chicago because "I fell in love with the gently rolling hills and woods and cornfields and being able to see the changing season."

The Old World heritage is still a part of Wisconsin. A 1970s survey revealed that 5 percent of Wisconsin residents were either born in Germany or had parents from Germany. However, 50 percent of the respondents claimed to be of German ancestry. Scandinavian ancestry is also above the national average throughout Wisconsin—La Crosse, Eau Claire, Stoughton, and Mt. Horeb are Norwegian, while Racine has been described as "the most Danish city in America." Wisconsin also has the nation's fifth-largest Polish population, centered mainly in the Milwaukee and Stevens Point areas.

Some of Wisconsin's small businesses have carried on the nineteenth-century tradition of pride in custom work. The W.C. Russell Moccasin Company, which has made handmade boots since its founding in 1898, was bought by Berlin's Bill Gustin in 1927. Resisting the trend of automation, his shoemakers have adapted styles for specialty catalogue companies such as L.L. Bean. In Kewaunee, Joseph Svoboda from Bohemia made church furniture in the 1880s, and a century later the family business, Svoboda Industries, specialized in traditional grandfather clocks; five different styles of clocks were named after Svoboda children. In Sturgeon Bay the Palmer Johnson company gained prominence as the world's largest builder of custom sailing yachts, their reputation for attention to detail impressing such clients as King Juan Carlos of Spain.

Wisconsin's strengths helped to cushion the economic turbulence of the 1980s in business and industry. The state's self-examination that culminated in the Wisconsin Strategic Development Commission reconfirmed the partnership between scholars, state government, and the risk takers of business. The Wisconsin Idea continues to create pathways as divergent as the tastes and opinions of Wisconsin residents.

Wisconsin's greatest strength lies in its diversity, from industry to landscapes and ethnic traditions. The people of this glacial land preserve Wisconsin's Old World values, but they also rely on Wisconsin's progressive tradition of experimenting with new ideas. Wisconsin is still a frontier state of opportunity. Perhaps Wisconsin's most enduring legacy is the pioneer's love for excellence and the optimism that all things are possible if one works hard enough.

The present capitol of Wisconsin was rebuilt in 1907 after a devastating fire in 1904. Among the traditions that have evolved on the capitol grounds are the annual farmer's market, summer evening concerts, and peaceful political demonstrations. Courtesy, Wisconsin Division of Tourism

Left
Fall colors reflecting in a peaceful lake are a pleasant sight enjoyed by Wisconsin residents and visitors alike. Photo by R. Hamilton Smith

Facing page left
A clear blue sky frames this photograph of Julian Bay in the Apostle Islands. Photo by R. Hamilton Smith

Facing page below
A bright sun sparkles through the trees above Trout Lake in Northern Highland State Forest. Photo by R. Hamilton Smith

Below
A Wisconsin sunset is framed by overhanging trees in this R. Hamilton Smith photograph.

Above
The Wisconsin River surges ahead, its quiet beauty a faint reminder of days long past, when fur traders plied its waters in search of their fortunes. Photo by R. Hamilton Smith

Right
Devil's Island is one of the northernmost islands in the Apostle Islands National Shoreline on Lake Superior in northern Wisconsin. Nature wears away at the shoreline, forming strange and beautiful shapes in the rocks. Photo by R. Hamilton Smith

A spectacular Wisconsin sunset reflects its beauty in the wetlands,
as another day comes to a close. Photo by R. Hamilton Smith

Ice fishing is a major winter sport throughout Wisconsin, along-side snowmobiles and cross-country skiing. Courtesy, Wisconsin Division of Tourism

Left
Wisconsin is ribboned by rivers and streams that first gave rise to the lumber industry and now give visitors opportunities for fishing, canoeing, or even whitewater rafting. These rafters enjoy the sport in Florence County. Courtesy, Wisconsin Division of Tourism

Below left
Wisconsin's tourist industry rests on its reputation for conserving its wildlife, resources, and water. Photo by Paul McMahon, courtesy, Wisconsin Division of Tourism

Below
Northern Wisconsin is the nesting place for the Common Loon, the beloved bird whose cry evokes crystal lakes and campfires. Photo by Richard Ver Bust, courtesy, Wisconsin Division of Tourism

Above
An Abbotsford barn, like many barns in Wisconsin, becomes a canvas as well as a place for dairy cows. Courtesy, Wisconsin Division of Tourism

Left
Wisconsin's agriculture land is some of the most productive in the nation. Photo by R. Hamilton Smith

Above
Birch trees cast soft shadows while the sun sets behind a Wisconsin pasture. Photo by R. Hamilton Smith

Right
Clouds promise rain above the windswept Cuex Meadow Wildlife Refuge. Photo by R. Hamilton Smith

Above
Stonefield Village near Cassville in western Wisconsin preserves a nineteenth-century town and the pioneer industries that helped build the frontier. Maintained by the State Historical Society of Wisconsin, this outdoor museum leaves behind the modern world. Photo by Hubert Franks, courtesy, Wisconsin Division of Tourism

Wisconsin's fall foliage is a brilliant spectacle at Lower Dave's Falls in Marinette County. Photo by Dave Heritsch, courtesy, Wisconsin Division of Tourism

Hot air ballons are familiar sights in Wisconsin during the summer, and one of the largest gatherings of hot air ballons occurs at the Wisconsin Dells. However, the quiet spots of Wisconsin's countryside are favorite places for hot air balloons. Photo by Richard Ver Bust, courtesy, Wisconsin Division of Tourism

Among the traditions of Wisconsin's state and county fairs is the promotion of Wisconsin as America's Dairyland. "Alice in Dairyland" is a contest open to young women that is decidedly different
from bathing suit contests. Courtesy, Wisconsin Division of
Tourism

This Eagle River cranberry harvest is part of a Wisconsin specialty that ranks Wisconsin second in cranberry production. Courtesy, Wisconsin Division of Tourism

As home of the Ringling Brothers Circus, Baraboo has since
become the center for the Circus World Museum, which preserves
and performs circus magic. Courtesy, Wisconsin Division of
Tourism

On Saturday mornings the Farmer's Market creates a ring of vegetables, flowers, cheese, and shoppers surrounding the Wisconsin Capitol. Courtesy, Wisconsin Division of Tourism

*Winnebago Indians have preserved many of their centuries-old tradi-
tions. Some of these dances can be seen by visitors at reservations
and also at the Wisconsin Dells. Courtesy, Wisconsin Division of
Tourism*

The Old Schlitz Brewery was commissioned by the New Deal's Federal Art Project, which employed artists during the Great Depression. Painter Paul Lauterbach apprenticed as an artist in Germany before coming to the United States in the 1920s and exhibiting at Milwaukee's Layton Art Gallery. Courtesy, Charles A. Wustum Museum of Fine Arts, Racine

Right
Kikkoman's factory in Walworth produces soy sauce. Kikkoman of Japan, Walworth's parent company, is 300 years old. Courtesy, Wisconsin Division of Tourism

Below
Old-time copper kettle vats used for brewing beer are still on display at the Pabst Brewery in Milwaukee. Modern brewing now favors stainless steel. Courtesy, Wisconsin Division of Tourism

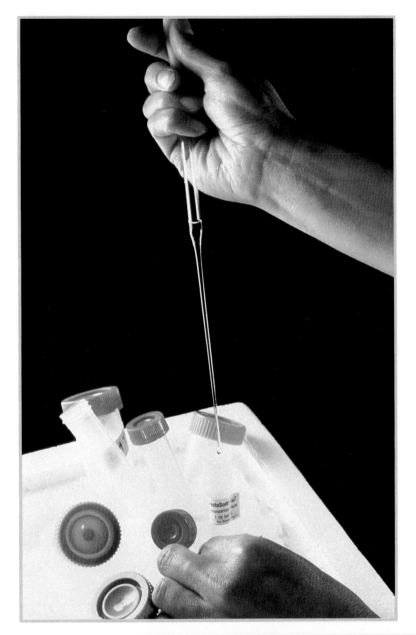

Left
Dispensing enzymes into test tubes is basic to biotechnology, a growing industry in Wisconsin and particularly in Dane County, where companies can draw on the resources of the University of Wisconsin-Madison. Courtesy, Promega

Below
In 1985 Promega of Fitchburg, Wisconsin, became the first company to enter into a joint venture with China to build a biotechnology industry, which would produce enzymes. Chang Chuan, left, was one of the first trainees from China to study with Promega scientists such as Tom Van Oosbree, right. Courtesy, Promega

Above
Founded in 1848, the University of Wisconsin-Madison attracts students from all over the state. Photo by R. Hamilton Smith

Right
While other downtowns have struggled for business, Milwaukee's Grand Avenue Mall has been very successful attracting shoppers with its airy skylights and lighting design, which give a feeling of the Gay Nineties. Courtesy, Wisconsin Division of Tourism

The Birkebeiner cross-country ski race at Telemark Lodge has become a tradition for skiers who enjoy the 55 kilometer trek from Cable to Hayward each February. Courtesy, Wisconsin Division of Tourism

Following page
This 1900 poster advertised the Wisconsin State Fair. Courtesy, State Historical Society of Wisconsin

PARTNERS IN PROGRESS

When people talk about doing business in Wisconsin, some points come up over and over again. The availability of good employees is one; business people in Wisconsin frequently praise the work ethic of their employees. Wisconsin's natural beauty and resources are also a boon. "You couldn't get us out of here with dynamite," Robert Cervenka (Phillips Plastics) insists from his office in the north woods.

The businesses in Wisconsin range from Old World craft industries like Gallun (the only calfskin tannery left in America) to space-age industries like Delco Electronics (which helped put the first man on the moon). Some businesses bear names associated with Wisconsin for many years (Oscar Mayer, Rayovac, Johnson Wax, Wausau Insurance, Peterson Builders, Nekoosa, Mosinee, Weyerhaeuser, Parker Pen).

Newer businesses are setting out to put their names on the national business map also. Harry Quadracci has convinced so many national clients to have their printing done in "some little town in Wisconsin" that companies ranging from *Newsweek* to *Playboy* now know where Pewaukee is.

But it is more than just good products and good ideas that make businesses thrive in Wisconsin. The people who make the products are also a rare find —hard-working, well-educated, skillful. As Marsha Kerley of Peterson Builders put it, "We've got a lot of good people. If we had to turn around and make widgets instead of boats, I think our people would be willing to do that."

Being adaptable to changing times has helped Wisconsin businesses change and grow. "We cannot survive in the past," Donald Taylor (Merrill Manufacturing) insists. "We must always be looking to the years ahead and the future of our company, our employees, and the community."

There have been a lot of changes and adaptations in Wisconsin business since the days when A.O. Smith was called C.J. Smith and Sons and manufactured parts for bicycles and baby carriages. Automobiles, computers, electronics, and all the other inventions that have made modern life possible have also changed the nature of Wisconsin business. The rise in foreign competition has been a recent challenge.

Changing times bring opportunities as well as challenges. A growing population has made possible the growth of new industries like Space-saver Corporation. Changes in the health care field have led to new ways of structuring the businesses of insurance, hospitals, and clinics. Changing laws and changing technologies have led to changes in the utilities industry.

Again and again business people talk about the "quality of life" in Wisconsin. Some mention the lakes; others the rivers, woods, or wildlife; still others the educational system. But whatever their definition, Wisconsin business people agree that whatever "quality of life" is—Wisconsin has it. And Wisconsin's businesses have made their own contribution to the state's development.

The organizations whose stories are detailed on the following pages have chosen to support this important literary and civic project. The civic involvement of Wisconsin's businesses, institutions of learning, and local government, in cooperation with its citizens, has made the state an excellent place to live and work.

WISCONSIN MANUFACTURERS AND COMMERCE

"Even the snow brings a few people to Wisconsin," says James S. Haney, president of Wisconsin Manufacturers and Commerce, which is headquartered just down East Washington Avenue from the capitol in Madison. While he suggests the snow may attract more winter sports enthusiasts than businesses, Haney says that there are many aspects of life in Wisconsin that attract people to live and work in the state.

The work force is one advantage to doing business in Wisconsin. "We probably have as good a work force available to anyone wanting to bring a business in or start a business as anyone anywhere," Haney says. He cites the level and quality of education, both in the university and in the vocational systems, which result in a well-educated work force. In addition to their educational level, Haney also mentions the impressive work ethic among Wisconsin workers.

The quality of life in Wisconsin is another draw for people to live and work in the state. "The quality of life here is almost unequaled," Haney believes. "That makes the area attractive to people."

James S. Haney, president of Wisconsin Manufacturers and Commerce.

A third advantage of doing business in Wisconsin is that the working relationship between business and labor in the state is very good. In addition, the apprenticeship program, which was developed jointly by labor organizations and vocational schools, is "one of the finest apprenticeship programs in the country," Haney asserts.

Haney's interest in the business atmosphere of Wisconsin stems from his role as leader of WMC, a private

nonprofit corporation dedicated to improving business conditions in Wisconsin. WMC has two subsidiaries, the WMC Service Corporation, a for-profit arm that publishes business directories, law handbooks on subjects of interest to Wisconsin businesses, employers' guides, and monthly newsletters, and the WMC Foundation, which includes all the educational programs WMC sponsors. These include Business World, a week-long summer conference for high school students and teachers, as well as safety training programs available to member businesses throughout the state.

WMC was founded in Milwaukee in 1911 as a group representing manufacturers only. The group was then called Wisconsin Manufacturers Association. The first treasurer was F.J. Sensenbrenner, who later became president and chairman of Kimberly-Clark and president of the University of Wisconsin board of regents. Another founder, G.F. Steele of Nekoosa-Edwards Paper Company, said that the purpose of the group was to "guide—in a practical manner on the basis of experience, sound economics, and equity—the evolving economy for the benefit of all." Two other groups that later merged into the renamed Wisconsin Manufacturers and Commerce are the Wisconsin State Chamber of Commerce and the Wisconsin Council of Safety.

Today, nearly 90 years after its founding, WMC has some 3,000 member firms, comprised of approximately 60 percent manufacturers and 40 percent service organizations. Although many of the big businesses in Wisconsin are represented, 80 percent of the members of WMC are small businesses with fewer than 100 employees.

Wisconsin Manufacturers and Commerce remains committed to strengthening the business climate of Wisconsin—despite the snow.

Wisconsin Manufacturers and Commerce headquarters at 501 East Washington Avenue in Madison.

MAUTZ PAINT OF MADISON

"Sometimes I think we have paint in our blood," says Biff Mautz, president of Mautz Paint of Madison. The Mautz family has been selling paint since 1892 and manufacturing it since 1922. More than one million gallons of Mautz paint are sold every year.

Millions of gallons of Mautz paint have been applied "to everything from football fields to space satellites," as Biff Mautz puts it. The third generation of his family to work with paint, Biff helped lead the way in marketing latex paints, which now account for about 80 percent of the company's sales.

When Rudolph and Bernhard M. Mautz opened the first Mautz Paint store on State Street in Madison in 1892, paint came in three colors—white, buff, and barn red. Since then the paint industry has changed enormously, and Mautz Paint has been among the innovators. Biff's father,

Bernie, began manufacturing paint in 1922 in a small plant on Murray Street. Mautz now manufactures about 2,000 different types of paints for the industrial and consumer markets. Mautz is in the top 5 percent of paint manufacturers nationwide.

As Mautz paints have become better known and widely respected, the firm has expanded its facilities and its payroll. The paint factory in Madison (where all Mautz paint is made) now occupies 150,000 square feet on East Washington Avenue. Mautz employs about 225 people, half at the Madison plant and half who work in the field at 31 company-owned retail paint stores.

"Wisconsin and Madison have been very good to us and very good for our firm's growth," explains Biff Mautz. From the factory in Madison, Mautz paints are shipped to clients all over the world, who apply them to everything from satellites, football fields, and corporate offices to zoos, film studios, and hotels.

The company manufactures and distributes both latex and oil-based exterior and interior coatings, as well as deck enamel, traffic-marking paint,

A horse, the mode of delivery in the late 1800s, patiently waits in front of the State Street store, the Mautz family's first venture into the paint business.

industrial enamel to be used on equipment, and even a fungicidal enamel that is used in the food industry.

Four full-time chemists and their assistants are kept busy testing all the batches of paint as they are manufactured. They also develop new formulas for future paints and coatings.

"Quality control is one of the most important facets of paint manufacturing," Biff Mautz emphasizes. None of the paint that Mautz produces is shipped until it has been tested.

As the Mautz family approaches its 100th anniversary in the paint business, there are signs that new family members will pick up the tradition of paint in the blood. Biff's son now works at one of the Mautz Paint stores.

Still headquartered in Madison, Mautz Paint of Madison's manufacturing and finished goods warehousing complex covers most of the city block shown.

MANSION HILL INN

"We've got to have a challenge," says Randall P. Alexander, president of The Alexander Company, Inc., which owns Madison's Mansion Hill Inn. "We can't just go out to the 'burbs and develop strip shopping malls or tract houses." Through their three corporations (The Alexander Company, Preservation Services, Inc., and Alexander Management Company, Inc.) Alexander and his wife, Terri (who is secretary of all the corporations), have renovated or constructed 50 projects since 1981.

Mansion Hill Inn was built in 1858 at 424 North Pinckney Street by Alexander A. McDonnell, who was also the contractor for the second state capitol, the one that burned down in 1904. The architects were August Kutzbock and Samuel Donnel. The house is an ornate example of the Rundbogenstil (round arch) style for which Kutzbock and Donnel were noted.

Between 1858 and 1986, when Alexander's renovation of the house was complete, Mansion Hill Inn had a variety of owners, residents, and reputations. At first the house was a showpiece, "the finest house money could buy," in the words of its first owner, McDonnell the builder. He imported cast iron from Sweden, marble from Carrara, Italy, and colored glass from Venice for his house. The mansion has four stories covering 9,000 square feet. A mahogany spiral staircase leads up to a belvedere that commands a view of the capitol. The mansion was surrounded by a grove of butternut trees, gardens, a wooden sidewalk, and a stable filled with Arabian horses.

The house was sold in 1868 to the Garnhart family. One of the Garnhart daughters married Orasmus Cole, a justice of the Wisconsin Supreme Court; they lived in the house until 1887.

When Sarah Fairchild Dean Conover (Governor Lucius Fair-child's sister) and her husband, a professor of Greek at the University of Wisconsin-Madison, moved into the house in 1887, it entered its heyday. The house became famous as the scene of many elegant dinners and receptions. Sarah's brother, Charles Fairchild, then owned the house for a few years, until he sold it in 1900 to the Griffith family, the last single family to live there.

When the house was sold to Carrie L. Pierce in 1906, it became a fashionable rooming house. Oscar Jensen bought it in 1938 and turned it into apartments. The house was sold in 1955, 1957, and 1967 to various owners. In 1985 The Alexander Company bought it and began a $1.4-million restoration.

There was a lot of restoring to do to make the famous old mansion elegant again. Generations of stu-dents and other transient tenants had parked their bicycles in the hallways and tacked posters to the walls. Air pollution had pitted the original stone carvings. The beautiful inlaid marble floor in the foyer was completely worn out from 130 years of foot traffic. Moldings had crumbled and glass had broken.

But Alexander knew a challenge when he saw one. He says that for years he had said to himself that the mansion "is the neatest building in the city and some day I'm going to buy it."

Alexander set about finding stone carvers, stained-glass artisans,

The Mansion Hill Inn is a $1.4-million restoration of an 1858 Romanesque-revival mansion, now on the National Register of Historic Places. Its charm and elegance is reminiscent of the luxurious, smaller European-style hotels. Photo by Zane Williams

and other crafts people who could restore the building to its original glory, and at the same time make it into a comfortable contemporary European-style city hotel. Alexander's restoration involved details such as tracking down a particular kind of marble first to Prairie du Chien and then to Iowa. At the same time Alexander's staff worked with the Kohler Company to make sure that the Mansion Hill Inn's 11 guest rooms and suites contained the luxurious bathrooms (complete with double whirlpools, skylights, even steam showers) popular in the 1980s.

Mansion Hill Inn opened as a luxury hotel in December 1985. The National Register of Historic Places listed the building. Today there are 11 guest rooms and suites, including the Craftsman Suite, the Garden Room, the Alexander A. McDonnell Room, the August Kutzbock Room, the Turkish Nook, the Sarah Fairchild Conover Room, the James Whistler Room, the Lillie Langtry Room, the Oriental Suite, the Carrie Pierce Room, and the Study. There is also a parlor, a wine cellar, a conference room, and, of course, the belvedere and spiral staircase.

Each of the rooms has been restored to a particular time and style. The Craftsman Suite, for example, is influenced by Gustav Stickley's arts and crafts philosophy of sturdiness and simplicity. In contrast, the Sarah Fairchild Conover Room is in the high Victorian style and is furnished with antiques of the Eastlake School.

Many of the rooms have marble fireplaces, French doors opening onto verandas, high ceilings, and a view of the capitol or Lake Mendota. Other amenities include complimentary continental breakfasts, afternoon tea, and an "honor bar"; whirlpool tubs with stereo headphones; state-of-the-art telephones; queen-size beds; cable television; and full valet service.

Alexander is pleased with the

results of the renovation. He says being a developer is a little like being a trial attorney. "You work on a case for a year and whether you win or lose, it's over." But, he adds, "unlike attorneys, we can savor that victory because we can drive by it."

Other people have also savored Alexander's development victories. His rehabilitation and new construction projects have received awards for

A view of the inn's foyer and parlor. The foyer floor consists of more than 2,000 hand-cut marble pieces. The parlor is furnished in the rococo style, probably most widely recognized as the Victorian look.

The Alexander A. McDonnell Room. Named for the mansion's builder, the elegance of the Empire style is seen in this spacious room with its ornate cornice, polished marble fireplace, tall round-arch windows, and French doors opening onto a veranda.

excellence from The Madison Trust for Historic Preservation, Historic Madison, Inc., Dane County Cultural Affairs Commission, Central Madison Council, Capital Community Citizens, Downtown Madison, Inc., Madison Newspapers, Inc., and *Madison Magazine*.

Randall and Terri Alexander talk about their business all the time; "the real challenge is to try to leave it all at the office," Alexander says. Their two sons, Joseph and Nicolas, are still in grade school, but they've already learned a lot about the family business. "The kids have really picked up a lot of architectural vocabulary," Alexander says. "They can pick out good contemporary architecture as opposed to boxes."

Alexander wants to continue building and restoring projects that are more than just boxes. Development "is an extremely stressful business and very risky," he says. "You have to be very, very careful, but you have to take risks. The more conservative you are, the less aesthetic your development will be. I want to be on the cutting edge."

PHYSICIANS PLUS MEDICAL GROUP

"The state of Wisconsin is a state with a heritage of many excellent group medical practices for three-quarters of a century," says Blake Waterhouse, M.D., president of Physicians Plus Medical Group. Some of the early physicians in Madison, such as the early Jacksons and Quislings, "were really visionaries," Waterhouse says. The group practices they set up many years ago are the foundation of today's Physicians Plus Medical Group, which now includes 180 physicians, as well as 650 non-physician colleagues.

"When the whole group-practice movement began 50 to 60 years ago, it was thought to be totally out of step with organized medicine," says Waterhouse. Until recently there were "many states that didn't have any group practices." When Physi-

The Jackson Clinic was named after Dr. James A. Jackson, Sr. One of the first surgeons in the area, he opened the clinic in 1917 along with four of his sons who were also physicians. Today the clinic is part of Physicians Plus Medical Group and is located downtown, covering 75,000 square feet on West Washington Avenue.

cians Plus Medical Group was formed in 1987, "our goal was to maintain individual patient care but also deal with the future of medical care—which is cost-effective managed health care. You can't do that as individual physicians or a small clinic." In the future "group medicine will become the norm rather than the exception," Waterhouse believes.

Physicians Plus Medical Group is made up of four longtime Madison-area medical groups: Jackson Clinic, founded in 1917; Quisling Clinic, founded in 1935; and Madison Medi-

cal Center and Odana Medical Center, founded in 1969. The larger group practice offers patients "many experienced physicians in multiple convenient locations, all now integrating their care to be more effective for patients," Waterhouse says.

Dr. James A. Jackson, Sr., arrived in Madison in 1853 at the age of 13. He served as a medical assistant in the Civil War and then attended medical school in New York on money his regiment had presented to him at the end of the war. Jackson returned to Madison and established

a medical practice; he was one of the first surgeons in the area.

Four of Jackson's sons became doctors—Reginald H. Sr., James A. Jr., Sydney C. Sr., and Arnold S. Jackson. In 1917 the father-sons group became the Jackson Clinic. By 1922 the clinic had 10 doctors, including non-Jackson family members. The original clinic was located at the corner of Pinckney and Hamilton streets, near the Capitol Square. In 1920 the clinic became affiliated with the old Stoeber Hospital and then with Methodist Hospital; in 1960 the hospital and clinic became independent of each other. In the late 1970s Jackson Clinic expanded from its downtown location. Jackson Clinic-West opened in 1979 and Jackson Clinic-East the following year. The current downtown facility, which covers 75,000 square feet, is on West Washington Avenue.

When the Quisling Clinic was established in 1935, it was also located in downtown Madison, on West Gorham Street. Its downtown clinic is still on the same site, although there have been five building additions since 1935. Quisling Clinic was started by four brothers—Sverre, Abe, Rolf, and Gunnar Quisling. Other staff physicians in the early days were A.D. Anderson, Arch Cowle, Norman Clausen, and William Ylitalo.

In the 1970s Quisling Clinic began to expand with the gradual addition of five new clinic locations. The Middleton clinic opened in 1974, the Waunakee clinic in 1979, the DeForest and Cross Plains clinics in 1981, and the Madison eastside clinic in 1984. The rapid expansion to six locations was in response to the changing medical environment wherein primary care and some specialty services were now coming to the patient, as opposed to the patient having to come to their physician in central Madison.

Board eligibility and certification became a prerequisite for the physician staff in providing quality specialty care.

Odana Medical Center was established in 1969 on its present site on Odana Road, in a building constructed by Marshall Erdman & Associates. By 1969 that part of Odana Road was rural; there were no sidewalks and there was so little traffic people could enter or leave the driveway on Odana Road without checking for cars. Cows grazed the fields next to the clinic.

There have been many changes since 1969. Odana Road is now a busy thoroughfare. Only two physicians—John Batson and Walter Washburn—remain from the original clinic group, along with four of the original employees. Dr. Dennis Oeth joined the group in 1975; Dr. Robert Cole in 1976; and Drs. Robert Kuritz, Bernard Micke, and Richard Schmelzer in 1978. In 1981 Dr. Bradley Manning became affiliated with the group informally.

In 1987 Jackson Clinic, Quisling Clinic, Madison Internal Medicine Associates, and Odana Medical Center joined together in Physicians Plus Medical Group. "The 'Plus' are the patients," Waterhouse says. "Our current configuration is simply an updating to provide even better patient care for the future." The current arrangement allows Physicians Plus to work with patients in the delivery of managed health care, which should be more cost effective. "The real mission of the organization is personalized health care," Waterhouse emphasizes.

Waterhouse is confident that Physicians Plus Medical Group can build on its tradition of long-term strong group medical practices. "We are proud to be part of the Wisconsin heritage of group practices and look forward with optimism to the future."

SPACESAVER CORPORATION

When Theodore W. Batterman acquired the insolvent Staller Cabinet Company, renamed Spacesaver Corporation, in rural Fort Atkinson in 1972, the operation was housed in a barn that covered some 8,000 square feet and employed seven people including the owners. Today the organization employs more than 200 people in three sites totaling 216,000 square feet. All facilities are now located within the city of Fort Atkinson.

Batterman's goal was to use his engineering and management skills—he had been corporate vice-president of Warner Electric Brake & Clutch Company of Beloit, Wisconsin—to develop an independent engineering, marketing, and manufacturing business. He wanted the firm's products to have a proprietary nature to them, and he sought to establish a unique marketing approach.

Not everyone shared Batterman's vision that the corporation he wanted to buy had the potential to realize his goals. When Batterman first applied for a loan to provide capital to operate the company, his loan application was denied by a local bank's loan committee. Batterman went back and requested of the bank president that he be given the opportunity to make a presentation to the loan committee, this time in person, to persuade them to approve his loan. He was successful. The loan committee consequently approved his loan.

Both Batterman and the bank (which has since appointed him a director and a member of its loan committee) are glad he persisted. Spacesaver Corporation's sales growth rate has far exceeded that of U.S. industry, averaging a growth rate since 1972 of 38 percent per year. Earnings have increased every year but one since 1972 and most of the profits have been reinvested in the company's growth. Spacesaver Corporation expanded its facilities nine

*Theodore W. Batterman, president
of Spacesaver Corporation.*

times during this period and acquired a subsidiary company. Its employee growth has more than doubled just since 1984.

Spacesaver has spearheaded the growth of a new industry—high-density, mobile storage units. There are now 20 firms competing in a market that totals approximately $100 million in sales and is growing at a rate of more than 15 percent annually. Spacesaver is by far the largest in the field. There are currently 14,000 Spacesaver systems in use.

Spacesaver systems range from very small, five feet long or less, for private offices to several hundred feet long for industrial applications. Load capacities range from less than a few hundred pounds to more than 250 tons. Spacesaver concentrates on 17 different user markets, including agricultural, fishing, and forestry; mining; construction; manufacturing; transportation; communications; public utilities; wholesale trade; retail trade; finance and real estate; insurance; professional services; health care; education; museums; architects and engineers; and public administration.

What Spacesaver offers to all of these diverse customers is a product to save on the increasingly expensive cost of space, particularly space required for storage and filing. Spacesaver systems, which eliminate the need for aisles between storage shelves, can store more than 100 percent more in the same space as traditional storage units. In addition to greatly reducing the space required for storage, these systems also sharply reduce the costs of construction, energy, and maintenance, and also improve operational productivity.

Spacesaver's marketing success is contributed directly to a unique marketing concept that has a network character all of its own defined as the Spacesaver Group. Sales, installation, and service functions are carried out by this network of small independent businesses (Spacesaver local area contractors). The product engineering, manufacturing, and marketing functions are concentrated in a separate but also small business (Spacesaver Corporation). This combination of small businesses networking together with a common purpose and commitment to each other provides a marketing strength of a much larger corporate network, but yet maintains the entrepreneurial flexibility of a smaller business.

After being nominated by the Fort Atkinson Chamber of Commerce, Batterman was recognized as Wisconsin's Small Business Person of the Year for 1985. This award is sponsored by the United States Small Business Administration and the Small Business Administration Advisory Council of Wisconsin, the Independent Business Association of Wisconsin, National Federation of Independent Businesses in Wisconsin, Wisconsin Association of Manufacturers and Commerce, and the Wisconsin Chamber of Commerce Executives Association. As a continued commitment to small business,

The barn that originally housed the fledgling Spacesaver Corporation.

Batterman served as a delegate from the State of Wisconsin to the White House Conference to Small Business in 1986 and was a member of the Governors Steering Committee for the Governor's Conference on Small Business for the State of Wisconsin in 1987.

Batterman attributes his success in launching a new industry to his entrepreneurial spirit. Even when he was very young, his mother and father put him in business with a roadside stand, selling produce from their garden. "They taught me how to run it," he says, "and business has been in my blood ever since.

"I have a basic desire for independence, which promotes the desire to utilize the talents that God has given me to achieve a dream."

Spacesaver Corporation has a continued commitment to growth. In 1987 it successfully put into operation its $7-million, state-of-the-art metal fabrication facility. In 1988 Spacesaver's corporate officers, Don Branz, secretary/treasurer and chief financial officer, and John Sattel, vice-president of operations, along with Batterman began planning additional new construction for 1989 to consolidate and expand all operations on a 37-acre site on the south end of the city of Fort Atkinson. Spacesaver has found that the city of Fort Atkinson has always been extremely progressive in supporting industry and creating a good economic environment, particularly for small business.

Spacesaver has spearheaded the growth of a new industry—high-density mobile storage units. Pictured here is one of Spacesaver's electric model high-density mobile storage systems. Spacesaver systems eliminate the need for aisles between storage shelves, and can store more than 100 percent more in the same space as traditional storage units.

WISCONSIN PHYSICIANS SERVICE

WPS is a service insurance corporation headquartered in Madison, Wisconsin, organized and regulated under Wisconsin laws and regulations. It was established in 1946 under the auspices of the State Medical Society of Wisconsin, which traces its history and tradition of medical service to Wisconsin residents to a time well before Wisconsin attained statehood.

The establishment of WPS was a direct outgrowth of an experiment by the State Medical Society called the Wisconsin Plan. Under the Wisconsin Plan, participating insurance companies were required to meet certain insurance benefits criteria before receiving the endorsement of the State Medical Society.

The physicians' purpose in establishing WPS was to provide a realistic insurance program for the reimbursement of medical care. The policies initially sold by WPS were "fee schedule" policies, i.e., benefits under the policies were determined

The Wisconsin Physicians Service (WPS) corporate headquarters at 1800 Engel in Madison. The building is called the Ray Koenig Building after WPS' late president.

Much of WPS' claims-processing operations are done here at the Broadway Building in Madison (below).

The lobby of the Broadway Building (bottom). Many times customers come in to see the WPS staff and personally discuss their claims.

by schedules of fees for medical and surgical procedures. The major portion of the schedule was included in the policy. Under this plan, physicians who elected to participate agreed to accept as payment in full for insureds who fell below a certain specified income level the schedule of fees provided under the policies. The insureds paid premiums to WPS, and WPS administered the insurance plan and guaranteed payment of fees to the physicians.

Initially WPS employed a handful of people, insured approximately 1,000 individuals and families, and made available two insurance plans; today, in its 42nd year of operation, WPS employs 2,300 people, processes 11.4 million health benefits claims annually, including benefit plans it administers but does not insure, and offers a full range of insurance benefit plans and administrative services. It also organized a wholly owned subsidiary life insurance company—The EPIC Life Insurance Company—to offer life insurance plans.

A significant portion of WPS' work force is involved in the administration of government health benefits programs—Medicare Part B in the State of Wisconsin, and the Civilian

Health and Medical Program of the Uniformed Services (CHAMPUS) in 12 states and the District of Columbia, covering retirees and dependents of active duty military personnel.

"WPS has had a record of innovation and leadership in health care benefit developments," says Mahlon Bontrager, president and chief executive officer. For example, as far as WPS can determine, it offered the first insurance plan with no fee schedule, i.e., paying "usual, customary, and reasonable" fees beginning in the 1950s; today nearly every health insurance company uses this approach. In the early 1970s WPS attracted national attention by the establishment of its Health Maintenance Program (HMP), which in most respects is what today is known as a Health Maintenance Organization based on the Independent Practice Association model. When the federal Medicare program became effective in 1966, WPS offered an in-

WPS employs 2,300 people and processes 11.4 million health benefit claims annually.

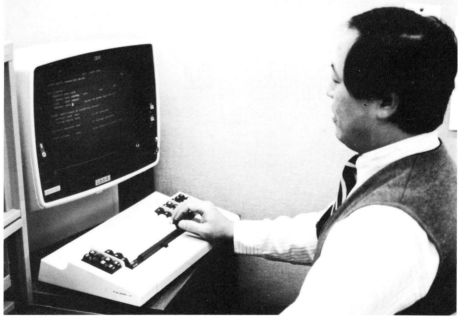

WPS relies on up-to-date automated systems for its claims, but also recognizes the value of its people and the personal touch that they provide.

surance plan to cover the Medicare "gaps" that many believed was the best and most comprehensive in the nation.

In addition to the two office buildings in the South Towne area in Monona and the one on Sherman Avenue in Madison that WPS owns, it currently leases office space in two locations in the Madison area, and is planning construction of a third building in the South Towne area; it also has sales and service offices in Milwaukee, Green Bay, Wausau, Kenosha, Appleton, Eau Claire, and La Crosse. "But our greatest resource is our employees," according to Bontrager. "People really make the difference for any organization but especially so for a labor-intensive, service organization such as ours."

WROUGHT WASHER MFG., INC.

A washer might seem to be just a slug with a hole in it, but washers are indispensable to the function of almost every machine or device with moving parts. Washers are so crucial, in fact, that the lack of a washer costing a penny can shut down a million-dollar machine.

Wrought Washer Mfg., Inc., has been making washers in Milwaukee since Fred Doepke founded the company in 1887 in a building measuring 30 feet by 60 feet. The firm was first called the Nut & Washer Mfg. Co.; later it became known as Milwaukee Wrought Washer. The early equipment was not very sophisticated. Every washer was laboriously produced by hand feed, which limited the output of the plant to approximately one ton per day.

Doepke realized that he needed more efficient machinery in order to supply the rapidly increasing demand. He designed new equipment and expanded the company's physical plant. In 1901 the first unit of the present plant on South Bay Street was built.

Doepke was an inventor and an optimist. In 1933, in the depths of the Depression, he explained his business philosophy: "In my business experience I have made practically every extensive improvement in our plant when everybody else had cold feet. I prefer to remain an optimist."

After Doepke died in 1934, the Doepke family continued as owners of the firm until they sold it in 1974 to Walter F. Borgess and his son, William. Jerome Fritsch purchased Wrought Washer from the Borgesses in 1981. And, in 1986, E.G. Pruim, with R.W. Allsop and Assoc. (a venture capital firm based in Cedar Rapids, Iowa), purchased the company from Fritsch.

Pruim, like founder Doepke, is an optimist. "As long as we can serve customer needs by providing a high-quality, low-cost product, we'll have sales," he says. "The customer is

E.G. Pruim (pictured here) purchased, along with R.W. Allsop and Associates, Wrought Washer in 1986.

number one, and we think we have the talent to service his needs."

Today Wrought Washer processes some quarter-million pounds of metal per day. About 45 percent of the steel processed is used for standard washers and 55 percent for custom and contract steel stampings.

The quality-control program at Wrought Washer meets or exceeds the quality standards of nuclear construction, some of the most stringent requirements a manufacturer will ever have to meet. Through statistical process control and operator involvement in manufacturing the product, the company monitors its manufacturing process from the beginning. Wrought Washer also satisfies ASTM, MIL-SPEC, SAE, and ANSI standards.

Wrought Washer today employs 235 people in its 220,000-square-foot facility (which has been enlarged many times since 1901). Annual sales total $20 million. The firm has more than 160,000 tool sets in inventory, so it can often provide cus-

tomers with an unusual washer without the expense of a new tool set. The corporation also maintains a large inventory of .010 through .750 thick steel, as well as substantial quantities of other materials.

The operation produces both metallic and nonmetallic washers. Metallic stampings include hot and cold rolled steel, high-carbon and alloy steels, spring steels, stainless steels, brass and all-copper-base alloys, lead, zinc, aluminum, and precious metals. Nonmetallic washers include fiber, nylon, and Bakelite. Wrought Washer has numerous specially designed, high-production stamping presses from 30 to 550 tons; they stamp at 16 to 300 strokes per minute. Size capabilities range from outside diameters of 5/32 inches all the way up to 26 inches. Gauges range from .010 to .750.

Wrought Washer puts a rust-resistant treatment on all plain-finish washers. Other available finishes include zinc plating with blue brite chromate (for added corrosion protection and better appearance), cadmium, phosphate, nickel, hot galvanizing, anodizing on aluminum, and passivation for stainless steel.

In 1986 Wrought Washer purchased Luebke Corporation of Brookfield, Wisconsin, from Dane and Greg Luebke. Luebke Corporation was founded by the Luebkes' father, Arthur, in 1945 as a contract screw machine business. When the sons took over the company in 1977, they changed its direction to more sophisticated contract machining. They sold the screw machines and purchased new multifunctional machining and turning centers. In 1982 Luebke Corporation developed a series of manufacturing cost-reduction services, in addition to its contract machining business, which today are the main focus of its operations. The Luebke subsidiary employs 60 people and has annual value-added sales

As part of Wrought Washer's growth and expansion, the firm purchased the Luebke Corporation in 1986. This subsidiary provides a series of manufacturing cost-reduction services in addition to its contract machining business. Pictured here is the Luebke Corporation headquarters.

product to our customers at a low cost with high quality in a short period of time." Pruim points to the capability and Wrought Washer's high standards of quality control as special pluses for the firm. Producing wash-

ers for the nuclear industry and other high-technology industries is challenging—especially when a washer can be crucial to the proper functioning of a million-dollar piece of equipment.

of more than $5 million.

Pruim sees many challenges ahead for Wrought Washer Mfg. Inc. "Other people can make what we do," he points out. But, he adds, "there is a good group of people in the area that can be relied on to design, manufacture, and deliver the

Located on the site of the original 1901 Wrought Washer facility, the Wrought Washer plant today has 220,000 square feet of space, processes approximately a quarter-million pounds of metal per day, and employs 235 people.

PARKER PEN USA LIMITED

Playwright George Bernard Shaw, General Douglas MacArthur, poet Carl Sandburg, Queen Elizabeth II, architect Frank Lloyd Wright, author Sir Arthur Conan Doyle, and U.S. Presidents Eisenhower, Kennedy, Nixon, and Reagan are just a few of the notables who have used Parker pens to help make their mark in history since George S. Parker devised his first fountain pen in Janesville, Wisconsin, in 1888.

Since that time Parker's quality writing instruments—which went from Janesville to the world—have been used routinely by millions of people around the globe for an infinite range of writing duties. Parker pens have been used for the great signings of world peace, the penning of poetry, the declarations of freedom for whole nations, and the composition of a simple shopping list. George S. Parker set out to make pens that would exemplify quality, craftsmanship, reliability, and the assurance of writing with the best writing instruments available. Parker's early goals are still the goals of the company today. Demand for Parker writing instruments continues to grow. Today they are sold in more than 150 nations.

Parker was born November 1, 1863, the son of pioneer parents who crossed the country from New England to Wisconsin and Iowa in the mid-nineteenth century. As a young man Parker decided to begin a career in telegraphy. He saved up $55 for tuition and moved to Janesville to become a student at the Valentine School of Telegraphy.

Within a year Parker was hired to teach at the school. To supplement his small income, he obtained the agency to sell John Holland pens to his students as a sideline. Parker was soon discouraged because the pens he sold needed frequent repair. He decided that he could make a better pen and began developing an

Parker advertising of the 1920s broadcast the results of torture tests proving the durability of the Parker Duofold pen. Introduced in 1921, the pen helped quadruple sales by 1926.

improved ink-feed bar with his pen-repair tools.

Parker patented his better writing system on December 10, 1889. Three years later, after arranging a financing deal with his lifelong friend and partner, W.F. Palmer (an insurance salesman), The Parker Pen Company was incorporated.

In 1894 the young company achieved a major milestone when Parker patented the most effective fountain pen-feed system available at that time. Parker's Lucky Curve feed was designed to drain ink back into the reservoir by capillary attraction when the pen was upright in the pocket of its owner.

In 1903 Parker convinced a shopkeeper in Copenhagen named Olsen to carry his pens. This was the first of a system of foreign distributorships that has become the envy of companies many times the size of Parker.

Sales increased dramatically when Parker earned the U.S. War Department's contract to sell his famous Trench Pen during World

War I to soldiers who needed a pen with a portable ink plant for writing letters in the field. The Trench Pen featured black pigment pellets that converted water into ink in the barrel of the pen.

In 1921 Parker launched the Duofold pen, which had twice the ink capacity of pens of the day—and it was offered in a burnt-orange color when most pens were staid black. The Big Red, as it was called, was promoted dramatically. It was dropped from planes and tall buildings to prove its durability. The Big Red helped quadruple sales by 1925. The Duofold was reintroduced in 1988 with the latest state-of-the-art technology as the Duofold Centennial to mark the company's first 100 years of business.

In 1924 Parker opened a subsidiary in England. That operation has prospered and today, at Newhaven, East Sussex, it houses the corporate headquarters and is the location of one of the company's two main manufacturing plants (the other is in Janesville).

To counter the lag in sales during the Depression, Parker, in 1933, launched the see-through Vacumatic pen, which boasted a new arrow-shape pocket clip that was to become the firm's most notable trademark.

Writing instruments produced at Parker's Janesville, Wisconsin, plant are sold in more than 150 nations. The company was founded in Janesville in 1888.

Parker will mark its centennial in 1988 with the reintroduction of the 1920s Duofold pen as the Duofold Centennial, using the latest in writing technology. The fountain pen is making its comeback in the United States as the writing instrument for those who prefer classic accessories and what has come to be known as the "power signature."

From the Parker Pen Archives
Italian composer Giacomo Puccini composed the opera La Boheme with a Parker around 1896.
Sir Arthur Conan Doyle created the famous Sherlock Holmes character and wrote his popular mysteries with a Parker in the late nineteenth century.
George Bernard Shaw used a Parker to pen the play, Pygmalion, in 1912.
In 1939 a young writer, Robert L. May, used his Parker to draft the original storyline for Rudolph the Red-Nosed Reindeer. Commander-in-chief of the Allied Forces in Europe, General Dwight D. Eisenhower used his Parkers to sign an end to World War II in Europe in 1945. Later that year General Douglas MacArthur used his Parker to conclude the war in the Pacific. Artist Norman Rockwell was commissioned by Parker to create art for magazine advertising in the late 1950s.
President Richard Nixon presented Chinese officials, during his historic 1972 journey to the Peoples Republic, Parker pens with traces of lunar dust brought back by the Apollo 15 astronauts. In December 1987 sterling custom-produced Parker 75 pens were used by General Secretary Mikhail Gorbachev and President Ronald Reagan to sign the treaty to ban nuclear missiles throughout Europe. The pens were used 16 times for signatures and counter-signatures and then exchanged ceremoniously as a gesture of accord.

George S. Parker died in 1937, but the company continued to grow under the leadership of his sons, Kenneth and Russell, and grandsons, Daniel and George.

In 1941 the famous Parker 51 line was introduced. Characterized by its sleek profile and new Lucite barrel, the 51 became Parker's flagship line of the 1940s and 1950s. It has been named one of the all-time best-designed U.S. consumer products.

The early ball pens of the late 1940s were of dismal quality. Parker finally entered the ball pen race in 1954 with a superior product, the Parker Jotter. In 1957 Parker introduced a major improvement—a porous tungsten carbide writing ball for blob-free, skip-free writing. The T-Ball Jotter refill has since become the industry standard.

Parker constructed a manufacturing plant on the north side of Janesville in 1953 and moved its American manufacturing operations there. The Janesville plant currently manufactures products for the Americas and Asia-Pacific markets.

Parker continued its product innovation in the 1960s, 1970s, and 1980s. Important new lines include the Parker 61, Parker 75, Parker Classic, Systemark (with the writing mode of the future, the new liquid ink roller ball refill), and the modern Parker Arrow (introduced in 1981).

During the 1970s company management initiated a diversification program into the leisure and temporary help fields. The 1976 acquisition of Manpower, Inc., proved to be most fortuitous. Manpower's annual sales mushroomed from roughly $300 million to nearly $900 million by 1986. The writing instrument business was sold in February 1986 to a group of Parker's British managers and an investment group for approximately $100 million.

In the early 1980s a major renovation of the Newhaven and Janesville plants was implemented, with Janesville operations designed to produce Jotters and the new Vector pens on fully automated lines.

Parker Pen Limited is now a privately held British company with writing instrument sales that grew from some $165 million to more than $205 million during the first year of new ownership. Parker today sells its pens in more than 150 nations by way of some 90 subsidiaries and distributorships. It is the leading brand in six of the top 10 global markets. Parker's 2,800 employees produce approximately 50 million quality writing instruments and 32 million refills each year.

As the company notes its centennial in 1988, it is a tribute to George S. Parker that his writing instruments have truly become the pens that write in any language.

NATIONAL GUARDIAN LIFE INSURANCE COMPANY

"What makes a company," says Lawrence J. Larson, chairman and chief executive officer of National Guardian Life Insurance Company, "is people who work together and want to see it grow." Larson has had a chance to watch National Guardian Life grow ever since he began work there as a junior accountant many years ago.

When National Guardian Life (then called the Guardian Life Insurance Company) opened for business in a little room on the first block of East Washington Avenue in Madison in 1910, its assets barely totaled $175,000. Today the firm has assets totaling more than $300 million.

National Guardian Life's employees have approached their task of selling and servicing life insurance, disability income, and annuities with both diligence and imagination. One early agent, Archie Hurst, went door to door on a bicycle to tell potential customers about his product.

Another early agent, George Sennett of Janesville, advertised his insurance business on the screen during silent movies. His slogan (perhaps playing on the similarity of his name to Mack Sennett's) was "See Sennett Soon." One of Sennett's competitors was more clever still, though. He bought space on the same screen to advertise "See Bill Smith now; soon may be too late."

The diligence of National Guardian Life's employees has resulted in outstanding growth for the company over the years. Under the guidance of George A. Boissard, president of the firm from 1910 to 1944, NGL outgrew its offices several times. NGL moved first to the Bank of Wisconsin building (now M&I Bank of Madison) on the Capitol Square. Then it moved to the Wisconsin Power & Light building (now the Hovde Building) on West Washington Avenue. Then, in 1941, the company built its own headquar-

George A. Boissard was president of National Guardian Life Insurance from 1910 to 1944.

ters—a three-story structure at 142 East Gilman Street.

National Guardian Life, which adopted its present name in 1920, has continued to grow in the years since George Boissard was president. Richard S. Boissard was president from 1944 to 1957; Lawrence J. Larson was president from 1957 to 1969 and chief executive officer since then; J. Clayton Howdle was presi-

dent from 1969 to 1974; and John D. Larson has been president since 1974.

NGL's sales today are in excess of $400 million. The firm is licensed in 31 states and its insurance in force exceeds $4 billion. Benefits provided to policyholders, beneficiaries, and people who receive annuities exceeded $66 million in 1987.

NGL continues to grow and now has 550 employees—400 agents and a staff of 150—in the home office in Madison. The firm moved to its present building at 2 East Gilman Street in 1965, where the home office staff enjoys a hilltop view of Lake Mendota.

"Life insurance is the greatest way in the world for people to save and protect things for themselves," says Larson. But, he adds, "Our product has to be sold; nobody buys it."

For more than 75 years National Guardian Life Insurance Company has been dedicated to "caring today about your financial tomorrow."

The home office of National Guardian Life Insurance at 2 East Gilman Street in Madison.

SNAP-ON TOOLS CORPORATION

"Corporations today will succeed only when change and improvement become a permanent way of thinking, and even a way of life," says William B. Rayburn, chairman and chief executive officer of Snap-on Tools Corporation. And, he adds, "the nuts and bolts of change still come down to how well and how quickly employees can absorb, accept, and implement change."

Nuts and bolts themselves have had a lot to do with Snap-on Tools

Sixty-eight years ago Joseph Johnson and William A. Seidemann founded Snap-on Tools by improving and innovating mechanics' tools.

Corporation's success. In the past 68 years the *Fortune* 500 firm has grown from two men with an idea to a large company with worldwide sales totaling $750 million. Snap-on markets a product line of 10,000 items, ranging from wrenches and pliers to metal storage cabinets and electronic testing equipment.

Snap-on's success over the years has relied on change and improvement in order to keep up with an evolving marketplace. From the very beginning 25-year-old Joseph Johnson wanted to offer an improved product to mechanics. Johnson looked at existing mechanics' socket wrenches, one-piece units with a socket permanently affixed to the handle, and wondered if they could be improved. Johnson wondered why a mechanic had to buy a handle for every socket. He set out to improve mechanics' tools by developing a set with five different handles and 10 sockets that would attach to provide a mechanic with 50 different combinations.

Johnson was working for American Grinder at the time, and he offered his employer the use of the idea. But American Grinder was not interested; the company believed it

Today the company's 10,000-plus products are distributed by 4,600 independent Snap-On dealers in 120 countries.

could make more money by manufacturing 50 wrenches per mechanic rather than 10 sockets and five handles. But Johnson still believed in his idea, and he enlisted the help of a co-worker, William A. Seidemann. The two men agreed that interchangeable sockets had the potential of universal acceptance by professional auto mechanics.

Johnson and Seidemann used crude bending jigs and muscle power to make a sample set of five handles with interchangeable sockets. They developed the slogan "Five Do the Work of Fifty" and soon found themselves with 500 C.O.D. orders and no way to fill them. They found some financial backers, incorporated the venture as the Snap-on Wrench Company in 1920, and moved into a rented building in Milwaukee.

A new idea in distribution was almost as important to the success of the Snap-on Company as the new wrench design. Stanton Palmer and Newton Tarble formed the Motor Tool Specialty Company in 1920 in order to distribute Snap-on tools. Their sales method was to approach mechanics directly, at their place of work. In addition to generating a lot of sales, this method allowed mechanics to tell Motor Tool directly about new products they were interested in acquiring. Motor Tool began distributing new tools under the name Blue-Point Tool Company. Eventually Blue-Point merged with Snap-on. The merged corporations moved to Kenosha in 1931.

The Snap-on name has come to be a symbol for mechanics. "It's kind of a badge to own the best tools," says Rayburn. "Mechanics work with a wrench or a screwdriver in their hand all day long and are serious about their livelihood. Our unparalleled success in the hand-tool industry proves that the demand for quality products and conscientious service will never change."

MOTOR SPECIALTY, INC.

When Henry E. Lund (along with investors George Forwark and Leo J. Orth) founded Motor Specialty, Inc. (MSI), in 1947, the firm's eight employees made motors for sewing machines as well as armatures and fields for large hair dryers. Today MSI's 125 employees make 12 different models (plus variations) of motors for a wide variety of applications. MSI's distinctive mottled grayish-silver fractional horsepower motors are used in vending machines, centrifuges, electric scroll saws, doctors' cast cutters, dentists' drills, portable whirlpools, electric door openers, and specialty ice cream machines.

These changes in MSI's business have come about to accommodate the changing needs of the company's customers. MSI works directly with its customers to develop motors for specific applications. "Customers come to us knowing they need a motor," says Robert Frank, who has been president of the privately held company since 1985. "We work with them to identify what type of motor will do the job for them. We're selling our engineering and technical knowledge along with our motors." Frank believes that the people who work at MSI help account for the company's success. "The product is very common," he says. "What we give our customers is service and attention."

MSI has made a deliberate decision to stay in Wisconsin. The firm quickly outgrew its original storefront

Henry Lund, founder of Motor Specialty, at his desk in the 1950s.

An employee dinner given by Motor Specialty in January 1960.

on State Street in Racine and then its 18th Street plant. Before the present manufacturing plant was built on Lathrop Avenue in 1959, Lund was approached with attractive state-sponsored industrial development offers from Alabama, Mississippi, and Nebraska. Lund said the decision to stay in Racine was based on the presence of a skilled and long-term work force. MSI was concerned that its loyal employees would face economic troubles if the company decided to leave Racine. The plant on Lathrop Avenue has grown to 57,000 square feet.

Lund, a native of Denmark who emigrated to America at the age of six, attended the Milwaukee School of Engineering and was a draftsman and engineer. He worked for other companies from 1926 to 1947, when he founded MSI. By 1957 Lund had bought out his two partners and was the sole owner of the operation.

Lund was president of MSI until he died in 1980. His wife, Florence, was vice-president of the company until her death in 1986. Their son, Phillip, was president of the firm from 1980 until he died in 1985. Today Florence and Henry Lund's oldest daughter, Jean Keiser, is vice-president/finance. Two of the Lunds' other daughters, Joan Sargent

and Carolynn Bass, work at MSI; their fourth daughter, Lynn Lund, is on the board. The four sisters own the company, which has annual sales of $5.5 million.

Various MSI employees are involved in the Lakefront Redevelopment, Kiwanis, the Boy Scouts of America, YWCA, the American Cancer Society, Big Brothers, Children's Hospital, Racine Rotary, and Junior Achievement.

Motor Specialty, Inc., plans to continue to grow. Says Frank, "We plan to grow at a nice controlled rate of growth, continuing to offer our customers what they want."

Motor Specialty's 40th anniversary ceremony took place in August 1987. Pictured here (from left) are Joan Sargent, owner and employee; Jean Keiser, owner and employee; Robert Frank, president; Lynn Lund, owner; and Carolynn Bass, owner and employee.

MULCAHY & WHERRY, S.C.

Mulcahy & Wherry was founded in 1966 in a small office in downtown Milwaukee with Charles Mulcahy its sole practitioner. Now one of the leading law firms in the state, the firm provides legal services through its regional offices located in Milwaukee, Eau Claire, Green Bay, Madison, Oshkosh, Sheboygan and Wausau.

The seven-office network is organized by practice areas into divisions: business, civil litigation, management labor relations, public finance, public law, and tax law. Shareholders, associates, and research associates staff each division, and when a case requires more than one expertise, a team approach is employed.

The Business Division has developed its general corporate and business practice through its work in business formation, mergers, acquisitions, commercial real estate, health care, bankruptcy, creditors' rights, and international business transactions. Through his roles as president of the Wisconsin World Trade Center and Honorary Consul of Belgium, division head and firm president Charles Mulcahy promotes international trade and economic development for Wisconsin.

Litigation is a major practice area of the firm. The Litigation Division represents both plaintiffs and defendants in personal injury and negligence cases, contract and complex commercial disputes and public issues, labor litigation, and appeals before state and federal courts and government agencies. Headed by Michael Wherry, the division has drawn national attention for prevailing in a landmark decision concerning access to sunlight for the purpose of solar energy and for its expertise in aircraft-related litigation.

The Labor Division represents employers in business, industry, government, and education, and is well known for its work in all aspects of management labor relations. The firm has authored a number of labor-related books, including *Comparable Worth: A Negotiator's Guide, Strike Prevention and Control Handbook* and *Public Sector Labor Relations in Wisconsin.*

The Public Finance Division is

Mulcahy & Wherry name partners Charles Mulcahy (below left) and Michael Wherry (below right).

nationally recognized bond counsel, providing opinions on all forms of general obligation, revenue, industrial revenue, and tax incremental financing obligations. The Public Law Division coordinates matters between private business and government, concentrating on general municipal, regulatory, administrative, and environmental law, land-use planning, and legislative matters.

In 1985 the tax firm of Meldman, Case & Weine, Ltd., merged with Mulcahy & Wherry. The Tax Division provides counsel on tax planning, audits and related litigation, criminal, foreign and state/local government tax matters, as well as personal, estate, and financial planning and employee benefits. Division members authored two editions of *Federal Taxation Practice and Procedure,* currently used in law schools nationwide.

Service with many statewide civic organizations, holding elected or appointed positions in government, and active participation in national, state, and local professional associations round out Mulcahy & Wherry's dedication to the practice of law and to public service.

GREENHECK FAN CORPORATION

"For a dream comes through much activity"
Ecclesiastes 5:3

One assumes that Bernard A. Greenheck and his brother Robert C. Greenheck never had a dream 40 years ago of building one of the largest businesses of its kind in the country. There is no doubt—for history demonstrates—that there was much activity.

The beginning of Greenheck Fan Corporation is the story of two men—one a salesman and marketeer, the other an engineer and a maker of things. Two brothers working together—succeeding where other like siblings would fail—because they believed in a simple axiom: "I don't want to have my own way, I want to succeed." And yet, if one follows in thoughtful steps the development of the company, one is led to believe that neither man thought much of future success. Success, if one is to call it that, flowed through a natural sequence of many dreams, tiny ideas, trial and error, hard-fought successes, painful failures. The story of the

business is to be found in the history of entrepreneurship.

The beginning in 1948 was tiny, unnoticed, obscure. An acre of land for $500, a block building of 3,200 square feet, a pitiful lot of hand tools—a tenuous launching, indeed.

But start they did, offering their services and skill in metal forming to any customer willing to hire them—metal doorstep boxes to house milk deliveries, milk tanks, and cage parts for the areas' rapidly growing mink farms. Their ability and willingness to produce innumerable metal products for a growing list of customers produced gross sales of $30,000 in the first year of business.

The company grew and prospered, though the going was slow, painful, and difficult. By 1951 it had

---

The corporate offices of Greenheck Fan Corporation are located near the extensive Schofield, Wisconsin, Industrial Park. Four of the company's five plants are also located in the park. The fifth plant is located in Ivyland, Pennsylvania. This building houses the offices of finance, sales, marketing, personnel, "The Center"—a seminar auditorium, and the heart of the company's computer network.

grown from a very few employees to eight, manufacturing furnace duct work and related products.

In the mid-1950s the firm made a significant step forward, destined to shape its future—the manufacture of the rooftop ventilator. This fan would prove to be the ancestor for one of the most complete lines of air moving products in the United States. The firm was incorporated as Greenheck Fan and Ventilator Company to emphasize its thrust toward air movement and particularly its development of rooftop ventilators. Robert, who had taken time out to earn his engineering degree, returned to the business to take charge of product development and manufacturing.

Bernard, in the meantime, traveled the country setting up an effective group of manufacturer representatives to sell the products of this small, unknown firm in Schofield, Wisconsin. This crisscrossing of industrial America was the university of on-the-job learning that Bernard entered into with great enthusiasm, using the time to learn the industry, to know the people in the industry, the

products needed, and the competition. This was a most difficult way to learn, as Bernard would later testify, but there was no other way.

Late in the 1950s the brothers were joined by Lawrence Grade, who added his financial expertise to running the company. The firm then moved forward with this unique trio, believing in a simple dictum: Risk failure bravely; view success positively; expect to succeed.

The firm grew steadily and dramatically through the 1960s and 1970s.

In 1968 it purchased 20 acres of land at the juncture of two main thoroughfares in Schofield on which to build a new plant. Since that time that new facility has been added to five times and now includes plants two, three, and four.

In 1977 increased demand prompted Greenheck Fan Corporation to build its National Distribution Centre. The goal of the center was to provide domestic customers with 24-hour shipment of its products.

In 1979 the corporate offices were expanded and plant one was modernized and enlarged. Five years later the firm built plant four for the manufacture of large centrifugal fans.

The growth continued with the building of the New Product Development Centre in 1986. This 17,000-square-foot building houses the most advanced research and development facility in Greenheck's slice of the air-moving industry. It boasts a modern prototype laboratory, plus a 45-foot by 15-foot by 14-foot wind tunnel designed to aid Greenheck engineers in producing at least three new products each year.

The customers for Greenheck products are a diverse group, geographically and structurally. They range from institutions in the mid-Wisconsin area to every state in the United States to firms in Canada, Taiwan, Korea, Kuwait, Pakistan, United Arab Emirates, Egypt, Saudi Arabia, and South and Central America. Within the United States, Greenheck customers are widely spread, with no one customer accounting for more than 3 percent of total sales.

The company that began as a two-man sheet-metal shop in 1948 has grown to employ some 481 workers in its four Schofield plants. The $30,000 in sales achieved in its first year has grown to some $60 million per year.

The story of Greenheck Fan Corporation is the story of three men, enforced by hundreds of team-spirited people, who seem to believe together that the road to continuing success is deciding to begin, getting excited about succeeding, and believing that the impossible can become possible through hard work and wise management.

Greenheck's "Vision of Excellence" has never been more exemplified than in its new Product Development Centre, located in the Schofield Industrial Park. This laboratory is the largest in Greenheck's slice of the industry. The wind tunnel shown here is 45 feet long, 14 feet wide, and 15 feet high. The readout room is equipped with the latest analysis tools available.

RACINE FEDERATED, INC.

"We believe in being in Wisconsin," says John E. Erskine, Jr., president of Racine Federated, Inc. "In fact, we're moving one of our operations up to Wisconsin rather than going the other direction." Although Racine Federated was established recently (in 1970), its two founders, John Erskine, Sr., and George Miller, were longtime industrialists in Racine.

When Erskine and Miller incorporated the company in 1970 as Racine Federated Industries Corporation, they brought together a number of former Racine Hydraulics/Rexnord personnel who began assembling a decentralized federation of diverse businesses and product lines.

The new team brought with it a management style that laid the foundation for an organization dedicated to quality and structured to serve its people and its customers. This management style utilizes a team concept in contrast to a traditional type of structure. Company management is headed by an executive committee that is firmly committed to "participative management." The company believes these principles provide an effective way to operate successfully in today's more competitive markets.

Today the firm has some 75 employees at three plants (two in Racine and one in Milwaukee) totaling 70,000 square feet. Racine Federated currently has sales of approximately $10 million and hopes to reach $25 million in the future, through both internal growth and diversified acquisitions. The operations of Racine Federated are divided into four divisions: Wyco Tool, Thiermann, Mark Line, and Hedland.

Wyco Tool, Racine Federated's largest division, was established in 1912. Wyco has long been the dominant manufacturer of concrete vibrators for the construction market. "Wyco has traditionally set the pace in both technology and design," according to Erskine. As the industry

Racine Federated's Hedland division manufactures a broad line of fluid and gas flow meters, some of which are pictured here.

leader, Wyco is committed to superiority in quality and performance for all its products.

The Thiermann division produces a unique line of specialized equipment for electric and telephone utilities. These machines greatly improve the productivity and safety of work crews operating in off-street

As the largest division of Racine Federated, Wyco Tool has produced the Wyco concrete vibrator, the first to be approved by Underwriters' Laboratories.

sites.

Mark Line, Racine Federated's smallest division, is a leading supplier of hydraulic strike-off extensions, an accessory for asphalt paving machines.

The Hedland division manufactures a broad line of fluid and gas flow meters, more than 800 different models in all. The company believes that the enormous popularity of these products made it the fastest-growing flow meter line in North America. Originally developed as an accessory for another product, Hedland flow meters soon became an important product line in their own right, and have now become an industry standard.

The success of Racine Federated's four divisions can be attributed directly to its employees. The firm believes its participative management philosophy provides employees with maximum freedom and authority, a prerequisite for being a top competitor. "It is only through our employees that the company can maintain its commitments to quality and to serving customers," says Erskine. "Our people build our successes."

TWIN DISC, INCORPORATED

"My father was a genius at sensing the direction demand would have to take in industrial manufacturing," says John H. Batten, chairman of Twin Disc, Incorporated. "He anticipated demand and was able to produce the right products at the right time." Batten's father, Percy Haight Batten, moved from Cleveland, Ohio, to Racine in 1915 to be works manager of the Wallis Tractor Company.

Wallis had begun to manufacture tractors with higher speed engines. These new engines required a different kind of clutch because the old ones were self-engaging at high idle speeds. In 1918 Percy Batten set up the Twin Disc Clutch Company in Racine to build the new clutch, using the design of inventor Tom Fawick of Iowa.

Percy Batten continued to work for Wallis for a while. But by the end of 1918 he began to work full time at Twin Disc and became president of the company. "As a little kid, I grew up in the company," says John Batten, who was born in 1912. "I came with my little sister and my mother on Sundays to help clean the office. Mother ran blueprints, and my sister and I emptied the waste-baskets."

Today Twin Disc is listed on the New York Stock Exchange; but despite its size (1987 sales totaled more than $129 million), it remains partially a family enterprise. Batten family members are the largest shareholders in Twin Disc, and a third generation of Battens is active in running the company. Michael E. Batten is president and chief executive officer of Twin Disc. There are also many employees who are third-generation workers at the firm.

Anticipating market demand remains important to Twin Disc today. The company's multimillion-dollar corporate research and testing area in Rockford, Illinois, works on new product development, often with customer involvement. Twin Disc products include hydraulic torque converters; power-shift transmissions; marine transmissions; universal joints; gas turbine starting drives; power takeoffs; mechanical, hydraulic, and pneumatic clutches; axles; and electronic control systems.

Twin Disc is active primarily in

Percy Haight Batten and the company he founded in 1918, Twin Disc, Incorporated.

four major market areas—construction, marine, industrial, and extractive. Overseas, the transportation market is also important. Twin Disc products can be found in a wide variety of off-highway vehicles, special equipment, heavy-duty machinery, and commercial boats.

Over the years Twin Disc has developed a worldwide reputation. "Our marine gears were on all major Allied landing craft during World War II," says John Batten. "Our machine-tool clutches were then standard in the industry. We received five Army-Navy 'E' awards." Batten says that after the war this record opened international markets for Twin Disc and led to the company's expansion overseas.

Today Twin Disc, like many American companies, has restructured in order to meet rising international competition. "We've had to reorganize our whole approach in order to be more competitive," says Batten. "We're generally thought of as the world's leaders in research and development of hydraulic torque converters. We're world-known for a variety of types of industrial clutches and transmissions that embody a high level of research and development."

PERCY H. BATTEN
January 12, 1877 – April 8, 1960

PIERCE MANUFACTURING INC.

"The best selling tool is a satisfied customer," says Douglas Ogilvie, chairman of the board and chief executive officer of Pierce Manufacturing Inc. Fire chiefs, who are Pierce's major customers, write to the company from all over the country to express their views of Pierce fire equipment. "The work done by Pierce is far superior to the workmanship done on any other apparatus," one fire chief wrote. "The workers at Pierce excel in building a quality fire engine," wrote another. "I now see why Pierce is the number-one fire apparatus manufacturer in the country," wrote a third.

Pierce has not always manufactured fire engines. Dudley Pierce founded the Auto Body Works in Appleton in 1913 to repair cars and other vehicles. Pierce set up shop in an old church that had been remodeled to include a ramp for driving vehicles in and out of both the first and second floors. In 1914 Humphrey Pierce, Dudley's father, became a

Eugene Pierce (pictured here) joined the company when it was still known as the Auto Body Works and ran it after his father, Dudley, the founder, retired in 1930.

The current leaders of Pierce Manufacturing Inc. are (from left) David A. Ogilvie, vice-president; Douglas A. Ogilvie, chairman and chief executive officer; and Michael R. Reese, president.

partner in the company as services expanded. The Auto Body Works began to concentrate on building custom truck and bus bodies to be mounted on Ford Model T and one-ton truck chassis. All bodies were hand made of oak, maple, and 20-gauge steel. By the end of 1914 the

firm had nine employees.

The Auto Body Works soon outgrew its church factory, and a new factory was built on Spencer Street in 1917. At the time the new location was so rural that the property was subject to a lease to a local farmer for pasture use. The company was incorporated that same year.

A catalog produced by the firm at this time advertised bodies that could be bolted onto the buyer's Model T to convert it for various uses. "Our standard color is dark olive green," read the catalog copy. "May be had in any dark color desired without additional cost, but if ordered in white or other light colors, an additional charge of five dollars is made for extra material and labor."

The company continued to expand, with various Pierce family members in control. Humphrey Pierce died in 1919, leaving Dudley as the controlling stockholder. Dudley retired in 1930 but served as president until his death in 1954. Dudley's son, Eugene, joined the firm in 1927; he ran the business after his father retired.

In the late 1920s the company started building bodies from steel. In the early 1940s it began building bodies for utility trucks; Eagle Manufacturing Company (a division of Four-Wheel Drive Company of Clintonville) made derricks and other equipment used by utility companies. Auto Body Works then branched out into beverage, bakery, beer, furniture, and refrigerated milk truck bodies. Among all the new kinds of trucks, the firm also began making what eventually became its main line of work—fire trucks.

Building these larger trucks required a larger facility, and in 1941 the firm constructed an addition to accommodate the larger trucks and the machinery necessary for handling steel.

When W.S. Darley Company of

Chicago approached Auto Body Works in 1957 to produce fire truck bodies under the Darley label, the organization agreed and began to concentrate exclusively on producing fire and utility trucks.

In 1957 Helen Haase, who joined the company in 1946, and Douglas Ogilvie, who joined the company in 1948, became officers and directors of Auto Body Works. When Eugene Pierce died in 1958, Ogilvie was elected president; Haase became secretary of the corporation. The company was renamed Pierce Auto Body Works, Inc., and the now-familiar oval logo was adopted.

One factor in the firm's growth (it now has annual sales exceeding $100 million) was an agreement it signed in 1959 with a Missouri snorkel apparatus company. This agreement gave Pierce a national marketing network, and Pierce has since become an aggressive marketer. Strong marketing is a necessity, says Ogilvie. "We're in a business where the type of product we build is used for 20 to 30 years," he points out. Finding new customers is of key importance because no one replaces fire

The old Auto Body Works plant in Appleton, which Dudley Pierce founded to repair cars and other vehicles, was set up in an old church that had been remodeled. Photo circa 1913

Pierce Manufacturing's current facility, where it employs more than 900 people and produces 60 fire trucks per month. Through quality control, aggressive marketing, and innovation, it has become the number-one fire apparatus manufacturer in the country.

trucks every couple of years.

But before marketing comes quality control. "Building a fine product is number one," Ogilvie believes. "But it takes a number of programs along with a fine product to be successful. Eugene Pierce was very quality conscious. Quality was the basis of the Pierce philosophy—the idea that extra effort will give your product satisfied customers."

Innovation has been another key to the growth of the Pierce organization. Pierce teamed up with the Snorkel Company of Missouri to develop a new fire-fighting unit called the Snorkel in 1959. The Snorkel utilized an elevating platform with a waterway piped to a 1,000-gallon-per-minute nozzle; it was available in 50-, 65-, 75-, and 85-foot lengths.

Another innovation was the Squrt. Helen Haase became well

known as a Snorkel-Squrt specialist. By the close of the 1950s Pierce was a nationally recognized builder of fire and utility apparatus.

The company's success necessitated building more facilities. There were more additions and land purchases until the main plant totaled 110,000 square feet. In 1970 a second plant was built on the west side of town that added 62,000 square feet of production capacity; it has now been expanded to 200,000 square feet. In 1969 the firm was renamed Pierce Manufacturing Inc. In 1970 the company acquired the rights to the name Pierce Arrow for fire apparatus and utility vehicles.

Pierce Manufacturing Inc. now employs more than 900 people and produces some 60 vehicles per month. It claims to produce "the finest paint jobs in the fire truck and utility industry." The company's standard color is no longer dark olive green. Utility vehicles and fire apparatus are now painted in a wide variety of colors. The firm's growth continues as it becomes the largest manufacturer in the fire apparatus market worldwide.

VALLEYCAST, INC.

"Everything we do here is custom work," says Geoffrey Palmer, executive vice-president and general manager of Valleycast, Inc., which produces more than 50 nonleaded copper alloys in wire form. "At a time when other companies in the wire industry are dropping alloys, Valleycast is adding them."

Copper is alloyed to enhance its properties. In some applications, for example, it is important that the metal used be both highly resistant to corrosion and able to conduct electricity. Valleycast can make a wire alloy of copper and other metals that will resist corrosion and still conduct electricity, though possibly not quite as well as copper alone. Creating an alloy "is always a trade-off," says Richard W. Cashman, president of Valleycast. "In order to improve certain properties, you have to give up something."

Valleycast produces finished copper alloy (brass) wire in sizes ranging from 0.040 to 0.650 inches in diameter. The finished wire is wound onto coils or reels in quanti-

A typical casting shop of the 1930s and 1940s. "Book molds" were used to cast three-foot-length rods, which were then rolled into wire.

ties weighing 1,000 to 2,000 pounds each. At each stage of processing the wire is wound onto special tubular carriers for transport. Otherwise, Palmer points out, those huge coils of wire could turn into "giant Slinkys."

Valleycast's customers use these huge rolls of custom-produced copper alloy wire for a wide variety of applications. Valleycast wire is ultimately used in toothbrushes, eyeglasses, circuit boards, batteries, screws, nails, rivets, zippers, high-grade electronics connectors, springs, welding material, and corrosion-resistant bolts and electrical fasteners.

When it was founded in 1964 as a vertical expansion of the Appleton Wire Works, Valleycast produced wire for one purpose only—to be used in making paper-machine screens. Appleton Wire Works (which was founded in 1895) originally purchased fourdrinier redraw wire and wove it into forming fabric for paper-machine screens. These screens were similar to window screens; the wire mesh was either larger or smaller, depending on the grade of paper they were used to make.

But in the early 1970s plastics began to replace metal wire in the fourdrinier industry. Valleycast, to

In this scene wire bars from the "book molds" are being passed repeatedly through rolls to reduce their diameter and increase their length. Photo circa 1940s

meet the realities of the changing marketplace, began to diversify into other brass mill wire products. Valleycast decided to buy the finest casting and annealing equipment available for its new endeavors. After a worldwide search Valleycast purchased an Outokumpu Upcast Machine, the state-of-the-art continuous strand casting equipment.

Valleycast also purchased the finest annealing equipment available, Ebner Bell Furnaces, along with other drawing machines and support equipment. The company constructed new buildings and added more employees. Valleycast entered the broader copper alloy wire market as a small but quality-conscious mill. The firm enjoyed steady growth throughout the 1970s.

The Appleton Wire Works had merged with the Albany Felt Company in 1968; the firm formed by this merger was called Albany International Corporation. In 1980 the company that is now Valleycast became known as the Cast Wire Division of

Albany International. At the end of 1983 the Cast Wire Division was sold to Division Management and Charterhouse International, Inc.

The new company, which was named Valleycast, Inc., continued to operate with the same people and the same approach; its growth and success continued.

Valleycast's success made it an attractive acquisition candidate. In 1985 all of the stock of Valleycast was acquired by Outokumpu Oy of Helsinki, Finland. Outokumpu is a leader in the production of copper, copper alloys, stainless steel, zinc, and a wide variety of other metals.

Valleycast is continuing to grow today. Its 50-percent expansion during the recession year of 1982 was followed by another major expansion in 1986. Additional expansion—well-planned, controlled growth—remains part of Valleycast's long-range objectives, according to Cashman and Palmer.

Another business pattern Valleycast intends to continue is its con-

The casting department today. Here large-diameter wires are being continuously cast to finish the chemical analysis process.

cern for the environment. "We are squeaky clean," says Cashman. "It's a lot less expensive in the long run to do it right the first time." Cashman points out that although Valleycast "is in an industry (primary metals processing) that's known for polluting, we were never in a position of polluting." And, he adds, "as we developed processes and products where pollution could be a problem, we made the choices to control it before it became a problem." Valleycast's policy, Cashman says, is that "if we're going to do anything, we do it

with the best technology that's available in the marketplace."

Both Cashman and Palmer expect that Valleycast's commitment to the latest technology will enable the company to continue its success. Valleycast has tripled its output during the past 10 to 12 years; it now serves 30 percent of the U.S. market for its products.

Part of Valleycast's commitment to keeping pace with the marketplace is its strong technical and metallurgical staff, which provides support to customers and backup production operations. Valleycast, Inc., also has an experimental caster, a functional continuous-strand caster similar to the production units. The experimental caster is used to develop new processes and alloys. A fully equipped and modern in-house laboratory also supports strong research and development efforts. The sophisticated equipment is used both for developing new alloys and for attaining high quality-assurance standards.

The Valleycast heat-treating department. The large-diameter coils are heated here to enable further work on them, to bring them down to smaller diameters.

LAKE GENEVA SPINDUSTRIES, INC.

Lake Geneva Spindustries, the largest privately owned metal-spinning shop in the United States, began 35 years ago in the basement of George Downing's house. Downing, who has been the sole owner and president of the company since 1974, says that he and his original partner, Don Petrie, really scraped to get the business started. "We had to have a truck right from the first," Downing recalls. Household Finance agreed to loan them $200 to buy a used truck, but only on the condition that they use all of their personal furniture—from both of their homes—as collateral for the loan.

"So we took the $200," Downing says, "and bought a dark green one-ton 1938 Chevrolet truck." They used the truck in the business, which was then called Lake Geneva Metal Spinning, for nearly 10 years. "We never had any trouble with it either," Downing adds.

In the early years most of their customers were in Chicago. "Lake Geneva is sort of a magic name in Chicago," Downing believes. "When I said I was from Lake Geneva, people would at least see me." Either Downing or Petrie would load finished product into the truck, haul it down to Chicago, and then pick up steel for the return trip to Wisconsin. Downing, who says that the 1938 Chevy, though sturdy, was not really big enough, can remember how the truck would sway on the trip, both to and from Chicago.

Whoever drove the truck to Chicago considered the trip there and back his day off for the week. "Other than those trips," Downing says, "we worked seven days a week." Downing's late first wife, Elaine, was the company's secretary during those early years.

Gross sales have grown from $38,000 in 1953, when there were six employees and four customers, to $7.5 million today, when there are 120 employees and 400 customers. The physical plant has grown, too. The Lake Geneva plant, after 11 additions to the original building (erected in 1956), now covers 43,000 square feet. There is also a second plant, which does tool-and-die work, in Fort Atkinson; it covers 40,000 square feet. A subsidiary, San Jamar, Inc., (formerly the Grif-Ho Company of West Allis), was purchased in 1984 and moved to Elkhorn.

Metal spinning is a traditional art form, dating back to the ancient Chinese potter's wheel. This same concept is used today to form a variety of metals, from brass to steel to sterling silver. The concept may be the same, but the techniques have changed. Spindustries, in addition to its more traditional lathes, also boasts a CNC machine that runs off of a Wang computer.

Spindustries is no longer located in Downing's basement, but it remains a family enterprise. Downing is president of Lake Geneva Spindus-

In 1956 Lake Geneva Spindustries was a small company called Lake Geneva Metal Spinning and used only traditional spinning lathes. From left are some of the company's early employees: Sam Veri, no longer with the company; George W. Downing, president and cofounder; and Ted Heusser, still an employee of the firm.

tries as well as chief executive officer of San Jamar, Inc. His wife Margaret is treasurer of Spindustries and president and treasurer of San Jamar. The next generation is well represented, too. Jeffery Downing, Susan Downing Wesner, Scott Wesner, and Jerry Arndt all work in Lake Geneva Spindustries.

The company is active in the community. It supports the Lake Geneva YMCA and awards several scholarships and prizes at local schools. The George W. Downing Endowment Scholarship was established in 1987 at the Milwaukee School of Engineering.

Today Lake Geneva Spindustries utilizes high technology along with the more traditional methods of spinning metal. Seen here are two generations of Downings in front of a modern lathe—a CNC controlled spinning lathe. From left are Jeffrey Downing, executive vice-president; Scott Wesner, purchasing agent; Gerald Arndt, sales manager of San Jamar, Inc., a subsidiary company; Susan Downing Wesner, assistant to the president of San Jamar, Inc.; Margaret Downing, president of San Jamar, Inc.; and George Downing, president of Lake Geneva Spindustries.

DEWITT, PORTER, HUGGETT, SCHUMACHER & MORGAN, S.C.

DeWitt, Porter, Huggett, Schumacher & Morgan, S.C., was formed in 1969 by merger of three Madison-based firms with practices dating from 1930. The firm has grown from 10 lawyers in 1969 to one of the 10 largest law firms in Wisconsin. In late 1987, having outgrown its original offices, the firm moved next door to the state capitol by relocating to the Manchester Place in downtown Madison. The firm also has an office on Madison's growing west side.

Close proximity to the state capitol is appropriate, given DeWitt Porter's special emphasis on governmental affairs, lobbying, and administrative law. From the beginning of its existence, the firm has identified the need to serve regional and national clients in specialty areas. Attorneys from DeWitt Porter have been instrumental in writing and assisting in the interpretation of many of Wisconsin's statutes and administrative regulations, particularly in the environmental and health care areas.

The national scope of DeWitt Porter's attorneys is illustrated by its commerce clause and transportation law attorneys' successful series of cases in the U.S. Supreme Court overturning state laws denying highway access to certain vehicles important to interstate commerce.

In addition to transportation, environmental, and health, other special concentrations include labor law (including school and municipal), taxation, pension and profit sharing, securities, corporations, partnerships, antitrust, real estate, municipal law, insurance and insurance regulation, utility regulation, energy, mining, banking regulation, white-collar criminal investigation and defense, computer law, intellectual property law, and civil litigation of all types. In addition to representation of major clients on selected issues, DeWitt Porter is a full-service law firm for a wide range of clients, including indi-

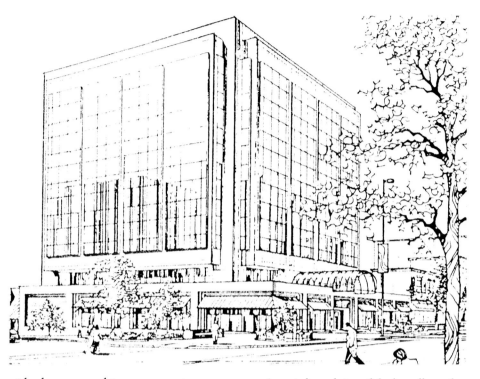

An artist's rendering of the law offices of DeWitt, Porter, Huggett, Schumacher & Morgan, S.C., at Manchester Place.

viduals, partnerships, corporations, municipalities, and professional and trade associations.

The firm's philosophy in representing its clients in litigation, negotiation, and legal action is to deliver cost-effective service through the use of its qualified, experienced profes-

Jack DeWitt, one of the original partners in the law firm of DeWitt, Porter, Huggett, Schumacher & Morgan, S.C.

sionals. Two attorneys are never used when one will do.

To provide this quality service, DeWitt Porter is committed to specialization by attorneys in their various fields of practice and to dependable attorney support functions. The firm prides itself on adopting state-of-the-art production techniques to fully utilize its computer capability both in researching and writing about the law. Having the needed information at the fingertips of an experienced professional helps to implement and expedite successful results.

The accelerating onslaught of information, technology, legislation, litigation, and administrative regulations continually carves out new areas and issues of the law, and the increasing complexity of life and business relationships requires a helping hand in the legal arena. DeWitt, Porter, Huggett, Schumacher & Morgan, S.C., is committed to effectively and efficiently providing this help.

THE AZCO GROUP LTD.

Four men—one a manager in industry, one a chief engineer from industry, one a company representative, and the other a refrigeration contractor—pooled $15,000 cash in 1949 and began a business. That initial investment has grown to approximately $3.4 million today.

Within the first 10-year period three of the four founders—Frank Jenkins, Harry Koller, and E.W. Bassett—sold their interests for various reasons, leaving F. John Barlow the only remaining founder of AZCO.

Since its beginning in 1949 and through a series of organizational structuring and acquisitions, THE AZCO GROUP LTD. is now the holding company of three wholly owned subsidiaries—AZCO HENNES INC., providing general construction for industry; AZCO ELECTRIC LTD., providing commercial, industrial, and instrumentation electrical construction; and PAFCO INC., a pipe and fitting supply company.

Jenkins and Barlow selected the name AZCO. They reasoned that in-

THE AZCO GROUP LTD. is a complete mechanical engineering contractor. Comprised of three subsidiaries, AZCO HENNES INC. (pictured at work here), AZCO ELECTRIC LTD., and PAFCO INC., these companies build, pipe, do electrical work, install sprinkler/fire-protection systems, and fabricate piping and other construction materials for use nationwide.

asmuch as their goal was to build a company that could provide mechanical contracting services from "A to Z," their "A to Z Company" should be named AZCO. Slogans such as "You Name It and We Do It," and "One Call Gets Them All" were frequently quoted in those early years.

By 1953 Barlow resigned a management position with Western Condensing Company and began to reorganize AZCO full time. His management background began to have a profound impact on AZCO. The organization was restructured and a well-planned expansion program was implemented. Departmentalization was the buzzword and Barlow set a strong path toward that management concept.

By June 1953 things were beginning to happen—a large ventilating contract was awarded by Kimberly-Clark and led to AZCO's own sheet-metal shop. Later that same year a local plumbing firm was acquired to add yet another service to meet the goals of organizational structure.

It became apparent that as Jenkins and Barlow gained experience in the contracting field, their previous business careers were a valuable asset, especially Barlow's strong management background in industry. Early in 1954 a subsidiary company was formed—Azco Fire Protection,

Inc., another service to fit into the big plan. Barlow comments that back then they were free to build and to grow in a way they chose, because they did not have the burden of, what he terms, ". . . insurmountable practices from an older company or from a family-owned company."

AZCO's industry orientation led to concentration on process and power piping to paper mills and industrial areas in northeastern Wisconsin. For its first five years of operation the firm had annual gross sales averaging $250,000. And for the next 30 years AZCO made a profit. The net worth increased to almost $3.4 million.

The first seven-figure contract was awarded in 1956 by Kimberly-Clark for the complete mechanical work for its corporate main office building. The following year a new management concept was introduced that transferred labor responsibilities to a fully oriented management person—quite a revolutionary move to make in the construction industry at that time.

Strong management principles led to control of tools, equipment, and materials. At the beginning of the second decade (1959), the annual volume approximated one million dollars. By the end of that decade the annual volume reached $6.5 million, and working capital was up to

THE AZCO GROUP LTD. began in 1949 and worked out of this office in Appleton. At that time the company had four partners, of which only one worked full time.

$800,000 with the net worth slightly more than one million dollars. Barlow's early organizational leadership was paying handsome dividends indeed.

In the early 1970s AZCO purchased a leading mechanical contractor in Milwaukee, The Downey Company, from the Downey family. The acquisition was known as AZCO DOWNEY. After 12 successful years AZCO DOWNEY was sold to the employees and is now known as DOWNEY INC..

In 1985 Hennes Erecting Company, Inc., an Appleton-based heavy-equipment and machinery-moving contractor, was acquired and merged with AZCO INC. under the leadership of Robert Helein. The new company, AZCO HENNES INC., was now the culmination of the long-term goal for an "A to Z Company." AZCO HENNES INC., the largest subsidiary of the holding company, provides general construction to industry with machinery moving and installation, pipe fabrication and erection, steel erection, boiler and turbine installation and repair, plant supplemental and contract maintenance, crane service, heavy-equipment specialist, sheet-metal fabrication and installation, fire protection, and construction management. The latest addition to the corporate holding company was the formation of AZCO ELECTRIC

LTD., headed by Daniel Coffey, to complete the installation construction service to industry and public utilities.

THE AZCO GROUP LTD. is now able to be of complete service to customers throughout the continental United States. Its clients range from breweries to chemical plants, food-processing plants, paper mills, power plants, and petrochemical operations, with construction services in 28 states.

THE AZCO GROUP LTD.

had $50.7 million in revenues for 1986 and was recognized by its peers through leading trade journals. One publication, *D.E. Journal*, placed the company at 27th in the nation in a group of 195, the eighth-largest process piping contractor, and the 17th-largest fire-protection contractor. Another publication, *Engineering News Record*, placed the firm 30th out of 99 leading contractors in the nation. Today John Barlow's dream is quite visible. He is now active as chairman of the board of THE AZCO GROUP LTD. Robert Helein is president of the holding company, and Don Baugh is president of AZCO HENNES INC. Depending on seasonal variations, the company employs between 500 and 1,000 people, with an executive and management staff of 100 based in the Appleton offices.

The "A to Z Company" idea has made a significant contribution to Appleton and the State of Wisconsin, where the entrepreneur and a strong work ethic spell success.

Today AZCO is still located in Appleton, but its headquarters, along with the number of people it employs, have grown considerably. Currently AZCO employs between 500 and 1,000 people, depending on seasonal variation.

BADGER WOOD PRODUCTS, INC.

"My dad was a carpenter and contractor who could build anything from houses to gymnasiums," says James L. De Broux, president of Badger Wood Products, Inc. De Broux says his father, Louis J. De Broux, quit school in the third grade to go to work in a shingle mill in Phlox, Wisconsin, so he could help support his family. Louis served in the Army in World War I and then apprenticed as a carpenter in De Pere, where he met and married his wife, Adele, in 1919.

Times were hard for the De Broux family in the early years. Louis worked as a carpenter and contractor, and managed to keep afloat during the Depression. But in the early 1940s he declared bankruptcy. "We lost our home and everything," says James. But Louis started over again and was soon working with wood in a workshop in his basement. "Dad always dabbled with ideas," remembers James. One of Louis' ideas, during World War II, was for a V-shaped wooden cribbage board that said "God Bless America with Victory." A large national beer company, impressed with the idea, said it would order 200,000 boards for samples if it could have an "exclusive" on them. "I used to drill the holes in those things with a drill press, one hole at a time," James says. "I can't stand to play cribbage to this day." One week after the order was received, and before one board was made, the war ended, and the order, of course, was cancelled.

The current Badger Wood Products, Inc., facility as drawn by an artist. This is the same facility that was built on Eighth Street in 1949 but with major extensions so that it now encompasses 30,000 square feet.

Things have gone better since then for the De Broux wood products company, which is now called Badger Wood Products. After the war Louis got enough business that he was able to rent a burned-out welding shop and employ several workers. In 1948 Louis built a house on Eighth Street in De Pere; the following year he built a plant next to the house.

The whole De Broux family lived in the house and worked in the plant. Adele cooked for the crews, and she, Louis, and all of the children ran the machines. A new generation soon went to work in the plant. James' wife, Lois, ran the office and

The Badger Wood Products, Inc., plant on Eighth Street in De Pere as it looked in 1962. The plant was built in 1949 with only 1,450 square feet and originally had the De Broux home next to it; over time the house became part of the Badger Wood Products facility. When this picture was taken, the building had a total of 4,500 square feet.

did the books for many years; three of their sons—Matthew, David, and Donald—are actively involved in running the business today. Lois and James' brother, Francis J., are on the board of directors.

The original plant was only 1,450 square feet; it has expanded to now cover 90,000 square feet. The old family home is part of the plant; Louis and Adele's old bedroom is now the employee nonsmoking lounge. "They would have liked that," James believes. "Neither of them smoked." Badger Wood Products also has an 80,000-square-foot facility with a sawmill in Drummond, Wisconsin. And the company has a third site, with a 3.5-acre lumber receiving warehouse, in De Pere.

Badger Wood Products has expanded its product line over the years. The firm started out making wood cove for linoleum floors, wood shelves for supermarkets, and wood moldings for kitchen counters, but changing technologies made those products obsolete. Today Badger Wood Products makes hardwood parts for kitchen cabinets. "We make every part that goes into a cabinet that's solid wood," De Broux says.

In the years since Louis De Broux built the first small plant, Badger Wood Products, Inc., has grown from 5 or 6 employees to 108. There are new machines, including computers and wood cutters accurate to plus or minus 5/1,000ths of an inch. And of the millions of hardwood products the company produces each year, not one is a cribbage board.

DECAR CORPORATION

In 1945 Dave, Ed, Charles, Art, and Robert, five former employees of the McDonnell Aircraft Corporation, set out to become manufacturers of a decorative slat for venetian blinds used in telephone companies nationwide. With a bank loan of $7,500 and an acronym created from their first names, Decar Corporation was born. The company purchased the old Blackhawk Dance Hall in Middleton and intended to turn the building into a production facility.

However, the venture was short-lived. Three partners bowed out before the business really got under way. Two remaining partners, Ed Weichmann and Charles Marschner, sold a half-interest in Decar to E.J. Elting, a Chicago-based investor. Elting turned the management of the business over to Ralph L. Fossier, Sr.

Elting, who gained control of Decar in 1947, found that the company could make only a flat decorative laminate—a surface now known as Formica. Fossier was given the responsibility to find a product Decar could manufacture and market successfully.

Gradually Fossier purchased the firm's stock from Elting and the remaining stockholders. Within three years he became sole owner of Decar.

By 1950 Decar became a major manufacturer of high-pressure laminate plastic, trade named Decarlite. Decarlite laminate was sold to dinette manufacturers throughout the country. Eventually the firm incorporated the Decarlite laminate into its own furniture, which was sold on a nationwide basis.

Fossier also founded Dentin Manufacturing Company in Corona, California, as a subsidiary of Decar in 1960. Dentin incorporates fiberglass in its production of picnic tables, playground and recreational equipment, and other indoor and outdoor furniture.

Today the Fossier family owns

Ralph L. Fossier, Sr., owner and chairman of the board of Decar Corporation.

and operates Decar. Fossier's eldest son, Ralph L. Jr., became president of Decar in 1984. Sons Mark and Daryl are president and vice-president of Dentin, respectively.

After a fire destroyed the original plant in 1970, Decar moved to a 66,000-square-foot facility that all current production and management functions—administration, manufacturing, financial, and marketing—call home. Executive and sales offices are located in Addison, Illinois, where Ralph L. Sr. continues to serve as chairman of the board, and his wife, Doloris, is chief executive officer.

Over the past 40 years Decar has shifted its manufacturing emphasis and become a leading library and

school, business, and original equipment manufacturer. Company products include the Bit-N-Byte and JobStream workstations, (ergonomically designed computer support centers), Imperial and OakQuest library furniture lines, and OEM high-pressure, low-pressure, vinyl, and wood component parts, ranging from tabletops and drawer fronts to completed cabinets and jukeboxes.

Under the parent Doloris Corporation, Decar continues to develop new products as technology and styles change. The company owns several patents on engineering designs such as the honeycomb core panel and the Magi-Kwik leg plate. The Honeycomb core provides a panel that is strong, yet lightweight and easy to move and maneuver. This production technique is now standard in many industries such as automobile and aerospace. The Magi-Kwik leg plate permits quick, simple leg attachment of adjustable or nonadjustable legs to Decar tabletops.

Standing behind its motto, "If we cannot be proud of the finished product—we don't make it," Decar Corporation advances into the future with goals of continued growth and success—based on the solid foundation built by Ralph L. Fossier, Sr.

Ralph L. Fossier, Jr., president, and Jack Schultz, vice-president/manufacturing, oversee the operation of the computerized CNC router.

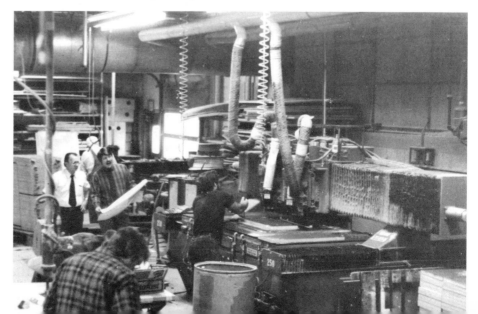

PETERSON BUILDERS, INC.

Fred J. Peterson, founder of Peterson Builders, Inc., of Sturgeon Bay, always wanted his own shipbuilding company. His father, Martin Peterson, started a company called Peterson Boat Works in 1907, but fire destroyed the firm in 1918. After the fire, Fred went to work building boats at other yards in Sturgeon Bay. However, he never forgot the many wooden ships, such as *Marion,* that he had helped build in his father's shipyard.

Fred Peterson set out to acquire experience both in boat building and in business practices in order to make the dream of his own shipyard a reality. Fred helped establish the first self-service grocery stores in Sturgeon Bay, started an insurance business, and organized the Sturgeon Bay Building and Loan Association. He also raised mink, ran trap lines for mink and muskrat, and built canoes.

In 1933 Fred and his wife, Irene, decided the time had come to put the name Peterson back on a Sturgeon Bay shipyard. Even though the economy was weak in 1933, Fred rented some land and buildings and named his new company Peterson Boat Works. Irene ran the busy office

Founded in 1933 by Fred Peterson, who is now retired at the age of 93, Peterson Boat Works was the predecessor to the present Peterson Builders, Inc.

while Fred was designer, builder, and salesman.

The first boat built at the newly opened Peterson Boat Works (today known as Peterson Builders, Inc., or PBI) was *Sally Lou,* a wooden fishing tug. Diversification from shipbuilding also began in 1933, when Fred and his crew, known as the Hungry Five of Peterson Boat Works, traveled to Frankfurt, Michigan, for their first boat repair job.

Business expanded rapidly, and by 1935 a large Quonset building was added to facilitate the growing production. That structure is still in use today at PBI, but is dwarfed by the

numerous modern PBI ship construction buildings.

Fred and Irene's teamwork built the foundation for a thriving company. Sons Ellsworth and Bob literally grew up in the shipyard. Ellsworth, who is today president of PBI, clearly remembers cleaning out bilges as a child. The family even posed for an ad in a PBI-built dinghy called *Peter Dink.* The eight-foot version, which cost $58.75 in the 1930s, was advertised as "a sturdy, lightweight, leakproof dinghy, an answer to the prayer of every yachtsman and sportsman in the country as well as the parents who want a safe boat for boys and girls." PBI also built sailboats up to 64 feet in length, gill-net tugs, and wood cruisers throughout the decade.

The advent of World War II brought change and expansion to PBI. The Army and the Navy, impressed with PBI's commitment to "quality production, on schedule," as Ellsworth Peterson puts it, ordered so many motor launches, submarine chasers, aircraft rescue vessels, and other ships from PBI that volume at the shipyard grew dramatically.

The number of employees had increased to 350 by 1942. Fred's sons were working full time by then. Dozens of launching and christening parties held at the yard during the war years were grand and proud occasions for the company.

In 1946 the firm was incorpo-

Located on Sturgeon Bay, Peterson Builders, Inc., is now under the direction of the second, third, and fourth generations of Petersons.

rated and renamed Peterson Builders, Inc. Officers were Fred J. Peterson, president; Ellsworth Peterson, general manager and treasurer; Robert Peterson, vice-president and head of production control; and Irene Peterson, secretary.

Employment at PBI had dropped to a dozen in the late 1940s. Fred decided that yacht building held potential for new business. PBI constructed the 65-foot schooner *Utopia* from Fred's design. In 1947 Fred, Ellsworth, and crew set sail on a nine-month cruise in the unique wood and steel-hulled vessel. They sailed to Europe, Africa, and the Caribbean to show off *Utopia* and demonstrate PBI's yacht-building expertise to the world. In the meantime PBI ventured into other kinds of work, building several houses and installing boilers and heating systems in businesses and homes.

By the early 1950s PBI was back to building ships. The company built and repaired commercial fishing and U.S. Coast Guard vessels. Although *Utopia* was successful in spurring orders for yachts, PBI built its last sailboat, *Westerly,* in 1954. Both are still sailing Door County waters.

PBI began constructing wooden minesweepers for the Navy in the early 1950s. In the process of building minesweepers and other craft, PBI helped develop special aluminum-welding technologies that formed the groundwork for today's industry standards.

To meet the increased volume in business, the firm purchased additional real estate and buildings. The 1960s and 1970s saw hundreds of vessels constructed of wood, steel, aluminum, and fiberglass at the yard. Oceanographic research vessels, municipal fire and rescue boats, amphibious vehicles, tuna seiners complete with helicopters, as well as ships for U.S. and foreign navies are but a

USS Grasp *(ARS-51) was built by Peterson Builders, Inc., and commissioned into the U.S. Navy in 1985.*

sampling of PBI's work during these years. Sizes of ships varied from 20 feet to 300 feet. Benefits for the skilled work force were also expanded during this time and included a profit-sharing program that had distributed more than $19 million to employees since it began in 1963.

Today PBI employs more than 800 people. Fred Peterson, at age 93, is now retired, but members of the

The boat yard is a beehive of activity with ships in various stages of construction.

second, third, and fourth generations of the Peterson family are active in the company. Many employees follow the Peterson tradition of multiple generations working together at the firm. Strong community involvement is yet another PBI tradition. In 1963 the Fred J. Peterson Foundation donated the indoor municipal pool (designed by Fred Peterson) to the City of Sturgeon Bay. The foundation continues in assisting various area projects and organizations.

Vast improvements in shipbuilding techniques and related technologies have occurred in the past five decades. Even greater advances loom on the horizon. Peterson Builders, Inc., intends to meet the challenges ahead as successfully as it has those in the past.

MARINE TRAVELIFT, INC.

"The old way of getting a boat out of the water was to use logs to roll the boat up onto the beach," says Allan J. Lamer, vice-president/marketing and sales for Marine Travelift, Inc. After that the two basic methods for boat handling were by marine railway or by crane.

In the late 1940s George "Butch" Baudhuin of Sturgeon Bay invented a truck-drawn straddle-type hoist for boats. Baudhuin, with the help of Arnie Petersen and a naval architect, Dick Stearn, of Sturgeon Bay, continued to improve on the development of the straddle hoist and designed it to be self-propelled for much-improved maneuverability in the boat yard. Baudhuin named the machine the Travelift and formed a new company, Travelift and Engineering Corp., to manufacture and market the machine to other boat yards and marinas for dry-docking large pleasure craft boats.

Baudhuin manufactured the Travelift machines in Sturgeon Bay and shipped them to locations in the Great Lakes area. As the reputation of the Marine Travelift grew, he began to sell the hoists on the East and West coasts also. In the late 1950s Baudhuin began building industrial units, which were used for handling prestressed concrete and steel.

In 1959 Drott Manufacturing Corp. of Wassau, Wisconsin, owned

In recognition for Marine Travelift's continuing emphasis on new product design, the company was awarded the Governor's New Product Award in 1984. Seen here receiving the award from Lieutenant Governor James T. Flynn (center) are president Gerald Lamer (left) and vice-president Allan Lamer (right).

by Ed and John Drott, purchased Travelift and Engineering Corp., and continued to improve and develop the machines for both marine and industrial use under the trade name Travelift.

In 1965 Petersen and Gordon Weber, both of Sturgeon Bay, purchased the rights to manufacture and market the marine units and formed a new company—Marine Travelift, Inc. Drott continued to market the industrial units and Marine Travelift marketed the Marine units.

In 1975 Gerald P. and Allan J. Lamer purchased Marine Travelift. Gerald Lamer, president and general manager, had worked for Drott for 23 years and was chief designer for hydraulic cranes. Allan Lamer had worked as account manager for Parker Hannifin Company in Minnesota for 10 years.

Marine Travelift, which is privately owned, builds some 100 units per year. "We have over 2,000 Marine Travelift units in service worldwide," Alan Lamer says. These include some of the earlier units and the bigger, more sophisticated designs being manufactured today. Until 1975 Marine Travelift had concentrated on building several different models ranging from 15-ton to 50-ton units. Since then the company

has developed 100-ton, 150-ton, and 250-ton models. A unit with a 500-ton capacity is currently being developed.

When that 500-ton unit is ready, "it will be the first and largest boat hoist in the world in that size and type," says Allan Lamer. In recognition of the firm's continuing emphasis on new product design, Marine Travelift received the Governor's New Product Award in 1984 for a new design for a 35-ton unit.

"We look for continuous growth in the marine field," says Allan Lamer, "and we are planning some new products for the marine and related markets." He adds that currently "we have 70 to 80 percent of the market for boat handling. Our units handle a full range of boats from pleasure boats all the way through 100-foot boats. In commercial and work boats, we can handle a range up to 200-feet-plus."

A Marine Travelift Model 250 AMO 250-ton-capacity boat hoist at Davis Boatyard in Virginia.

A Marine Travelift Model 100 BFM 100-ton-capacity boat hoist at a boat yard in California.

Marine Travelift Model 35 BFM, 35-ton capacity, and 70 BFM, 70-ton capacity (in the background), are pictured here at a marina in Stuart, Florida.

KEWAUNEE ENGINEERING CORP.

Kewaunee Engineering Corp. was founded in 1941 as Kewaunee Engineering and Shipbuilding Corporation by Fred J. Peterson, Sr., and a group of investors. During World War II the company primarily built freight carriers and other naval craft for government use. Today the firm, which was purchased by Gerald P. Lamer and Allan J. Lamer in 1985, offers a variety of products and services, ranging from components for mine-sweeping equipment to metal trailers, heavy steel fabrications, and custom machining work for other manufacturers. One of its major customers is Marine Travelift, Inc., which is also owned by the Lamer brothers.

"Kewaunee Engineering Corp. has achieved steady growth through a record of quality, dependability, and customer service," says Gerald P. Lamer, president of the firm. "We acquired the company in 1985 because the owner, Fred J. Peterson, Sr., was 94 years old and wanted to sell the business."

Today one-third of Kewaunee Engineering's production is for Marine Travelift. The organization has 170,000 square feet of office and production facilities on a 75-acre site located on Kewaunee Harbor. Since the town of Kewaunee has only some 3,000 people, Kewaunee Engineering is the dominant employer, with approximately 200 employees. "We have a low rate of job turnover," Gerald Lamer claims. "Many of our employees have been here 20 years or more."

Kewaunee Engineering specializes in the fabrication of heavy steel. It works with 96-inch by 240-inch plates that range in thickness from one-quarter inch to six inches. The plates range in weight from 1,634 pounds to 39,200 pounds. The company shears the steel or cuts it, forms it in a press, then drills or bores it as necessary before it is welded into a

Adjacent to Kewaunee Harbor, Kewaunee Engineering Corp. is located on the northern outskirts of Kewaunee, Wisconsin, 30 miles east of Green Bay on the shore of Lake Michigan.

finished product. The firm ships out in excess of 2 million tons of product a year.

There have been some famous milestones in Kewaunee Engineering's past. In 1944 the company launched a general-purpose supply vessel for the U.S. Army Transportation Corps. The ship was at first called FP-344. When FP-344 was transferred to the Navy in 1962, it was renamed the USS *Pueblo* and put under Commander Lloyd Bucher. In 1968 the *Pueblo* was seized by the North Koreans in the Sea of Japan and entered the history books.

A major fire in December 1965 destroyed the plant and almost meant the end of the company. However, Peterson, who had been the sole owner of the corporation since the end of the war, decided to rebuild the plant. The new plant was dedicated in a special Fred J. Peterson Appreciation Day celebration on October 28, 1966.

The loss of Kewaunee Engineering would have been a major blow to the town of Kewaunee. Allan Lamer

thinks that the people of Kewaunee are as important to the success of the company as the company is to the well-being of the town. "We have good access to skilled labor here. We find that the work force is very skilled and interested in the company they work for. There's good talent available here."

For the future the Lamers are actively seeking new customers for Kewaunee Engineering Corp., and they are diversifying as well. They recently constructed a small-boat marina for 32 boats; they plan to expand the marina.

Although it specializes in the fabrication of heavy steel, Kewaunee Engineering offers a variety of products and services ranging from components for mine-sweeping equipment to metal trailers and custom machining work for other manufacturers.

BRILLION IRON WORKS, INC.

"Quality is number one and we have to deliver it at an affordable price," states Karl Gabler, president and chief executive officer of Brillion Iron Works. The company, which currently employs approximately 700 people in three plants that total more than 550,000 square feet, is "dedicated to producing the highest quality tillage tools and castings with superior machinability and dimensional stability to provide our customers with the finest product possible," Gabler adds.

Brillion manufactures its own line of quality crafted farm equipment marketed nationally and worldwide under the Brillion name. Brillion's seeding, tillage, and shredding equipment is well recognized as a leader in the farm equipment and agricultural industry. Farm implements produced by Brillion are a major factor in minimum and no-till farming, which is important in conservation of land and resources and reduction of chemical use.

Satisfying its customers has become a challenge for Brillion Iron Works as is true of iron foundries all over the world today. "Foreign competition has put lots of pressure on us," Gabler says. "We've developed new cost-saving techniques because customers do not accept price in-

creases. So in order to keep prices down, or even lower them, we have to find our cost savings in the plant." Brillion is aggressive both in technology and in terms of cost savings.

The Brillion Iron Works has long been a landmark in the city of Brillion. The predecessor of today's company began in 1893 as a foundry and machine shop established to build power packs for threshing machines and cream separators. This shop was organized as Brillion Iron Works in 1895 by Henry Ariens, president, and his partners, John Thompson and Emil Loos. (Loos withdrew as a company shareholder in 1901.) The firm was incorporated in 1902.

The company grew. In 1903 the physical plant was expanded. Four years later Brillion purchased the Young Loader Manufacturing Company of West Bend. The organization expanded further after its invention of the Brillion Gasoline Engine, which required no battery, in 1912.

Brillion Iron Works has long been a landmark in the city of Brillion. In 1895 Henry Ariens (president) and partners John Thompson and Emil Loos organized a foundry and machine shop into Brillion Iron Works. The business was incorporated in 1902. This artist's rendering shows the Brillion plant circa the late 1930s.

The company's expansion required further additions to the physical plant. In 1913 Brillion built three concrete structures, including a fireproof foundry room with updated equipment, a pattern shop, and a warehouse. The firm built an office building in 1914.

Innovations in its product line assured further growth for Brillion. In 1916 the foundry introduced a front-wheel-pull tractor that could be operated by one person and pull three to five plows. This new Brillion tractor provided 15 percent more load per horsepower than other drive tractors.

Despite its earlier successes, economic conditions during the Depression pushed Brillion Iron Works into voluntary bankruptcy in April 1933. Reorganized in January 1934, Brillion resumed operations under the name of Brillion Pulverizer Company. Officials of the firm were R.D. Peters, secretary/general and general manager; A.F. Paustian, president; C.F. Pritzl, vice-president; and O.M. Russell, general superintendent.

The company was soon renamed Brillion Iron Works, Inc., and began to grow again. A foundry addition was built by employees in the plant. In 1963 a 13,000-square-foot addition expanded the machine shop facilities. Four new line-frequency

coreless induction melting furnaces with gas-fired preheaters were added in 1966.

Daily production of iron increased substantially when a ductile iron plant was built in 1973. The plant was again expanded three years later when the Farm Equipment Division was moved to a new facility. Additional automated horizontal molding units were added in 1977 and 1981 and a DISA unit in 1985.

The company merged with Beatrice Foods in 1969, operating as an independent division of Beatrice until Brillion became part of the Robins Group of La Jolla, California, in 1985.

During all of these changes—automation, expansion, new ownership—Brillion's work force has remained remarkably stable. "Our work force has an employment longevity that is unusual in the modern day," says Gabler. "We have some workers who have been here 40 years. We have three generations from some families. We have every family combination you can think of—husband and wife, mother and daughter, father and son, many brothers and sisters." And, he adds, Brillion's work force is more than just loyal. "We have a very good aggressive work force—hardworking and here when you need them."

In the 550,000 square feet of manufacturing area, Brillion's work force can melt and mold 1,200 tons of iron a day. Brillion's three plants now utilize mostly computerized machinery. Some parts of the operation are still labor intensive. The molten iron is still manually poured into the molds; however, the new Disamatic utilizes an auto-pour. And making patterns (Brillion has more than 3,700 patterns in use or in storage) cannot be automated. Brillion employs a staff of 25 journeymen patternmakers to keep the pattern equipment in first-class shape. They

Today Brillion Iron Works, Inc., employs 700 people in three plants that total more than 550,000 square feet. Its work force can melt and mold 1,200 tons of iron per day.

also make new patterns every month, as new needs arise.

Brillion melts and pours both gray iron and ductile iron into molds. The molds, which are made of green sand, are produced on five separate molding lines in plant 1 and four separate lines in plant 2. All of these molding lines are fully mechanized. The high green sand mold strength assures excellent dimensional qualities in the casting and a very fine surface finish. Brillion's recently installed Disamatic machine employs three on-board computers that manage sand control, mold density, shake-out time, pattern changes, and other process specifications. The Disamatic can produce up to 420 molds per hour.

The company has developed the Brillion Pledge to communicate its commitment to quality to its customers. "To help our customers be successful," it reads, "we pledge to supply the most reliable castings

available. We will accomplish this through use of only the finest raw materials and the strictest process controls. We will demonstrate this by supplying the highest quality castings that are readily machinable, dimensionally reliable, and competitively priced. We will listen to our customers' needs and requirements and do our utmost to answer questions, solve problems, and provide service they can depend on."

As Gabler puts it, Brillion's commitment to quality and productivity ensures that "we're here to stay."

Here are some of the high-quality castings that Brillion produces.

CRESCENT WOOLEN MILLS CO.

When Archibald M. Webster left his home in Winona, Minnesota, in 1923 to establish a woolen mill in Two Rivers, he had planned to go alone. But on the morning Archibald was to leave his brother, L.E. "Ted" Webster said, "Just a minute, Arch, I'm going to go with you." The firm the two brothers founded, Crescent Woolen Mills Co., is still going strong in Two Rivers today, and employs 50 people in a 52,000-square-foot plant on School Street a block from Lake Michigan.

Archibald and Ted Webster came from a long family tradition in the wool industry. Their father, William Walter Webster, founded a woolen mill in Rushford, Minnesota, that later was moved to La Crescent and then to Winona. Known as the W.W. Webster Company, it was a landmark in Winona for many years. Although the Minnesota woolen mill is no longer owned by the Webster family, the company that currently operates in the building (Winona Knitting) is a customer of Crescent Woolen Mills.

Crescent Woolen Mills sells its spun yarn to companies all over the Upper Midwest. "Today we manufacture about 35,000 pounds of spun yarn weekly," says William Webster, one of Archibald's five children (Robert K. Sr., Leland, Charles M. Sr., Jeanne Webster Groessl, and

Archibald M. Webster (1885-1957), founder of Crescent Woolen Mills Co.

The Crescent Woolen Mills Co. School Street plant in Two Rivers, which has seen four additions since it was built in 1955. The company currently employs 50 people who blend the woolen fibers, then card, spin, twist, and wind them into shippable cones.

William). Since Archibald's death in 1957 and Ted's death in 1970, Archibald's children have run the firm. William is currently president of the company; Robert K. Sr. is chairman of the board; Charles M. Sr. is secretary/treasurer; and Guy, son of Robert K., is a vice-president. (Leland died in 1987.) A fourth generation of Websters is now becoming active in the wool business also.

Crescent purchases virgin wool fibers from sheep-growers cooperatives throughout the Midwest and wool brokers who represent sheep producers in the United States, England, and Ireland. In its factory on School Street (which has seen four additions since it was built in 1955) Crescent employees blend the fibers, then card, spin, twist, and back wind them onto shippable cones. Customers include knitters of socks, sweaters, hats, and gloves.

There have been some changes in the way wool is spun and the machinery used. Rubberized V-belts have replaced leather belts, for example, and electronics have been introduced to a limited degree. The equipment has gotten bigger, and more operations can be done on one machine.

The biggest change is the introduction of synthetics into blended fibers. Crescent has experimented with innovations such as cotton-wool blends and polypropylene-wool blends. "But," says William Webster, "we are not getting away from wool. It will probably continue to be the basic mainstay of the company." Webster points out that the addition of a little synthetic fiber to the yarn used to make socks increases durability without appreciably affecting the comfort and soft feel of the product.

Their long family tradition in the wool business has left the Websters with a deep appreciation for the diversity of fibers, sheep, and spinning. "Sheep are no different from people," says William Webster. "They have different coarsenesses of hair. Fibers come in different lengths and thicknesses, just as garden hoses do."

Crescent's employees are one of the real assets of the company, Webster says. "We have a good, knowledgeable, loyal, well-trained work force." Many of Crescent's employees also have a long family tradition in the wool industry.

VERSA TECHNOLOGIES, INC.

"The vitality of a business is directly proportional to its profitability, not its size" says James E. Mohrhauser, president and chief executive officer of Versa Technologies, Inc. (Versa/Tek). "If you ask employees to forge a career with you, you have an obligation to be as profitable as possible in order to be able to withstand adversity. No matter how hard an employee works, a job is insecure if management doesn't have its priorities straight."

In order to ensure the profitability of its three operating divisions (Milwaukee Cylinder, Moxness Products, Inc., and Mox-Med, Inc.), Versa/Tek concentrates on niche markets where customers' needs for technological and engineering expertise, product quality, and superior service will result in above-average profitability.

Versa/Tek works with the development and engineering departments. "We get in on the ground floor of product development," Mohrhauser explains. "It might be two, three, or four years until we get our first order." In this way, Mohrhauser says, Versa/Tek often "develops a rapport and trust with customers that makes them unwilling to leave for better pricing." The approach that Versa/Tek tries to convey to its customers is that "we're willing to extend ourselves. We're not just selling product by the pound."

Versa/Tek is engaged in the manufacture of engineered fluid power components and the specialized molding and extrusion of silicone rubber products. The company's headquarters is in Racine. Its shares are publicly held and traded over the counter. Versa/Tek's common stock is held by approximately 1,200 stockholders of record. Its three operating divisions serve diverse markets.

Milwaukee Cylinder manufactures custom-engineered cylinders for

James E. Mohrhauser, president and chief executive officer of Versa Technologies, Inc.

the aircraft, automotive, robotics, petrochemical, machine tool, and capital goods industries. It also manufactures hydraulic devices that raise, lower, or level semitrailers, trucks, and medical vans, as well as a line of specialized material-handling equipment for factory applications under the trade names Pow'r Arm and Pow'r Lift.

Moxness Products, Inc., fabricates silicone rubber components for special sectors of diverse industrial markets. Some of its markets include business and data-processing equipment, consumer electronics, automotive, electrical distribution, home appliance, and aerospace.

Mox-Med, Inc., extrudes, molds, and fabricates silicone components for the health care/medical and food-processing markets. Mox-Med is currently the sole operating unit of Versa Medical Technologies, Inc.,

which was established to concentrate on opportunities of above-average potential in its selected markets.

Mohrhauser has been guiding Versa/Tek since he, together with financial backers no longer involved with the company, purchased Milwaukee Cylinder in 1967, and two years later became president of publicly held Plastics Corporation of America. The two predecessor components merged in 1970 and became Versa Technologies, Inc. Moxness Products, Inc., was part of Plastics Corporation of America. In 1978 Mox-Med, Inc., was established to concentrate on serving the health care/medical market in a separate manufacturing plant in Portage, Wisconsin.

Mohrhauser's goal for Versa/Tek has been an after-tax profit of 8 to 10 percent; Versa Technologies, Inc., has consistently reached that goal since the mid-1970s. "And," says Mohrhauser, "we continue to challenge ourselves to find better ways of doing our jobs."

PARAGON ELECTRIC COMPANY, INC.

In 1905 Edward M. Platt of Manitowoc was in the coal business in Chicago. He advanced some money to friends who owned a business, Paragon Sellers Co., that sold telephone specialties. When they defaulted on the loans, Platt took over. He and several investors incorporated the firm in Illinois, with the main office in Chicago and a second office in Manitowoc.

The company did not manufacture—it represented other manufacturers in the sale of lightning rod grounding devices, telephone wire (later known as Paragon Ironite), battery boxes for dry cells, and clamp-on bed lamps. Platt developed a focus for the firm and a product of its own—he purchased the patent for a time switch, a rather new invention that started electric heaters automatically. The switch was maufactured in Manitowoc and sold to the Mergenthaler Linotype Company, which used the device to preheat lead pots for hot metal type.

Operations began with one employee, Herbert Menge, who assembled purchase machined parts. Output was one to three units per day, and each sold for $45. When power companies realized that money could be saved by using the switch to control generators, the demand for time switches grew, and Paragon with it. August Ohm, destined to remain with Paragon for many years, was hired as Menge's assistant. Failure of one of Paragon's competitors brought about the employment of Paragon's first officially titled engineer, Harold Haines. The timers Haines conceived were "fearful in appearance, but wondrous in design." The most famous was the Model E, better known as the Paragon Bee's Nest. Haines passed away at the peak of his career, and August Ohm's son-in-law, Emil Swenson, became the design engineer. He developed the first synchronous motor time switch, which

Paragon introduced in 1932. Now switching could be controlled with the accuracy and convenience of an electric clock instead of relying on spring-wound power.

Paragon outgrew its little shop in Manitowoc and larger quarters were found. In 1936 employment jumped to 40, including many of the men who were to help develop Paragon's future.

In 1938 Paragon designed the first time switch for controlling the automatic defrosting of refrigerators; the De-frost-it would turn the refrigerator off during nighttime hours, allowing ice to melt and water to evaporate. From this add-on unit sprang the expansion of time switches in the commercial and domestic refrigeration market. Paragon is still prominent in the manufacture of automatic defrosting control timers for both commercial and domestic refrigeration.

The advent of World War II proved to be a critical time for Paragon. A contract was obtained, however, to build timers and switches that would control demagnetization devices on mine sweepers. That work made it necessary to hire more workers and created a need for expansion. The City of Two Rivers solved the

Today Paragon occupies 360,000 square feet in the city of Two Rivers. Additional facilities are located in Bristol, England, and Ontario, Canada.

problem by offering a plant that provided four times more space.

Paragon moved into electrical box manufacturing for use in sub-

Paragon started in 1905 as a telephone specialty company and expanded into wire and electrical items. The first plant was located here at 502 North Ninth Street in Manitowoc.

marines and smaller naval vessels, and manufacturing began for shipboard electric panels that supported switches, meters, and connection points. Time switches were used in radar apparatus and ship switchboards. Paragon was in the right place at the right time and contributed greatly to the nation's wartime efforts.

When the war ended in 1945, Paragon began the task of building for peace. However, the plant was stacked from floor to ceiling with switchboards, boxes, and parts previously destined for the war effort. The War Department advised Paragon to take inventory and scrap them. The large factory was empty and Paragon faltered. Civilian markets had been lost, designs were outdated, and Paragon needed working capital to get back on its feet.

Paragon Electric Company became a Wisconsin corporation in 1945. By the end of 1948 new products were flowing into an expanding market, and stockholders were receiving a return on their investments. When the De-frost-it was taken off the shelf and redesigned, it became a tremendous success. A thermostat setback control called Nitrol promised tremendous savings in heating cost. The Elec-Trivet, designed to keep coffee hot without a stove, was an overnight success at trade shows and department stores nationwide, contributing to Paragon's success in the mid-1950s.

In 1954 Paragon reintroduced an improved version of its famous 300 Series time switches. Labeled the 3000 Series and marketed under the name Memory Master, the switches incorporated all the features of the competition—yet Paragon could make them better and sell them cheaper.

The following year Paragon began production of the DRV synchronous timing motor, a development of

crucial importance to Paragon's subsequent growth. Manufacturing its own motor allowed Paragon to develop highly integrated and efficient controls, and revenues from the sale of the motors to other firms provided capital for expanding other product lines. Paragon pioneered the development of automatic defrost controls for frozen-food cases and storage lockers, and still leads in that field today.

In 1960 George Platt, son of Edward and president of Paragon, began negotiations with the American Machine and Foundry Company. On February 2, 1961, Paragon became AMF/Paragon. Sales continued to grow, and by the end of 1964, after fewer than three years with AMF, sales had jumped 50 percent. The product line diversified: Consumer products were stressed by adding inexpensive home lighting timers, and commercial lines were expanded. AMF/Paragon was successful in gaining new customers in the water-conditioning field with new, advanced controls. A full line of electronic time controls ranging from one to 32 channels was developed. Interest in energy management led to the development of energy optimizers for HVAC controls, electronic lighting controls, and energy-management systems.

In 1985 Minstar, a company headed by Irwin Jacobs, acquired AMF. Paragon was offered for sale. The management group at Paragon, headed by Robert E. Horn, president and chief executive officer, negotiated the purchase of Paragon from Minstar. The sale was effective

Paragon is a leader in electronic controls. From single-channel timers to complex energy-management systems like the one shown here, Paragon manufactures state-of-the-art equipment for industrial, consumer, commercial, and international markets.

March 19, 1986. Paragon also purchased facilities in Canada and England, and established representatives worldwide. Paragon Electric Company, Inc., is beginning a new era, with ownership returned to the Lakeshore community where it began in 1905.

The De-frost-it, introduced in 1938, turned refrigerators off at night, allowing ice to melt and evaporate. This add-on unit led to an expanded use of time switches in the commercial and domestic refrigeration market, establishing Paragon as a prominent manufacturer of automatic defrost controls.

H.G. WEBER & CO.

"We pride ourselves on quality, workmanship, innovation, and service," says Gerald Chopp, president of H.G. Weber Company. The firm, which employs some 85 people, was founded in 1925 by Herman Gustave Weber (1878-1943). Emigrating from Germany in 1899, Weber worked for a succession of companies in the printing and paper-converting machinery field. He started as a draftsman, working his way up to designer and chief engineer. In 1925 Weber established the H.G. Weber Co. in Sheboygan; moving the company to its present site in Kiel, Wisconsin, in 1936 to be near his customers and the paper industry, Weber's goal was to produce a better bag-making machine.

In its 60-plus years the H.G. Weber Company has manufactured more than 1,000 bag-making and paper-converting machines. Weber machines are sold worldwide, with equipment installed in 42 countries.

"We have increased our sales approximately 20 percent each of the past two years, owing mostly to the development of new products," says Chopp. "We don't base our long-range goals on quotas or percentages. Our aim is to design and manufacture machines easier to operate with increased productivity and respond to the needs of the packaging and converting industry."

In recognition of its accomplishments, the H.G. Weber Company has received two Wisconsin Governor's new product awards (Up-Ender Roll Handler and Patch Applicator), and the President's "E" Award for Excellence in Export.

Bag-making equipment was once the sole product of the H.G. Weber Company. Bag machines convert bags from bulk rolls of paper, cutting, folding, and gluing in one continuous operation. Some Weber machine models produce more than 500 bags per minute. The company also manufactures auxiliary components for custom printing, rotary die cutting, and adhesive laminating during the bag-making process.

"Our corporate goal is to develop four new products a year," explains Chopp. "We're aiming for world leadership through craftsmanship, service, and product development." To accomplish these ambitious goals, the H.G. Weber Company recently expanded its facilities to 50,000 square feet.

Currently Weber bag machines are producing more than 80 percent of the bags used in North America for the packaging of pet food products. Over the years Weber has become a leader in the manufacture of specialty square-bottom bag-making machines. Bags made on Weber machines are used for packaging products such as salt, cookies, chemicals, corn, grain, rice, coffee, frozen foods, and microwave popcorn. Weber assisted in the development of the current microwave package design, which includes the applying of a metalized heating patch with Weber's award-winning patch applicator.

Weber also produces machines that manufacture multi-ply bags up to five-ply construction. These bags are used for the packaging of charcoal, chemicals, granular rubber, potatoes, carbon black, onions, compressed asbestos, animal feeds, and powdered milk.

Other Weber machines manufacture a wide variety of office file folders, pocket files, and X-ray envelopes. Some of the same equipment can produce gaskets, carton blanks, or products requiring die-cut formation.

At H.G. Weber Company, Chopp says, "We are proud of our employees, products, and the facilities we work in, and we know our employees appreciate being appreciated."

In 1925 Herman G. Weber founded the company that still bears his name, the H.G. Weber Company.

A commemorative 1,000th paper-converting machine, which makes microwave popcorn bags at the rate of 300 bags per minute, or five per second, was dedicated on April 7, 1987.

GRAEF, ANHALT, SCHLOEMER & ASSOCIATES, INC.

"I can remember when I was 10 years old, going down to the Plankinton Arcade with my mother and watching the fish swim in the pool at the bottom of the spiral staircase," says Luther W. Graef, president of Graef, Anhalt, Schloemer & Associates, Inc., consulting engineers. "Only the fish change," adds Graef, whose firm was involved in every aspect of the structural design of the Grand Avenue, including the renovation of the Plankinton Building.

For the Grand Avenue the firm designed a new, three-story Retail Center extending between Second Street and the Boston Store, designed foundation repairs and a new mall entrance for the Boston Store, did an analysis for renovation of the first and second floors of the Majestic Building, designed the restoration of the Plankinton Building to its original 1915 appearance, did an analysis of the Woolworth Building (a six-story retail and office structure) for renovation, designed two new pedestrian skywalks over city streets, and designed two new five-story parking garages connected to the mall.

For its work on the Grand Avenue, the firm received the 1982 Engineering Excellence Award from the Wisconsin Association of Consulting Engineers and the 1983 Engineering Achievement Award from the Wisconsin Section of the American Society of Civil Engineers.

Since 1961, when Graef, Anhalt, Schloemer was founded, the firm has received many other awards for its less-famous projects. The three founding partners, all registered professional engineers, were Robert E. Schloemer, Leonard P. Anhalt, and Graef.

The firm began with the three partners and two employees in an office above a bakery. Today Graef, Anhalt, Schloemer, with 17 partners, works on 600 projects a year, has annual sales well exceeding $5 million, and has a staff of 115 people, including both architects and engineers.

The company is no longer located above a bakery; it now owns a building on a four-acre, parklike site near the Milwaukee County Zoo. The structure, the Milwaukee Engineering Center, also houses an electrical engineering firm, a mechanical engineering company, and a drafting firm. "By having our electrical engineer, mechanical engineer, and drafting consultants in our building, we can offer our clients complete service under one roof," Graef points out.

The Graef, Anhalt, Schloemer staff is able to assist clients through all phases of a project, from field surveys and project design to on-site

The Grand Avenue, located in the heart of Milwaukee's downtown commercial district, presented a challenge to Graef, Anhalt, Schloemer engineers. In this view of the interior of the Plankinton Building, fish swim in the pool at the bottom of the spiral staircase, as they did in 1915 when the building was new.

construction services. Staff professional registrations are held in 33 states. Services include site selection, architectural design, structural design and analysis, plant engineering services, facilities mapping, building renovation and restoration, municipal public works design, sewer and water systems, sewage-treatment facilities, industrial pollution control, solid-waste studies, site engineering, storm-water-control systems, field surveying, streets and highway design, bridge design, and construction inspection.

The firm's recently completed and current projects in Milwaukee include involvement in the Milwaukee Water Pollution Abatement Program, structural engineering for the Summerfest Amphitheatre, foundation walls for the First Wisconsin Center, and buildings on both the University of Wisconsin and Marquette University campuses.

The three founding partners of Graef, Anhalt, Schloemer & Associates, Inc., are (from left) Robert E. Schloemer, Leonard P. Anhalt, and Luther W. Graef. Today the firm has 17 partners and a total staff of 115.

MADISON BUSINESS COLLEGE

"Success Spoken Here" reads a sign on the bulletin board outside the library at Madison Business College's Spring Harbor campus. MBC has a specific definition of the success it seeks for its graduates. "We have been providing professional education for business careers since 1856," says Dr. Stuart E. Sears, president and chairman of the board. "Our school is the fifth-oldest business college in the United States and by far the oldest this far west." Business education, Sears adds, "is all we do and that's where we put all our resources."

In the past 131 years MBC has prepared approximately 35,000 students for careers in business. Things have changed since MBC opened its doors in a small building on the square across from the capitol in 1856. "The technological explosion has had a profound effect on what we do and how we do it," Sears explains. In the early days MBC (then known as Northwestern Business College) offered courses in penmanship, bookkeeping, and arithmetic. The typewriter had yet to be invented.

But as soon as machines such as typewriters and adding machines became common in business offices, MBC began teaching students to use them. Today all students are required

---

Northwestern Business College, the forerunner of Madison Business College, on North Pickney Street in 1875. Today a YWCA stands beside this site.

to take at least one course in the use of computers in order to graduate.

Because the school has seen so much change in its 131 years, MBC is committed to a philosophy of teaching students to expect change in their later work lives. "If you teach people that this is a computer and you press this button and this happens," Sears believes, they learn to run one particular computer. But later they may end up working on a different computer, one that is operated differently. "So we try to teach them that this is the purpose of the button," Sears says. "The button doesn't have to be in a particular place."

MBC has not stayed in one particular place either. Over the years it has been located in several different buildings on the square, on West Washington Avenue, and now on Spring Harbor Drive on the west side of Madison. It has changed names several times also, from Northwestern Business College, to Capital City Commercial College (popularly known as the "4C" College), to Madison Business College.

Today Madison Business College is a private, independent, coeducational two-year institution. Its graduates most frequently earn the Associate of Arts (A.A.) degree in business administration (accounting, accounting/data processing, general business management, and sales and marketing majors), and secretarial studies (executive, legal, and medical majors). Diploma programs are offered in bookkeeping and in general secretarial studies and general clerical studies. A certificate program is offered in stenographic studies. In addition to courses in their major field of study, students are also required to complete a general education core of courses.

"We don't attempt to be all things to all people," says Sears. "We don't spread our offerings out over

This building was home to Madison Business College for 60 years until the college was moved to its present location in 1980. The college stood across West Washington Avenue from the Valley Bank building.

car repair and fly-fish tying and nursing. All we do is what we do—business."

Such dedication to preparing its students for a business career pays off for MBC graduates when they look for a job. MBC estimates that 90 to 95 percent of its graduates find jobs in the fields in which they were trained by the time of graduation. "We don't wait for six months to compile those statistics," Sears says. "Our graduates have jobs right at the time of graduation."

MBC has a full-time employment officer who helps students with the job hunt. This employment service is a lifetime free service for graduates of MBC.

Because MBC has been in existence for such a long time, many generations of students have graduated from the school. Students frequently mention that their grandmother or grandfather also attended MBC, and it is not at all unusual for siblings to follow each other through.

There have been several instances of mothers and daughters enrolled at the same time at MBC.

The personal atmosphere of the school is one reason people choose to go there. The largest class ever allowed is 40, according to Sears, and most classes are much smaller. The student and faculty populations as a whole are also small, which contributes to the overall informal friendli-

An aerial view of the parklike setting of the Madison Business College campus near the shores of Lake Mendota. Photo by Skot Weidemann. Courtesy, Sutter Weidemann Photography

ness. "Everyone knows everyone else at MBC," claims Sears. "The teachers know all the students by name. No one is just a number here."

As befits a school preparing its graduates for careers in business, Sears says that MBC is "marketplace oriented. If the market says we're no good, then we are out of business. If we don't do the job that we're here to do and do it at least as well as anybody else who does it, then we are out of business. And we haven't been out of business in 131 years."

Education is always a cycle. Students graduate, new students take their place, times change, and technology and information requirements change. MBC has kept up with the changes in business education over the years. As Sears is fond of saying, "You run awfully fast to stay even and you have to run even faster than that to get ahead." But one thing has stayed the same at MBC: its commitment to the successful business careers of its students.

As Sears puts it in an open letter to students published at the front of the Madison Business College course catalog: "My office is always open. Please feel free to come in at any time and discuss your plans with me or with any member of our staff. We are dedicated to your success."

A.O. SMITH CORPORATION

When Arthur O. Smith met Henry Ford in 1906, neither man had yet become famous for the mass assembly line techniques their companies later developed. Smith's company (founded by his father, C.J. Smith, in 1874) had been producing parts for baby carriages and bicycles. When the automobile craze began, the Smith Company began to furnish parts for Cadillacs, Packards, Elmores, Locomobiles, and Fords.

When Ford came to tour Smith's plant in 1906, Smith boasted that they were manufacturing several automobile frames a day, with an eye to eventually making as many as a dozen a day. "But I want 10,000 frames," Ford is supposed to have said. "And I want them in four months. Can you do it?" Smith replied optimistically, "Of course. That's what we're here for." Smith's optimism was well-founded. The company filled the order for 10,000

Henry Ford and Arthur O. Smith toured Milwaukee streets in a new 1906 Ford Model N car. Ford had driven from Detroit to show Smith one of the first 10,000 frames in use, the first major production order for passenger frames for A.O. Smith.

frames and has been making great quantities of parts for automobiles ever since.

A.O. Smith's son, L.R. Smith, became president of the company when his father died in 1913. L.R. Smith was as optimistic and ambitious as his father, and he shared the family's engineering ability. L.R. Smith set out to design and build, with the help of hundreds of engineers, the first fully automatic frame plant.

In 1921 a plant was designed in which 552 separate mechanical operations could be performed, each within the rigid framework of a 10-second cycle. Flat sheets of steel were fed automatically into one end of the machine, which was nearly two city blocks long, and black painted finished frames came out the other end at the rate of one every eight seconds. Millions of frames—more than 10,000 a day—were manufactured thus in the world's first fully automated assembly line.

After 37 years the South Frame Plant finally stopped using the famous machine in 1958. But its influence on assembly-line construction in industry is still being felt today. The A.O. Smith Corporation today uses robots, computers, and electronics in its highly automated assembly lines, but the principles date back to the early experiments by Smith engineers.

The Smith Corporation developed other innovative technologies as well. Shortly after C.J. Smith, an emigrant from England who had been an indentured engineering apprentice, founded the company in 1874, it developed the technology of forming steel tubing from sheet metal. This steel tubing was used at first to build lightweight bicycle frames. Then C.J.'s son, A.O., applied the principle of the tubular bicycle frame to the development of the first automobile frame. This innovation was one reason car manufacturers like Ford were interested in the small specialty hardware manufacturer in Milwaukee.

Other technological breakthroughs included a process for fusing glass to steel. This technology has applications in the manufacture of home water heaters, large brewery storage tanks, and large silos. Smith also pioneered in the development of pipelines for crude oil, and in welding techniques and equipment.

During World War II the firm became a major government contractor; it made bomber landing gears

The final assembly station of the famous 1921 A.O. Smith car frame machine, the world's first fully automated assembly line. The giant jaws automatically closed cold rivets of the car frames, one frame every eight seconds.

and torpedo air flasks, as well as 80 percent of all the bomb casings used by the Allies.

After the war the company developed and introduced small fractional horsepower electric motors, petroleum metering systems, and the revolutionary Harvestore® agricultural feed-processing system.

Today A.O. Smith continues to emphasize research and development. Its newly constructed Corporate Technology Center is a 56,293-square-foot facility located at Park Place in Milwaukee. The Corporate Technology Center includes a Chemical Systems Group, an Electrical/Electronic Systems Group, an Energy Systems Group, a Design and Prototype Group, a Manufacturing Assessment Group, an Advanced Manufacturing Methods Group, and other research offices.

A.O. Smith still maintains its headquarters in Milwaukee, but it is a far larger company than it was in the late 1800s, when it was called C.J. Smith and Sons, and manufactured parts for bicycles and baby carriages. Today the *Fortune* 500 company employs more than 12,000 people worldwide and manufactures products in 22 plants both in the United States and abroad. In 1986 the firm had net sales of well over $910 million. C.J.'s great-grandsons, L.B. and A.O. Smith, are on the board of directors of the company; several members of the fifth generation are employees of the firm.

The Automotive Products Company, a division of the A.O. Smith Corporation, is the largest operating unit of A.O. Smith. It is the leading manufacturer of automotive and truck structural products in North America and has a leading presence in Mexico as well. The division's sales are approximately $600 million annually.

The Automotive division's three plants (in Milwaukee; Granite

This 3,000-ton press, installed in 1986 at the A.O. Smith Automotive Products Company in Milwaukee, forms side rails for one dozen different light truck frames. The press can produce more than 300 parts per hour.

City, Illinois; and Milan, Tennessee) have more than 6,000 employees.

The Automotive Products Company manufactures full-size passenger car frames, front-engine cradles, rear suspension systems, and suspension components. Its truck products include fully assembled frames for light and medium trucks, as well as heat-treated side rails for heavy trucks. The company also produces suspension components used on trucks.

The Automotive Products Company recently received Q1 awards from the Ford Motor Company for excellence in the quality production of the Ranger truck frame, which is produced at the Milwaukee plant, and the front-engine cradles for the Ford Taurus and Mercury Sable passenger cars.

In its century-plus history the A.O. Smith Corporation has seen many changes. Product lines such as

bicycles and baby carriages gave way to full automotive frames commonly used in rear-drive cars. When U.S. automakers switched to front-drive models in the 1970s, the Smith Corporation began to make the "engine cradles" that have replaced full frames in many cars.

As in the old days, when A.O. Smith told Henry Ford, "That's what we're here for," the company retains its commitment to innovation and optimism.

A.O. Smith's Research and Engineering Building opened in 1931. Pioneering the use of acres of outside curtain wall glass and the absence of inside columns marked the beginning of an epoch in contemporary office architecture. The building is now headquarters of the A.O. Smith Automotive Products Company.

A.F. GALLUN & SONS COMPANY

"Calf is to leather as diamonds are to jewels," says Tony Gallun, managing partner of A.F. Gallun & Sons Company. "Calfskin is one of the most expensive and best quality leather there is." Gallun, the fourth generation of his family to convert calf hides into tanned leather calfskin, is convinced that calfskin is "the most leathery product there is. It looks, feels, and smells like leather."

In the mid-nineteenth century, when German immigrant August F. Gallun started his tannery in a small building on Wisconsin Avenue at the river, now downtown Milwaukee, calfskin was in great demand. There were calfskin tanneries all over the United States and in Europe; there were even other calfskin tanneries in Milwaukee. "The Gallun company is the only surviving American calf tannery," Tony Gallun points out. "There were probably 15 American calf tanneries when I started here in 1955."

Gallun's great-grandfather moved the tanning operation to its present site on North Water Street, still on the Milwaukee River, in approximately 1885. August F. Gallun's son, Albert F., became president of

The Gallun Tannery, circa 1875.

the firm in 1890, when his father retired. Albert F.'s son, Edwin A. Gallun, served as chief executive officer of the company from his father's retirement in 1933 until 1978. The firm became a limited partnership in 1986; the three general partners are Edwin A. Jr., Arthur B., and Tony Gallun.

The periodic lack of availability of calves for veal has contributed to the decline of the calfskin tanning business in the United States. Tony Gallun thinks his family's operation has survived while others have not because "when business was good my father put most of the profits into outside investments to diversify the profit base of the company. And he really had the right approach to making leather. He didn't invest in costly machinery that couldn't tan leather any better or any faster than the machinery that was already in place."

The calf tanning business has sped up. Gallun tans between 400,000 and one million calfskins per year. In the old days it took 6 months for a skin to go through the whole tanning process. Today that process takes from six to eight weeks. And every single skin goes through approximately 65 separate processes, including trimming, soaking, unhairing, shaving, coloring, toggling, drying, weighing, and measuring.

"What we sell and ship out of

here is the same shape as we get it from the packinghouse," Gallun says. Unhairing and tanning is standard for all the skins, but many of the 65 processes, such as coloring and finishings, are done to a customer's specifications. "We're in the fashion business," Gallun points out. As an example, he says that 10 years ago 75 to 100 percent of all Gallun's calfskins were glazed, a process in which the grain surface is polished several times in order to develop the classic calfskin color and gloss. Today only about 25 percent of the skins are glazed.

Ten years from now some other finish for calfskin may well be popular. But Gallun is convinced that there will always be a place for calfskin, "the most leathery product there is."

August F. Gallun, founder of A.F. Gallun & Sons Company, in 1857.

The Gallun Tannery today.

OSCAR MAYER FOODS CORPORATION

When Oscar F. Mayer of Bavaria arrived in America in 1873 at the age of 14, he went right to work, first as a butcher's boy in Detroit and later as a worker in Chicago's stockyards and retail meat markets. No one but his friends, relatives, and employers knew his name. When he died in 1955 (he had moved the headquarters of his meat-processing company to Madison in the early 1950s), Oscar Mayer's name was a household word all over America.

People knew about Oscar Mayer bologna, sausages, luncheon meats, and smoked and canned meat products. But most of all, they knew the German-American's name from Oscar Mayer wieners. Ten years after his death Oscar Mayer's name was immortalized in "The Wiener Song." Variations of "Oh, I wish I were an Oscar Mayer wiener . . ." have been performed by the Vienna Symphony Orchestra, a teenage rock band, a string ensemble, and a Nashville country-western group, among others.

In 1974 Oscar Mayer's name was again put to music in the "My Bologna Has a First Name . . ." song. Giving hot dogs, bologna, and other processed meat products a name has been a key to the company's success over the years. As early as 1904 the Mayer brothers (Oscar, Gottfried, and Max) decided to use a brand name for their products. Edelweiss, one of their early trademarks, was used for bacon slabs, on boxes of pork sausage, and on lard pails. Another early trademark, Moose, went on baker's lard and heavier bacon.

In an era when many foods were sold without labels or wrappings, trade names such as Edelweiss and Moose were an effective way of helping the consumer pick out Oscar Mayer products. By the 1920s the firm was using more sophisticated trademarks—Approved Brand and Meats of Good Taste. In 1929 the

Oscar F. Mayer & Bro. was started as a retail meat market in rented quarters on Chicago's near north side in 1883. Five years later the firm moved two blocks away, and that is still the site of the Chicago plant. Shown here is the retail store on the site where the Chicago plant now exists.

name Oscar Mayer was added in a band around every fourth wiener. Other attention-getting devices included the introduction of Little Oscar, the midget chef, and his sausage-shaped vehicle, the Wienermobile, in 1936.

What all of these devices did was bring to the attention of the public the products produced by the Mayer family, which included sons, grandsons, nephews, and other descendants of the original founders. The business that started in a rented shop in Chicago has grown to be the sixth-largest meat company in the United States and the nation's largest producer of brand-identified, processed meat products. Today Oscar Mayer has sales exceeding $2 billion, primarily in the United States but also through five overseas operations, and it is known for the high quality and convenience of its products.

Headquartered in Madison, it is

Oscar Mayer, founder of the company that bears his name.

the largest private employer in Dane County. The Madison facility was purchased in 1919 from a farmers' cooperative and now employs 1,700 people in a 1.3-million-square-foot processing plant. In addition, the corporate office, which employs 900 people, is located there and has more than 400,000 square feet of office space.

The company is made up of several divisions, including consumer products, foodservice, specialty sales, operations, international, and technical services. The consumer products division distributes Oscar Mayer, Louis Rich, Claussen, Chef's Pantry, and Kemp food products.

In 1981 the Oscar Mayer Company was acquired by General Foods Corporation, which was acquired by Philip Morris Companies, Inc., in 1985.

Recent Oscar Mayer product innovations include cheese hot dogs and center-cut bacon, and the company's most famous production system—the "hot dog highway," which produces 36,000 wieners in less than an hour. They all carry the now-familiar name of the founder.

STEVENS POINT HOLIDAY INN CONVENTION AND ENTERTAINMENT CENTER

The Stevens Point Holiday Inn Convention and Entertainment Center is a statewide convention center and vacation spot. Located exactly in the middle of Wisconsin, it draws people from Superior to Madison, Milwaukee, and Chicago, and from Green Bay to La Crosse and Eau Claire. The Stevens Point Holiday Inn, surrounded by 15-acre grounds, has the largest Holidome in the United States and is one of the largest Holiday Inns, according to Lawrence Zenoff, its president. The hotel complex is "a landmark—famous all over the state," Zenoff adds.

One key to the Stevens Point Holiday Inn's success is its location right on Highway 51, the major north-south highway in Wisconsin. People do not have to drive out of their way if they are traveling farther north; the Holiday Inn is visible from the nearby freeway exit. If a convention is the destination, the Holiday Inn convention complex is roughly a two-hour drive from most parts of

the state. And many people heading north from Milwaukee, Madison, and Chicago consider the Stevens Point Holiday Inn and Holidome the halfway point in their trip.

The hotel, with 300 beautifully appointed guest rooms and suites, was newly remodeled in 1987. Changing times require changes in a hotel complex, according to Zenoff. For example, "female travelers are concerned with safety and security," he notes. The $6-million remodeling project resulted in spacious rooms and brightly lit corridors.

The convention center, also newly remodeled, can accommodate conventions as large as 2,500 (in 15 function rooms). Civic, government, business, and religious organizations come to the Stevens Point Holiday Inn convention center for two- to

The newly remodeled convention center attracts civic, government, business, and religious organizations.

The Stevens Point Holiday Inn Convention and Entertainment Center is a statewide convention center and vacation spot.

five-day conventions, as well as exhibits and trade-association meetings.

All of the dining and bar areas were completely redone as part of the renovation. The new Mesquite Grill is a dinner house with an open-hearth mesquite grill. The chefs cook in the middle of the dining room, so diners can watch the chefs at work. Entrees include mesquite-grilled baby back ribs, fresh chicken, beef ribs, and salmon. Grilled foods are first smoked in a mesquite smoker and then finished on the mesquite grill. Other featured entrees include steaks, as well as lobster and other seafood.

Zenoff says that the Mesquite Grill has a "California-style atmosphere," including western stone and a lot of greenery in the decor. The California influence extends to the breakfast and lunch menus. A massive salad bar and a famous Friday-night fish fry are other features of the new restaurant. "We've been known for our Sunday brunches for more than 18 years," Zenoff claims, and that tradition continues with a Sunday brunch containing more than 120 items. People come from as far away as Merrill and Portage to try the omelettes, French toast, appetizers,

The new Mesquite Grill is a dinner house with an open-hearth mesquite grill.

and juice bar. All of the bakery products are homemade, and ice carvings add to the air of festivity on Sundays.

Five nights per week Mortimer's Show Palace "Mort's," a Las Vegas-style show lounge, features floor shows. Mort's is "known as the hottest nightclub in northern Wisconsin—the place where all the action is," Zenoff enthuses. Mort's seats 300 and features entertainers such as the Platters, the Drifters, and Motown groups. The flashy decor features bright brass appointments and neon signs. "It's flash city," according to Zenoff.

The Concert Center can seat 1,400 people in a theater-style setting and features four to six big shows per year, in addition to the smaller nightclub shows booked into Mort's.

The Holidome is probably the most famous feature of the Stevens Point Holiday Inn. "We guarantee the weather!" is the Holidome's slogan. "It can be 30 below outside, but inside it's a tropical climate," Zenoff explains. The Holidome, which is all glass enclosed and heat controlled, is filled with tropical plants and trees that thrive under its sunlamps even in the middle of the winter. Ninety hotel rooms, including 10 of the 15

suites, overlook the Holidome.

The Holidome's amenities include a heated, Olympic-length swimming pool, double whirlpool, sauna, tanning machine, and a game area, with Ping-Pong, pocket billiards, shuffleboard, miniature golf, electronic games, and an exercise gym. There is also a soft play enclosure for small children.

A restored antique wagon from the 1920s serves hot dogs, ice cream,

Among the inn's amenities is a heated, Olympic-size swimming pool.

popcorn, sodas, and pizza to Holidome guests who cannot bear to leave the Holidome even to eat.

Outside the Holidome there are other attractions. The grounds of the Holiday Inn were newly landscaped in 1987. And, Zenoff points out, "the finest golf course in the state of Wisconsin is across the street." Indeed, Robert Trent Jones II considered his design for the 6,900-yard SentryWorld golf course to be his "Mona Lisa." The SentryWorld Golf Tennis Sports Center features championship golf, indoor and outdoor tennis, and racquetball. There are many lakes in the area surrounding Stevens Point, so fishing and boating are available. Winter attractions include skiing and snowmobiling.

Lawrence Zenoff's parents, William and Jean Zenoff, built the Stevens Point Holiday Inn Convention and Entertainment Center in 1968. Zenoff Inns, Inc., owns the Stevens Point Holiday Inn as well as other businesses; Lawrence is president (his sister, Hedda, is not active in the company). The Zenoffs donated Zenoff Park and Softball Complex to the city of Stevens Point.

HILLSHIRE FARM

Hillshire Farm is one of the largest producers of quality processed meat products in the United States. It all began when Friedrich "Fritz" Bernegger and Billy Schmidt bought a small meat market in New London, Wisconsin, in 1929. By 1934 the business had grown to include two supermarkets, and a slaughterhouse, which was located on a one-acre farm site just outside New London. The partnership was dissolved in 1953, when Fritz Bernegger took over sole operation of the business. The supermarkets were sold, and the packing plant was incorporated as Quality Packing Company.

In 1971 Sara Lee Corporation (then known as Consolidated Foods) purchased Quality Packing Company, and soon the official name was changed to Hillshire Farm. The main production facility at New London now employs more than 1,300 people. The firm has been a major economic factor in the growth of New London and area communities. A limited amount of Hillshire Farm products are also produced at one other facility—Kahn's Claryville

plant in northern Kentucky.

In 1972 Hillshire Farm Smoked Sausage was first introduced outside Wisconsin. Since that time Hillshire Farm Smoked Sausage has grown to be the national leader in market share in the category. In addition to a complete line of endless and link smoked sausage products distributed nationwide, Hillshire Farm is a leading regional marketer of a broad line of processed packaged meat items in the Midwest and West. These products include skinless and natural casing wieners, fresh bratwurst, pork sausage links, and Italian sausage, hams, bacon, and specialty items such as braunschweiger.

Hillshire Farm employees take pride in producing consistently high-quality products. All employees are responsible for ensuring that only the finest packaged finished goods leave the plant. They are backed up by a large, well-trained team of quality-control inspectors who monitor every

Friedrich "Fritz" Bernegger, founder of Hillshire Farm.

Hillshire Farm's corporate headquarters, located in New London, employs more than 1,300 people.

phase of processing to include analysis of each batch. Raw materials inspection and rigid microbiological standards are among the many areas where Hillshire Farm exceeds industry standards to produce fast-selling, high-quality products that are recognized as leaders in the processed meat categories throughout the country.

EMPLOYERS HEALTH INSURANCE

Their American Dream began in Freedom.

From the basement of a home in the hamlet of Freedom, Wisconsin, Ron Weyers and Wally Hilliard opened for business in 1969 to sell group health insurance. With approximately 1,300 established health insurance companies already selling the same thing, Weyers and Hilliard didn't have a chance—or so it seemed.

It didn't take long for the two to find a niche in that crowded market. With an overriding commitment to customer service, their dream became reality. In just 17 years their venture grew from the smallest to the 16th-largest group health insurance company in the United States.

When the firm opened for business as Wisconsin Employers Group, Weyers and Hilliard solicited the small business owners in and around the Fox River Valley. "It's difficult for small businesses to administer a health insurance program," Hilliard explains. "We simply provided a service that those businesses desperately needed." And the word quickly spread.

With a market that included nearly 4 million potential customers (U.S. businesses with fewer than 100 employees), Wisconsin Employers Group soon became the largest commercial group health insurance company in Wisconsin. By 1982 Wisconsin Employers was a force in Minnesota and Indiana as well.

That same year the American Express subsidiary, Fireman's Fund Insurance Company, was looking to buy a strong, regional group health insurance company. Soon after the November 1982 purchase, Fireman's Fund Employers Health Insurance became a strong, national company.

Since 1982 group health premiums increased 266 percent to $491 million per year. The number of insureds increased 200 percent to nearly three-quarters of a million people. Insurance industry watchdog, the A.M. Best Company, said the company earned an "A" rating in only its first year of eligibility. At the home office in De Pere, floor space doubled, then doubled again to 360,000 square feet. Regional sales offices increased from

five to 30 sites. Employment reached 1,300.

Despite the explosive growth and profitability, American Express was only interested in the group health insurance as a short-term investment. In December 1986 Lincoln National Corporation purchased the operation, and American Express headed to the bank with a 650-percent return on its original 1982 investment.

Today the Weyers and Hilliard dream machine is called Employers Health Insurance. As a Lincoln National Company, it's poised to take off from the sixteenth-largest position to become a billion-dollar company (in premiums) by 1991.

Amidst all the new, billion-dollar changes, Weyers and Hilliard are determined to keep the business philosophy of Employers Health Insurance. "Two principles have guided this company through its first 20 years in business," Weyers says. "Outstanding customer service is our greatest competitive strength and overriding commitment." He adds proudly, "Our employees, the people who deliver such outstanding service, are our greatest assets."

The Employers Health Insurance headquarters in De Pere.

MERITER HOSPITAL

Name changes are nothing new in the history of Meriter Hospital. Over the years the predecessors of Meriter Hospital were known as Stoeber Hospital, Gill and Boyd Hospital, Hayes Hospital, Hicks Hospital, Hayes-Hicks Hospital, and, most recently, Methodist Hospital and Madison General Hospital.

When Meriter Hospital was created in 1987 with the merger of Methodist and Madison General, people were puzzled at the choice of the name Meriter. The new name was derived from the root word "merit," which means worth, value, excellence. Meriter aspires to provide quality services and personal care to patients, residents, and customers.

The hospital is an operating company of Meriter Health Services, Inc., which came into being with the merger of Methodist Health Services and General Health Services, the parent corporations of Methodist and Madison General hospitals. Meriter Health Services, Inc., is a not-for-profit parent corporation of Meriter's

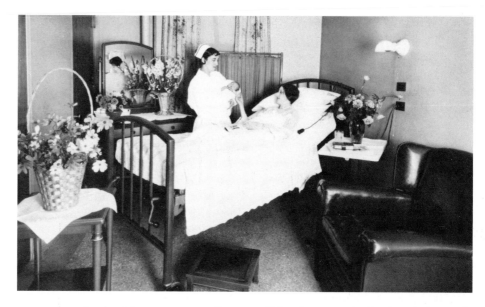

This private room in the obstetrical unit of Methodist Hospital cost five dollars per day in 1936. A staff nurse's salary at that time was about $50 per month.

comprehensive health care system. It sets policies and oversees operations for Meriter Hospital, Meriter Retirement Services, Meriter Foundation, Madison General Hospital Medical and Surgical Foundation, and Meriter Health Enterprises.

Meriter Hospital is a not-for-profit, locally directed 500-bed community hospital serving patients of all ages at two Madison locations. Meriter Hospital/Methodist is located at 309 West Washington Avenue; Meriter Hospital/Madison General is located at 202 South Park Street. Meriter Hospital has 2,800 em-

ployees, 400 physicians on the active medical staff, 135 clergy members from more than 15 denominations, and 650 volunteers. Meriter is a major teaching affiliate of the University of Wisconsin Medical School; it trains medical residents in many specialties.

Fewer than 100 years ago, Madison had no hospitals at all. It was believed that sick people belonged at home and that hospitals were places for charity patients to go to die. With the advent of modern medicine, attitudes began to change. In 1898 a group of Madison citizens, who had tried for years to build a hospital, organized the Madison General Hospital Association with D.K. Tenney as the first president. At the time a nine-bed facility managed and owned by Mary Hayes was the only small hospice-type hospital in Madison. In 1900 the association purchased the hospital and its furnishings from Hayes. A group of Women's Club members, headed by Minnie Hobbins and Rachael Jastrow, supervised the hospital under the auspices of the association.

The operating room at Madison General Hospital, circa 1921. The original Madison General Hospital began operating in 1903.

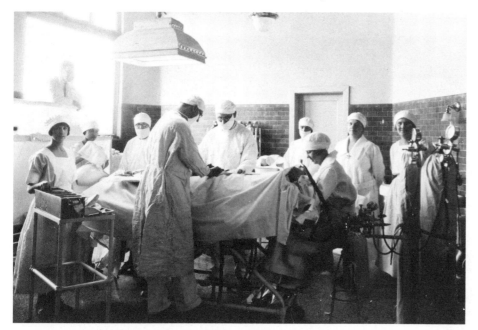

The hospital almost immediately proved too small, and another house was rented and equipped for 16 patients; it had facilities for general surgery. The addition was called the Hicks Hospital, after its matron, Emma F. Hicks.

Finally, in 1902, the Madison General Hospital Association obtained an option on the land where the hospital now stands. The Women's Committee and the Attic Angels Association raised the money first for the land and then for well in excess of half the cost of the hospital building. The city appropriated $10,000, giving it a permanent interest in the hospital.

The original Madison General Hospital was in use by 1903. The patient load grew so fast—from 228 in 1903 to 738 in 1910—that porches and hallways were used to accommodate the overflow. In 1912 a fireproof annex that held 60 to 70 patients was built. More space was added in 1917, 1921, 1928, 1929, 1938, 1952, 1963, 1966, 1969, and 1972.

The city held a "reversionary interest" in the hospital's land and buildings tracing to its original pledge to building the hospital in 1903. The hospital purchased the city's reversionary interests in 1986.

Madison General's School of Nursing dates back to 1899; it received N.L.N. accreditation in 1955.

Methodist Hospital's history goes back to 1918, when the West Wisconsin Conference of the Methodist Episcopal Church gave permission to establish a Methodist Hospital in Madison. By 1919 the association was running the Stoeber Hospital, a 12-bed maternity institution located on Wisconsin Avenue next to the First Methodist Church. In 1920 the association purchased St. Regina's Convent at 309 West Washington Avenue.

Stoeber Hospital became affiliated with the Jackson Clinic in 1920.

When the operation of Stoeber Hospital was discontinued in 1922, Methodist Hospital continued the affiliation with the Jackson Clinic. Methodist's School of Nursing was begun in 1921; a house at 345 West Washington Avenue was purchased and remodeled into a nurses' home.

In 1923 Methodist purchased a nearby property that added 20 more beds, but the hospital still needed more space. By 1927 the organization had constructed a 110-bed facility for one million dollars. The old 40-bed hospital was then converted into a student nurses' dormitory and named Maude Sager Hall. Another building was purchased in 1942 to accommodate the Cadet Program, which trained nurses for the war effort. Other modifications followed in 1950, giving the hospital a total of 147 beds. The agreement with Jackson Clinic was canceled in 1960; the hospital then had an open staff arrangement.

A new addition to Methodist Hospital increased the institution's capacity to 280 beds in 1968. Methodist's School of Nursing closed in 1974 after merging with Madison Area Technical College's program. Other milestones in Methodist's history include the first eight-bed intensive care unit in Madison (1963); the first coronary artery bypass surgery (1967); hemodialysis center (1971); 26-bed psychiatry program (1972); mobile hemodialysis (1977); Birth Place (1978); CT Scanner (1983); Women's Center (1985); and the Shared Magnetic Resonance facility (1986).

In 1987 the long histories of two of Madison's oldest hospitals merged with the establishment of Meriter Hospital. The institutions now share a history—and a name.

Today's Meriter Hospital is a result of the merger of Madison General (below) and Methodist Hospital (bottom). Meriter is a not-for-profit locally directed 500-bed community hospital serving patients of all ages at these two Madison locations. Photo of Methodist Hospital courtesy Brent Nicastro

WISCONSIN PACKING COMPANY, INC.

Morris Segel came to America from Eastern Europe at the approximate age of seven. He and his sister crossed the ocean alone and their parents came later. The Segel children lived at first with their sponsoring family who ran a small butcher shop in Sheboygan. Morris Segel helped in the butcher shop by building fires and cleaning up. The butcher sometimes sent him out to drive cattle on foot from the countryside farms back to the shop in Sheboygan. When Morris turned 16 he began to drive a little truck and would tie a cow to the back of the truck and drive slowly back to town. Morris would sometimes buy a calf for himself and then butcher it and sell the meat.

"My father made many friends as a youngster, visiting all the farmers," says Segel's son, Floyd A. Segel, who is now chairman of the board of Wisconsin Packing Company, Inc., the large company that grew from Morris Segel's early work in the meat business. "Later," says Segel, "when he opened his own business, he would do business with them strictly on his honor."

When Morris Segel and Blanche

Grimson were married in 1923, they opened a small grocery store. But the business did not suit Segel; he wanted to get back to the meat business. "My grandfather liked the action of the cattle business—retail didn't suit him," says Justin Segel, Floyd's son, who is secretary/treasurer of Wisconsin Packing and president of Milwaukee Tallow Company, one of its divisions.

Morris Segel eventually built a slaughtering plant and the business grew from there. Blanche Segel was the company's bookkeeper for many years.

The firm was incorporated as Wisconsin Packing Company, Inc., in 1938, succeeding a partnership between Morris and his brother formed in 1925. Wisconsin Packing Company, Inc., was reincorporated in Delaware in 1976 to consolidate the separately incorporated businesses of the Segel family. Wisconsin Packing is engaged in the meat, food, and related industries.

The firm operates through six wholly owned subsidiaries: New Glarus Foods, Butler Capital, Butler Beef, Wis-Pak Foods, Wis-Pak Transport, Inc., and the Milwaukee Tallow Company.

New Glarus Foods was formed in 1978 to purchase the business known as Strickler's Markets. Eugene Strickler, a Swiss sausage maker, be-

Morris Segel (left) and Floyd Segel (right), father and son, respectively, at work at the company Morris co-founded with his brother in 1925.

gan the business in New Glarus in 1909. New Glarus Foods makes sausages and smoked meats and is a major supplier to the specialty food trade.

Butler Capital is a venture capital firm investing in insurance agencies.

Butler Beef markets both imported and domestic meats. Butler Beef's worldwide information resources include permanent field personnel, Telex reports, and its own satellite communications equipment.

Wis-Pak Foods produces portion-controlled frozen meat products for all phases of the food service industry. Wis-Pak is a primary supplier of frozen meat products to national and regional fast-food restaurants, national and regional distribution organizations, and contract food service companies for educational, business/institutional, and health care facilities. Wis-Pak has three processing plants, located in Butler, Wisconsin; Jacksonville, Florida; and Kansas City, Missouri. They employ the latest technology with state-of-the-art equipment, such as Formax patty machines and liquid nitrogen freezing tunnels.

Wis-Pak Transport, Inc., was

The original Wisconsin Packing Company plant (pictured here) was located at South Second and West Oregon streets. The building has since been demolished. Photo circa 1952

formed in 1972 to meet Wisconsin Packing's trucking needs. It ships Wis-Pak's products nationwide and back-hauls other organization's products.

Milwaukee Tallow Company, Inc., renders and recycles animal waste products in a process that yields tallow and meat meal. Milwaukee Tallow was formed in 1875; the Segel family acquired complete control of it in 1949. The firm takes waste products from livestock such as beef, hogs, and calves, and separates it into raw blood or bones, fat, and offal. The rendering process makes further refinements, resulting ultimately in components that can be used in farm animal feed and pet food, fertilizer, and consumer products, including soap, paint, synthetic fibers, tires, waxes, polishes, shaving cream, and lubricants.

Wisconsin Packing has grown 300 percent in the past 10 years, according to G. Woodrow Adkins, president. The company employs 700 people in facilities that total some 425,000 square feet.

Prior to 1977 Wisconsin Packing was in the slaughter and boning

Wisconsin Packing Company, Inc., operates through six wholly owned subsidiaries along with an international department. Here a computer operator works in the international trade department, which mainly imports meat products.

A Wisconsin Packing Company management meeting with Floyd Segel, chairman of the board, at the helm.

business, but the killing operation was discontinued in 1977. For the future Adkins sees a trend toward further diversification. "We will continue to grow in the sausage business and internationally, both in terms of importing and exporting," he says. "We've moved out of primary supply (live animals) and into value-added products. We are not as dependent on the ups and downs and whims of the farmer, the price of land, or the grain supply."

Justin Segel sees a strong future for Milwaukee Tallow also. "Less than 45 percent of the average steer is sold for food consumption," he says. "Over 100 million pounds of

by-products are paid for and recycled by the rendering industry each day." Segel points out that the rendering industry does a service for the environment. "Milwaukee Tallow Company processes over 6 million pounds weekly," he says, recycling everything from restaurant waste grease to animal remains. Those 6 million pounds are enough to fill County Stadium to the six-foot level, he says. "It is clear there would be a health emergency if this material were not processed on an immediate basis."

Despite the service his company performs, though, Segel doesn't take things too seriously. Milwaukee Tallow, he points out, is otherwise known as "The Fat People."

The corporate headquarters and flagship plant of Wisconsin Packing Company, Inc., in Butler, Wisconsin.

JOHN DEERE HORICON WORKS

John Deere Horicon Works manufactured its one-millionth lawn and garden tractor in 1984. The world's largest manufacturer of lawn and garden tractors, the Horicon Works is located on the edge of the 33,000-acre Horicon Marsh, a beautiful haven for waterfowl, fish, and other wildlife. The Horicon Works has doubled output in the past five years and tripled it in the past 10 years. Employment is at an all-time high—there were more than 1,800 workers during peak periods in 1987.

Dave Westimayer, mayor of Horicon and a third-generation Horicon Works employee, remembers when the factory was referred to as "the John Deere toy factory." But, he adds, "I don't hear that any more." The factory today manufactures or markets roughly 200 separate models of grounds-care equipment, the broadest line of home-owner and commercial machines offered by any company in the grounds-care equipment industry.

The Horicon Works is a leader in utilizing technological and manufacturing advances to make the most of factory space and production time and is a leader in just-in-time manufacturing. Waste-elimination practices have also helped reduce inventories. The Horicon Works just completed building a new 77,000-square-foot paint facility that is the most advanced of any vehicle factory.

When Daniel and George Van Brunt founded the Horicon Works factory in 1861, they probably never expected that the company they formed to produce seeders and grain drills would become the world's leader in lawn and garden tractors. The Van Brunts invented the broadcast seeder (using a carved turnip as a model) and then the first seeding device to help farmers keep birds from eating their seeds. (Their fundamental design is still used on modern grain drills.)

A view of the John Deere Horicon Works from across the Rock River.

Some of the buildings erected by the Van Brunts in the early days of the organization are still in use at the factory today. The firm has experienced steady expansion throughout its history, particularly after its acquisition by Deere & Company in 1911. Today the factory covers 1.3 million square feet.

Known as the Van Brunt Company until 1947, the operation changed its name to the John Deere Van Brunt Company, and in 1958 was renamed John Deere Horicon Works.

Over the years the Horicon Works has made many innovations, and it continues to introduce new products and new techniques today. Horicon Works was the first nonautomotive plant to introduce the use of automatic guided vehicles (AGVs) on assembly lines. These robotic transporters follow directions broadcast from wire embedded in shop-floor guide paths to move the product frame and some components from station to station for assembly. When the AGV line reaches full capacity, one riding lawn tractor will be produced every minute.

Production of the small lawn and garden tractors began at Horicon Works in 1963. They were so well received and widely admired that the Smithsonian Institution in Washington, D.C., requested one for its museum.

Back in the late 1970s the John Deere Horicon Works reassessed its position. "We recognized that we had to change," says Lauren Miller, personnel manager. "In the long run our traditional methods just wouldn't be enough to meet the challenges of foreign competition on the world market." To remain competitive, the company instituted just-in-time manufacturing, new production technology, and participative management.

These lawn and garden tractors are just two of the many quality products manufactured at the John Deere Horicon Works.

THE WORTH COMPANY

"We make the Cadillac of the creepy crawlers," says David R. Worth, president since 1987 of The Worth Company, which developed a proprietary process for injection molding fishing lures. "Our worms, lizards, and crawdads are the most lifelike lures in the world," claims Worth. "But," adds his father, Robert W. Worth, chairman of the board, "people don't understand the sophistication of the equipment we have. Most people still think of us as fly tyers."

In fact, Stevens Point was once considered the fly-tying capital of the world. "They called it Tackle Town, U.S.A.," says Robert Worth. The Worth Company is the only surviving tackle firm in Stevens Point—and it no longer ties flies (although it still manufactures fly-tying kits). The firm went from an intensive hand labor process to a state-of-the-art metalworking operation, with facilities including high-speed production equipment and support operations, to function as a completely self-contained manufacturer.

The Worth Company has been manufacturing fishing tackle and related products in Stevens Point since

1940, when Joseph Worth (Robert's father), purchased the Olsen Bait Company of Chippewa Falls from Rhyder Olsen. Worth continued working full time as a heating engineer for a while. His wife, Edythe, managed the new company on West Clark Street, and Olsen moved to Stevens Point to help run the production end.

During World War II The Worth Company began to manufacture emergency survival kits containing fishing flies, spinners, spoons, and leaders. It also made G.I. "dog tags," belt buckles, gun-cleaning rods, and draft diverters for tent stoves.

In 1943 the company moved to a larger building on West Main Street where it continued its government contract work. There was so much work that the operation expanded into the east wing of the old armory as well as the village hall in Amherst.

After the war the firm decided to consolidate its facilities. In 1945 it purchased the Elmer Pendergast property and built a well-lighted, air-conditioned plant. The first building was finished in 1946 and a second in 1948.

The Worth Company continued to manufacture tied flies until foreign competition made it impossible to continue. During the Korean War the firm again worked on government contracts.

In 1957 the entire operation was moved to a 10.5-acre site in Whiting. Robert Worth rejoined the company as sales manager in 1957 and became president in 1959 when his father died. His brother, Joseph E., became vice-president. In 1973, when Joseph E. died, the company endowed a scholarship in his name at the University of Wisconsin-Stevens Point to benefit a graduate student in the Department of Natural Resources' fishery program.

Today The Worth Company is privately held and run by David R. Worth (right), grandson of Joseph Worth, president and chief executive officer. Robert W. Worth (left), the son of Joseph Worth, is the retired chairman of the board.

The Worth Company, which is privately held, has sales of $4.1 million today. The company manufactures more than 18,000 products, which it sells to 4,000 customers. Its 65 employees work in a facility covering 36,000 square feet.

The consumer division of The Worth Company manufactures lures, fish scalers, and other accessories for all types of sport fishing. The Anchormate® line of anchor-control units is available in three different models. Worth Manufacturing, a division of the company, produces metal and wire products for the OEM lure-component market, as well as for home and commercial use worldwide.

The Worth Company also manufactures more than 2 million split and key rings per week. These are used in the aerospace and automobile industries as well as in airplanes, helicopters, computer printers—and fishing lures.

Joseph Worth purchased the Olsen Bait Company of Chippewa Falls in 1940 and turned it into The Worth Company, which has been manufacturing fishing tackle and related products in Stevens Point ever since. The firm had sales of $4.1 million in 1987.

NEKOOSA PAPERS INC.

Nekoosa means "swift-running water" in the Chippewa Indian language. It was originally the name for a small stagecoach stop built near a section of rapids on the Wisconsin River. In 1831 the first sawmill on the Wisconsin River was built at that site in the middle of the thick, central Wisconsin forests. The sawmill eventually became a part of the Nekoosa Paper Company, which built the third paper mill on the river in 1893. Today Nekoosa is a name known by paper users all over the country as the brand name for top-quality writing and printing paper.

Centralia Water Power and Paper Company built a pulp mill and the first paper mill on the Wisconsin River near Port Edwards, four miles north of Nekoosa, in 1887. A third paper mill was built in 1896 at Port Edwards. These and related properties were incorporated in 1908 into Nekoosa-Edwards Paper Company.

Newsprint was the primary product of Nekoosa-Edwards until World War I, when the company began to manufacture protective papers for foods. Kraft wrapping, specialty paper, and butcher papers were then the main items of production.

In the late 1930s Nekoosa-Edwards Paper Company began to make fine and printing papers. It

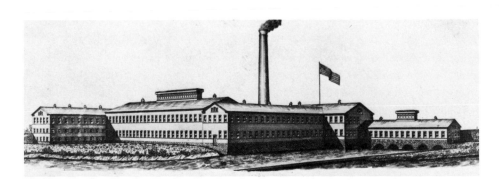

This artist's rendering of the John Edwards Manufacturing Company, a parent company of Nekoosa Papers Inc., shows the mill as it looked in 1900. At that time the mill manufactured about 50 tons of newsprint.

introduced a line of watermarked papers known as Nekoosa and a companion group of unwatermarked papers called Ardor. This move into the fine paper market brought growth and prosperity for the company.

Nekoosa's leading product lines today are business communication papers, which include copier, carbonless, business forms, paper, check, uncoated printing, converting, technical papers, and paper for all types of business office equipment. Nekoosa benefits from the great increase in the volume of information being generated today and the rapid technological changes occurring in the field of information transmission. Less expensive computers and copiers, fiber optics, and satellite transmission all offer new opportunities for transmitting information worldwide.

Nekoosa sees a business oppor-

tunity in this great increase in the volume of information being generated. The company believes that most of this information will ultimately be presented as words printed on paper—mainly copier paper. And Nekoosa Paper Inc. is one of the world's largest manufacturers of copier paper.

Anticipating customers' future needs for paper products requires a lot of listening. One of the fundamental objectives of Nekoosa's management is to stay close to the customer, to treat him as a business partner, to listen carefully to what he says about his needs and problems, and to anticipate his future requirements.

Management members are also convinced that up-to-date equipment and high-quality employees are essential to Nekoosa's success. Their second objective is to have efficient

A current aerial view of Nekoosa Papers Inc.'s Port Edwards, Wisconsin, mill and administration offices.

Bare feet and wooden floors would appear to be conducive to foot slivers in this early 1900s view of a paper machine crew in the Centralia Water Power and Paper Company plant. The machine is producing newsprint.

Centralia Waterpower and Paper Company was a Nekoosa Papers Inc. parent company. The firm built this groundwood pulp mill at Centralia (now Wisconsin Rapids) in 1887. It was the first paper mill on the Wisconsin River, and after becoming part of the Nekoosa-Edwards Paper Company in 1908, the mill was destroyed by fire four years later.

plants with state-of-the-art equipment so that the company can compete successfully with any competitor firm in the business. Thanks to a talented, industrious group of employees who are committed to high standards, Nekoosa has been successful in accomplishing both these objectives.

Nekoosa Papers' main office is located in Port Edwards, Wisconsin. Thousands of tons of Nekoosa papers leave the mills in Port Edwards and Nekoosa, Wisconsin, and Ashdown,

Nekoosa Papers was a pioneer in industrial reforestation, having started a program of tree replacement in 1926. The first nursery was this planting on the shore of the company's man-made Nepco Lake. Lack of space has caused the planting operations to be carried out at two other sites in Wisconsin.

Arkansas, by train or truck. Nekoosa has tremendous warehouse facilities, and often an order can be filled from paper already in stock. The company produces hundreds of varieties of weights, colors, sizes, and finishes of Nekoosa papers. Nekoosa produces more than 120 grades of paper in a spectrum of colors and whites with 12 paper machines.

Nekoosa Papers today has three manufacturing facilities, two in Wisconsin and one in Arkansas. Nekoosa's Wisconsin mills (in Port Edwards and Nekoosa) are especially suited to the production of technical specialty papers, as well as the huge range of white and colored products required by the company's merchant distributors. The mill in Ashdown, Arkansas, has three large, modern paper machines, as well as a state-of-the-art finishing department. The Arkansas mill produces quality, high-volume white papers.

Nekoosa Papers sells its business communication papers through a network of more than 200 merchant distributors who represent Nekoosa throughout the United States. Some volume grades, such as busi-

ness forms papers, are sold to converters who produce finished forms and other products for the end user. Quality envelope papers are also sold to envelope converters.

With high-speed, automated finishing equipment at all three of its mills, Nekoosa can convert approximately two-thirds of its production into precision-size sheets. This is one reason Nekoosa has become a major supplier of superior quality copier paper.

Nekoosa Papers is also a leading supplier of check paper. The equipment used to scan and sort checks magnetically can run at speeds in excess of 40 checks per sec-

This is one of Nekoosa Paper's newer paper machines in its Wisconsin mills. The paper manufacturer produces more than 820,000 tons of business communications papers annually.

ond. These high speeds require paper made to exacting specifications. Nekoosa participated in the development of national standards for check paper.

In 1970 Nekoosa-Edwards Paper Company merged with Great Northern Paper Company to form Great Northern Nekoosa Corporation (GNN), creating a company with an annual capacity of 1.75 million tons of paper.

PHILLIPS PLASTICS CORPORATION

When Phillips Plastics Corporation began business in a rented former cheese factory in 1964, it had two employees—Robert Cervenka and Louis Vokurka, the company's founders. The firm is still based in Phillips, county seat of Price County, but today it employs 1,400 people in 10 facilities that occupy a total of 350,000 square feet. Annual sales exceed $60 million. Phillips Plastics produces plastic parts for some 1,000 manufacturers, ranging from automakers to producers of computer equipment. Phillips Plastics has had steady growth since 1964, with the exception of the recession periods in 1974-1975 and 1981-1982. Most of the company's growth over the years has been internal; very little of it has been achieved through acquisitions. The current corporate goal is to grow at a rate of 20 percent per year.

Phillips Plastics started as a custom injection-molding shop producing thermoplastic parts. Today the operation offers concept design

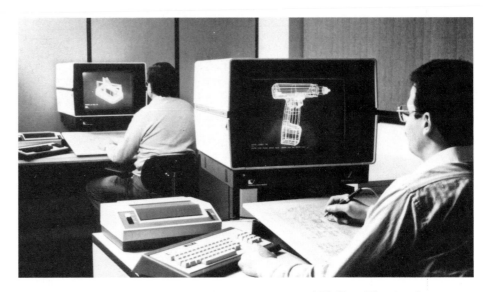

One of the two CAD/CAM systems used at Phillips Plastics to improve quality and reduce costs at the early design stages.

through production. Phillips now offers product design and development; model making; prototyping; engineering and tooling; production, decoration, and assembly of thermoplastic parts; and production of decorative overlays. Leading manufacturers in the automotive, electronics, data-processing, medical, appliance, tele-communications, and instrumentation industries use the products and services of Phillips Plastics Corporation.

A stand-alone technical center in Prescott, Wisconsin, south of Hudson, was opened in early 1988. Research and development are crucial to Phillips' continued success, according to Cervenka, president of the firm. "We really have developed a reputation as a high-quality producer." But, he adds, the company "has to pay constant attention to making our products and service better."

Well-established statistical process control systems at Phillips have resulted in exceptional quality ratings from major customers. Some customers have eliminated incoming inspections of Phillips products, based on past product quality and the firm's quality process procedures.

Quality is key to Phillips' success, Cervenka claims. "At Phillips, we do not audit the product; we audit the process. This ensures the highest quality level attainable for the final product." The first step in the quality-assurance process is evaluation of the product's design. Phillips works with customers to modify designs in order to improve product quality, reduce part cost, allow a faster molding cycle, reduce part weight, or reduce the number of parts required.

A view of the central molding area of one of the Phillips Plastics plants. Phillips Plastics has molding presses of up to 700-ton capacity.

"People involvement has always been part of our quality program," states Cervenka. "The company tries to make all workers aware of quality attitudes." A third important part of the quality process is equipment maintenance. Equipment is evaluated frequently for proper operation, accuracy, and repeatability. Presses used to be replaced every eight years; today Phillips replaces them every seven years, and a six-year replacement period is being considered.

Presses today work harder than in the past, but, as in the past, accuracy degrades with use. Phillips runs its machines 24 hours a day, since start-up and shut-down would generate scrap. It is most efficient to start up once and keep going. Phillips currently evaluates presses with a computer, which can sense material and mold temperature and injection speed or pressure. The computer automatically compensates for variations and provides a frequency of adjustment record. It is important to keep on top of quality issues all the time, Cervenka believes. "If you don't put quality in in the beginning, you're going to have a hard time trying to force it in at the end."

Phillips Plastics Corporation is privately held; 25 percent of the stock is currently owned by employees through a plan tailored especially for the firm. The employee retirement fund also invests in Phillips stock, so that virtually every current employee is a stockholder of the company. Cervenka says that such a strong employee investment in the organization is a good incentive. "If the value of our stock increases by 20 percent, the retirement fund also grows by 20 percent."

The firm also established the Ann Marie Foundation approximately 15 years ago. Set up to honor Cervenka's mother, Ann, and Vokurka's mother, Marie, the foundation makes gifts in the communities where

Test and evaluation along with in-plant product inspections enable Phillips Plastics to maintain the highest quality levels.

Phillips Plastics has manufacturing plants. Typical grant recipients include school scholarships, nursing homes, Boy and Girl Scouts, and Big Brothers and Sisters programs in the local areas. In addition, the foundation will continue to grow as the company grows.

Phillips Plastics' 10 locations are in Phillips, the corporate headquarters and custom division; Eau Claire, insert/multishot molding division; Hudson, preproduction services division; Medford, knob division;

Chippewa Falls, engineered fastener division; Fredonia, Graphic Technologies, Inc.; Eau Claire, assembly division; Oak Grove, technical center; Prescott, fastener production division; and Bloomington, Minnesota, the national sales office.

But corporate headquarters of Phillips Plastics Corporation is likely to stay in Phillips, particularly with the completion of a cedar-sided corporate office building overlooking Long Lake in 1987. "You couldn't get us out of here with dynamite," Cervenka insists.

Each production facility has its own quality-control department with the instruments and data-processing equipment required to monitor quality process procedures.

WORZALLA PUBLISHING COMPANY

December 31, 1986, is a milestone date for Worzalla Publishing Company employees. On that date employees became 100-percent owners of their company, culminating a rich corporate history that has relied on the strength of its employees.

Worzalla, with roots dating back to 1891, is a modern-day printer and book manufacturer. Charles W. Nason, company president, says employee ownership gives Worzalla a major advantage in the marketplace.

"Our people make us different; they are our major strength," Nason points out. "Historically, there has been a superb work ethic here that gives us a quality and flexibility advantage over our competitors. Employee ownership simply has enhanced everything that we do."

Worzalla has taken a flexible approach to business since the early days of the company. Zygmunt Hutter and Trefoil Krutza began publishing a Polish newspaper called *Rolnik* (Farmer) in 1891. *Rolnik* was edited entirely for farmers in the central Wisconsin area, and by the end of its first year of operation had 300 subscribers.

Joseph and Stephen Worzalla purchased *Rolnik* in 1898. The brothers called their business Worzalla Publishing Company and operated from a second story at Main and Third streets in Stevens Point. Soon they began to diversify.

In 1908 a new publication was created called *Gwiazda Polarna* (The Polar Star), which was designed to appeal to people living in cities. With its broader editorial appeal, *Gwiazda Polarna* soon had Polish-reading subscribers nationwide.

As business increased, the Worzallas needed more space. They purchased the former Hoffman Piano Company land and buildings on Second Street in 1912. They also moved a vacant structure to that site and then purchased the Stiley-Riley Laundry adjacent to the Hoffman building, which formerly was the Blue Ribbon Carriage Factory. This unlikely combination of old buildings was to house company operations for the next 45 years, until the entire complex was razed and the firm moved to its current site in 1957.

The Worzalla brothers immediately began expanding the printing operations. They entered the bookbinding field with a new branch of the corporation—The National Bookbinding Company. The separate name was intended to reassure printers who needed bookbinding services that Worzalla would not pirate their printing customers.

Worzalla continued to expand in 1925, when it began publishing a Spanish magazine called *Cultura*. The magazine was published only until 1932, but did reach a circulation of 30,000. In 1927 the firm added a Polish magazine called *Jaskolka* (The Swallow). *Jaskolka* would reach a circulation high of 22,000.

Point Paper Products was another Worzalla venture; it got its start

The original location of J. Worzalla & Sons. A general store occupied the first floor, and the printing and publishing business was headquartered on the second floor.

in 1932. This company sold household paper products as well as meat and kraft wrapping papers. In 1935 Worzalla began to publish *The Central City Herald,* a weekly English-language newspaper. It was later renamed *The Central Wisconsin Herald* and reached a circulation of 8,000 by the time it ceased publication in 1938.

Job printing took on greater emphasis at the beginning of World War II, when the company expanded letterpress operations. After World War II the binding and printing operations grew quickly, and additional

This picture was taken in 1912 while operator Vincent Prychla sets type on a Linotype machine, which etched each character out of hot metal.

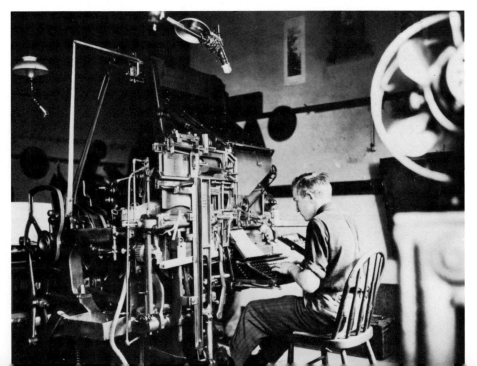

warehousing was constructed in 1945 and again two years later. Offset printing was added in 1955.

A holding company called Walter Williams Realty Company was formed. The name came from Walter Worzalla, son of Stephen, and William Worzalla, son of Walter. The second- and third-generation Worzallas built a new plant in 1957 on Jefferson Street. The realty firm owned the building and published the weekly Polish newspaper and also purchased equipment to lease to the company. In 1973 Worzalla Publishing purchased all the assets of Walter Williams Realty Company and dissolved it back into Worzalla.

The Worzalla family retained ownership of the operation until May 1983, when John Riddell and Graham Core bought the firm from Bill "Skip" Worzalla. Just over two years later the employees would buy the company through an Employee Stock Ownership Program (ESOP).

Worzalla has grown over the

years. When the firm moved to its new plant on Jefferson Street in 1957, there were 67 employees; today there are more than 225. The company did not reach one million dollars in sales until 1964 and did not reach $3 million until 1975. Sales in 1987 exceeded $18 million.

Today Worzalla prints and binds books, magazines, catalogs, pamphlets, posters, and maps for nationwide customers and several international accounts. Worzalla manufactures Wisconsin's *Blue Book* and is particularly well known in the juvenile book field, which accounts for two-thirds of its current business.

Worzalla's present facility is a 119,000-square-foot building on Jefferson Street in Stevens Point. The main office and manufacturing facility are located here.

Worzalla's production and warehouse facilities occupy more than 130,000 square feet. Modern four-color sheet-fed presses help feed a versatile book bindery that produces millions of books each year. And the Polish newspaper *Gwiazda Polarna* is still published weekly in Stevens Point, although not by Worzalla, and has the largest weekly circulation of any Polish-language newspaper in the free world.

People and a full-service production capability are at the heart of Worzalla's success, Nason believes. "Worzalla has a total capability under one roof," he says. "There's not a lot in the book publishing business that we can't do."

Nason says controlled growth fueled by the strength of employee ownership will point Worzalla into the twenty-first century. While the book publishing industry undergoes major changes, Worzalla will have to remain flexible to ensure independence and survival.

As always, it will rely on its employees. Except now, they own the company.

Nettie Skibicki and Pearl Golla operate smyth sewing machines (as part of the publishing process) that sewed book sections together at the spine. Photo circa 1938

SCHREIBER FOODS, INC.

The chances are that anyone eating a cheeseburger in America today is enjoying Schreiber cheese. Schreiber Foods, Inc., founded in Green Bay in 1945, is now the largest privately held cheese company in the world. Schreiber processes and packages more than 8,500 cheese products.

Schreiber Foods is a leader throughout the United States in the marketing and manufacturing of natural, processed, and substitute cheese products, and precooked bacon and bacon bits. Serving the food service, retail, industrial, and military markets, products are sold through 25 sales offices and manufactured in 11 plants across the nation.

The operation was named after L.D. Schreiber, who owned a butter and egg brokerage in the Chicago Mercantile Exchange. In 1935 Schreiber started a small wrapping operation for natural cheese. A decade later Merlin G. Bush formally organized the Schreiber Company's cheese division in Green Bay, recruiting Daniel D. Nusbaum from the University of Wisconsin to help form the company. The cheese division remained a part of Schreiber's Chicago operation until 1962, when 13 em-

Merlin G. Bush, founder of Schreiber Foods, Inc.

ployees purchased the business and incorporated it as the L.D. Schreiber Cheese Company.

There were two Schreiber cheese plants by 1962, one in Green Bay and one in Carthage, Missouri (added in 1950). In operation today are eight cheese manufacturing plants—in Green Bay and Wisconsin Rapids, Wisconsin; Curwensville, Pennsylvania; Carthage, Clinton, and Monett, Missouri; Logan, Utah; and Tempe, Arizona.

Schreiber's early cheese production was largely turned out in loaf or canned form. Much of Schreiber's

cheese in the early days was purchased by the government for military and foreign aid programs.

Quality was important at Schreiber from the beginning. Two of Bush's quality watchwords were "16 ounces in every pound" and "If you don't like it, send it back!"

An unchanging guarantee of customer satisfaction and a reputation for prompt delivery also helped in the building of the organization. Aggressive sales efforts in the 1950s led to gradual but constant gains in commercial markets, particularly grocery chains.

Schreiber increased its market penetration by manufacturing its own innovative machinery for production and packaging. The cheese casting line and individually wrapped slice machine were great successes. Schreiber launched a subsidiary, Green Bay Machinery, to manufacture and sell these machines to international customers.

M.G. Bush was president of the firm until 1969, when Robert K. Deutsch became president. In 1978 Robert G. Bush (Merlin's son) became president. In 1985 Robert Bush was elected chairman of the board and John C. Meng elected president.

Schreiber Foods has continued to grow over the years. Acquisitions included the Clearfield Cheese Company and Westland Foods Company (producer of precooked bacon slices and bits).

In the mid-1980s Meng reorganized the company in order to meet the needs of a changing economy. He divided the firm into two divisions. The retail division serves supermarket chains, wholesalers, and the military. The food service division serves fast-food chains, distributor markets, and the prepared food and frozen food industries.

The cheese industry is changing, and Schreiber is increasing its research and development efforts in

Schreiber Foods' Green Bay plant in the 1960s.

Daniel D. Nusbaum was recruited by Merlin Bush to help build the company in its fledgling years.

bel inventories. Flexible films, corrugated and semirigid containers, and labels are tested for quality in terms of material performance, sealing capability, label adhesion, and keeping qualities.

Schreiber's cheeses and other products are continually tested during actual production runs by on-line inspectors to assure quality in flavor, texture, and appearance. In-plant facilities are directed by graduate engineers to provide highly effective preventive maintenance programs. Each of Schreiber's facilities has a fully equipped quality-control laboratory staffed with expertly trained technicians to assure customers that high-quality standards are consistently maintained.

In recognition of unique customer needs, Schreiber has trained its sales force to analyze customer programs and plan new marketing strategies useful in contemporary merchandising.

Schreiber can supply its customers with a full line of cheese products with more than 680 different variations based on customers' marketing requirements. Mild cheddar, for example, comes in the forms of block, daisy, midget, split midget, longhorn, split longhorn, print, loaf, chunks, sticks, wedges, shreds, and rippled chips. Swiss comes in the

John C. Meng, president and chief operating officer of Schreiber Foods, Inc.

forms of sandwich cut, baby wheel, and shreds. All that cheese is destined to cover a lot of cheeseburgers, tacos, pizzas, salad bar salads, home cooking, snacking, and parties.

Schreiber is striving to maintain a strong and growing company by working and communicating together to find solutions to problems—to continue to make Schreiber better today than yesterday, and better tomorrow than today.

Schreiber Foods' Green Bay cheese plant today.

order to keep pace. The company recently moved into the brand-name market with Clearfield's Cooper Brand, American Heritage, Schreiber Deluxe, Schreiber, and Valu Line cheese. The Schreiber Brand program has also recently been introduced.

Schreiber purchases cheese and ingredients from more than 175 suppliers all over the world. The company also purchases packaging supplies and maintains customer la-

Robert G. Bush, current chairman of the board and chief executive officer.

STA-RITE INDUSTRIES, INC.

In 1934 a group of Delavan business people collected $10,000 to construct a 3,200-square-foot building on the city's east side to house a new pump company. Called Sta-Rite Products, Inc., the firm began business as a manufacturer of pumps for home and farm water systems. During its first 25 years it expanded to become the largest manufacturer of pumps for suburban and farm water systems. The company also established a base for penetrating into broader fluids-handling markets.

Sta-Rite's initial product line was made up of shallow well piston pumps and deep well reciprocating pumps. In 1939 the firm began marketing a jet-type pump and water system that proved to be a turning point for sustained growth.

By 1957 Sta-Rite was manufacturing four-inch submersible-type water pumps complete with oil-lubricated motors designed by the company. In the 1960s the growth in housing developments beyond city water mains enlarged the market for pumps for both new and replacement construction. Sta-Rite also began producing large-capacity water supply pumps for motels, industrial plants, cluster home developments, small communities, and agricultural enterprises.

Sta-Rite pioneered the plastics technology that made it the industry leader in swimming pool pumps and filters.

In 1959 Sta-Rite moved into a new one-million-dollar building on a site just off what was to become the Rock Freeway. This structure has been expanded at least seven times through the years. Another new manufacturing/warehouse facility was constructed in 1968. Today the firm has two buildings (a total of 338,000 square feet under roof) on an 86-acre property.

Sta-Rite acquired several companies beginning in the 1960s, including the Skidmore Corporation, manufacturer of low-pressure steam-heating pumping systems, in 1965. With the merger with Webster Electric Company, Inc., in 1966, the name was changed to Sta-Rite Industries, Inc. Some of the other businesses and product lines acquired in the 1960s were sold after a decision was reached in 1973 to concentrate resources in markets that offered the greatest growth potential—water and fluid power.

By 1971 Sta-Rite had grown to international status; sales were $172 million and earnings close to $6 million. (That year Sta-Rite was ranked 907th in sales in the *Fortune* 1,000.) In 1980 Sta-Rite acquired Fluid Con-

trols, Inc., a Mentor, Ohio, manufacturer of hydraulic valves and fluid power systems. In 1982 Sta-Rite Industries became a subsidiary of WICOR, Inc., a Wisconsin holding company. (WICOR's other two subsidiaries are WEXCO and Wisconsin Gas Company.)

Today Sta-Rite Industries, Inc., manufactures pumps for the swimming pool/spa, water well, turf and irrigation, sewage, municipal, industrial, plumbing, retail, and do-it-yourself markets. These products are marketed under such brands as Sta-Rite, Flotec, Town & Country, Berkeley, Tait, and Swimquip.

Sta-Rite Industries, Inc., also produces hydraulic power and control systems for use in industrial, agricultural, construction, materials-handling, and mobile equipment markets; oil-heating pumps, ignition transformers, and boiler-feed and condensate return systems for the heating industry; and hydraulic steering and engine controls for marine craft. Other products include filters, softeners, and control valves for home, municipal, and industrial water-treatment markets.

State-of-the-art manufacturing equipment is used to maintain the close tolerances required for hydraulic components made by Sta-Rite's Fluid Power Group.

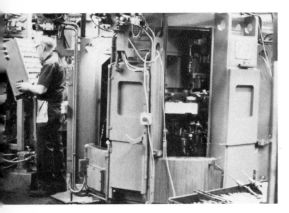

Sta-Rite is a market leader in the agricultural irrigation market with submersible turbines (shown here) and Berkeley-brand centrifugal pumps.

WISCONSIN GAS COMPANY

Wisconsin Gas Company was the first public utility in the state of Wisconsin. John Lockwood, an engineer from Cincinnati, and four Milwaukee citizens formed the then Milwaukee Gas Light Company in 1852. Lockwood had proposed in 1851 to build a gas works that would furnish "good gas for all the public lamps that might from time to time be installed."

The Wisconsin State Legislature in 1852 granted the company the right to perpetual existence and an exclusive franchise to serve the city of Milwaukee.

By the fall of 1852 the Third Ward Gas Works (the original gas-manufacturing plant) was manufacturing gas from coal. The entire network, which included seven miles of buried gas pipes, 100 meters, and the plant, cost $150,000.

On November 23, 1852, the firm turned on the gas and the city celebrated. As the *Milwaukee Daily Sentinel* reported, "It was the biggest thing that ever happened to Milwaukeans, as for the first time in city history, the streets were brilliantly lighted."

Gaslights soon found their way indoors. Before gas, buildings had

Today the Wisconsin Gas service area encompasses 388 communities in 43 Wisconsin counties.

been poorly lit with tallow dips and whale-oil lamps. Two months after the "turn-on" celebration, the company was offering indoor lighting service to the public. Within five years the firm had 889 customers. Total annual gas sales exceeded 16 million cubic feet.

Milwaukee Gas Light expanded between 1863 and 1926 by acquiring one competitor (Fifth Ward Gas Light Company), which had failed, and establishing four affiliated suburban Milwaukee companies.

In 1901 Milwaukee Gas Light became a part of the American National Gas Company System, known then as American Light and Traction Company, and today as American Natural Resources Company.

In 1930 Milwaukee Gas Light completed construction of its present general office building, located at 626 East Wisconsin Avenue in downtown Milwaukee. In 1956 the giant "gas flame" replica on top of the building began passing on weather predictions to residents of a 25-mile area. The flame flashes different colors to forecast weather.

In 1949 natural gas was introduced to Wisconsin. Within a three-month period some 1,300 Milwaukee Gas Light service people converted more than 500,000 appliances from the use of manufactured to natural gas.

In 1960 Milwaukee Gas Light began to expand outside of the city; five years later it adopted the name Wisconsin Gas Company to reflect its statewide role.

On June 30, 1975, the utility became independent from ANR, and Wisconsin Gas stock began to be traded on the New York Stock Exchange. In 1980 the firm's shareholders approved the formation of a holding company, WICOR, Inc. WICOR's other two subsidiaries are Sta-Rite Industries, a Milwaukee-based manufacturer, and Wexco, a

In 1903 the then Milwaukee Gas Light Company was growing rapidly in the city of Milwaukee.

small gas and oil exploration and development concern.

Wisconsin Gas Company today is the largest natural gas distributor in the state, serving 432,500 customers in 43 counties. The firm delivers dependable, clean, and efficient natural gas to heat homes, businesses, industries, and institutions; for food preparation, water heating, and clothes drying; and for industrial processes, drying crops, and fueling fleet vehicles.

The lighted "gas flame" atop the Wisconsin Gas Building beams a friendly warmth and forecasts the weather by changing colors: When the flame is red, it's warm weather ahead; when it's blue, there's no change in view; when it's gold, watch out for the cold; and when the flame is in agitation (flashing), expect precipitation.

ST. JOSEPH'S HOSPITAL

In 1890, when six Sisters of the Sorrowful Mother established their order's second American hospital in Marshfield, the city had a population of only 3,435. The woods surrounding Marshfield were full of lumberjacks harvesting the timber that formed the basis of the area's economy. Civil War veterans were moving into the area to redeem their government land grants. And dairying, which was to replace lumber in the area's economy, had just begun.

The Sisters responded to Father Paul Geyer's plea on behalf of St. John's Catholic Church. Many loggers were suffering from typhus fever. Mother Mary Francis Streitel, foundress of the order, and five other Sisters arrived in Marshfield in 1890 and set up a temporary hospital and convent in a rented house on North Central Avenue.

In 1891 the Sisters (including six more newly arrived from Rome) opened a brick hospital building they had commissioned on the outskirts of Marshfield. Those 10 acres are still the site of St. Joseph's today.

A forest fire, a dry well, and a lack of patients were early challenges. A water cure called the Kneipp Water Cure was so popular that it drew patients from several states, but it was discontinued in 1895. The hospital needed the space the sanitorium (water cure) took up.

In 1901 the hospital began the first of six major building programs that transformed the 40- by 80-foot original brick building into today's large medical facility that employs 1,970 people, admits nearly 18,000 patients, and records nearly 50,000 outpatient visits each year.

The original St. Joseph's Hospital building, outside of Marshfield, was completed in 1891 and had six patient rooms.

A chapel was completed in 1902. At the dedication in mid-May the superior general, Mother Mary Johanna, asked the Sisters to pray that the occasion not be marred by rain. Their prayers were answered—it snowed instead!

Marshfield's central Wisconsin location has enhanced the hospital's unique niche in medicine. It has become a critical care center for northern Wisconsin and Upper Michigan, an area estimated to contain more than 2 million people. Today St. Joseph's contains 524 active beds; it is an acute-care referral and teaching hospital providing "the healing touch of Christian care" to its patients. Marshfield has grown, too, to surround it.

St. Joseph's does four tons of laundry per day; 1,200 babies are delivered at St. Joseph's each year. The hospital medical staff practices in the departments of medicine, surgery, obstetrics/gynecology, orthopedics,

St. Joseph's Hospital today contains 524 beds and is an acute-care referral and teaching hospital.

neurosciences, pathology, pediatrics, psychiatry, radiology, oncology, otalaryngology, anesthesia, cardiology, family medicine, and cardiovascular and thoracic surgery.

The medical staff is, for the most part, made up of specialists and subspecialists of Marshfield Clinic, Wisconsin's largest private practice group and one of the five largest in the nation.

The Joint Venture Laboratory is a combined service of St. Joseph's Hospital and Marshfield Clinic. Begun in 1973, it is the largest medical laboratory in Wisconsin, consisting of 10 physicians/pathologists/Ph.D.s, 145 professional/technical staff members, and 80 support personnel. The lab performs more than one million tests per year for the hospital, the clinic, and hundreds of outreach clients.

Today St. Joseph's Hospital is a not-for-profit corporation with 250 physicians. It is a teaching hospital with a national reputation. And it is continuing to grow, adding new buildings and new services, such as a home health care program, a hospice, a day-care center for employees' children, and an alcohol and drug abuse treatment program.

WEYERHAEUSER COMPANY

Frederick Weyerhaeuser.

When Frederick Weyerhaeuser made his first investment in the timber of the Pacific Northwest he said, "This is not for us, nor for our children, but for our grandchildren." Weyerhaeuser was a man of great vision; he knew the country was expanding and that the expansion would require millions of feet of timber to build the homes and businesses of the future.

A German immigrant, Weyerhaeuser began his historic career in the timber industry in 1857 as a night watchman in a sawmill in Rock Island, Illinois. His employers soon recognized his strong work ethic and business sense and promoted him to yard manager. In 1858 Weyerhaeuser borrowed money to purchase the Rock Island mill and assumed its debts.

Weyerhaeuser at first bought his logs on the open market. When the supply became scarce, he looked for the source of the timber—the white pine forests of Wisconsin. "When I first saw the fine timber on the Chippewa," he once said, "I wanted to say nothing about it. It was like the feeling of a man who has found a hidden treasure." Beginning in 1868 Weyerhaeuser built up considerable assets in Wisconsin. Throughout the 1870s and 1880s he owned logging companies in the Chippewa and Rusk County area.

Weyerhaeuser built the first

railroad in Wisconsin in 1884. That same year the village surrounding one of Weyerhaeuser's logging headquarters was established as the town of Weyerhaeuser. Logging practices in the nineteenth century were wasteful. Weyerhaeuser was among the few who realized that if logging practices did not change, there would be no forests for the future. As Weyerhaeuser told a Congressional committee in 1908, "Every time you cut a tree, there is one tree less." His testimony helped change America's forestry practices.

Today there are nine Weyerhaeuser Company locations in Wisconsin, employing more than 1,800 people (out of 41,700 total Weyerhaeuser employees). Operations include hardwood lumber (Dorchester and Onalaska), pulp and paper (Rothschild), corrugated shipping containers (Manitowoc), architectural doors (Marshfield), molded door skins and particle board (Marshfield), building products wholesalers (Green Bay and Wauwatosa), and hardwood lumber sales office (Wausau).

Weyerhaeuser Company is a worldwide marketer, supplying the globe with wood and paper products, personal care products, real estate development and construction, and financial services through unconsolidated subsidiaries. Weyerhaeuser Company is ranked number 62 on the *Fortune* 500 list and had net sales of $5.652 billion in 1986.

George Weyerhaeuser is the president and chief executive officer of the company. Like his great-grandfather, Frederick Weyerhaeuser, George Weyerhaeuser is a man of vision. In his words, "The men who founded our company, and the directors and managers who followed them, have consistently been concerned with the future. We have no less responsibility to those who will follow."

George H. Weyerhaeuser, president and chief executive officer, plants the commemorative 2-billionth tree under Weyerhaeuser Company's 20-year-old high-yield forestry program; he is assisted by John P. McMahon, vice-president/timberlands. The cloned superior Douglas fir tree also commemorates the completion of Weyerhaeuser reforestation in the Mount St. Helens volcano-damage zone, where it was planted on June 28, 1986.

E.C. STYBERG ENGINEERING COMPANY, INC.

E.C. Styberg Engineering Company, Inc., has done business in Racine for more than 60 years. When E.C. Styberg, Sr., founder of the company, emigrated to America from Sweden at the age of 20, he and his parents settled in Racine because they had relatives living there. For 17 years Styberg worked for various Racine industries before starting his own business.

In 1927 Styberg started a tool-and-die shop in a two-car garage behind his house on Winslow Street in Racine. Business was good at first, and Styberg hired several toolmakers. The business quickly outgrew the garage, and Styberg bought lots on DeKoven and Kearney avenues and erected a redbrick factory building. Styberg and his eight toolmakers settled into the new factory just months before the Stock Market Crash of 1929.

After the crash, orders dried up and Styberg set to work soliciting business throughout the Milwaukee and Chicago areas. By 1933 his business was again going well, and he began to diversify. In addition to the jobbing tool-and-die work, Styberg began fabricating production parts on his punch presses. His early production parts included products for the Johnson Wax Company and the Schwinn Bicycle Company.

During World War II Styberg's operation produced precision components for several types of military products, including dies for cartridge shells, bearings and cooler parts for aircraft engines, valves for ships and submarines, electromechanical assemblies for radar units, and many other specialized components. During the war Styberg expanded with the purchase of an additional building, on Junction Avenue.

In 1950 the firm consolidated its facilities when it moved to the former Wright Rubber Company plant on Gould Street. With various additions, the facility today totals more than 135,000 square feet.

E.C. Styberg, Jr., was elected president of the company in 1968. E.C. Styberg, Sr., was chairman of the board until his death in 1974. The junior Styberg remains president of the privately held company; his wife, Bernice, serves as secretary.

Two postwar advances in transportation contributed to the firm's growth from a couple of employees in a backyard garage to a company employing more than 200 people in a 135,000-square-foot facility. The first advance was the jet engine. Styberg has been an important manufacturer of precision components for military and civilian jet engines since the late 1940s. These parts are generally

E.C. Styberg, founder, started a tool-and-die business in 1927 that grew to become E.C. Styberg Engineering Company, Inc.

The original building, a converted garage on Winslow Street, out of which E.C. Styberg started his business on October 1, 1927. Three years later he moved to a new facility on DeKoven Avenue.

made from special alloy steels and require a variety of precise fabricating processes.

The second advance is the automatic transmission for motor trucks and off-highway-type vehicles. Automatic transmissions require a number of precision components, which Styberg produces. These include such Styberg specialty items as clutch plates, clutch housing, Belleville disc springs, brake and clutch discs, and connecting drums.

E.C. Styberg, Jr., attributes the success of E.C. Styberg Engineering Company, Inc., to a strong commitment to excellence. "For over a half-century," he says, "we've dedicated our efforts to being progressive, flexible, and customer oriented."

KENOSHA SAVINGS & LOAN ASSOCIATION

When Kenosha Savings & Loan Association opened for business in 1902, it offered its customers only two services. It made mortgage loans and offered share-draft accounts. Today Kenosha Savings & Loan is a full-service diversified financial institution, offering virtually every kind of banking service available. One-third of all the people living in Kenosha County are customers of Kenosha Savings & Loan; just about any type of investment, loan, or insurance product imaginable is available from KS&L.

Banking has changed a lot since KS&L began in 1902 as the Kenosha County Building Loan & Investment Association. (The name was shortened to Kenosha Building & Loan Association in 1926 and later took on its present name.) In the early days the purpose of the company was to make long-term home loans to the working public. Most banks made only three-year loans, and people wanted longer-term loans to bring down the cost of financing.

KS&L has been located in various buildings over the years, including the Schwartz Building and the Commercial Exchange Bank building. In 1957 the company built its current main office building on 59th Street and Seventh Avenue across from historic Library Park in downtown Kenosha. The structure was completely remodeled in 1972.

KS&L began adding branch services in 1968 with the opening of the Pershing Plaza branch. Today Kenosha Savings & Loan has seven offices and is one of the largest financial institutions in Kenosha County. Its assets total more than $300 million, and its reserves exceed $30 million.

Kenosha Savings & Loan has grown tremendously since the late Don Corr became manager of the association's three employees in 1946.

Despite its small size, Corr once said, "We worked hard so we got lucky."

When Corr, who was then chairman of the board, died in 1987, Kenosha Savings & Loan established the Donald T. Corr Endowed Scholarship Fund, which will be used to award Kenosha-area high school students scholarships to the University of Wisconsin-Parkside.

Corr used to tell stories about the changes at Kenosha Savings & Loan over the years. He recalled the time, for example, when the assets of another financial institution were being transferred to the ownership of KS&L. "They literally rolled the vault down the street under heavy police protection to our building," he said many years later.

Despite the many changes, Kenosha Savings & Loan Association continues to be owned by its shareholders (depositors), as it always has been. And, says Paul P. Gergen, president and chairman of the board, "We will continue our tradition of solid financial leadership."

In 1902, when Kenosha Savings and Loan opened its doors, the twentieth century had just begun and the Industrial Revolution had come into being. At that time Kenosha Savings and Loan was located in this building at 5617 Sixth Avenue.

THE CHENEY COMPANY

From a basement workshop manufacturing a single product to a modern 59,000-square-foot plant with more than 100 employees producing nine product lines, The Cheney Company has grown since it was founded in 1935.

Today The Cheney Company produces a full line of stairway elevators for public buildings and private residences—from inclined stairway lifts to vertical lifts, from deluxe custom-designed lifts to affordable rental units. Its products are designed to give Freedom of Movement® to people who have difficulty climbing stairs.

The company was founded by Wallace E. Cheney in the basement workshop of his home. Its first product, the Wecolator, was named for Cheney whose initials were W.E.C. Wallace was an engineer and an inventor. He made the first Wecolator for a family friend who had suffered a heart attack and was advised not to climb stairs.

The first Wecolator featured a compactly designed machine that contained an electric motor and special gearbox. It was mounted on a cog rail and could negotiate complex stairway curves and landings. An upholstered wooden chair was fitted on top of the machine, which also contained a drum for the power cord and a switching device to reverse the chair's direction automatically at the end of travel.

Wecolators became so popular that in 1938 Wallace resigned from his full-time job at Allis Chalmers to devote all his time to the business. Advertising was through word of mouth, and it was so effective that four Wecolators were installed on one particular city block within several months. Today the Wecolator is the only completely custom-built lift on the market.

In 1966 T. Clayton Cheney (Wallace's brother) became presi-

An original Wecolator stairway elevator designed and invented by Wallace E. Cheney in the basement of his home. Photo circa 1935

dent, and two years later his sons, Robert and Ted, purchased the business. Wallace died in 1969. Two years later Ted became Cheney's third president, and in 1985 the company moved to its current New Berlin, Wisconsin, headquarters. In 1987 Darlene Lewis became president.

As the need for quality accessibility equipment grew, Cheney grew—with new leadership, new products, and a distributor network that today covers the world.

The firm introduced the affordable Liberty I and II Stairlifts for straight, uncomplicated stairway applications.

The Liberty Wheelchair Lift was designed to meet the need for wheelchair accessibility in public buildings and private residences. It fulfills the need for an inclined platform lift to transport the disabled from one level to another.

For areas where space is limited, Cheney developed the Handi-Lift. This vertical wheelchair lift complements many decors in public and private buildings. An optional Handi-Enclosure is available.

Wecolators became popular, and The Cheney Company expanded and diversified. Here a Cheney crew stands in front of the beginnings of a Cheney stairway elevator. Photo circa 1952

The present headquarters of The Cheney Company, a modern 59,000-square-foot plant employing more than 100 people and manufacturing seven product lines.

Pictured here is one of the newest Cheney products—a Liberty Lift LX—designed in 1988.

For unmatched versatility, Cheney designed the Victory Wheel'n Chair Lift. It is a wheelchair lift and a seat lift. It negotiates curved stairways as well as straight stairways. And it features state-of-the-art electronic controls and a contemporary design.

Lewis attributes the success of Cheney products to a combination of factors. The U.S. population is aging, and there is more recognition of the needs and rights of disabled people. "But most of all, we spend a lot of time on research and development for a company our size," Lewis says. "We have to be sure our products maintain Cheney's reputation for reliability and high quality. It's a strong tradition—there still are some Cheney units in operation that were installed in the 1940s."

Cheney's growth accelerated when the company was acquired by Mediquip Healthcare of Toronto, Canada, in 1987. "We met our long-term goals immediately instead of in five or 10 years," says Lewis. "The acquisition gave us greater resources to meet the rapidly expanding need for durable medical products."

Cheney is on the move, improving existing products as well as expanding product lines and marketing strategies. Product improvements include new seat designs for easier, more comfortable transport and for a more contemporary look.

Through the acquisition, The Cheney Company became the sales and marketing arm for subsidiaries of Mediquip, namely, Concord Elevator, Inc., in Toronto and Toce Bros. Mfg. in Louisiana. In addition, Cheney redesigned a residential porch elevator formerly marketed by the Ricon Corporation in California. The year 1988 saw the merger of Toce Mfg. into the Cheney-Louisiana manufacturing facility for the Ride-A-Stair and Handi-Porch Elevator.

Because of the new relationships, consumers now can rent or purchase the economical Ride-A-Stair for as little as $2.50 per day. For public buildings with a high concentration of people, Cheney offers the Handi-ProLift (a Concord product). It is a step above Cheney's Handi-Lift.

To market the products, Cheney works with a network of more than 250 distributors worldwide. "Cheney is very, very professional and stands behind all of its products," says Tony Filippis, a Michigan-based Cheney distributor since 1982. "I've been in this business for 54 years, handling a competitor's product. When I competed against The Cheney Company, I just didn't feel good about it because the product was inferior to Cheney's. I can't say enough good things about Cheney—the product, the company, and the people."

The Cheney Company is committed to continue developing products that give Freedom of Movement® to people who cannot climb stairs. "People have tried to copy us over the years," states Lewis. "But no one has been able to match our quality. We plan to continue that tradition."

QUAD/GRAPHICS, INC.

"Many companies talk about their five-year plans," says Harry V. Quadracci, president and founder of Quad/Graphics. "At Quad/Graphics, we used to have our five-minute plans. But we replaced that years ago with our 'Ready, Fire, Aim' plan. That may sound outrageous, but we at Quad/Graphics believe that if the bull's-eye is already in sight, we have probably already missed an opportunity."

Making the most of opportunities has helped Quad/Graphics grow from a small printing operation with 11 employees and a single printing press in 1972 to one of the nation's top 10 magazine and catalog printers with more than 3,000 employees in 1987. The company's first building covered a modest 20,000 square feet in Pewaukee. Today Quad/Graphics has four facilities—in Lomira, Pewaukee, and Sussex, Wisconsin, and Saratoga Springs, New York—encompassing more than 2 million square feet.

Quadracci, who founded the business using a $35,000 second mortgage on his home and capital raised from 15 associates, did not find immediate success. When Quad/Graphics opened for business, both a paper shortage and a recession contributed to a very slow start. Quadracci and his co-founders had targeted newspaper inserts, but that market was in a slump. And, in any case, their first press could not be relied upon to give the required quality.

The first five years were difficult, but the company gradually moved out of the newspaper-insert business and into its present specialty, printing magazines and catalogs. In addition to finding its niche, Quadracci says that another key to Quad/Graphic's success is its list of satisfied customers. "The most important asset we have," he says, "is a continually growing list of satisfied customers. It's not a question of

"He may be the only chief executive officer in the country who runs a school for his customers and sells his latest technology to his competitors," said INC. *magazine of Harry V. Quadracci in 1986.*

price or cost, it's a question of trust and value."

Getting customers in the first place was a challenge for Quad/Graphics. "At one point we had only two customers—and only one of them paid," Quadracci says. "We printed one magazine, which had a

press run of 15,000. Normally it would have taken only a few hours to print and bind, but every time a prospective customer wandered in, we cranked up the presses and kept running it, just to make it look like we were busy. In the end, we stretched that tiny press run of about four hours into a 30-day marathon."

Quad/Graphics no longer has a shortage of customers. The firm has grown at a rate exceeding 50 percent per year compounded annually since its founding. Today it prints some of the biggest national magazines, including *Newsweek, Harper's, U.S. News & World Report, and Playboy.*

Convincing prestigious national clients to have their printing done in "some little town in Wisconsin," as some of them said, was not easy at first. Quadracci launched an advertising campaign with the tag line "Where in the world is Pewaukee?" that both poked fun at easterner's provincialism and showed, on a satiric map, where in fact Pewaukee is. Quadracci includes a list of satisfied customers, including Jacques Cousteau, the National Football

Pressmen Dave Calmes and Karl Zeirke examine signatures.

League, and other names readers would recognize.

Today print buyers nationwide know where Pewaukee and Quad/Graphics are. The company's innovations have become legendary in the printing industry. Employees, for example, work a three-day, 36-hour work week (three 12-hour shifts), which allows Quad/Graphics to run its presses 24 hours a day. (Employees take turns working Sundays). Productivity rose 20 percent when this new schedule was installed.

Unlike most printers, Quad/Graphics makes its own inks. The firm is quick to update equipment; none of its presses is more than five years old. Quad/Graphics is also known for its employee stock ownership plan, profit-sharing program, extensive benefits, employee education and training programs, and the art collections in its facilities.

Quad/Graphics is perhaps best known, though, for its management methods. Quadracci believes that both managers and employees should take responsibility for the success of the company. "Anybody who sees that something needs to be done ought to assume the responsibility for doing it," he says. One of the rea-

Harry V. Quadracci with his partners in the Sussex Pressroom.

Enterprise has the latest in high-technology preparatory equipment, and technicians such as Roger Heathcote guarantee every job will meet with the customer's satisfaction.

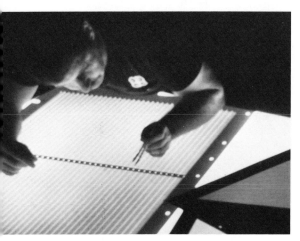

sons he founded Quad/Graphics was that he was fed up with traditional management methods. Quadracci, who has a law degree from Columbia University, served as a corporate counsel and manufacturing manager in the printing industry for nearly a decade before founding his own company.

Quadracci and his father, Harry R. Quadracci, have a long history as printers. Harry R. founded the Standard Printing Company with a single letterpress in a garage behind his father's grocery store in Racine. Harry R. eventually sold Standard Printing, and then worked for many years at the W.A. Krueger Printing Company, which he co-founded. In 1972 he left Krueger, where he had installed the first four-color web-offset press with long dryer and chilled water system in 1957, to co-found Quad/Graphics with his son. Today Harry R. is chairman of the board of Quad/Graphics.

Harry V. also began printing as a very young man. At the age of 14, he organized Quad/Photo, which was directed at the first communion and

eighth-grade picture market. At age 16 Harry V. formed Quad/Litho, which specialized in calling cards, church bulletins, and tickets. In 1961 Harry V. also joined the W.A. Krueger Company. When he resigned from the firm in 1970, he was vice-president and general manager of the Wisconsin division.

In addition to Quad/Graphics, the Quad Technologies Group includes Quad/Marketing, Inc., Enterprise Graphics, Martin Colorplate, Press, CR/T, Finishing, Duplainville Transport, Quad/Tech, Werkes/Tech, Quad/Construction, *Milwaukee* magazine, Quad/Care, Quad/Rail, Quad/Text, and Quad/Communications.

The firm is active in the community through its direct corporate giving program and its annual community fund matching gift program. In 1985 Quad/Graphics, Inc., resurrected the Great Circus Train and laid the groundwork for the return of the Great Circus Parade to the streets of Milwaukee.

WISC-TV

When WISC-TV (Madison's Channel 3, a CBS affiliate) went on the air for the first time at 7 p.m. on June 24, 1956, it did not get off to an auspicious start. Only one camera was set up; it rested on the packing crate of the unopened second camera. The announcer sat on the floor throughout the broadcast. And when it started to rain, the sound of the drops on the steel roof of the Quonset hut nearly drowned out the announcer's voice.

Despite its humble beginnings, WISC-TV has gone on to become the number-one TV station in the Madison market. "Sign on to sign off, we're number one," says Elizabeth Murphy Burns, president of the broadcasting group of the Evening Telegram Company, which owns WISC-TV. "Channel 3 has consistently been the number-one-rated station in the market, even though CBS has not always been the number-one-rated network."

WISC-TV has held the number-one position in the ratings because of its emphasis on producing quality local programming—local newscasts and public affairs programming. Pictured here is the "Live at Five" local newscast.

WISC-TV's headquarters on Raymond Road in Madison. WISC-TV is Madison's CBS affiliate.

Burns attributes the station's success to its emphasis on producing quality local programming, including local newscasts and public affairs programming. She believes that part of the responsibility of having a broadcast license is providing local programming. The station budgets one million dollars per year for local newscasts alone.

People look to television for information, and Burns believes it is important that a station provide good quality local news. "TV is like the newspapers of the 1930s. It's where most people go to get informed."

WISC-TV's local programming includes "News 3 Mid-Day," which is the longest-running live local program in Madison. Other WISC-TV local productions are "Live at Five," "News 3 at 6," "News 3 at 10," "For the Record," "Apostolate to the Handicapped," the Easter Seals telethon, the Leukemia telethon, Badger State games and specials, "Great Wisconsin Quiz Show," "Steve Yoder Show," "Don Morton Show," "Newscurrents Challenge," and "Doctor on Call."

The station no longer broadcasts from a steel-roofed Quonset hut. In 1981 WISC-TV consolidated its production and broadcast facilities in a new 22,500-square-foot building on Raymond Road, next to its transmitter building. The transmitter tower is 1,107 feet tall and is approximately 2,300 feet above sea level.

The station has owned the land on Raymond Road since roughly 1955, when Ralph O'Connor, the first general manager, saw a land survey that indicated it was the highest elevation in that part of Dane County. "High terrain is a big advantage in TV," says Richard Nickeson, who recently retired as executive director of marketing for the Morgan Murphy

TV Stations.

Nickeson thinks that WISC-TV has other advantages in the Madison market besides its high tower. "We're privileged," he says. "We have a fine working environment, good esprit de corps, and talented people." Nickeson also points to enlightened management as a boon to the station. "Elizabeth Murphy Burns and, before her, her parents, were willing to make capital investments in the company that have helped it to pioneer. We have state-of-the-art equipment."

WISC-TV has pioneered in the market in several ways. It is the only VHF station in its market; it had the first remote broadcasts in Madison; it was the first stereo television station in Wisconsin; and it was the second in the nation to provide automated closed captioning of its local news for the hearing impaired.

WISC-TV was founded in the early 1950s by Morgan Murphy (Elizabeth Murphy Burns' father), who owned 50 percent of the company, and by a group of Madison investors who owned the other 50 percent. George A. Nelson, the son of one of those early investors, who is today vice-president/administration and finance, remembers the early days of the station. "I worked as a laborer on the first studio. I carried bricks. We were all frantically trying to get everything ready before the first broadcast." Nelson remembers that people were expecting the station to sign on with a test pattern and were surprised when they broadcast the news. By 1981 the Madison group of investors had sold their interests in the station back to the Morgan Murphy family.

Today the Murphy family (Burns and her brother, John B. Murphy, who is president of the Evening Telegram Company and runs the family's newspapers) own five television stations, four newspapers, and one radio station in markets all over the country.

Other local programming includes "News 3 at 10" (top) and "News 3 at 6" (above).

Burns thinks that a lot of changes lie ahead in the television industry, particularly regarding the impact of cable, satellites, computers, and electronics. Still, she enjoys the challenges of the field. "It's an incredible business. It's of the moment and it's powerful. It can inform and entertain." Burns particularly enjoys the challenge of the Madison market. "Madison is an exciting community. It has government, the university, a vital business community. The people are diverse and sophisticated—it's a very good television market."

Today there are some 100 employees at WISC-TV, broadcasting local and syndicated programming to the southern Wisconsin area. Burns thinks that the Madison market will continue to demand good, exciting local television programming, and that all of the local stations will try to fill that demand. Burns thinks that competition in the marketplace is good: "We have to scurry to remain number one."

WEATHER SHIELD MFG., INC.

Edward L. Schield, who graduated from Medford High School in 1952, came back to his hometown in 1955, borrowed $300, and began to sell aluminum combination doors and windows. After making his sales calls, Schield went back to a 12-foot by 24-foot garage and assembled the doors and windows. Today the company Schield originally called Weather Shield Aluminum is known as Weather Shield Mfg., Inc., and is the third-largest wood window manufacturer in the country.

Weather Shield is still based in Medford where it started. The corporation's headquarters, main assembly facilities, as well as a millwork plant, vinyl extruding plant, and glass assembly plant are all located in Medford. Weather Shield also operates millwork plants in Ladysmith, Wisconsin, and Logan, Utah. Other assembly divisions are located in Loveland, Colorado; Logan, Utah; and Camp Hill, Pennsylvania. Weather Shield also has several distribution centers throughout the United States in addition to the assembly locations.

Edward L. Schield owns Weather Shield today, having bought out two early investors, David Schield (his brother) and Robert Spencer. The privately held company has facilities totaling 1.1 million square feet. There are now 2,074 employees, including Schield, who is president. Edward and Clarice Schield (who also graduated from Medford High School) have three sons—Mark, Kevin, and Brian. Mark is vice-president/sales, and Kevin is vice-president/western operations. Brian is an attorney in California.

Schield's decision in the late 1950s to expand Weather Shield from the aluminum door and window business and into wood proved prophetic. The firm began manufacturing wood windows and doors with features such as maintenance-free exterior and triple insulating glass be-

Edward L. Schield, founder of Weather Shield Manufacturing, Inc.

fore energy efficiency became extremely popular. At first Weather Shield supplied wood windows primarily for homes, but today a good portion of its business is for the commercial and residential markets, including large historic renovation projects.

Schield has always been interested in new product development and automation of production. Weather Shield's engineering department and machine tool division are continually working to improve existing products and develop new products and processes. "If you don't do that, you can't stay in business," Schield believes. "You don't have a product that will outsell and outperform the competition if you're satisfied with the status quo, because every successful company is improving on their product line and methods."

At the heart of Weather Shield's product line is its status as a prestige producer. Its slogan, "Better Ideas in Wood Windows," extends beyond energy efficiency and low maintenance. Many of its windows are custom built or special designs.

An example of a Weather Shield wood window. Weather Shield windows are not only used in homes but also in commercial and residential markets, including large historic renovation projects.

Shapes range from rectangles to ovals, octagons, cloverleafs, eyebrows, full circles, half-circles, and half-ellipses. Detailing includes patterned glass, beveled glass, true leaded glass, removable wood grilles, metal grilles, and true divided lite construction.

Weather Shield's product line is one of the largest in the industry. Weather Shield wood windows and

Weather Shield's corporate headquarters, main assembly facilities, millwork plant, vinyl extruding plant, and glass assembly plant are all located in Medford, where the company started.

doors are available in hundreds of styles, sizes, and options.

Weather Shield extrudes its own vinyls for weatherstripping and manufacturing maintenance-free exterior window and door parts. The company has 20 vinyl extruders (all in Medford) that extrude vinyl products for doors and windows.

The company does all of its own millwork at three plants in Medford, Ladysmith, and Logan, Utah. Medford and Ladysmith are the two biggest millwork plants in Wisconsin. Weather Shield imports Ponderosa pine from the West Coast and ma-

The original Weather Shield Mfg. plant in Medford.

chines it into wood parts for its windows and doors.

Weather Shield also makes all of its own insulating glass at its four glass-fabricating plants (two in Medford, one in Ladysmith, and one in Logan), in order to have more glass options. Glazing options include insulating glass, triple insulating glass, low "E" glass, and Williamsburg true divided lite. Insulating glass is 5/8 or one inch thick overall, depending on window or door style. The two lites of glass are sealed together with a primary seal consisting of polyisobutylene and an additional secondary glass sealant. An aluminum spacer filled with desiccant to absorb moisture separates the glass and creates an airspace between the two lites.

Triple insulating glass is one or 1.5 inches thick, depending on window or door style. The three lites of glass are sealed together with a primary seal consisting of polyisobutylene and an additional secondary glass sealant. Aluminum spacers filled with moisture-absorbing desiccant separate the glass and create two airspaces between the three lites.

Low "E" glass—low emissivity glass—has a special reflective hard coating that is applied to the glass while it is being manufactured. This reflective coating becomes a part of the glass and creates a harder surface than glass itself. Low "E" glass is 5/8 inch, one inch, one inch triple, and 1.5 inches triple thicknesses, depending on window or door style.

Williamsburg true divided lite consists of glass units that are separated by 1 3/8-inch-wide clear pine muntin bars. Glass is available in 7/16 inch, 5/8 inch, or one inch thicknesses, depending on the window or door style.

By combining different shapes, details, sizes, and colors, as well as glazing, wood, screen, and finishing options, hundreds of different window and door configurations are possible. Interiors are unprimed, natural wood that can be painted or stained to match the purchaser's decor. Exteriors are available as unprimed wood, ready for painting or staining, or primed on frame, trim, and sash.

Low-maintenance exteriors feature Lifeshield®, a general term referring to Weather Shield's White Vinyl, White Aluma, Adobe Aluma, or Desert Tan Aluma Thin Fin Trim. Low-maintenance units feature vinyl exterior frames. A rigid vinyl or aluminum nailing fin on the head and side jamb perimeters make installation easy. The siding overlaps the fins to provide a neat, clean appearance and also to create a layered seal

for extra protection against air and water infiltration. A continuous drip cap at the head (on most unit types), flexible vinyl flange at the sill, and an aluminum glazing bead also help assure a tight seal.

Weather Shield's many window and door options allow the company to manufacture units ranging from classic tilt windows to state-of-the-art Lee Haven® fire doors and insulated glass cloverleaf windows with true leaded glass centers.

Weather Shield's Better Ideas in Wood Windows have long been ahead of their time. The company's philosophy is that a window can be more energy efficient than a wall. With the possibility of solar energy, a window can achieve a positive energy gain, whereas a wall can do only one thing—lose energy. This approach to windows and doors fits in well with the 1980s emphasis on both natural light and energy efficiency in residential and commercial buildings.

In addition to an innovative product line, Weather Shield benefits from its emphasis on quality produc-

Today, as the third-largest wood window manufacturer in the country, Weather Shield has assembly divisions and distribution centers throughout the United States, but remains based in Medford.

tion. The company inspects its doors and windows at every point along the way, but Schield's philosophy is that "quality cannot be inspected into a product; it must be built in."

Weather Shield windows and doors are manufactured according to a just-in-time (JIT) schedule. The organization has a large inventory of parts. But, "we don't manufacture just in case somebody wants to order one like that," Schield says. Scheduling is crucial in a business such as Weather Shield's, and the JIT program, rather than increasing delivery times, has improved delivery schedules by a week since it was instituted two years ago.

Weather Shield Transportation, Ltd., a wholly owned subsidiary, transports the firm's doors and windows in more than 400 semitrailers and 80-plus leased tractors to locations nationwide. Weather Shield wood windows, sliding and hinged patio doors, and steel entry systems are sold by a sales force of some 120 people, as well as independent sales representatives in outlying areas.

Schield began his business career calling directly on his customers, and his business grew from there. Even today he believes that "customer satisfaction is the one most important ingredient in the success of any company."

NU-LINE INDUSTRIES

Nu-Line Industries, a division of Memline Corporation, proudly promotes the fact that all of its products are "Made in the U.S.A." Nu-Line manufactures quality juvenile furniture from dense domestic hardwoods such as maple, beech, birch, oak, and ash. All of the company's products are manufactured in Suring, which is near the sources of hardwood used in its products.

Nu-Line's "Made in the U.S.A." business approach has met with success. The firm received the Governor's New Product Award for a newly designed gate that won national recognition in 1971. Today Nu-Line has diversified its products in the juvenile furniture line. Its products include security gates, kiddie swings, guard rails, kiddie yards, step chairs, nursery chairs, storage chests, portable pen-cribs, play-yards, table and chair sets, rockers, high chairs, and changing tables.

Kenneth R. Stuart, president of Nu-Line, purchased the company in 1959; it had been incorporated in Milwaukee in 1947. Stuart moved the firm to Suring to be near sources of hardwood.

Three people ran the company for a few years, until, in 1968, the Suring Area Development Corporation (SADC) was formed. From 1969 to 1985 Nu-Line worked with SADC to put up buildings needed for expansion, and in 1985 Nu-Line purchased SADC.

Over the years the plant in Suring has been greatly expanded, and Nu-Line currently operates in an approximate 144,000-square-foot facility that includes a factory outlet store. Nu-Line's sales today total approximately $20 million. With 330 employees, Nu-Line is one of Oconto County's largest employers.

Nu-Line produces about 35,000 units in its juvenile furniture line each week. The company recently gained national recognition when a

Nu-Line manufactures quality children's furniture from a range of domestic hardwoods. From guard rails to kiddie yards to storage chests and high chairs, Nu-Line manufactures a diversified line of juvenile products from its Suring, Wisconsin, plant. It is the leading manufacturer of gates and portable cribs in the United States.

leading consumer magazine rated Nu-Line gates the strongest, safest gates on the market. The firm is the leader in the manufacture of gates and portable cribs in the United States.

Nu-Line was acquired in January 1988 by Huffy Corp., headquartered in Dayton, Ohio. Huffy is a manufacturer of bicycles under the Huffy and Raleigh brand names. Huffy basketball backboards are also manufactured in Waukesha, Wisconsin.

Nu-Line will continue as a separate company and remain in Suring, according to the announcement by officials of Huffy. It will operate as a part of the Huffy juvenile products business under the direction of Charles S. Wilke, president of Gerico Inc.

"We plan to maintain Nu-Line as a separate wood products company and build upon its excellent business foundation with expanded new product introductions," said Wilke.

Stuart cites location as a factor in the company's success. "Nu-Line juvenile products are the very best you can buy—partly because they are American made in Suring, Wisconsin, where people still take quality and craftsmanship seriously. Our products are constructed of select northern hardwoods."

Nu-Line's most recent recognition was being voted Manufacturer of the Year in October 1987. Stuart was honored to receive this award during the Juvenile Products Manufacturers' Association annual trade show.

Nu-Line Industries is also concerned about product safety. "Nu-Line's outstanding reputation comes from our 40-year commitment to providing only the highest quality and safest products possible," Stuart says. "Nu-Line is involved in establishing industry safety standards for juvenile products." Product safety seals go right next to the "Made in the U.S.A." labels on Nu-Line products.

WAUSAU INSURANCE COMPANIES

Located almost precisely in the center of Wisconsin, Wausau may very well be the best-known small city in the United States. Since January 1954, when the famous Wausau depot made its debut in *TIME* and other leading magazines, the "Wausau Story" advertising campaign of Wausau Insurance Companies has put the name before millions of American readers with literally billions of impressions. The association of this major insurance organization with its hometown has been beneficial to both.

The Wausau story has its beginnings in Madison in 1911, when the legislature passed into law the first workers' compensation law able to meet the test of constitutionality.

Up in Wausau, 150 miles to the north, a group of businessmen, primarily lumbermen, decided to form a mutual insurance company to cover their liabilities under the new law. They named the fledgling insurance company Employers Mutual Liability Insurance Company of Wisconsin. Today it is officially Em-

ployers Insurance of Wausau—A Mutual Company. Most people, however, are more familiar with the trade name that appears with the famous depot, Wausau Insurance Companies.

The firm opened for business on the day the law became fully effective, September 1, 1911. The first policy issued was to the Wausau Sulphate Paper Company, known today as the Mosinee Paper Corporation. That policy, the first valid workers' compensation policy in the nation, has been continuously in force ever since.

The company has had six corporate headquarters since the first one—a rented room above a cigar store at the intersection of Third and Scott streets in downtown Wausau. The present four-building complex, enclosing 500,000 square feet, has been home to the company since 1967.

The first employee was Jay C. Youmans, whose task was to work with policyholders to prevent industrial accidents. Youmans became well known among safety professionals as Mr. Safety. In 1913 he helped to establish the National Safety Council.

The company is now staffed by 6,000 employees who provide virtually every kind of coverage needed by the nation's businesses and other

This picture was taken on May 15, 1926, in the Hans Weik Saloon Building at Third and Jackson streets, the third home office of the company. H.J. Hagge, who was to become company president in 1931, is standing directly under the fan at the rear.

enterprises. Workers' compensation is still the mainstay of Wausau's line of insurance products, accounting for more than 40 percent of the $1.3 billion of earned premium the firm puts on the books each year.

From the beginning, Wausau insisted that policyholders work diligently to provide a safe work environment. This attention to what is called "loss control" is a continuing hallmark of the Wausau/policyholder relationship.

In 1928 Joanna Johnson joined the company as an industrial nurse. She was the first nurse in the insurance industry to work with policyholders in developing in-plant medical care for the work force. That same year Wausau Insurance opened a physical therapy center that was also a first for the insurance industry. It worked to restore victims of industrial accidents to the highest level of physical capability and productivity possible. A Wisconsin Historical Society Registered Landmark plaque in

Leon J. Weinberger, president and chief executive officer of Wausau Insurance Companies since 1985. Weinberger is also a vice-president of Wausau's parent corporation, Nationwide Insurance.

downtown Wausau calls attention to the site of this historic and humanitarian endeavor.

In 1932 a new crisis swept a nation already in the throes of the Great Depression. Silicosis, a non-communicable disease caused by long-term exposure to silica dust in the so-called "dusty trades," was causing a wave of workers' compensation claims as an industrial illness. Many insurers were refusing to write coverage for foundries, quarries, and other industries with silica dust exposures. In keeping with its own credo, Wausau Insurance dug in its heels and established an industrial hygiene laboratory in Milwaukee to research the problem. Under the direction of Dr. E.G. Meiter and in consultation with O.A. Sander, M.D., the laboratory developed methods of ventilation and personal protection that, in conjunction with periodic physical examinations, made it possible for workers to avoid the disease. That laboratory, now located in Wausau, has grown into a highly sophisticated facility where a staff of chemists works to find answers to a host of complex problems faced by policyholders.

During the 1950s Wausau Insurance pioneered in studying industrially induced hearing loss. Dr. Roger Maas, an audiologist, advocated a national education program, in-plant noise level surveys, preemployment hearing assessments, engineering controls, and personal hearing protection equipment.

In 1982, when the company moved into the Westwood Training and Conference Center, its state-of-the-art training facility just up the hill from the corporate headquarters, the building included both a fire-protection laboratory and a loss-control laboratory. The first is devoted to the latest fire-protection equipment and techniques; the latter concentrates on methods of protect-

ing workers from industrial machines as well as displaying and demonstrating personal protection gear. Both laboratories are used to train company employees and representatives of policyholder firms.

In 1985 Wausau Insurance Companies affiliated with Nationwide Insurance of Columbus, Ohio. The Wisconsin firm serves as the business insurance supplier for the giant insurance organization. Wausau itself now boasts assets of $3 billion and annual revenues approaching $1.5 billion. As a part of the Nationwide Group, it has joined itself with a $17-billion enterprise, giving it even more muscle to serve the needs of American society.

In September 1986 Wausau Insurance celebrated its 75th anniversary. Paul Donald, president of Nationwide's property/casualty affiliates, and chairman of the Wausau Insurance Board of Directors, noted on that occasion, "Seventy-five years is a significant milestone, one that the people of both the Wausau companies and the Wausau community should truly cherish. Three-quarters of a century is a level no business can reach unless it successfully established genuine bonds of trust with its employees, its townspeople, and the public it serves. Wausau's past has been outstanding, and the future should be even better."

A replica of the Wausau train depot as it looked in 1901. This replica was built about 1980 on the grounds of Wausau Insurance Companies from the original plans and is used as a meeting facility for the firm. The original building is still located at the base of East Hill in Wausau.

President Lee Weinberger extended his thanks to the firm's hometown, commenting that, "Wausau has been such a good place to grow an insurance company . . . We can draw much widsom from those who built this company as we move confidently toward our 100th anniversary. I am proud of this company, its traditions, its potential, and its role in the continued growth of our hometown and of our society."

The corporate headquarters of Wausau Insurance Companies totals 500,000 square feet.

MOSINEE PAPER CORPORATION

The Wausau Sulphate & Fibre Company was founded in 1910 and became the first integrated kraft mill on the North American continent. It was the first wood room, pulp mill, and paper mill designed specifically to produce paper by the kraft, or sulfate, process. In those early days the company employed 150 people who produced 12 to 15 tons of natural kraft paper per day on one paper-making machine.

Another first came about when the company was issued the first workers' compensation policy in the country from Wausau Insurance Companies on September 1, 1911, the same day the first workmen's compensation law went into effect.

In 1914 the No. 2 paper machine was added to the mill; the new machine had an average production of 54.9 tons per day. The No. 3 paper machine was erected in 1918, and by 1920 the company experienced another first—No. 3 paper machine was the first in the world to produce paper at a sustained speed of 1,000 feet per minute.

From the beginning, the kraft wrapping papers were marketed under the trade name "Mosinee." In order to ensure that the firm would be identifiable with it major product, the Wausau Sulphate Fibre Company changed its name to Mosinee Paper Mills Company in 1928. The origin of the name "Mosinee," however, is a matter of opinion. Some local citizens claim it was derived from an Indian name meaning "moose's knee,"

James L. Kemerling, president and chief executive officer of Mosinee Paper Corporation.

so named for a particular bend in the Great River (the Wisconsin River), while others say that the name belonged to an old Indian chief renowned in the area.

In 1928 Mosinee acquired the Bay West Paper Company and also purchased a water-creping machine for the mill at Mosinee. The resulting creped paper was manufactured for use as vacuum cleaner bags. The company purchased 4,500 acres of jack pine in northwestern Wisconsin; this land eventually developed into the Mosinee Industrial Forest. Mosinee also helped finance the Institute of Paper Chemistry at Lawrence College in Appleton. But when the Depression arrived, business declined. The selling price of kraft paper dropped from $5.25 a hundredweight in 1926 to $2.75 a hundredweight five years later. Mosinee Paper was forced to cut wages as well as the number of employees.

Expansion began again at

Mosinee's kraft mill as conditions improved in the country. In 1944 the company started operating the Mosinee Industrial forest in Solon Springs, Wisconsin, and by 1946 was also undergoing the largest modernization program of its history in Mosinee. By 1950 the mill was producing an average of 177 tons of paper per day. In 1964 a fourth paper machine was installed (rebuilds of the first three paper machines took place in 1952, 1953, and 1966). The Converted Products Division was added to the organization in 1966, followed by the Calwis and Green Bay Plastics operations two years later.

In 1911 Mosinee Paper Corporation purchased the first workers' compensation policy in the country from Wausau Insurance.

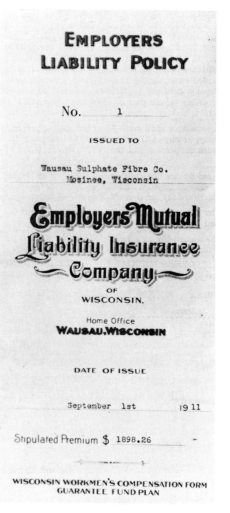

EMPLOYERS LIABILITY POLICY

No. 1

ISSUED TO

Wausau Sulphate Fibre Co.
Mosinee, Wisconsin

Employers Mutual Liability Insurance Company

OF
WISCONSIN.

Home Office
WAUSAU, WISCONSIN

DATE OF ISSUE

September 1st 1911

Stipulated Premium $ 1898.26

WISCONSIN WORKMEN'S COMPENSATION FORM GUARANTEE FUND PLAN

The predecessor of the Mosinee Paper Corporation was the Wausau Sulphate & Fibre Company, the first integrated kraft mill on the North American continent. Photo circa 1911

The company reorganized on a divisional basis in 1971 and was renamed the Mosinee Paper Corporation. Today the corporate office and the Pulp and Paper Division (the original kraft mill facility) are still headquartered in Mosinee. Three regular Fourdrinier machines and a Yankee Fourdrinier (with a 90-ton drying drum) allow the Pulp and Paper Division to custom produce up to 300 tons a day of a wide variety of industrial specialty papers in runs as low as 20 tons. The pulp mill can produce 240 tons a day from both soft and hard woods. Much of the wood is procured locally or from the company's industrial forest.

Producing one ton of kraft paper requires 2 to 2.6 tons of wood, 260 tons of water, 60 tons of air, 2.1 tons of coal, .24 tons of chemicals, and 725 kilowatt hours of electricity. With this in mind, the Pulp and Paper Division has long recognized the importance of forest conservation and pollution abatement. The company began a program of conservation in the mid-1940s with 30,000 acres of virgin forest. Today the organization scientifically harvests and replants approximately 90,000 acres of industrial forest to supply more than 30 percent of the mill's softwood needs. The forest also provides recreational opportunities for area residents. The program of air and water recovery plus energy self-generation began in the late 1960s and cost more than $35 million. As a result, clarified water is returned to the Wisconsin River and particulates have been reduced by 90 percent and reducible sulfur by 99 percent. This program, which resulted in a new pulp mill/power plant, was completed in 1977 and was the largest single capital investment in the Pulp and Paper Division's history. Recently, the Pulp and Paper Division also became involved in stocking the Wisconsin River with muskellunge.

Mosinee's Pulp and Paper Division today. Mosinee comes from the Indian word meaning "Moose Knee" for which the Indians had named a bend in the Wisconsin River. The plant is still located at that bend in the river.

With the acquisition of The Sorg Paper Company of Middletown, Ohio, in 1983, the corporation has doubled its size to include five operating facilities, 1,400 employees, and annual revenues exceeding $200 million. The Bay West Division in Green Bay markets high-quality toweling and tissue products along with "cost-control" soap and towel dispensers. It also markets windshield wipes and dairy towels. The Mosinee Converted Products Division, in Columbus, Wisconsin, specializes in custom converting by means of laminating, saturating, and coating processes resulting in end products such as product wrapping, laminated fiber stock for cans, and moisture barrier protective wrappings. It has also entered the nonwoven fabric converting industry, developing products for industrial and consumer uses. The Green Bay Plastics Division manufactures specialty plastic products. The Sorg Paper Company, a wholly owned subsidiary, is a large, nonintegrated manufacturer of a diverse line of specialty fine and coarse papers. It also operates a de-inked pulp mill.

Today Mosinee Paper Corporation is one of the nation's leading manufacturers of specialty papers. Many of Mosinee's specialty paper products are produced for national and international industrial custom-ers who, in turn, convert and market their own finished products. As a corporation, Mosinee Paper produces or converts more than 250,000 tons of paper each year. In 1986 Mosinee was recognized by *Forbes* magazine as "one of the 200 best small companies in America."

Precision process control at Mosinee's Pulp and Paper Division has allowed the company to set the highest quality standards for excellent basis weight, moisture, and caliper.

MERRILL MANUFACTURING CORPORATION

"We cannot survive in the past," says Donald F. Taylor, chairman of the board of Merrill Manufacturing Corporation. "We must always be looking to the years ahead and the future of our company, our employees, and our community." Taylor's son, Richard L. Taylor, president of the firm, agrees. "We have embarked on an aggressive capital investment program to modernize our facilities and maintain our competitive position," Richard L. says.

Merrill Manufacturing, a privately held company with sales of approximately $7.5 million per year, is in the midst of a long-term major capital investment program. New equipment and updating of the company's facilities will help keep Merrill Manufacturing competitive in a changing market. The capital investment, which will total roughly $1.5 million in the next two years, will help the firm retain its strong position as a custom manufacturer of welded wire assemblies.

Merrill Manufacturing and its predecessors have played a prominent role in the economy of Merrill for more than 100 years, and Richard L. Taylor intends to keep it that way. "Our roots are here," he says, "and we feel very strongly about that. We've got the best quality of life anybody could ask for. It's not even worth thinking about moving."

The company's original plant was built on Genesee Street (a block from Merrill Manufacturing's current plant) in approximately 1880 by a man named Christenson. The plant was originally used as a foundry and machine shop servicing the many sawmills and logging operations then operating in the Merrill area. In 1900 John O'Day, a prominent logger, purchased the business and incorporated it under the name Merrill Iron Works. The foundry poured standard gray iron casting. It also included a pattern shop, a small machine shop, and

Merrill Machinery & Supply Company, the predecessor of Merrill Manufacturing Corporation, in 1916. The building, which still stands, is located one block from the present plant. The company was housed in this building and later additions until the current facility was built in 1958.

possibly a few items of mill supply.

In roughly 1914 the firm became deeply indebted to one of its suppliers, the John Deere Plow Company of Milwaukee. Francis E. Taylor (Donald F.'s father) worked for John Deere as an accountant in Milwaukee. He was asked to take over the active management of the company. By 1916 the firm's debt was again manageable, and the principal stockholder/owners, Patzer and Richmond, asked if Taylor would like to buy the company.

In 1916 Taylor and W.J. Tesch acquired the majority stock of the Merrill Iron Works. The firm continued to furnish mill supplies for the logging industry. During World War I the company furnished castings for the war effort, including parts for submarines.

Donald Taylor worked in the business as a grade-school child, helping take inventory during his vacations from school. "We had a rolling ladder," he says. "We would count the bolts in the bins by counting them out into weighing pans."

The 4-Slide Automatic Department in 1948 in the building on Genesee Street, one block from the current facility.

There was a drive-on scale in the street outside the store, and one of Donald's jobs was to help weigh loads of hay. Drivers would drive the wagon onto the scale, he says, and "we charged them 10 cents for weighing" the load. Despite his early work in the firm, Donald did not join the company full time until 1939.

By the early 1920s it was apparent to Francis Taylor and W.J. Tesch that the logging industry had little future in this area of Wisconsin. By the late 1920s the company, which was then called Merrill Machinery & Supply Company, changed from a foundry to a manufacturing operation. By 1928 the old foundry had been torn out, and manufacturing machinery purchased and installed.

The company faced hard times during the Depression and made a settlement with its creditors in order to continue in business. In 1933 the mill supplies portion of the business was sold to the D.J. Murray Company at Wausau.

In 1935 the manufacturing company was renamed Merrill Manufacturing Corporation. Annual sales figures reached $89,000. "If we can push this to $100,000," Tesch commented, "we'll have a fine little business here."

During World War II the firm worked seven days a week, 24 hours a day to manufacture "quartermaster findings"—wire-formed products

The 1958 ground breaking for the current Merrill manufacturing facility, which today totals 110,000 square feet. From left are R.P. Tesch, W.J. Tesch, Don F. Taylor, and Francis E. Taylor.

used by the military. After the war the operation expanded rapidly.

In 1958 ground was broken to build a larger plant facility one block from the original building on Genesee Street. Francis Taylor died four days later. In 1982 the Taylor family purchased Tesch's share of the company, and it is today owned entirely by the Taylors. Richard L. joined the corporation in 1967.

Today Merrill Manufacturing is one of the largest companies of its kind in the United States. Its manufacturing plant and office now total 110,000 square feet. It does in excess of 90 percent of its own tooling. The

These are just a few of the thousands of wire forms developed and manufactured by Merrill Manufacturing Corporation.

firm has 200 employees and anticipates hiring more as the capital investment program continues.

Merrill Manufacturing specializes in special applications for wire-form products. The firm has developed and manufactured thousands of different wire forms. "There's a basic betterness to wire," Richard L. Taylor says. He points out that tooling costs for a wire-form component can be less than one-tenth of what they would be for the same part made of stamped metal or molded plastic. "And, since most wire is steel, it's strong. Wire forms reduce cost significantly, they reduce weight, and they have a long life," he says.

Each year Merrill Manufacturing Corporation, whose roots in the community go back more than a century, among other things, donates a piece of needed equipment to the local hospital on behalf of Merrill employees and customers. Richard Taylor says, "We must remain a good corporate citizen."

The fourth generation is now in school with plans to keep up the family tradition.

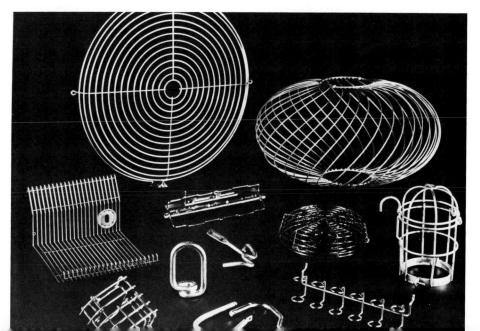

GENERAL MOTORS IN WISCONSIN

General Motors Corporation, based in Lansing, Michigan, operates three divisions in Wisconsin—the B-O-C Group Janesville plant, Delco Electronics, and AC Spark Plug.

JANESVILLE PLANT, BUICK-OLDSMOBILE-CADILLAC GROUP

General Motors operations in Janesville date back to 1918, when W.C. Durant, prompted by the trend toward mechanization in farming, moved the Samson Tractor Company from Stockton, California, to Janesville. The original building was completed in 1919; production of tractors began immediately.

In 1922 the plant stopped producing tractors and began to manufacture Chevrolet automobiles. The first Chevrolets were produced in February 1923 by the Chevrolet and Fisher Body divisions of General Mo-

tors. The Oldsmobile Division took over this facility in 1942 for wartime shell production.

Early in 1946 the Chevrolet and Fisher Body divisions resumed production of Chevrolet cars and trucks. The two divisions were merged into a single operation in 1968 and became part of the GM Assembly Division. In 1984 General Motors reorganized its divisions, and the Janesville facility became part of the Buick-Oldsmobile-Cadillac Group.

Today the Janesville facility assembles Chevrolet Cavalier and Cadillac Cimarron cars, as well as Chevrolet and GMC crew cab and cab chassis for the GM Truck and Bus Group. The plant employs about 5,600 people and operates on two production shifts. The facility contains two assembly lines, one for cars and one for trucks. The plant is 3.2 million square feet in size.

B-O-C Janesville makes approximately 52 cars per hour and 15 trucks per hour. The Janesville plant had a payroll of $196 million in 1987 and made purchases of more than $84 million from local suppliers. Employees contributed more than $302,000 to the local United Way in 1987. Among General Motors plants, the Janesville facility is particularly known for the consistently high quality of its products.

Beginning with the 1989 model year the car line will assemble Chevrolet Cavaliers and Buick Skyhawks (the Cimarron is being discontinued). Following the 1989 model year the truck line will be converted for production of a medium-duty truck that is planned for introduction in the 1990 model year.

DELCO ELECTRONICS

Delco Electronics is best known for its contributions to putting a man on the moon. Delco was the prime building contractor for the guidance

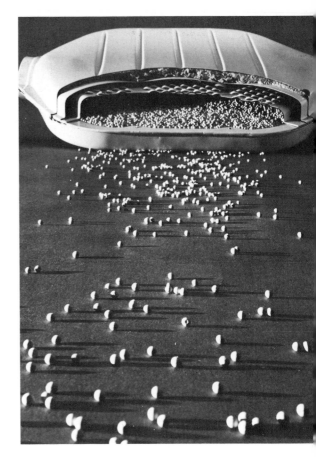

Catalytic converters, built by AC Spark Plug Division for all GMC passenger cars since the introduction of 1975 models, continue to roll from AC assembly lines in Oak Creek, Wisconsin, site of the division's one-million-square-foot converter-manufacturing facility.

and navigation system for the Apollo spacecraft. In 1969 the Apollo Inertial Guidance System, manufactured by Delco Electronics, was flown on the first man-on-the-moon mission; Delco's system was also successfully used on all subsequent Apollo flights.

Delco Electronics was formed in 1970 by a merger of two GMC divisions, AC Electronics and Delco Radio. The new name was formed by dropping "AC" and "Radio" from the two former titles. Delco Electronics currently ranks as the world's largest producer of digital computers. In 1983 Delco Electronics delivered its 12-millionth electronic control module.

Delco's commitment to quality

AC Spark Plug's assembly line in Oak Creek, Wisconsin.

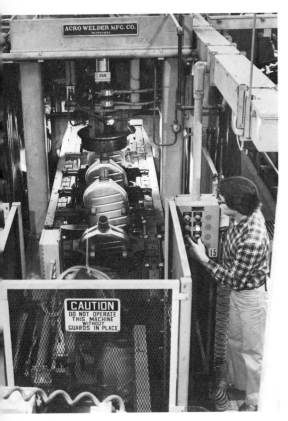

has frequently been recognized. The Department of Defense presented its Defense Quality Excellence Award to Delco in both 1984 and 1985. And in 1987 Delco was chosen to participate in McDonnell Douglas Corporation's Delegated Supplier Inspection Program, one of only 25 out of 6,000 suppliers to achieve the DSIP designation, which is based on the supplier's "overall attitude toward quality."

Catalytic converters and exhaust oxygen sensors, supplied by AC Spark Plug Division for all GM passenger cars since the introduction of 1981 models, continue to roll from AC assembly lines in Oak Creek, Wisconsin, and Wichita Falls, Texas. AC-Milwaukee operations builds more than 25,000 catalytic converters daily to equip Chevrolet, Buick, Oldsmobile, Pontiac, and Cadillac passenger cars and some Chevrolet and GMC light trucks.

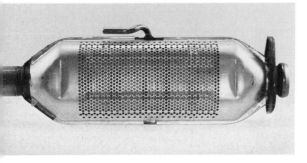

AC SPARK PLUG

Albert "AC" Champion, a French bicycle, motorcycle, and automobile racer who had been making spark plugs and magnetos in a small garage in Boston, moved to Flint, Michigan, in 1908 to head the new Champion Ignition Company. France, at that time, was the world leader in ceramic products, and Champion had researched spark plug manufacture there. Champion Ignition eventually became a subsidiary of the GM Corporation, and its production of spark plugs increased as GM's production of cars grew.

AC began adding product lines during World War I, when it branched into aviation spark plugs. In 1922 the organization was renamed AC Spark Plug Company. AC began operations in downtown Milwaukee in 1948, building gunsights and gyroscopic bombing-navigational computer systems. In 1959 AC-Milwaukee Operations moved into larger quarters in Oak Creek, as AC began production of inertial guidance systems for Titan, Thor, Mace, Regulus, and Polaris missiles, as well as guidance systems for space exploration and commercial navigation.

An aerial view of the Buick-Oldsmobile-Cadillac Group Janesville plant.

AC-Milwaukee operated as a separate division (AC Electronics Division) from 1965 until 1970, when Delco Electronics Division was formed. In 1973 AC reassumed operational control of most of the Oak Creek facilities for the manufacture of catalytic converters. (Delco continues to use about one-third of the building's space.)

Following a joint AC and GM Research Laboratories catalytic converter development program, GM equipped all 1975 model (and later) passenger cars and some light trucks with the AC-built emissions-control devices. AC today is the world's largest producer of catalytic converters. AC-Milwaukee builds more than 25,000 catalytic converters daily to equip Chevrolet, Buick, Oldsmobile, Pontiac, and Cadillac passenger cars and some Chevrolet and GMC light trucks. By the start of 1988 model production the one-million-square-foot converter-manufacturing facility in Oak Creek had manufactured nearly 82 million catalytic converters.

TOMBSTONE PIZZA

When Tombstone pizzas were first produced in 1962 by Joseph "Pep," Ronald, Frances, and Joan Simek, they were served to customers in the Simek's country tavern, the Tombstone Tap. The tavern was located across the road from a cemetery just outside Medford. Today the pizzas that began as a food item to augment the income for the Tombstone Tap are still being made in Medford, but they are now being shipped, frozen, to retail customers in 23 states. The pizza company with the unusual name has grown to become one of the largest manufacturers of frozen pizza in the country.

There have been changes as the company has grown. The Tombstone Tap is now an apartment building. The 1959 Cadillac that functioned as the company's first delivery vehicle has been replaced with a large fleet of semis, trailers, and freezer-box delivery trucks, needed to move Tombstone-brand products to more than 45,000 retail outlets in the firm's marketing area. All of the Simeks have retired from the pizza business. In 1986 the privately held company was acquired by Kraft, Inc. Tombstone Pizza is now a freestanding operating unit within Kraft's Frozen Foods Division. At the time of the sale to Kraft, Tombstone Pizza

employed more than 1,000 people and had sales in excess of $100 million.

Some things have not changed, however. Twelve-inch cheese and sausage was the original kind of Tombstone pizza, and it is still the company's best seller. It still contains Pep's secret tomato sauce. D. David "Dewey" Sebold, who had worked at the Tombstone Tap during college, who had sold Tombstone pizzas on a route during those early years, and who had been executive vice-president and general manager of Tombstone Pizza during the Simeks' ownership, is now the firm's president and chief executive officer. He is committed to maintaining the quality that has made Tombstone Pizza so successful.

A new three-level corporate headquarters now overlooks the cemetery that inspired the corporate name. The large quarry stone building, completed in 1986, is located just down the road from the former Tombstone Tap.

The headquarters' contemporary design is based on the prairie

---

The old Tombstone Tap Tavern where Joseph L. "Pep" Simek developed his famous pizza recipe. The tavern was so named because of its proximity to a cemetery.

school of architecture. Extensive interior landscaping, including 550 tropical plants, vaulted skylights, and more than 50 specially commissioned artworks, highlight the 60,000-square-foot building.

Approximately one-fifth of Tombstone Pizza's Medford employees works in the new headquarters building. But the pizzas are made at a plant elsewhere in Medford and at a second plant in Sussex, which opened in 1983 and four years later underwent an expansion that tripled its size and led to the doubling of its work force.

Sebold attributes Tombstone Pizza's tremendous success—it has enjoyed double-digit growth in sales in every year since its founding—to its emphasis on quality products, quality people, and the direct-store-delivery sales system. Tombstone Pizza, which competes in the "premium" end of the frozen-pizza market, uses top-quality natural ingredients, with no extenders and only 100-percent real cheese.

A second key to Tombstone Pizza's success, according to Sebold, is that the company takes responsibility for transporting the frozen pizzas from the plants in Medford and Sussex all the way to their final retail destinations in stores, taverns,

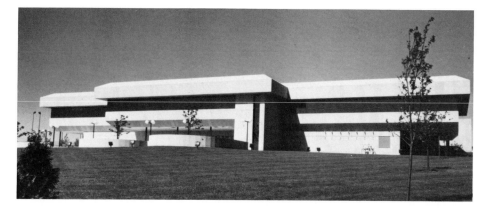

The new corporate headquarters of Tombstone Pizza—a visible symbol of Tombstone Pizza's success.

and other outlets. Sebold, who joined Tombstone full time in the mid-1970s, advocated a direct sales force because it gave the firm direct control over its product. All Tombstone products are shipped by the company's own trucks and trailers to regional warehouse facilities, and then delivered directly to retailers by route salespeople via freezer trucks.

Although its product line is expanding, Tombstone has not taken shortcuts with quality. The firm processes all the meat it uses in its line of meat snacks, Italian sausage, Canadian-style bacon, and pepperoni used on its pizzas. The sausage is a very lean beef and pork mixture, cooked to remove excess fat. The meat snacks, Canadian-style bacon, and pepperoni are smoked in Tombstone Pizza's own smokehouses. Only 100-percent real cheese is used on Tombstone pizzas. Close attention is given to the quality of the company's sauce and crusts.

Tombstone Pizza, which began in Medford, is committed to enhancing the quality of life in the Medford area. The Tombstone Pizza Foundation distributes funds to local educational institutions and medical causes, including the Marshfield Medical Research Foundation, and annually awards college scholarships to a local high school graduate and graduating son or daughter of a Tombstone Pizza employee. Individually, Tombstone Pizza employees at all levels are encouraged to participate in local civic and charitable organizations.

Pep Simek invented Tombstone's secret pizza sauce when he was laid up with a broken leg (from dancing the Peppermint Twist too energetically in early 1960 at the Tombstone Tap). He was not entirely surprised at the success of Tombstone pizza. "Because we had a good product," he said years ago, "there was demand, and it was easy to sell."

Tombstone Pizza has an ambitious mission: to become the leading frozen pizza company in the United States. Sebold says, "That mission is achieveable because there is a tremendous spirit in this organization, a spirit that thrives on challenge. Leadership is the key. Tombstone Pizza has always been a leader in quality products, quality people, and quality service. Leadership in the industry is a challenge we have the spirit to meet."

Assembly-line workers arrange pepperoni on Tombstone pizzas as part of the pizza-making process. Photo by John Alley, Wisconsin Gas Company

CHURCH MUTUAL INSURANCE COMPANY

Dieter H. Nickel, chairman and president of Church Mutual Insurance Company.

"We're proud of the fact that 95 percent of our claims are paid within 24 hours of receipt of final proof of loss," says Dieter H. Nickel, president of Church Mutual Insurance Company. "It's a record that has prompted many unsolicited letters of commendation." Church Mutual is also proud of its financial stability, which has consistently earned the organization an "A+" rating from the A.M. Best Company, independent analyst of the insurance industry.

Church Mutual was founded in 1897 in Merrill, where it is still based. The original incorporators of the company were pastors F.J. Siebrandt and Herman Daib, as well as Gustav Wenzel, John G. Wenzel, H.R. Fehland, William Rehfeld, August Piske, F.E. Brown, and Julius Thielman. It was called the Wisconsin Church Mutual Fire Insurance Association.

In the early years of the firm coverage was restricted to church, church society, or pastor of the synods constituting the Evangelical Lutheran Synodical Conference and the Norwegian Evangelical Lutheran Church of America. But the company has not been affiliated with or sponsored by any religious denomination.

Daib was president of the firm beginning in 1912 and a member of the board of directors for 44 years, until his death in 1941. The company operated as an assessable mutual until 1939, when it established a guarantee fund of $125,000 and became a nonassessable legal reserve mutual company.

Between 1897 and 1945 all business was solicited by mail through one annual direct-mail release. The letter remained the same except for the addition of current statistics. Another barrier to growth in the early days was that all policies expired permanently each year. In order to renew a policy, a new application had to be filled out, submitted, and approved. Today, with an automatic policy-renewal procedure, 95 percent of policyholders renew their policies with Church Mutual.

W.W. Schuster took over management of the firm in 1945, first as Church Mutual's executive secretary and treasurer and then, in 1951, as president. When Schuster was elected his mandate was to "turn around the company by increasing premium production, assets, surplus, and to establish an image of aggressiveness," he wrote many years later. "A period of five years was granted to bring about the new trend."

In 1945 the organization had three employees—Schuster, Laura L. Clausen, and E.A. Pophal. (L.J. Kohlhoff was an inactive president until 1951.)

The company, which adopted its present name in 1952, now underwrites general insurance risks. Church Mutual absorbed all of the assets and assumed all of the liabilities of the Lutheran Mutual Fire Insurance Company of Burlington, Iowa (1949); the Mutual Fire Insurance Society of the Michigan Conference of the Evangelical United Brethren Church, Ltd. (1953); the American Church and Home Mutual Insurance Company of Madison, Wisconsin (1962); and the Furniture Mutual Insurance Company of Milwaukee and the Cheese Makers Mutual Insurance Company of Madison (1963).

Today Church Mutual employs 400 people, both in Merrill and in

The first policy issued by Church Mutual on June 3, 1897. The insured, St. John Lutheran Church of Merrill, paid a premium of $1.60. This church is still insured by Church Mutual.

the field, and does business in 30 states. Direct premiums written are $116 million, and policyholder surplus is approximately $40 million. The company's growth has required larger facilities. A building project now under way will double the 54,000-square-foot home office facility in Merrill.

"People are our most important asset," says Nickel, who has been president of Church Mutual since 1971. "The various departments at our home office are staffed by experts in underwriting, policy rating and coding, insurance law, accounting, loss control, claims, investment and finance, data processing, sales and marketing, training, and other policyholder support services."

Church Mutual's efficient service is one of the most important parts of its reputation, Nickel believes. "The individual attention and care our people provide have built

our reputation for service. Modern computer and word-processing systems keep records and statistics readily available. It's another facet of our effort to offer our policyholders efficient service."

The company still primarily insures churches, as it did in the early days of its history. But today it insures other institutional properties as well, such as schools, camps, nursing homes, and related dwellings. Some commercial risks are also covered. Coverages include fire, allied lines, inland marine, medical malpractice, multiple peril, commercial umbrella, workers' compensation, automobile and general liability, glass, burglary and theft, computer, directors, officers, and trustees.

This artist's rendering shows the preliminary design of Church Mutual Insurance Company's building addition.

The firm solicits business by mail and through direct representatives and agents. Church Mutual's 54,000 policyholders include churches of every size, from little country churches to multibuilding complexes in large cities. Church buildings today are in use seven days a week, which exposes them to complex and changing insurance needs. It is the challenge of Church Mutual Insurance Company to continually meet these needs.

Regardless of the nature of an insurance loss, all institutions need prompt settlement of their claims, according to Nickel. "When misfortune strikes a church," he points out, "many lives are disrupted. We try to help a church resume its normal activities as soon as possible. It's important to us that our Claims Department work swiftly and fairly, because it's important to the churches we protect."

S.C. JOHNSON & SON, INC.

When Samuel C. Johnson, great-grandson of the founder of S.C. Johnson & Son, Inc., joined the family business in 1954 at the age of 26, his assignment was to find a new product to diversify the company, which had built its reputation on wax. After roughly nine months Johnson, now chairman and chief executive officer, brought a new product into his father's office. "Well, now, here's my first new product—Johnson Aerosol Insect Spray," he said. His father, Herbert Fisk Johnson, Jr., was skeptical.

"Don't you know we don't make anything without wax in it?" he asked. "I told him we could put some wax in it, but it wouldn't make it any better," S.C. Johnson says. "He sent me back to the lab and told me not to come back until I had something that was really good and different, where the consumer could tell the difference." Johnson came up with Raid House and Garden Insecticide, an aqueous-based system that was a big improvement over existing solvent-based bug killers.

Today the privately held company makes many products that do not contain wax, although its popular name is still "Johnson Wax." The $2-billion corporation, with subsidiaries in 45 countries, manufactures and sells a broad range of consumer products, from floor finishes to laundry specialties to insecticides. It also makes heavy-duty commercial and institutional products, as well as a line of specialty chemicals.

The firm, which employs 11,500 people worldwide (2,600 in Wisconsin), began modestly in 1886 in Racine with four employees. The founder, Samuel Curtis Johnson, purchased a parquet-flooring system from the Racine Hardware Company in 1886. Johnson, at age 53, was the survivor of two business failures.

Johnson's big break came when he learned that his customers did not

The Johnson Wax Administration Center, built in 1939, and Research Tower, completed in 1950, were designed by Frank Lloyd Wright and are listed in the National Register of Historic Places.

know how to care for their elaborate parquet floors. "My great-grandfather had heard that in some castles in France the wooden floors had lasted 300 years, preserved with beeswax," says Johnson. His great-grandfather mixed a batch of wax in his bathtub, called Johnson's Prepared Wax, and began to sell it. The new wax was so popular that Johnson was soon selling it all over the country.

Four generations of Johnsons have led the corporation. Herbert Fisk Johnson, Sr., joined the firm in 1892; he succeeded his father as president when S.C. Johnson died in 1919. Herbert F. Sr. died in 1928; Herbert F. Jr. (the company's first chemist) then became president. Samuel C. Johnson joined the organization in 1954; he became president in 1966 and chairman in 1967. "Two things turned us from being a small midwestern family-owned floor wax business to a major national manufacturer," S.C. Johnson says. "They are the Frank Lloyd Wright office building built in Racine in 1939 and our sponsoring the 'Fibber McGee and Molly' radio program." Johnson continues, "The building says to people that there is something creative about this company, something special and venturesome. It has been important in attracting good, creative people to Johnson Wax."

Now more than 100 years old,

Johnson Wax is one of the 200 largest industrial manufacturers in the United States. Its profit-sharing plan began in 1917. The Johnson Foundation, based at the Frank Lloyd Wright-designed Wingspread just north of Racine, sponsors conferences on education, cultural growth, and improvement of the human environment. The Johnson's Wax Fund is a company-sponsored philanthropic organization.

The Great Workroom, located in the Johnson Wax Administration Center, was intended by Frank Lloyd Wright "to be as inspiring to live and work in as any cathedral ever was to worship in."

RAYOVAC CORPORATION

For more than 80 years the name RAYOVAC has been synonymous with the state of Wisconsin and innovations in batteries and flashlights. RAYOVAC is a major force in the expanding, multibillion-dollar portable power and lighting industry. Started in Madison in 1906 as the French Battery Company, the RAYOVAC Corporation has grown to be the nation's third-largest battery and battery-operated lighting products manufacturer.

RAYOVAC offers a wide array of round cell batteries, miniature button cell batteries, specialty batteries, and battery-powered lights in a wide variety of sizes and shapes. RAYOVAC's round cells include high-performance alkaline, dependable heavy-duty, and economical general-purpose batteries and rechargeables. RAYOVAC has been the leader in development and miniaturization of button cell power systems, including state-of-the-art lithium, long-lasting premium zinc air, dependable mercury, and silver.

RAYOVAC has also led the way in flashlights. From the revolutionary Sportsman flashlight in 1949 to the brighter Krypton-powered Workhorse of the 1980s, RAYOVAC has changed the way consumers perceive flashlights.

The key to the company's success has been its ability to be in the forefront with new products and merchandising concepts. Throughout its history, RAYOVAC has been an innovator. The firm introduced many historic products. RAYOVAC innovations include the first portable radio with high-fidelity reception, 1933; the first wearable vacuum-tube hearing aid, 1937; and the world's first lead-proof "sealed in steel" dry cell battery, 1939. RAYOVAC continued its technological breakthroughs in the 1940s, 1950s, 1960s, and 1970s with improvements in battery and flashlight performance.

In 1970 RAYOVAC worked with Polaroid to develop a totally new type of flat battery to power the SX-70 instant camera. RAYOVAC introduced the first heavy-duty all zinc chloride battery in 1972.

In the 1980s RAYOVAC introduced the Workhorse premium flash-

RAYOVAC Smart Packs™ are multipacks of six or eight batteries packaged in convenient zip-tab containers. Smart Packs are available in the most popular battery power systems (alkaline and heavy duty) and in three heavy-user battery cell sizes (D, C, and AA).

light. This new light, with its lifetime product warranty, 70-percent-brighter Krypton bulb, and advanced Fresnel lens, revolutionized the entire flashlight industry. Following the lead of RAYOVAC's Workhorse, the entire market began to change to premium-priced, quality-built lights. Today Workhorse is the number-one selling premium flashlight.

RAYOVAC introduced two battery breakthroughs in 1985, including the Pro Line premium zinc air battery. This totally new battery gave superior performance to any other hearing aid battery on the market.

RAYOVAC's Smart Pack, six or eight batteries in an easy-to-open zip-tab container, revolutionized battery packaging and merchandising.

RAYOVAC followed with the Checkout Pack Merchandising System. Designed for store checkout lanes, this system combined non-carded, shrink-wrap, battery packages in a gravity feed display—another first in the industry.

LUMA 2, RAYOVAC's latest innovation, is the first flashlight with its own emergency backup system built right in. The backup system is powered by a lithium battery.

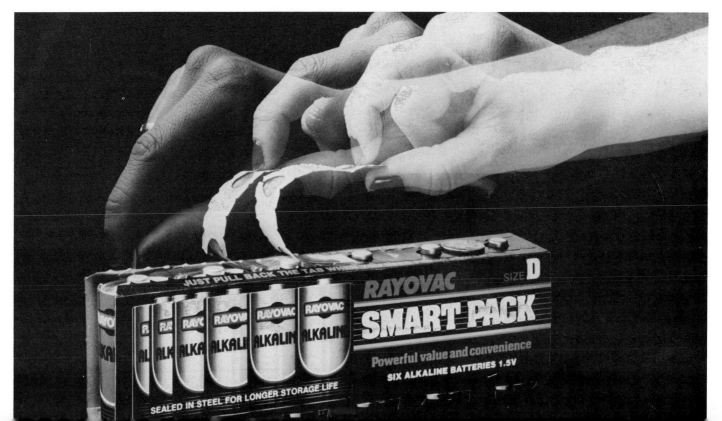

EVCO PLASTICS

"Our lunchroom was our manufacturing facility at one time," says Dale M. Evans, executive vice-president of EVCO Plastics. Before that the company founded by Donald L. Evans (Dale's father) was located in the basement of the family home in Windsor. Today EVCO is a division of Don Evans, Inc., and has three facilities in Wisconsin (in DeForest, Oshkosh, and Vienna Township), as well as in Calhoun, Georgia, and Sparks, Nevada.

EVCO, which remains privately held, employs 350 people. To meet current business demands, it operates its machinery 24 hours a day, seven days a week working in three shifts.

The Evans family has guided the firm through tremendous growth since its formation in 1948. Donald L. Evans is president and chairman of the board of Don Evans, Inc.; his wife, Joan, is secretary/treasurer. Of their five children, Dale, Steve, and Chris are active in the company. Two others, Jim and Rick, pursue other endeavors. The lineage continues with Chris' wife, Karen, who is marketing manager of the office products division.

Dale Evans attributes the suc-

This photograph of the EVCO Plastics DeForest facility was taken in 1978 after the original facility was expanded.

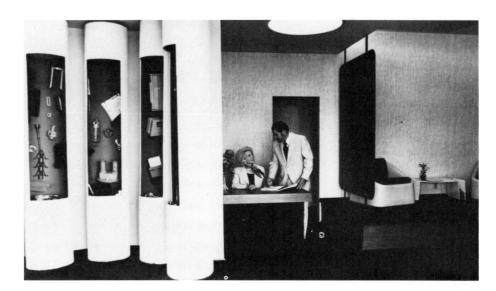

cess of the custom-molding company—which has average annual sales of $20 million to $25 million—to the "hard work and creativeness of my father. He worked 16-hour days, six days a week to build the company," Evans says. "Nothing made him think that he couldn't do it." Evans also credits his mother's contribution. "My mother not only took care of five kids but also did the book work and the invoicing" in the early days.

The firm has grown tremendously since then and is continuing to grow. "The past six years we've basically tripled in size," Evans says, adding that "a lot of that has to do with the groundwork that my father laid." EVCO is building a new 50,000-square-foot production facility

EVCO Plastics is a division of Don Evans, Inc., which was founded by Donald L. Evans. The Evans family still runs the company and its subdivisions, with Donald Evans serving as president and chairman of the board and his wife, Joan, as secretary/treasurer.

that will be completed in November 1988. It will be located north of Madison and will involve 50 to 100 new employees.

The new plant has been designed around EVCO's new computer-controlled Automated Molding Plant (AMP), made by Netstal of Switzerland. The AMP is state-of-the-art equipment in molding automation. A laser-guided, robotic overhead crane swaps molds and injection units between several molding machines. A

host computer automatically feeds set-up and production data to the molding machines. Parts are robotically removed.

EVCO believes that the AMP flexible manufacturing technology will enable the firm to run short-run jobs as economically as long-run jobs. It will also afford higher part quality and productivity. In addition to the AMP, EVCO also operates 50 other molding machines.

Over the years EVCO has built in excess of 1,000 molds, including some molds that other sources considered impossible to make. The company is a certified supplier for many of the major corporations in the United States.

The EVCO quality-control plan has specific procedures for the control of all incoming materials, proper storage and identification, in-process controls during production, documentation of all processes, and complete traceability via a lot numbering system. EVCO is able to work with customers who employ a just-in-time inventory-control program.

EVCO's machines and molds have the capacity to turn out a wide variety of products, from 3.5-ounce to 168-ounce shots, (the amount of molton plastic a machine is capable of injecting per cycle) and 75 to 1,000 tons of clamping pressure. EVCO has in-house quality control of all its production, including development and secondary operations. Handling so many operations in house results in cost and time advantages for EVCO's customers. Many finishing steps, such as assembly, sonic welding, hot stamping, drilling, and tapping are handled in house. There is a full-time, fully staffed finishing department, which has the same quality-assurance controls as earlier stages of design and production.

"Today's age is the age of plastics," says Donald Evans. "We at EVCO pride ourselves in our capacity to work successfully in this exciting medium. For more than 25 years we have innovated in sound, successful plastic design capability and manufacturing expertise. Our products range from the highly technical to the most simple."

EVCO has four operating divisions, including three custom-molding departments; Evco Office Products; an engineering department that does tooling, makes molds, and does design work; and a restaurant that opened in 1973.

EVCO's custom-molding capabilities include design, engineering, tooling, manufacturing, and secondary operations. The company's industrial designer works on product, graphics, and concept design projects to ensure an integration of styling and engineering. The firm's tooling and plastics engineers develop complete mold drawings with every job. EVCO's range of molding materials includes standard thermoplastics as well as engineering plastics such as glass, fiber, and Teflon-filled resins and some conductive plastics.

EVCO also maintains its own tool room with standard lathes, grinders, mills, and EDM equipment, and machining centers that can run around the clock unattended. All this is backed up by a CAD-CAM (computer-aided design/computer-aided machining) system.

The EVCO Office Products division designs and manufactures office accessories. These include an interlocking desk set, letter and legal stacking trays, vertical trays, calendar holders, pencil cups, pencil cubes, file boxes, letter files, wastebaskets, magazine files, and open files.

The plastics age is "a unique age where a versatile material can be formed to meet more product needs than ever before," says Donald Evans. "Products can be delicate or unbelievably strong, intricate or starkly simple, colorless or blazingly colorful." EVCO Plastics' success with plastics is evident in the DeForest lunchroom, where employees taking a break fill as much space as the whole company used to occupy.

(Right) Today a second generation of Evans participate in the business founded by their father. Chris (left) and Steve Evans are active in the company while Dale (below) is executive vice-president of EVCO Plastics.

GODFREY COMPANY

When Edwin R. Godfrey formed the commission firm of Wharton & Godfrey in Milwaukee in 1870, supermarkets did not yet exist. Today the firm Godfrey founded supplies in excess of 20,000 different products to Sentry and Sun Warehouse Foods stores. Supermarkets carrying such a vast array of products—from meats to flowers, and from vegetables to paper towels—were not even dreamed of in the 1870s.

Godfrey Company—which was acquired in late 1987 by Fleming Companies, Inc., a food-distribution firm based in Oklahoma City—is primarily engaged in the retail distribution of food and related consumer products through corporate-owned and affiliated full-service supermarkets and super-warehouse stores located in southern and eastern Wisconsin. The company also supplies independent grocers with a full line of goods and services through its distribution centers in Waukesha and Marshfield. The retail stores supplied by the company's two distribution centers accommodate the needs of more than 100 million customer

shopping trips each year.

There have been a lot of changes since Edwin Godfrey bought out his partner in 1872 and continued the commission business under the name of E.R. Godfrey & Sons Co. The firm was officially incorporated in 1889. Godfrey Company began operating as a wholesaler in 1903. It operated a dry grocery business from a new, eight-story building on the corner of Broadway and Detroit streets in Milwaukee.

For a while the company expanded the number of warehouse locations in order to make its goods more accessible. The firm established its first branch, in Calumet, Michigan, in 1903. Soon the company was operating 14 individual warehouses in strategically accessible locations. But improved transportation and chang-

Pictured here is the Godfrey Company distribution center in Waukesha, Wisconsin. As a retail distributor of food and related consumer products, the Godfrey Company operates through corporate-owned and affiliated full-service supermarkets and superwarehouse stores located in southern and eastern Wisconsin.

ing supply conditions led the firm gradually to phase out the branch operations.

In 1925 Godfrey Company was one of three wholesalers in the country to become part of the Independent Grocers Alliance (IGA). To satisfy a growing consumer demand, Godfrey Company entered the frozen-food business in 1936, one of the first companies in the Midwest to do so.

In 1949 the operation moved to a much larger and more efficient one-story warehouse on North Port Washington Road in Glendale. It was one of the most modern warehouses in the United States. In 1959, to meet another growing consumer demand, the firm entered the fresh meat business.

Faced with the threat of being pushed out of its metropolitan markets by chain store heavyweights, Godfrey Company formed a retail division known as Sentry Markets in 1953. Three independent, affiliated retailers worked in conjunction with the wholesaler in the formation of Sentry. Today Sentry Foods consists

Godfrey Company's egg farm, Artesian Farms, Inc., in Palmyra, Wisconsin.

of 86 retail operations, 32 of which are owned by the company and 44 operated by independent retailers.

In 1964 Godfrey Company constructed and moved into a one-story, 550,000-square-foot warehouse, considered to be one of the most modern facilities of its kind in the United States, in Waukesha.

Under the trade name Sun Foods, the company operates four super-warehouse food stores. Three Sun Foods stores are in the metropolitan Milwaukee area; the fourth is in Kenosha. These stores average some 60,000 square feet in area and offer extended lines of food and non-food products. Sun Foods stores are designed to attract high-volume sales, which are essential to this type of food retailing.

Godfrey Company is in the midst of a major corporate expansion program that will entail an investment of almost $35 million. The first stage involved major remodeling and expansion of 15 existing Sentry Foods stores and decor enhancements of 18 other Sentry stores. In addition, three new Sentry super-

stores will open in Racine, West Milwaukee, and West Bend. The superstores will range in size from 48,000 to 60,000 square feet, and will offer a dramatic new presentation of meats, bakery, produce, and floral departments. Other new attractions include a New England-style fresh seafood department offering a wide variety of fresh and saltwater favorites, freshly baked pie by the slice, an extensive deli department, and a large video rental center.

Hub City Foods, Inc., a wholly owned subsidiary of Godfrey Company, distributes food and nonfood products to independent retailers in north-central Wisconsin and services convenience stores throughout the state. Located in Marshfield, Hub City Foods operates a distribution center of 135,000 square feet and distributes products to more than 400 retail outlets.

Godfrey Company, along with its affiliated Sentry stores, employs almost 7,000 people and has annual

sales approaching $750 million. The firm offers many goods and services to its affiliates, including fresh-cut flowers from its own greenhouses, Crestwood Bakery products from its bakery in West Allis, fresh eggs from its own egg farm (Artesian Farms, Inc., in Palmyra), and grocery products marketed under the Sentry- and Sunrise-brand labels.

The company also owns and operates two Sentry drugstores, two retail liquor stores, and a hardware store, all of which are located in shopping centers with Sentry Foods stores. The firm is also engaged in the development and marketing of land for residential building sites in Walworth County.

Today Godfrey Company provides services for customers in every county of Wisconsin. The Sentry stores are the highest-volume floral outlet in Wisconsin, furnishing flowers for 3,000 weddings per year. The egg farm's 350,000 laying hens produce more than 6 million dozen eggs per year. And the 115,375-square-foot bakery operation is the largest retail bakery operation in Wisconsin.

WISCONSIN ELECTRIC POWER COMPANY

The history of electric service in Wisconsin has been marked by risk taking, competition, innovation, and massive technological changes. Only days after Thomas Edison's first power plant went into service in September 1882, one of Wisconsin Electric Power Company's earliest predecessors began operating the Vulcan Street Plant in Appleton—the world's first Edison hydroelectric power plant.

Milwaukee's first power plant (1885) went into operation in the midst of a very disorderly system. A number of small electric utilities served Milwaukee. Customers in the same buildings sometimes were served by different companies.

The incorporation of many of those utilities (1896) into The Milwaukee Electric Railway & Light Co. (TMER&L, Wisconsin Electric's predecessor) brought some order.

With the acquisition of Commonwealth Power Co. in 1917,

TMER&L began serving downtown Milwaukee with steam for heating and processing. In 1919 the first successful experiments using pulverized coal as fuel were conducted at the firm's Oneida Street (later the East Wells) plant.

In the early years, however, TMER&L's main business was rail transportation, not electricity. During the first decade after 1900, TMER&L extended electric railway service into suburban areas, bringing electricity with it and helping to develop those communities.

In the early 1900s the demand for electricity rose as new uses for the service were discovered. Lakeside Power Plant, in St. Francis, was built to meet the growing demand. It was the first power plant designed to burn pulverized coal only. A new holding company—the Wisconsin Electric Power Company—was formed to finance the construction of Lakeside. Wisconsin Electric Power Company owned the plant and leased it to TMER&L. In 1938 TMER&L changed its name to Wisconsin Electric.

The demand for electricity continued to grow rapidly. The firm built

Port Washington Power Plant (1935) to help meet that demand. After World War II local industries flourished and home appliances became popular. Kilowatt-hour sales tripled between 1945 and 1965. An ambitious power plant construction program at Port Washington and at a new location—Oak Creek—created the backbone of Wisconsin Electric's generating system.

The company entered the nuclear age with generating units at Point Beach Nuclear Plant (1970 and 1972). The coal-fired Pleasant Prairie Power Plant was added in 1980.

When inflation and interest rates soared in the 1960s and 1970s, Wisconsin Electric responded by adopting a new strategy based on conservation. That effort resulted in control of the growth in electric peak demand, which led to rate reductions in the 1980s. Today Wisconsin Electric Power Company is a subsidiary of Wisconsin Energy Corporation, a holding company established to create nonutility diversification opportunities in the utility's service area.

Interurban trains rolled out of the Public Service Building in Milwaukee in 1936. The PSB remains Wisconsin Electric's headquarters today.

Line crews help maintain the thousands of miles of power lines that serve the company's 850,000 customers in Wisconsin and Upper Michigan.

WISCONSIN BELL, INC.

When Alexander Graham Bell invented the telephone in 1876, many people first regarded it as "an amusing little instrument," a toy.

Charles H. Haskins, however, was quick to realize the telephone's commercial potential. Haskins, author of a book on electrical principles, brought the first telephone to Milwaukee in the spring of 1877. He started Milwaukee's first telephone exchange with 15 customers.

On July 7, 1882, Haskins and two associates created the Wisconsin Telephone Company, the forerunner of Wisconsin Bell, Inc. Today Wisconsin Bell has added more than a million customers to its original list. The company now serves most of the metropolitan areas of the state, including greater Milwaukee, Madison, Appleton, Beloit, Eau Claire, Fond du Lac, Green Bay, Janesville, Kenosha, Oshkosh, Racine, and Superior.

From the early years of this century, when customers needed a heavy dose of patience while using the old "crank 'n cuss" magneto phones, through the days of the "number, please" operators, to to-

Wisconsin Bell's digital network provides high-speed data transmission for business customers. The company's digital network is a state-of-the-art communications service that serves as a gateway to the Information Age.

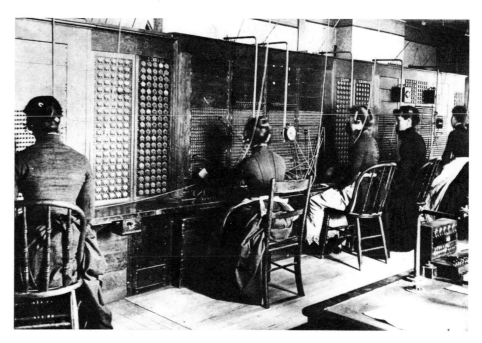

Operators sit at Wisconsin Bell's Milwaukee switchboard in this 1887 photograph.

day's digital transmission of information, telephone service has gone through a staggering series of improvements and modernizations.

For more than 100 years Wisconsin Bell has applied the latest technological advances to the everyday needs of its customers. Since the seven regional Bell holding companies were formed following the breakup of the Bell System in 1984, Wisconsin Telephone has been known as Wisconsin Bell. The company is part of American Information Technologies Corporation (Ameritech).

Wisconsin Bell today functions as an electronic gateway to the world. Technological advances such as the commercial use of fiber optics, high-speed data transport over conventional telephone lines, and digital electronic switching of voice, video, and data signals give customers services they want. Applications include electronic banking, home computer access to faraway data bases, and medical diagnostic reports over the telephone.

Schools are using data communications to cut administrative costs. Businesses in the travel and leisure industry use sophisticated communications systems for ticketing, reservations, car rentals, and package tours. Wisconsin Bell has helped manufacturers set up integrated voice and data communications with suppliers to assure timely delivery of materials.

As part of its commitment to Wisconsin, the company has been instrumental in surveying businesses to determine the factors that would cause them to leave the state or stay. The studies have pinpointed problem areas for businesses, and are used by local governmental officials to resolve those concerns. These efforts have convinced dozens of businesses that had planned to leave to stay and expand instead.

Wisconsin Bell's century-old tradition of contributing to the economic health and vitality of Wisconsin and providing quality service to its customers is carried out by the company's thousands of employees. Wisconsin Bell men and women each day bring their knowledge and skill to the goal of providing the best in communications services.

GREEN BAY AREA CHAMBER OF COMMERCE

Just over 100 years ago, on March 29, 1882, a small group of east side businessmen gathered to organize the area's first business organization, which became the ancestor of the Green Bay Area Chamber of Commerce.

It was called the Green Bay Businessmen's Association, and its 72 charter members pledged to "advance the commercial, mercantile, and manufacturing interests of Green Bay . . . and to promise the general prosperity of the city . . ." The first president was F.W. Hurlbut, a wholesaler of coal, oil, cement, fish, pork, and salt.

Among the organization's most important activities was developing community support for construction of the waterworks in 1886, unification of Green Bay and Fort Howard, and the location of the State Reformatory. It also purchased and platted a tract of land along the Fox River as the community's first industrial park.

In 1908 the association was reorganized as the Green Bay Commercial Club, with John F. Martin as president. Among the community projects it helped initiate were the laying of the first concrete pavement in the county, along Cedar Creek Road, now University Avenue. It also directed the Perry Centennial Celebration in 1913.

The club was dissolved eight years later when, on November 13, 1916, the Green Bay Association of Commerce was incorporated. A.E. Winter was elected president, with F.E. Burrall, Joseph P. Neugent, and Nic Bur as officers. Frank H. Smith was employed as the first full-time secretary. There were 173 firms and individuals on the original roster.

The association soon took on the task of leading the community's war effort. The first Liberty Loan Drive, the City War Garden program, the Brown County War Board, the Fuel and Food Administration, and the fight against the influenza epidemic were among the group's efforts.

As the country moved out of the Great Depression, the association helped organize the biggest community celebration since the Perry Centennial, the Tercentennial Celebration marking the 300th anniversary of the visit of the first European, Jean Nicolet. Highlight of the festivities was the appearance of President Franklin D. Roosevelt.

In 1941 the country was again at war, and the Association of Commerce spearheaded war loan drives, raising more than $5 million annually.

Following World War II the city resumed its growth and development, becoming the state's third-largest retail center and second-largest wholesale center. The association's efforts were directed at the construction of a new airport, post office, federal building, and veterans' memorial arena. In 1948 the association formed an Industrial Development Corporation, which sparked interest in formation of what is now the Packerland Industrial Park.

The organization relocated its offices in 1957 to the former Milwaukee Road depot at 400 South Washington Street, its present office. In the 1960s the group made a major effort to change its course, and on August 30, 1966, became the Green Bay Area Chamber of Commerce.

Benjamin J. Teague was president of the chamber from 1975 to 1985. During his tenure the group was involved in a major downtown redevelopment program, support for local government reorganization, and consolidation and formation of an aggressive legislative program, including a Political Action Committee to stimulate the participation of members in the legislative process.

Nevin R. Limburg has been president of the chamber since 1985. Current priorities of the chamber include economic development, better member communications, and a remodeling of the Washington Street office.

The chamber's historic office at 400 South Washington Street has just been remodeled.

GREATER KENOSHA AREA

"Kenosha's abundant natural resources have benefited us," says William B. Rayburn, chairman of the board of Snap-on Tools, a *Fortune* 500 company that has been based in Kenosha for more than 50 years. "But to a greater extent," Rayburn adds, "it's the people in and around Kenosha and their dedication, energy, vision, and spirit that have made us what we are today."

Howard D. Cooley, president of Jockey International, also based in Kenosha, agrees. "A primary advantage for our business is the availability of a well-educated and motivated work force with a strong sense of loyalty. Additionally, Kenosha is a fine community in which to live and raise a family. Our employees enjoy living here."

Kenosha today is a city of 77,685 people located in a county with a population of 123,137. Kenosha County covers 278.5 square miles and consists of one city, three villages, and eight towns. Kenosha is bordered on the east by Lake Michigan and is 36 miles from Milwaukee, 55 miles from Chicago, and 104 miles from Madison.

Indians were the earliest inhabitants of Kenosha (named after an Indian tribe); some of the largest roads and highways in the area go back to Native American trails. The first white settlers came from New England in 1835. In 1850 Kenosha was incorporated as a city and designated the seat of Kenosha County.

Today Kenosha has many major industries, including American Brass, Chrysler, Eaton, Frost, Jockey International, Kenosha Beef International, Macwhyte, Tri-Cover, G. Leblanc, Manu-tronics, Ocean Spray Cranberries, Snap-on Tools, and Wisconsin Electric Power. The Kenosha Municipal Airport is a general aviation airport recently upgraded by a $9-million capital improvement program to a new jet runway, expanded lighting and instrument landing systems, a new terminal building, and hangar facilities for large aircraft.

Another sign of Kenosha's industrial strength is the Lakeview Corporate Park currently being developed by Wispark Corporation, a wholly owned subsidiary of Wisconsin Energy Corporation. The 10- to 15-year development plan calls for creation of between 7,000 and 12,000 jobs, ranging from industry and manufacturing to warehousing, office space, and retail and commercial business.

There are three institutions of higher education in greater Kenosha. Gateway Technical College is part of one of the oldest vocational/technical education systems in the country. The University of Wisconsin-Parkside, offering four years and graduate degrees, is a center for research and development. Carthage College is a small, private, liberal arts college on the lake.

In addition to its miles of lakeshore, the Kenosha area also contains 6,000 acres of parkland. The Bong Recreation Area is a 4,500-acre state park used for camping, hang gliding, motorcycling, hot air ballooning, dog trails, ski and horse trails, and nature trails. The many farms in the Kenosha area mean miles of open green spaces. The Warren J. Taylor Memorial Gardens at Lincoln Park are famous for their floral displays.

"Kenosha is an area for all seasons," says Louis J. Micheln, executive director of the Kenosha Area Chamber of Commerce.

Scenes of progress in the Kenosha area: Carthage College (below), Gateway Technical College (right), and the Kenosha County Courthouse (lower right).

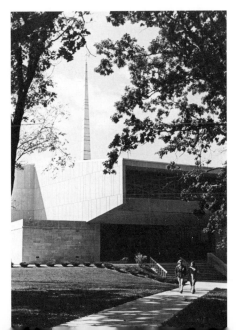

THE MARCUS CORPORATION

The Marcus Corporation traces its beginnings to November 1, 1935, when Ben Marcus, who emigrated from Poland at age 14, opened a movie theater in an abandoned department store in Ripon, Wisconsin. His entrepreneurial urge was fueled by a fascination with motion pictures that has formed the foundation for what has become Wisconsin's largest theater chain.

The Marcus Corporation's multistate group of Budgetel Inns is one of the country's most successful economy motel chains. Introduced in 1973, Budgetel will become even more visible as the result of a franchising program begun by the company in 1986.

The Marcus name has been identified with the lodging industry since 1960, most notably since 1962, when Ben Marcus acquired the Pfister Hotel in downtown Milwaukee. Under the leadership of his son, Stephen H. Marcus, the Pfister was transformed into the jewel it had been when it originally opened on May 1, 1893. In 1972 a second downtown hotel was acquired, renamed the Marc Plaza, and restored to its rightful place as one of the city's finest hostelries.

Food service is the final aspect of The Marcus Corporation's three-cornered presence in leisure-time industries. The company holds the Big Boy Restaurant franchises for four states—Wisconsin, Illinois, Minnesota, and Iowa. The first, Wisconsin, was granted in 1958 and was one of the first issued anywhere by the California-based Bob's Big Boy. Two years later the company obtained a franchise from Kentucky Fried Chicken, and still holds that franchise for the state's populous southeastern corner.

The Marcus Corporation ranks as one of Wisconsin's most successful business organizations; as one of the state's largest employers, its Wiscon-

Stephen H. Marcus,
president, chief operating officer,
and treasurer of The Marcus Corporation.

sin payroll exceeds 5,000.

Under the leadership of Ben Marcus, chairman and chief executive officer, and Steve Marcus, president and chief operating officer, the company has rightly earned a reputation as a good corporate citizen. "We will continue our personal and corporate involvement in activities benefiting the community, state, and nation," reads a cornerstone of the company's philosophy.

Ben Marcus has been involved with Variety Clubs International and its children's charities for decades. In 1985 he headed the Wisconsin campaign to raise funds for the restoration of the Statue of Liberty. He joined some highly select company in 1982 when he was named one of the recipients of the prestigious Horatio Alger Award.

Steve Marcus' activities have

ranged from chairing Milwaukee's United Performing Arts fund campaign to personal involvement with the United Way to the presidency (in its early years) of Summerfest, now a nationally renowned music festival.

The Marcus Corporation has recently made available more than a half-million dollars' worth of restaurant coupons and movie tickets to Wisconsin's public and private school districts, to be used to encourage student performance.

The corporation's home since 1953, The Marcus Amphitheater, a 23,000-seat outdoor performing facility located on Milwaukee's lakefront, has moved the city into the front ranks of entertainment centers. Ben and Steve view The Marcus Amphitheater as a monument to the thousands of employees who have helped the company grow and prosper.

"We take great pride in our dedicated management teams and employees. We are people pleasing people."

SENTRY INSURANCE

In 1903 members of the Wisconsin Retail Hardware Association met in Milwaukee and agreed to form a mutual fire insurance company—Hardware Dealers Mutual Fire Insurance Company of Wisconsin. Business formally began in 1904 in Berlin, Wisconsin. Hardware stores felt they needed their own fire insurance because the presence of bulk supplies of oil and turpentine in their stores caused them to be charged high rates. C.A. Peck became part-time manager of the new insurance company and leased office space for $50 per year, including light and heat. In 1911 P.J. Jacobs, a director of the company and hardware store dealer, moved the headquarters to Stevens Point.

Today the firm (which was renamed Sentry Insurance in 1971) is one of the largest mutual insurance companies in the country. Sentry is owned by its policy owners. The organization is licensed to do business in every state and has service and claims offices throughout the country. More than 1,000 full-time professional sales representatives and almost 30,000 independent agents distribute Sentry products.

Sentry still sells insurance to hardware stores, but it has expanded far beyond commercial coverages. Sentry today is an all-lines insurance company offering a wide variety of personal and commercial insurance coverages, including auto, home owners, life, commercial property and casualty, group life and health, and more.

Today Sentry is a national leader in nonstandard auto and preferred motorcycle insurance through its Dairyland subsidiary. Other subsidiaries include Sentry Life, which offers individual and group health, life, and equity products; Parker Services, Inc., which provides risk management services and environmental laboratory services; and Middlesex In-surance (based in Concord, Massachusetts), which provides property and casualty coverages.

Over the years Sentry has been an innovator in the insurance business. About the time the firm moved to Stevens Point (in 1912), it decided to form a casualty company to meet the need created when the Wisconsin legislature passed the nation's first workmen's compensation law. In more recent times Sentry was one of the first insurers to offer a Variable Universal Life product, and was an early innovator in the field of 401(k) retirement plans. Through its Sentry Plain Talk® policy, it pioneered simplified insurance policy language. A recent innovation is the Payback℠ auto policy. Good drivers enrolled in the payback plan promise not to drink and drive. After five years of claim-free driving, they are rewarded with the return of half of their first year's insurance premiums and for each subsequent year the good driving record continues.

Sentry's assets today exceed $2.5 billion. Sentry Insurance headquarters in Stevens Point serves as the center for corporate operations of the Sentry complex. Constructed in 1977, the headquarters totals more than 1.8 million square feet of building area on an 80-acre site. The natural ecology of the site has been preserved as much as possible. The

From 1904 until 1910 the Hardware Dealers Mutual Fire Insurance Company of Wisconsin conducted business from space in this Berlin, Wisconsin, building. Rent was $50 per year, including light and heat.

native landscape provides a home for mallards, Canada geese, swans, pheasants, and even deer.

Sentry also owns and operates SentryWorld golf course and sports complex. The nationally recognized, 18-hole golf course designed by Robert Trent Jones II is open to the public. Indoor tennis, racquet, and squash courts are available, as well as a pro shop and dining and banquet facilities.

On Wednesday, August 2, 1922, the new home office of Hardware Mutual Companies was formally opened in Stevens Point, Wisconsin, consolidating units from the fire company and casualty company into one building.

*A parade of elephants down one of Milwaukee's residential streets
proclaimed that the circus had come to town in 1915. Photo by
Sumner Matteson, courtesy, Milwaukee Public Museum*

PATRONS

The following individuals, companies, and organizations have made a valuable commitment to the quality of this publication. Windsor Publications and Wisconsin Manufacturers and Commerce gratefully acknowledge their participation in *Wisconsin: Pathways to Prosperity.*

A to Z Printing Co., Inc.
      Frank J. Marek
Anamax Corporation
THE AZCO GROUP LTD.*
Badger Wood Products, Inc.*
H.O. Bostrom Company, Inc.
Brillion Iron Works, Inc.*
Castle Metals
The Cheney Company*
Church Mutual Insurance Company*
Crescent Woolen Mills Co.*
Decar Corporation*
John Deere Horicon Works*
DeWitt, Porter, Huggett, Schumacher & Morgan, S.C.*
Employers Health Insurance*
Essential Industries Inc.
EVCO Plastics*
A.F. Gallun & Sons Company*
General Motors in Wisconsin*
Godfrey Company*
Graef, Anhalt, Schloemer & Associates, Inc.*
Greater Kenosha Area*
Green Bay Area Chamber of Commerce*
Green Bay Packaging Inc.
Greenheck Fan Corporation*
Hillshire Farm*
S.C. Johnson & Son, Inc.*
Kenosha Savings & Loan Association*
Kewaunee Engineering Corp.*
Kremers Urban Company
      Division of Schwarz Pharama
Lake Geneva Spindustries, Inc.*
Madison Business College*
Mansion Hill Inn*
The Marcus Corporation*
Marine Travelift, Inc.*
Mautz Paint of Madison*
Meriter Hospital*
Merrill Manufacturing Corporation*
Mosinee Paper Corporation*
Motor Specialty, Inc.*
Mulcahy & Wherry, S.C.*
National Guardian Life Insurance Company*
Nekoosa Papers Inc.*

Nu-Line Industries*
Oscar Mayer Foods Corporation*
Paragon Electric Company, Inc.*
Parker Pen USA Limited*
Perlick Corporation
Peterson Builders, Inc.*
Phillips Plastics Corporation*
Physicians Plus Medical Group*
Pierce Manufacturing Inc.*
Quad/Graphics, Inc.*
Racine Federated, Inc.*
RAYOVAC Corporation*
Reed Lignin Inc.
Regal Ware, Inc., Kewaskum, WI
St. Joseph's Hospital*
Schreiber Foods, Inc.*
Schwaab Inc.
Sentry Insurance*
A.O. Smith Corporation*
Snap-on Tools Corporation*
Spacesaver Corporation*
Sta-Rite Industries, Inc.*
Stevens Point Holiday Inn Convention and Entertainment Center*
E.C. Styberg Engineering Company, Inc.*
Tombstone Pizza*
Twin Disc, Incorporated*
Valleycast, Inc.*
Versa Technologies, Inc.*
Vulcan Chemicals
Wausau Insurance Companies*
Weather Shield Mfg., Inc.*
H.G. Weber & Co., Inc.*
Weyerhaeuser Company*
Weyerhaeuser Paper Company-Manitowoc Branch
Windsor Homes Inc.
Wisconsin Bell, Inc.*
Wisconsin Electric Power Company*
Wisconsin Gas Company*
Wisconsin Packing Company, Inc.*
Wisconsin Physicians Service*
Wisconsin Power & Light Company
WISC-TV*
The Worth Company*
Worzalla Publishing Company*
Wrought Washer Mfg., Inc.*

*Partners in Progress of *Wisconsin: Pathways to Prosperity.* The histories of these companies and organizations appear in Chapter X, beginning on page 217.

BIBLIOGRAPHY

Alexander, J.H.H. "A Short Industrial History of Wisconsin." *The State of Wisconsin Blue Book.* Madison: Wisconsin Legislative Reference Bureau, 1929.

Bowman, Francis. *Why Wisconsin.* Madison: F.F. Bowman, 1948.

Clark, James I. *Chronicles of Wisconsin.* Madison: State Historical Society of Wisconsin, 1955.

Current, Richard N. *Wisconsin: A Bicentennial History.* New York: W.W. Norton & Co., 1977.

————— .*The History of Wisconsin, Vol. 2: The Civil War Era, 1848-1873.* Edited by William Fletcher Thompson. Madison: State Historical Society of Wisconsin, 1976.

Glad, Paul W. *Progressive Century, The American Nation in Its Second Hundred Years.* Lexington, Mass.: D.C. Heath and Company, 1975.

Nesbit, Robert C. *Wisconsin: A History.* Madison: State Historical Society of Wisconsin, 1973.

————— .*The History of Wisconsin, Vol. 3: Urbanization and Industrialization, 1873-1893.* Edited by William Fletcher Thompson. Madison: State Historical Society of Wisconsin, 1985.

Paul, Justus F., and Paul, Barbara Dotts, eds. *The Badger State, A Documentary History of Wisconsin.* Grand Rapids, Mich.: William B. Erdmans Publishing Company, 1979.

Smith, Alice E. *The History of Wisconsin, Vol. 1: From Exploration to Statehood.* Edited by William Fletcher Thompson. Madison: State Historical Society of Wisconsin, 1985.

Still, Bayrd. *Milwaukee: The History of a City.* Madison: State Historical Society of Wisconsin, 1965.

CHAPTER ONE

Black, Robert F. "The Physical Geography of Wisconsin." *The State of Wisconsin Blue Book.* Madison: Legislative Reference Bureau, 1964.

Clark, James I. "Wisconsin: Land of Frenchmen, Indians and the Beaver." *Chronicles of Wisconsin.* Madison: State Historical Society of Wisconsin, 1955.

Gilman, Rhoda R. "The Fur Trade." *Wisconsin Magazine of History.* 58 (Autumn, 1974): 3-18.

Hodge, William H. "The Indians of Wisconsin." *The State of Wisconsin Blue Book.* Madison: Legislative Reference Bureau, 1975.

Kellogg, Louise P. *Early Narrative of the Northwest, 1634-1699.* New York: Charles Scribner's Sons, 1917.

————— .*The French Regime in Wisconsin and the Northwest.* New York: Cooper Square Publishers, Inc., 1968.

Ritzenthaler, Robert, and Ritzenthaler, Pat. *The Woodland Indians of the Western Great Lakes.* Garden City, New York: American Museum of Natural History, 1970.

————— . *Prehistoric Indians of Wisconsin.* Revised by Lynne G. Goldstein. Milwaukee: Milwaukee Public Museum, 1985.

Schultz, Gwen. *Wisconsin's Foundations, A Review of the State's Geology and Its Influence on Geography and Human Activity.* Madison: Kendall/Hunt Publishing Company, 1986.

Snow, Dean. *The Archeology of North America, American Indians and Their Origins.* London: Thames and Hudson, 1976.

U.S. Geological Survey and Wisconsin Geological and Natural History Survey for the Committee on Interior and Insular Affairs, U.S. Senate. *Mineral and Water Resources of Wisconsin.* Washington, D.C.: U.S. Government Printing Office, 1976.

CHAPTER TWO

Andersen, Theodore A. *A Century of Banking in Wisconsin.* Madison: State Historical Society of Wisconsin, 1954.

Blanchard, W.O. *The Geography of Southwestern Wisconsin.* Wisconsin Geological and Natural History Survey. No. 65, 1924.

Clark, James I. "The Wisconsin Lead Region." *Chronicles of Wisconsin.* Madison: State Historical Society of Wisconsin, 1955.

Current, Richard N. *Wisconsin: A Bicentennial History.* New York: W.W. Norton & Co., 1977.

Gilman, Rhoda R. "The Fur Trade." Wisconsin Magazine of History. 58 (Autumn 1974): 3-18.

Kuehnl, George J. *The Wisconsin Business Corporation.* Madison: The University of Wisconsin Press, 1959.

Lurie, Nancy Oestreich. *Wisconsin Indians.* Madison: The State Historical Society of Wisconsin, 1980.

Miller, David Harry, and Savage, Jr., William W., eds. *The Character and Influence of the Indian Trade in Wisconsin: A Study of the Trading Post as an Institution.* Norman, Okla.: University of Oklahoma, 1977.

Mollenhoff, David V. *Madison: A History of the Formative Years.* Dubuque: Kendall/Hunt Publishers, 1982.

Nesbit, Robert C. *Wisconsin: A History.* Madison: State Historical Society of Wisconsin, 1973.

Nichols, Roger L. "The Black Hawk War in Retrospect." *Wisconsin Magazine of History.* 65 (Summer 1982): 239-246.

Smith, Alice E. *The History of Wisconsin, Vol. 1: From Exploration to Statehood.* Madison:

State Historical Society of Wisconsin, 1985.

Still, Bayrd. *Milwaukee: The History of a City.* Madison: State Historical Society of Wisconsin, 1965.

Turner, Frederick Jackson. *The Frontier in American History.* New York: Henry Holt and Co., 1920.

CHAPTER THREE

Alexander, J.H.H. "A Short Industrial History of Wisconsin." *The State of Wisconsin Blue Book.* Madison: Wisconsin Legislative Reference Bureau, 1929.

Andersen, Theodore A. *A Century of Banking in Wisconsin.* Madison: State Historical Society of Wisconsin, 1954.

Balasubramanian, D. "Wisconsin's Foreign Trade in the Civil War Era." *Wisconsin Magazine of History.* 46 (Summer 1963): 257-262.

Clark, James I. "Wisconsin Grows to Statehood, Immigration and Internal Improvement." *Chronicles of Wisconsin.* Madison: State Historical Society of Wisconsin, 1955.

————— ."Farm Machinery in Wisconsin." *Chronicles of Wisconsin.* Madison: State Historical Society of Wisconin, 1955.

————— ."The Wisconsin Pineries, Logging on the Chippewa." *Chronicles of Wisconsin.* Madison: State Historical Society of Wisconsin, 1955.

Current, Richard N. *The History of Wisconsin, Vol. 2, The Civil War Era, 1848-1873.* Edited by William Fletcher Thompson. Madison: State Historical Society of Wisconsin, 1976.

Fries, Robert F. *Empire in Pine: The Story of Lumbering in Wisconsin 1830-1900.* Madison: State Historical Society of Wisconsin, 1951.

Merk, Frederick. *Economic History of Wisconsin During the Civil War Decade.* Madison: The Society, 1916.

Nesbit, Robert C. *Wisconsin, A History.* Madison: State Historical Society of Wisconsin, 1973.

Raney, William F. "The Building of Wisconsin's Railroads." *Wisconsin Magazine of History.* 19 (1935-1936): 387-404.

Rice, Herbert W. "Early Rivalry Among Wisconsin Cities for Railroads." *Wisconsin Magazine of History.* 35 (Autumn 1951): 1-15.

Smith, Alice Walker. *The History of Wisconsin, Vol. 1: Settlement and Statehood.* Edited by William Fletcher Thompson. Madison: State Historical Society of Wisconsin, 1985.

Smith, Guy-Harold. "The Settlement and the Distribution of the Population in Wisconsin." *Transactions of the Wisconsin Academy of Sciences, Arts and Letters.* 24 (1929):

53-107.

Walsh, Margaret. *The Manufacturing Frontier: Pioneer Industry in Antebellum Wisconsin, 1830-1860*. Madison: State Historical Society of Wisconsin, 1972.

CHAPTER FOUR

Alexander, J.H.H. "A Short Industrial History of Wisconsin." *The State of Wisconsin Blue Book*. Madison: Legislative Reference Bureau, 1929.

Archdeacon, Thomas J. *Becoming American: An Ethnic History*. New York: MacMillan, 1983.

Baron, Stanley. *Brewed in America, A History of Beer and Ale in the United States*. New York: Arno Press, 1972.

Cochran, Thomas C. *The Pabst Brewing Company, The History of an American Business*. New York: New York University Press, 1948.

Downard, William L. *Dictionary of the History of the American Brewing and Distilling Industries*. Westport, Conn.: Greenwood Press, 1980.

Holubetz, Sylvia Hall. *European Immigrants*. Madison: State Historical Society of Wisconsin, 1984.

Korman, Gerd. *Industrialization, Immigrants and Americanizers: The View from Milwaukee 1866-1921*. Madison: State Historical Society of Wisconsin, 1967.

Lawrence, Lee E. "The Wisconsin Ice Trade." *Wisconsin Magazine of History*. 48 (Summer 1965): 257-267.

McDonald, Sister M.J. *History of the Irish in Wisconsin*. Washington, D.C.: Catholic University of America Press, 1954.

Merk, Frederick. *Economic History of Wisconsin During the Civil War Decade*. Madison: The Society, 1916.

Nesbit, Robert C. *Wisconsin, A History*. Madison: State Historical Society of Wisconsin, 1973.

——— . *The History of Wisconsin, Vol. 3: Urbanization and Industrialization, 1873-1893*. Edited by William Fletcher Thompson. Madison: State Historical Society of Wisconsin, 1985.

Paul, Barbara, and Paul, Justus, eds. *The Badger State, A Documentary History of Wisconsin*. Grand Rapids, Mich.: William B. Erdmans Publishing Company, 1979.

Rippley, La Vern J. *The Immigrant Experience in Wisconsin*. Boston: Twayne Publishers, 1985.

Schafer, Joseph. *A History of Agriculture in Wisconsin*. Madison: State Historical Society of Wisconsin, 1922.

Schefft, Charles E. "The Tanning Industry in Wisconsin: A History of Its Frontier Origins and its Development." Master's thesis, University of Wisconsin, 1938.

Scott, Franklin D. *The Peopling of America: Perspectives on Immigration*. Pamphlet No. 241. Washington, D.C.: American Historical Association, 1963.

Walsh, Margaret. "Industrial Opportunity on the Urban Frontier: 'Rags to Riches' and Milwaukee Clothing Manufacturers, 1840-1880." *Wisconsin Magazine of History* 57(Spring 1974): 175-194.

Zeitlin, Richard H. *Germans in Wisconsin*. Madison: State Historical Society of Wisconsin, 1977.

CHAPTER FIVE

Alexander, J.H.H. "A Short Industrial History of Wisconsin." *The State of Wisconsin Blue Book*. Madison: Legislative Reference Bureau, 1929.

Anderson, W.J., and Bleyer, Julius, eds. *Milwaukee's Great Industries: A Compilation of Facts Concerning Milwaukee's Commercial and Manufacturing Enterprises, Its Trade and Commerce, and the Advantage It Offers to Manufacturers Seeking Desirable Locations for New or Established Industries*. Milwaukee: The Association for the Advancement of Milwaukee, 1892.

Baldwin, William. "Historical Geography of the Brewing Industry." Ph.D. dissertation (microforms), University of Illinois, 1966.

Bowman, Francis. *Why Wisconsin*. Madison: F.F. Bowman, 1948.

Branch, Maurice L. "The Paper Industry in Lake States Region 1834-1947." Ph.D. dissertation, University of Wisconsin, 1954.

Clark, James I. "The Wisconsin Pineries, Logging on the Chippewa." *Chronicles of Wisconsin*. Madison: State Historical Society of Wisconsin, 1955.

Cochran, Thomas C. *Pabst Brewing Company: History of an American Business*. New York: New York University Press, 1948.

Current, Richard N. *Pine Logs and Politics: A Life of Philetus Sawyer*. Madison: State Historical Society of Wisconsin, 1950.

——— . *Wisconsin, A Bicentennial History*. New York: W.W. Norton & Co., 1977.

Davies, Ayres. "Wisconsin, Incubator of the American Circus." *Wisconsin Magazine of History*. 25 (March 1942): 283-296.

Fries, Robert F. *Empire in Pine: The Story of Lumbering in Wisconsin 1830-1900*. Madison: State Historical Society of Wisconsin, 1951.

Garland, Hamlin. *A Son of the Middle Road*. Edited by Henry M. Christman. New York: Macmillan, 1961.

Hilton, Robert T. "Men of Metal: A History of the Foundry Industry in Wisconsin." Master's thesis, University of Wisconsin, 1952.

Kaysen, James P. *The Railroads of Wisconsin, 1827-1937*. Boston: The Railway and Locomotive Historical Society, 1937.

McDonald, Forest. *Let There Be Light: The Electric Utility Industry in Wisconsin, 1881-1955*. Madison: American History Research Center, 1957.

Nesbit, Robert C. "Making a Living in Wisconsin." *Wisconsin Magazine of History*. 69 (Summer 1986): 251-283.

Peterson, Walter F. *An Industrial Heritage: Allis-Chalmers Corporation*. Milwaukee: Milwaukee County Historical Society, 1978.

Raney, William F. "The Building of Wisconsin Railroads." *Wisconsin Magazine of History*. 19 (June 1936): 387-404.

Rath, Sara. *Pioneer Photographer, Wisconsin's H.H. Bennett*. Madison: Tamarack Press, 1979.

Stark, William F. *Ghost Towns of Wisconsin*. Sheboygan, Wis.: Zimmerman Press, 1977.

Still, Bayrd. *Milwaukee, The History of a City*. Madison: State Historical Society of Wisconsin, 1949.

CHAPTER SIX

Carstensen, Vernon Rosco. *Farms or Forests: Land Policy for Northern Wisconsin, 1850-1932*. Madison: University of Wisconsin College of Agriculture Press, 1958.

Clark, James I. "Farm Machinery in Wisconsin." *Chronicles of Wisconsin*. Madison: State Historical Society of Wisconsin, 1955.

——— ."Wisconsin Agriculture: The Rise of the Dairy Cow." *Chronicles of Wisconsin*. Madison: State Historical Society of Wisconsin, 1955.

——— ."Cutover Problems, Colonization, Depression, Reforestation." *Chronicles of Wisconsin*. Madison: State Historical Society of Wisconsin, 1955.

——— ."Farming the Cutover, The Settlement of Northern Wisconsin." *Chronicles of Wisconsin*. Madison: State Historical Society of Wisconsin, 1955.

Current, Richard N. *Wisconsin, A Bicentennial History*. New York: W.W. Norton & Co., 1977.

Ebling, Walter H. "A Century of Agriculture in Wisconsin." *The State of Wisconsin Blue Book*. Madison: Wisconsin Legislative Reference Library, 1940.

Kane, Lucille. "Settling the Wisconsin Cutovers." *Wisconsin Magazine of History*. 40 (Winter 1956-1957): 91-98.

Lampard, Eric E. *The Rise of the Dairy Industry in Wisconsin: A Study in Agricultural Changes, 1820-1920*. Madison: State Historical Society of Wisconsin, 1963.

Osman, Loren. *W.D. Hoard, A Man for His Times*. Fort Atkinson, Wis.: W.D. Hoard & Sons, 1985.

Schafer, Joseph. *A History of Agriculture in Wisconsin*. Madison: State Historical Society of Wisconsin, 1922.

CHAPTER SEVEN

Acrea, Kenneth. "The Wisconsin Reform Coalition, 1892-1900: La Follette's Rise to Power." *Wisconsin Magazine of History*. 52 (Winter 1968-1969): 132-157.

Asher, Robert. "The 1911 Wisconsin Workmen's Compensation Law: A Study in Conservative Labor Reform." *Wisconsin Magazine of History*. 57 (Winter 1973-1974): 123-140.

Brownlee, Jr., W. Elliot. "Income Taxation and the Political Economy of Wisconsin, 1890-1930." *Wisconsin Magazine of History.* 59 (Summer 1976): 299-324.

Campbell, Ballard. "The Good Roads Movements in Wisconsin, 1890-1911." *Wisconsin Magazine of History.* 43 (Summer 1966): 273-293.

Carstensen, Vernon. "The Origin and Early Development of the Wisconsin Idea." *Wisconsin Magazine of History.* 39 (Spring 1956): 181-188.

Clark, James I. "The Wisconsin Labor Story." *Chronicles of Wisconsin.* Madison: The State Historical Society of Wisconsin, 1955.
——— ."Farm Machinery in Wisconsin." *Chronicles of Wisconsin.* Madison: The State Historical Society of Wisconsin, 1955.

Clark, Victor S. *History of Manufactures in the United States, 1860-1914.* Washington, D.C.: Carnegie Institute of Washington, 1928.

Cooper, Jr., John Milton. "Robert M. La Follette: Political Prophet." *Wisconsin Magazine of History.* 69 (Winter 1985-1986): 91-105.

Crabb, Richard. *Birth of a Giant: The Men and Incidents that Gave America the Motorcar.* Philadelphia: Chilton Book Company, 1969.

Epstein, Ralph C. *The Automobile Industry, Its Economic and Commercial Development.* New York: Arno Press, 1972.

Glad, Paul W. *Progressive Century, The American Nation in Its Second Hundred Years.* Lexington, Mass.: D.C. Heath and Company, 1975.

Gurda, John. *The Quiet Company: A Modern History of Northwestern Mutual Life.* Milwaukee: The Northwestern Mutual Life Insurance Company, 1983.

Hoeveler, Jr., J. David. "The University and the Social Gospel: The Intellectual Origins of the 'Wisconsin Idea.' "*Wisconsin Magazine of History.* 59 (Summer 1976): 282-298.

Holbrook, Stewart H. *Machines of Plenty.* New York: Macmillan, 1955.

Korman, Gerd. *Industrialization, Immigrants and Americanizers, The View from Milwaukee, 1866-1921.* Madison: The State Historical Society of Wisconsin, 1967.

Nesbit, Robert. *The History of Wisconsin, Vol. 3: Urbanization and Industrialization,*

1873-1893. Edited by William Fletcher Thompson. Madison: State Historical Society of Wisconsin, 1985.

Ozanne, Robert. *The Labor Movement of Wisconsin.* Madison: State Historical Society of Wisconsin, 1984.

Peterson, Walter F. *An Industrial Heritage: Allis-Chalmers Corporation.* Milwaukee: Milwaukee County Historical Society, 1978.

Rae, John B. *The American Automobile Industry.* Boston: G.K. Hall & Company, 1984.

Rock, James M. "A Growth Industry: The Wisconsin Aluminum Cookware Industry, 1893-1920." *Wisconsin Magazine of History.* 55 (Winter 1971-72): 86-99.

Stevens, John D. "Suppression of Expression in Wisconsin During World War I." Ph.D. dissertation, University of Wisconsin, 1967.

Stone, Fanny S. *History of Racine County, Vol. 1.* Chicago: S.J. Clarke Publishing Co., 1916.

"Wisconsin Played a Pioneer Role in Development of Automobiles." *Wisconsin Then and Now.* 21 (March 1975): 4-6.

CHAPTER EIGHT

Blake, Peter. *The Master Builders.* New York: Alfred A. Knopf, 1960.

Christensen, Chris L. "The Future of Agriculture in Wisconsin." *The State of Wisconsin Blue Book.* Madison: Legislative Reference Bureau, 1937.

Danbom, David B. "The Professors and the Plowmen in American History Today." *Wisconsin Magazine of History.* 69 (Winter 1985-1986): 106-128.

Fried, Orrin A. "Wisconsin Manufacturing Since 1929." *The State of Wisconsin Blue Book.* Madison: Legislative Reference Bureau, 1933.

Glad, Paul W. "When John Barleycorn Went into Hiding in Wisconsin." *Wisconsin Magazine of History.* 68 (Winter 1984-1985): 119-136.

Goldberg, Robert. "The Ku Klux Klan in Madison, 1922-1927." *Wisconsin Magazine of History.* 58 (Autumn 1974): 31-44.

Lurie, Nancy Oestreich. *Wisconsin Indians.* Madison: State Historical Society of Wisconsin, 1980.

Marshall, Douglas G. *Wisconsin's Population, Changes and Prospects.* Madison: Wisconsin Agricultural Experiment Station, 1959.

Nesbit, Robert. *The History of Wisconsin, Vol. 3, Urbanization and Industrialization, 1873-1893.* Madison: State Historical Society of Wisconsin, 1985.

Ozanne, Robert. *The Labor Movement in Wisconsin.* Madison: State Historical Society of Wisconsin, 1984.

CHAPTER NINE

Corporation for Enterprise Development. "Taken for Granted: How Grant Thornton's Business Climate Index Leads States Astray." Washington, D.C.: Corporation for Enterprise Development, November 1986.
——— ."Making the Grade: The Development Report Card for the States." Washington, D.C.: Corporation for Enterprise Development, March 1987.

Eisinger, Peter. "Business Location Factors." *Task Force Report to Wisconsin Strategic Development Commission.* State of Wisconsin, 1985.

Krikelas, Andrew, and Mondschean, Thomas. "An Economic Analysis of Wisconsin Regions." Madison: Wisconsin Department of Development, 1987.

Krueger, Lillian. "Waukesha, the Saratoga of the West." *Wisconsin Magazine of History.* 24 (June 1941): 394-424.

McKay, Tom, and Kmetz, Deborah E., eds. *Agricultural Diversity in Wisconsin.* Madison: State Historical Society of Wisconsin, 1987.

Malin, Steven R. "Service Sector Growth and Regional Economies: New Concerns and Opportunities." *Regional Economies and Markets* 1 (Spring 1987): 1-7.

Myers, Dowell. "Our Best Weapon." *Corporate Report Wisconsin.* 2 (February 1987): 22-24.

Rath, Sara. *Pioneer Photographer, Wisconsin's H.H. Bennett.* Madison: Tamarack Press, 1979.

Strang, William A. *Wisconsin's Economy in 1990: Our History, Our Present, Our Future.* Madison: University of Wisconsin-Madison, 1982.

Wisconsin Agricultural Statistics Service. *1986 Wisconsin Agricultural Statistics.* Madison: Wisconsin Department of Agriculture, 1986.

Wisconsin Strategic Development Commission. *The Final Report.* State of Wisconsin, 1985. (See also Task Force Reports at the Legislative Reference Bureau.)

INDEX